Badiou and Communicable Worlds

Also Available from Bloomsbury

Badiou and Indifferent Being: A Critical Introduction to Being and Event, William Watkin
Badiou and His Interlocutors: Lectures, Interviews and Responses, ed. A.J. Bartlett, Justin Clemens
Badiou, Poem and Subject, Tom Betteridge
Badiou and the German Tradition of Philosophy, Jan Völker

Titles by Alain Badiou

The Pornographic Age, Alain Badiou
Happiness, Alain Badiou
Being and Event, Alain Badiou
Logics of Worlds: Being and Event II, Alain Badiou
Mathematics of the Transcendental, Alain Badiou

Badiou and Communicable Worlds

A Critical Introduction to Logics of Worlds

William Watkin

BLOOMSBURY ACADEMIC
LONDON • NEW YORK • OXFORD • NEW DELHI • SYDNEY

BLOOMSBURY ACADEMIC
Bloomsbury Publishing Plc
50 Bedford Square, London, WC1B 3DP, UK
1385 Broadway, New York, NY 10018, USA
29 Earlsfort Terrace, Dublin 2, Ireland

BLOOMSBURY, BLOOMSBURY ACADEMIC and the Diana logo
are trademarks of Bloomsbury Publishing Plc

First published in Great Britain 2021
This paperback edition published in 2022

Copyright © William Watkin, 2021

William Watkin has asserted his right under the Copyright, Designs
and Patents Act, 1988, to be identified as Author of this work.

Cover design by Irene Martinez Costa
Cover image © William Watkin

All rights reserved. No part of this publication may be reproduced or transmitted in any form or by any means, electronic or mechanical, including photocopying, recording, or any information storage or retrieval system, without prior permission in writing from the publishers.

Bloomsbury Publishing Plc does not have any control over, or responsibility for, any third-party websites referred to or in this book. All internet addresses given in this book were correct at the time of going to press. The author and publisher regret any inconvenience caused if addresses have changed or sites have ceased to exist, but can accept no responsibility for any such changes.

A catalogue record for this book is available from the British Library.

A catalog record for this book is available from the Library of Congress.

ISBN:	HB:	978-1-3501-7794-9
	PB:	978-1-3502-1437-8
	ePDF:	978-1-3501-7795-6
	eBook:	978-1-3501-7796-3

Typeset by Integra Software Services Pvt. Ltd.

To find out more about our authors and books visit www.bloomsbury.com
and sign up for our newsletters.

Contents

Abbreviations	ix
Introduction: Categories of Indifferent Communicability	1
Being and Event	2
Choice of category theory as mathematical basis for *Logics of Worlds*	3
The new event	4
The problem with category theory and Badiou's *Mathematics of the Transcendental*	7
Overview of category theory	9
Definition of category	11
Relation as function	14
POSets	17
Arrows or morphisms	19
Associative composable commutative (ACC)	21
Diagrams	23
Categories and communicability	24
The Preface: The Invariant Exception of Truth	29
Dialectical vs democratic materialism	29
'except that'	32
For a didactics of eternal truths: Invariance	33
Mathematical invariance	35
Distinctive features of truths	41
Book I Formal Theory of the Subject (Meta-Physics)	45
Referents and operations of the faithful subject	49
The four subjective destinations	56
Typology	60
Subjectivation summarized	62
Book II Greater Logic, 1. The Transcendental	65
Necessity of a transcendental organization of the situations of being	67
Exposition of the transcendental	69

The origin of negation	72
Section 1: The concept of transcendental. Inexistence of the whole	74
Derivation of the thinking of a multiple on the basis of that of another multiple	75
A Being is thinkable only insofar as it belongs to a world	76
Appearing and the transcendental	82
It must be possible to think, in a world, what does not appear in that world	85
The conjunction of two apparents in a world	87
Regional stability of worlds: The envelope	90
The conjunction between a being-there and a region of its world	93
Dependence: The measure of the link between two beings in a world	94
The reverse of an apparent in the world	95
There exists a maximal degree of appearance in the world	96
What is the reverse of the maximal degree of appearance?	97
Section 3: Algebra of the transcendental	101
The inexistence of the whole: To affirm the existence of a set of all sets is intrinsically contradictory	101
Function of appearing and formal definition of the transcendental	103
Equivalence-structure and order-structure	106
First transcendental operation: The minimum or zero	107
Second transcendental operation: Conjunction	108
Third transcendental operation: The envelope	110
Conjunction of a being-there and an envelope: Distributivity	112
Transcendental algebra	112
Book III Greater Logic, 2. The Object	**115**
Transcendental indexing: The phenomenon	119
Existence	123
Analytic of phenomena: Component and atom of appearing	125
Real atoms	129
Definition of an object	131
Atomic logic 1: The localization of the one	132
Atomic logic 2: Compatibility and order	135

Atomic logic	139
Function of appearing	140
The phenomenon	141
Existence	141
Phenomenal component and atom of appearing	142
Real atom and postulate of materialism	144
Definition of the object	144
Localizations	146
Compatibility	147
Order	147
The relation between relations	148
Real synthesis	150
The transcendental functor	152
Book IV Greater Logic, 3: Relation	**159**
Section 1: Worlds and relations. The double determination of a world: Ontology and logic	161
Every world is infinite and its type of infinity is inaccessible	163
What is a relation between objects?	165
Logical completeness of a world	167
The second constitutive thesis of materialism: Subordination of logical completeness to ontological closure	169
The inexistent	171
Diagrams	174
Book V The Four Forms of Change	**179**
Subversion of appearing by being: The site	181
Ontology of the site	185
Logic of the site 1: Consequences and existence	186
Logic of the site 2: Fact and singularity	188
Logic of the site 2: Weak and strong singularity	190
Logic of the site 4: Existence of the inexistent	191
Logic of the site 5: Destruction	196
Beings and events	197
Book VI Theory of Points	**201**
The scene of the points: Three examples	205
Point and the power of localization	207

Interior and topological space	208
The space of points, 1: Positivation of a transcendental degree	211
The space of points, 2: The interior of a group of points	214
Atonic and tensed worlds	214
Being, event, consequences	218

Book VII What Is a Body? 221
   Birth of a body: First description 227
   Birth of a body: Second description 229
   First formal sketch: Definition and existence of a body 232
   Second formal sketch: Corporeal treatment of points 233
   Scholium: A political variant of the physics
      of the subject-of-truth 235
   Conclusion: What is it to live? 237

One Conclusion: Communicability and Commutativity 243
Another Conclusion: Badiou's Politics of Communicability
   or Three Functions of Power Structures 249
Coda 253

Notes 255
Bibliography 264
Index 269

Abbreviations

LW   Alain Badiou, *Logics of Worlds*, trans. Alberto Toscano. London: Continuum, 2009.

MT   Alain Badiou, *Mathematics of the Transcendental*, trans. A.J. Bartlett and Alex Ling. London: Bloomsbury, 2014.

Introduction: Categories of Indifferent Communicability

To think of one thing in terms of itself, yet also in terms of another, has ever been the task of the philosopher. There is a long-standing intuition that what things are in essence can only be thought of as regards the properties they possess, which relate them to other objects in the world that possess the same properties, in which case they are identical objects, similar properties, so we can say they are related, or have nothing in common with our initial object whatsoever, marking a point of absolute difference. This harmful intuition is grounded intractably in Aristotle's theory of classes, and its reliance on Plato's views on essence, propositions that cursed the occupation of philosophy for millennia, maledictions whose nefarious influence over our communities only began to be dispelled around a century or so ago.

With the foundation, thanks to Boole and then Frege, of extensional reasoning in the nineteenth century,[1] it became possible to think of a thing in terms of what it is, not as regards the properties it possesses relative to the ideal of the essence of the thing it is taken to be, problematic because essence is little more than superstition, but rather due to the abstract, indifferent position of the object in question, in relation to the world and other objects therein, thanks to functions. Functions replace essence in the nineteenth century, at the same time that infinity usurps God, and a revolution in thought ensues at the same time as Nimrod Bar-Am's 'Revolution in Logic'. Cantor's set theory, and its subsequent axiomatization, provides us with a manner by which we can say what an object is, in terms of its composition, relative to other objects, due to simple functions like belonging, inclusion and rank. At the same time, set theory solves the aporias and problems one finds in such an immanent system by founding a non-decomposable 1 (the void set), and an actual, rather than romantically inconceivable, infinity. After two and a half millennia, the theory of classes due to essence is replaced by the theory of sets due to belonging.

Badiou's *Being and Event* (1988) was the first work to fully understand the impact of axiomatic set theory's indifferent extensionality on the long-standing problems of continental philosophy. In handing ontology over to mathematics, he was able to suture philosophy to set theory and transform our discipline forever. Things that were impossible to think before now became possible. Beings were superseded by multiples, and identities based on differences or essences became functions, thanks to indifference.

Being and Event

As our first study, *Badiou and Indifferent Being*,[2] argues, Badiou's application of set theory to ontology resulting in an entirely consistent yet non-closed structure has an ulterior motive. He does not care for a philosophy of ontological stability, except because of its potential to make credible one of the impossible-to-think topics of continental thought, singularity or, as he prefers to call it, the event. Badiou observed the many torturous, conceptual ouroburos of our forebears and peers as they tried to demonstrate real differential change, against the propensity of stability to overwhelm singularity as soon as it is broached, such that thinking singularity becomes, in Derrida's hands, for example, a mournful pursuit of the difference 'to come' that never fully transpires, or in Deleuze's a feverish affirmation of every small perturbation as a potential line of flight. Either the event never arrives or it is perpetually arriving, either way negating the very concept and purpose of events, which is to bring about unique, radical, lasting, but occasional change. Badiou's astonishing observation is that it is not the stability of logocentrism or territorialization that hamstrings the event, but rather consistent stability is the only potential for there to be a lasting theory of the event. His mathematized ontology, therefore, has one purpose only for Badiou to create an ultra-stability, against which a true event can finally be discerned.

The impact of Badiou's theory of the event is significant for three reasons that are in accordance with Badiou's own transformation of epistemology, namely that impossible ideas can become possible if they are in agreement with the conditions of the community these ideas serve, they fulfil a desire in that community and they allow said community to do new things. The formalism of set theory answers to the first demand of conditional communicability, the widespread assumption in theoretical circles that singularities are essential, and disruptive answers to the second. As for the third requisite, as yet it is not clear to me that theoretical communities around the world have been innovating their areas in reference to the work of Badiou, certainly not to the degree that they are, thanks to Agamben, Butler, Zizek, Hardt and Negri.

One reason for this is that the communicability of Badiou's event was hampered by its extensional abstractness, what I call the indifference of being and the event. Another is that there were elements of the theory of the event that did not quite convince. So the story goes, criticisms such as those found in the work of Desanti and Hallward led Badiou to the conclusion that the theory of the event was incomplete in *Being and Event* because it was too intrinsic, whereas the impact of events on worlds has to be in some way extrinsic.[3] More specifically, it is the intrinsic nature of set theory, from which an entire ontology of cardinal infinites can be composed from within the confines of the empty set or number 1, that is the origin of its radical, indifferentiated modality. Belonging as a primitive allows us to determine the composition of beings because all beings emanate from that single empty set. While his concentric, alliumatic, radiating generation of multiples (what I term CAR) allows us to construct and indifferentiate ontology such that an event can finally be thought, such indifferentiation and intrinsic-ness disallow events to occur from within the empty set, such that there can be no ontological events. Nor does the event's radically indifferential nature, all events are both content-neutral yet unique and thus indifferentially the same ontological speaking, bode well for an extrinsic statement such as: This specific event occurring in this world at this time with the following effects after which said world could never be the same again. In short, events are impossible to describe ontologically, because they are extrinsic, and multiples are fundamentally intrinsic. Badiou went away to think about his, and twenty years later he published *Logics of Worlds*.[4]

Choice of category theory as mathematical basis for *Logics of Worlds*

The application of a new kind of mathematical formalism in *Logics of Worlds*, one which is far less well-known outside of mathematical circles and much more obscure for the non-specialist, might explain in part why the book has not yet had the impact one might expect.[5] This formalism is called category theory and in reality while it informs *Logics* it does not dominate it in the same way that set theory orchestrates *Being and Event*. Criticisms of the early work besides, there are two essential components of category theory that make it inevitable that Badiou would turn to it to make events extrinsically possible. The first is that if sets concern the composition of objects, categories describe the relations between objects, meaning they are, by definition, extrinsic. If the primitive of the multiple is belonging, then the primitive of the category is relation, a perfect situation for understanding how objects relate to each other differentially, sharing everything in common, something in common or nothing in common, yet still existing in the same world. If philosophy has indeed been dominated by two questions for two millennia, the essence of an object or what it is composed of, and the relation of the object to other objects within a world, sets solved the first issue, while categories answer the second point, again by radicalizing an intuitive approach to existence. If essence is replaced by belonging, then relation due to properties is replaced by relation due to functions. It doesn't matter what two objects are, when it comes to relation, only what one does to the other is the basic premise of Badiou's reading of category theory.

The second essential aspect of category theory is that it is part-founded on set theory. This has two very important implications. The first is that it can rely on some of the basic axioms of set theory such as a minimum, and actual infinities. Categorical worlds are, in many ways, as stable as set-theoretical beings. The second is that while many philosophers have built credible, if ultimately flawed, theories of being and existence, this ontico-ontological difference, between pure being and how it manifests in actual existence, has proved a consistent stumbling block for thought. In that categories present meta-mathematical diagrams of sets and are themselves set-compositional; the entire purpose of category theory is to translate other large-scale theories, such as set theory and topology, into one single language. Thus the ontico-ontological difference ceases to be Heideggerian obfuscation and neatly becomes describing multiples in terms of functional relations rather than compositional embeddedness. One way of looking at multiples is intrinsic, sets, the other is extrinsic, categories. One multiple, two ways of looking, each perspective being entirely consistent with the other because category theory was, initially, a method of categorizing sets. And so an entire, I think lamentable, chapter in modern continental thought is permanently closed.

The new event

If we return to the event we can now say the following. Events cannot be disproved, thanks to set-theoretical ontology, which delimits the conditions for the assertion of the event, while denying the opportunity to construct an event from within ontology alone. In nature, there is nothing new, so there are no events. In the world, however, new things do appear to occur, and so category theory provides the event with a language that is willing to speak of events. However, to create a theory of the event as categorical relation, quite a large portion of the architecture of the event exposed in *Being and Event* has to be abandoned or radically re-presented. For example, the impression given that worldy situations are power-based impositions, thanks to the representation of belonging in terms of inclusion due to the function of the recount of the state, a proposition that opens states up to the errancy of the multiple, such that they must admit to the potential for intermittent evental disruption as the price to pay for otherwise stable, easy to dominate worlds, is gone from the pages of *Logics of Worlds*. Worlds are not actually anything like this description, so that events' impact on worlds has to be completely rethought. This is, in a sense, the point of the second volume of the Being and Event project.[6]

The super-consistency of natural being is the correct backdrop for a singularity which is evental. You need a super-consistent ontology for any event to be credible. Yet the super-consistency of nature or ontology literally permits no gaps where events can come into being. Category theory presents a second, ultra-consistent language, this time for describing beings in relation, rather than beings in composition. Again the assumption is that singular events need an ultra-consistent world in order to appear. This time, however, the nature of the consistency of categories has aspects which, while equally intolerant of events, cannot disallow events the possibility of appearing because categorical worlds are only partially ordered, so-called POSets. If, in set theory, there are no gaps – there is nothing between 5 and 6, for example – except as regards the empty set, and between finite and infinite sets, in category theory the purpose of the category is to be able to diagrammatically present clumps, clots, islands of being, as all consistently part of the same world, even if they do not in any way relate to each other directly. Category theory therefore speaks the language of sets, meaning the preconditions for events are carried over from being into worlds without any controversy, but it describes worlds covered in archipelagos of POSets leaving space for events to appear.

If you remember, the ontological interdiction on events is that they are self-mentioning multiples and the only self-mentioning multiple is the void set. Self-mentioning multiples are also banned from category theory which depends on set theory and often uses the classical logic which, for example, in the form of Russell's paradox of Gödel's incompleteness theorems, makes self-predication impossible. Yet they also use intuitionist logic, hence the plural *Logics of Worlds*, which states that a proposition is possible only if you can present it, only if you can conceptually 'see' the said proposition.[7] This loosens the hold of classical logic on categories, for example, there is no assumption of the excluded middle in categories; you need to be able to show that not-not-A is the same as A, and in many instances it is not. It also means if you can draw a consistent diagram of a self-mentioning multiple, then it exists. Finally, all objects that appear in the world are self-relational; this is the arrow of identity which we will come to in due time. An object can appear in a world simply by being the object that it is, self-relation, seen from the position of universal exposition, which is the category as a whole.

Thus an object can in-appear in a world, yet with such self-relational intensity that the power of this intensity can force it to appear, through the means by which it attracts other objects. This is not a new being, which is ontologically impossible, but that doesn't matter because multiples which appear in worlds can appear in an infinite variety of intensities from minimum to maximal. What this shows us is that it is how multiples appear, their degree of self-relation, that allows them to become, potentially, evental. Events are multiples that appear minimally in the world; they do not relate to any other multiples and only relate to the world by being the world's minimum, yet do so with maximal self-relational intensity. If this intensity can be taken from inappearance to appearance, without negating said maximal self-intensity, then finally we can say that events exist. This is the aim of the second volume of the Being and Event project and the crucial importance of *Logics of Worlds*.

Let us present our thesis, no proper understanding of Badiou's event without a full engagement with *Logics of Worlds*, and hence no full conception of Badiou's ontology, philosophical importance and certainly no appreciation of his much-vaunted politics, as a simple set of deductions. If the purpose of Badiou's ontology is to found a theory of radical change called the event, and we accept that *Being and Event* presents the abstract possibility that we cannot rule events out, meaning it is incumbent upon us to retroactively prove that they occur, then the intrinsic and indifferential nature of Badiou's ontology is insufficient. Ontology cannot rule events out, but we need a formalism that can rule them in. This extrinsic formalism is category theory. If, therefore, there can be no real understanding of events without the innovations of categorical thinking, then we cannot understand the event outside of the pages of *Logics of Worlds*. Making *Logics* by far Badiou's most important book in going to press.[8] As a community we have tended to avoid reading *Logics of Worlds*, but we cannot indulge ourselves in this luxury of avoidance anymore. The purpose of the rest of this book, therefore, is to make *Logics of Worlds* appear as the transcendental category of Badiou's philosophy of the event and to convince you to be militants to this cause.

The problem with category theory and Badiou's *Mathematics of the Transcendental*

The presence of category theory within the book is far less pronounced than that between set theory and *Being and Event*. Across the entirety of *Logics of Worlds* there is only one book that engages in any detail with the peculiarities of categories, commutative triangles, pull-backs and so on, that is 'Book IV Relation', and only one book that is defined by a categorical concept, 'Book VI Theory of Points'. While there is much made in the greater logic of envelopes, conjunctions and the reverse, none of these are seen as concepts peculiar to category theory according to Goldblatt's seminal and vast study *Topoi*, a text we know influenced Badiou's work extensively.[9] In contrast to the prominence of set theory in *Being and Event*, the fundamentals of categories are not theorized with the same rigour as the axioms of sets, for example. Function is not debated in particular; the dynamic and diagrammatic aspects of categories are assumed but not developed; morphisms in their rich variety pay fleeting visits at best; indeed, morphism, domain, codomain and arrow all lack entries in Badiou's own glossary so that while Badiou tells us that category theory is essential to his logics of appearing, dig a little deeper and this claim seems hard to fully support. Which means one has to dig very deep to fully comprehend the rather complex relation *Logics of Worlds* has with categories.

A simple detail in the brief introduction to one of Badiou's perhaps less-read books, *Mathematics of the Transcendental*, provides one with the vital clues for the solution of this conundrum. The short, dense, brilliant study of categories is an essential companion to *Logics* in the same way as *Number and Numbers* is vital for a full comprehension of *Being and Event*. Yet although it is presented as one book, in truth it is two essays, separated by a span of two decades and which stand, in effect, at odds with one another. In a way the book lays bare the process of the assimilation of categories into Badiou's thought so that 'Part One: Topos, or Logics of Onto-Logy: An Introduction for Philosophers' is easily the best introduction to category theory ever written, while 'Part Two: Being There: Mathematics of the Transcendental' is a preparatory sketch for *Logics of*

Worlds. Only a tiny portion of the first part makes it into the major study, where practically all of the second features there. The division between the books is so stark that, for example, the first part stipulates that diagrams and categories struggle to be called actual infinities, that the generic has no role there and that categories are entirely extrinsic. While *Logics* makes it clear early on that worlds are all actual infinities, it has a pronounced role for the generic and forcing and presents a whole section on the internalized nature of categories that is not, however, tied to the function of spreading.[10]

It would require a different kind of study to unpick the dependence of Badiou's mathematics of the transcendental on category theory, so here I will just make a couple of explanatory comments. First, it is obvious that Badiou has taken category theory and created a greater logics of appearing based on its axioms, maxims and functions. Just as set theory does not explain the void set in terms of being is-not, so category theory does not define the universal exposition of the category as a transcendental functor. In effect, Badiou is extrapolating ontology from sets and transcendental functions from categories. Going further, although the terminology is at odds, Badiou's greater logic is composed entirely in accord with category theory and so is, in a sense, yet another language that the meta-mathematical processes of categories can describe. If it is the case that set theory can function as a description of being, so category theory can function as a description of being-there.

'Part Two' perhaps shows this most clearly through the way in which it translates 'Part One' from its strictly topological presentations that clearly show the difference between categories and sets into algebraic formulae, which also begin to be directed to the task at hand, a mathematical formalism for the problem of the transcendental as a function of being-there in a world.[11] By the time we get to the concepts of the greater logic which occupy the first four books of *Logics*, they are still tied to categorical ideas, but are no longer category theory in the strictest sense of the word. What we discover is that the transformation of categories into a greater logics of appearing, which in part leaves categories behind, is actually one of the greatest achievements of Badiou's career. If ontology is to be handed over to mathematics, then both elements of ontology, Being and beings in a world, need to be mathematized, the former by sets, the latter by categories. Category theory then both founds the greater logics of beings' appearance in worlds and provides concepts which Badiou is able to suture to philosophy to literally remake categories, in the same manner he remade multiples. Yet this is far from obvious when reading *Logics of Worlds*, primarily because Badiou favours the algebraic rather than topological mode of categories.

Overview of category theory

Having reconciled ourselves to the rather complex relation the book has to categories, the dilemma is how much time to spend explaining them. My first take on this was leave categories to one side as much as possible, as, for example, Badiou's idea of order relation, a central primitive in the study, while categorizable, as all mathematical functions are, is in no way a core part of categories, so why do we even need categories to explain that?[12] Returning to the text after a sojourn away, however, I found myself uncomfortable with this relegation. The ideas behind categories support, I realized after further study, the fundamentals of Badiou's greater logic, providing a skeleton of cans and cannots without which the mathemetization of worlds and transcendental functions wouldn't hold together such that Badiou's objective phenomenology, as he calls it, would be as open to critique as say Husserl's consciousness-based phenomenology. For example, although Badiou does not analyse commutativity, associativity, composability and partial-ordering in immense detail, these concepts determine how the greater logic operates and without them the overall system would founder. This being the case, and because actually within *Logics* itself little time is given to really explaining categories, for example, the basic diagrammatic definition of the category is not even used in the book, we do need to spend time on category theory early on.

A category is nothing other than the mathematics of meta-structural relation between objects in the same world that, however, solves the logical paradoxes, impasses and aporias attendant on philosophies of the immanence of beings in a world since, shall we say, the Greeks. And an event little more than a 'diagram' that, failing the basic requirements of visibility and relation, for example, discernibility and classification as it is termed in *Being and Event*, still exists in a world taken as a category. This then is the simple purpose of a far from simple book to define all worldly situations as consistent due to the mathematics of categories and then to demonstrate how an inconsistent event can establish relations in such a world that are by definition impossible, for example, self-relation or non-relation to the transcendental definition of the world it is appearing in, such that it can be said to exist indiscernibly and yet with real functions.

The central philosophical question we glean from categories is not to think of one thing in terms of another as regards properties they share in common in relation to a being that they do not, which is how pre-mathematical ontology used to pose the problem, but rather to think of one thing in terms of how it acts on another, and how this functional relation defines worlds such as they are and differentiates beings not in terms of *what* they are, but what they do to each other. Categories then formalize the basic existential function of all beings in all worlds, a function we shall call relation. *Logics of Worlds* is, therefore, a book about the fundamental driver of all kinds of thought: the means by which units are bound together into a larger unit they share in common with each other, and other units with which they share little or nothing in common, but which have something in common with that shared-in-common larger unit. All considered from the perspective of how one unit is tied to another not in terms of what they are or what they are like, but what one does to another. On the surface this might sound like another way of describing sets. But sets allow us to know what things are, by breaking them apart to see what they are composed of, whereas categories allow us to know what things do, by looking at the relations between them, leaving the object as such untouched, fully composed, devoid of analysis. Put *Being and Event* and *Logics of Worlds* together, as Badiou insists we must do, and you have a means of showing what things are, based on their composition, and what things do, thanks to their interrelation.

A category is a transcendental function located in the least-largest position above all of its components. These smaller components are called diagrams. The transcendentally located category oversees the degrees of relationality between the objects in its line of sight, gifted to it by its position of only-just superiority. A category is defined solely by being the transcendental least-largest position from which all diagrams of a world can be related to by at least two objects: the object in relation to itself and the category the object is included in. Being visible is a function, the fundamental function; Badiou calls it universal exposition. It is what is meant by being included in the set-theoretical sense of worlds that Badiou's earlier work describes. Inclusion on this reading still means being re-counted,[13] when you speak of multiples, but it also means being visible when it comes to diagrams which, by definition, means being relatable. If you can be 'seen' in a world, this asserts, in fact, being held in a functional relation with at least one other object, such that this larger object acts on you with a basic existential operation: as a being, you exist, to some degree of intensity, in this world, relationally speaking. A category structures relations between the diagrams it oversees, and between itself and all its diagrams even if, within the world, these varied diagrams do not all relate to each other. This is because categories entertain POSets. It organizes relation by showing it in diagrams of visibility.

Introduction

What a thing actually is, and how it acts on another thing, without changing its 'essence' or that of the thing it is influencing, dominating, while being able to register that the existence of these two so-called 'things', is entirely dependent on what a thing does, not what it is, is the quintessence of the entirety of the Being and Event project up to the present moment.

Definition of category

A category consists of objects and arrows, provided that, given two arrows: there always exists the composite of these two arrows; this composition is associative; and for every object we have an identity arrow, which is neutral in any composition in which it operates.

(*MT* 20)

Unlike set theory, where there exist excellent introductions for the non-specialist that begin with simple statements such as Potter's sets are aggregates or Tiles' location of sets within the Aristotelian tradition of classes,[14] there is no introduction to categories written for the non-specialist. Most definitions of a category follow Simmons' lead in simply listing what a category consists of,[15] and Badiou's definition in *Mathematics of the Transcendental* is similarly descriptive and minimal. Indeed, Badiou himself marvels at the '"lean" and startlingly general' nature of the definition of categories (*MT* 20). If categories are hard to define, easier to simply describe, they do have the great advantage of being relatively simple in make-up; they possess far fewer axiomatic elements than sets, for example. They also benefit from being a mode of visually mapping functions across different domains; so if you wish you can see an actual picture of a category when you struggle to picture it in your head. Here, for example, is the classic diagram of a so-called commutative triangle, a central function in nearly all categorical worlds, as I said curiously not reproduced in *Logics* itself[16]:

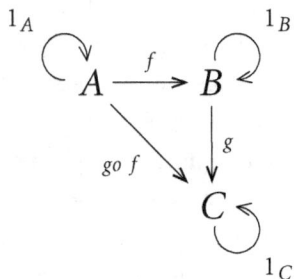

Taking this basic diagram we can map it on to Badiou's rather bland definition. We have here our objects, A, B and C, and the arrows that travel between them: $A \to B$, $B \to C$ and $A \to C$. These are commonly called morphisms. We also have a composite arrow. The arrow from A to C is functionally the same as the combined arrows from A to B and B to C making the arrow combination A to B to C a composite or composable. It is composed of more than one function, here written f and g, and this composition of functions is, functionally, the same as the function directly from A to C, called $g \bullet f$. In category theory notation you read from right to left. Thus we can say the line between A and C is composed of the two functions that exist between A and B and B and C, so that the two directional choices are functionally the same. This is called a commutative diagram and while not all diagrams commute, the ones that primarily concern our study mostly do.[17] Commutative means you can swap the two sides of an equation, for example, and get the same result. For example $A \to C = A \to B \to C$, or here $C \bullet B \bullet A = C \bullet A$.

Thinking some more about Badiou's definition we can also say of this composite of functions that it is associative, which means that the directionality from A through B to C has to be preserved, in that order, although you have no need to consider this particular composite function in any specific order. For example, you can look at it first and then look at A to C, or look at A to C first if you wish. But when you choose to look at A through B to C, then that local order has to be maintained. This is important as the function A to C is not the same as the function C to A, if such a function exists. If two sets of functions can be said to be the same and thus placed on either side of an equation, then one can replace the other but only if the direction and order of the functions are preserved. Categorical functions are asymmetric in their composition: direction matters.[18]

The dynamic between the symmetry of commutation, each side of the equation is the same, and the associative asymmetry of the side in question, it does matter which order you move through its functions, drives a certain philosophical conception of categories. Just as sets, for Badiou, are doubly determined thanks to the dynamism of belonging and inclusion which means, miraculously, the entirety of beings can be generated from the void set alone, so here, although I do not believe he ever says this, the same is true of commutation and association. Commutation captures the symmetry of relation between two objects; what they share in common is equivalent whether you compare A to C or A to B to C. Association captures the associative asymmetry of functions 'within' the relative compositions of A and B. This is important because commutation translates the multiple from ontology to appearing by being classical, while association converts the multiple into a category by being intuitive. For example, while classically we might say $C \bullet B \bullet A = C \bullet A$ in our triangle, we cannot say that $\neg\neg(C \bullet B \bullet A) = C \bullet A$, because while the two sides are functionally the same, they are not functionally equivalent, for example, $C \bullet B \bullet A$ has twice the number of functional relations than $C \bullet A$. You can make them equivalent, but you cannot assume equivalence.

As we shall see, this movement between symmetry of equivalence and asymmetry of association pertains directly to the basic function of existential relation, there in the world because relates to at least one other unit in said world, and that of categorical complexity, there in the world in relation to another unit in the world both of which share in common some form of relation to a least one other unit that is there in the world. Such as the world itself as categorical maximal, a unit just larger than the two which envelops them, something just smaller than both units they share in common that conjoins them, or something neither has in common, which is their minimum in this world. If it can be said that the entirety of what there is can be generated from the void set alone, thanks to the dynamic interchanges between belonging and inclusion, or sets and subsets, is it possible that the entirety of all worlds made up of what there is can be presented by the dynamism between commutation and association, or relation and co-relation (taking co-relation to mean a relation two objects share in common with a third)? Possibly.

Leaving such a massive question to one side for now, finally we can say that each of the objects here has to have a functional relation with itself represented by the self-enclosed or self-returning arrow attached to each object. This gives us the very basic sense of the duality of all relational functions in a world. Each object in the world has to relate to itself, it exists in a world to a certain degree of intensity, and to the categorical world itself. The first relation is ontological, why is there something rather than nothing, the second categorical, if there is something it exists in this world by relating to at least one other thing, the world itself.

Thanks to these two basic ways of defining categories, all categories are doubly determined as regards their modes of presentation (algebraic and topological), we end up with a five-part description of a category as (1) **objects** linked together by (2) directional **arrows** or **morphisms**. These arrows are assigned to (3) **functions** which travel from a **domain** to a **codomain** or from a **source** to a **target**. We can combine functional arrows across several objects not just ordered pairs, as in sets. When we do, we say these operations are

(4) **composable,** in a manner that is **associative** such that diagrams formed will be **commutative**. Thus diagrams of categories are 'larger' on the whole than the ordered pairs of sets, comprising at least three elements. These 3+ elements form composite units; two functions combined to arrive at a final codomain can be taken to be the same as a single function made up of two stages. There are, in most diagrams, two paths to the waterfall to paraphrase Raymond Carver, or as Goldblatt says, 'the diagram offers two paths from A to C,'[19] either via B, or direct from A to C. That said, whichever path you take, the order of the compositional elements of that path must be taken in order, which is what is meant by associative. Finally, (5) all diagrams also possess **identity functional arrows** from themselves to themselves. To repeat: **objects, arrows, functions between objects, associativeness** and **identity functions**, these five concepts determine all categorical diagrams and each has its own philosophical story to tell of which Badiou narrates only some. If you wish, we can sum up these five concepts by saying that if sets are determined by belonging, categories are defined by relation. Thus *Logics of World* is, ostensibly, a radical reappraisal of the modality of relation, while *Being and Event* is a radical presentation of the ontology of nonrelation.

Relation as function

We now have a basic definition of the composition of a category, a definition that is actually more of a description, a description that is primarily a depiction in diagrammatic form: the famous commutative triangle. One thing that is often said about categories is that they are structure-preserving, in the same way as logic is truth-preserving.[20] Nothing can exist in a category outside of the structure meaning beyond its diagrammatic visibility. Another is that they are meta-mathematical. Category theory is, in this sense, a language into which other mathematical languages can be translated, such as set theory most centrally, but also other forms of mathematics like topology (categories are a bit set-like and they are very topological). As such then category theory is a meta-language for maths that makes different ways of doing maths for different communities using disparate languages, universally transmissible. It is, therefore, the mathematics of communicability. In our case, category theory is the meta-language that allows Badiou to construct his greater logic of appearing which he calls his mathematics of the transcendental; he also refers to it as an objective phenomenology.[21] The meta-mathematical essence of categories means they support a concept of communicability which is central to Badiou's ideas and our own. If category theory is a means by which different ways of describing worlds can be mapped on to each other, then it is clear why, for Badiou, category theory is a suitable basis for his idea of logics of worlds. If there are many different ways of constructing worlds, category theory allows one to overlay these different languages in a single, consistent manner that can be seen. Categories allow diverse worlds to be intelligible across one single, diagrammatic language, so that all their complex relations are universally transmissible, visible, for example, from what is often called the universal position of the name of the category itself,[22] and thus communicable, definable in terms of what these worlds allow to happen, functions, rather than the content they communicate. It is not what categories say that matters but what they do, and in this sense they are the quintessence of communicability as I have defined it.[23]

The traditional drawing of a category is composed of objects and arrows. Although in our diagram this was not the case, in general objects are usually represented by dots. This is a visual clue towards the true nature of the category. Within category theory, the objects in question are rendered as dots so that they remain indifferent, quality neutral, impervious to analysis.[24] In category theory what matters is not what the object is, that is the question set theory asks, but what is the relation between one object and another. Relationality then is the key component of category theory so that all the effort of depiction is centred not on the objects but what goes on between them. Objects are reduced to dots so as not to distract from the lines of force that travel from one dot to another. This visible attenuation and indifferentiation of the object raises an important question: If categories are all about relations between objects, how can said relations be established if the object itself remains indifferentiated, abstracted, unopened, without quality and so on? The fact that the relations between objects are called arrows is another clue. A relation is taken as movement between one object and another, and this movement is called a function. In category theory objects are defined by directional, functional relations between one object and another, what they are does not matter, nor does their internal composition,[25] rather what they can do is the point. Categorically speaking, objects are indifferential in and of themselves, but relationally differential between each other.

Goldblatt describes a function as 'an association between objects, a correspondence that assigns to a given object one and only one other object. It may be thought of as a rule, or operation, which is applied to something to obtain its associated thing'.[26] He goes on to describe it as a black box where 'for a given input a function produces a uniquely determined output'.[27] If we have a domain, that is the input, the arrow or morphism represents the function, and the codomain is the output or result. His example is the function [multiply by 6] from which the input 2 will result in 12. Lawvere and Schanuel give two relatively straightforward examples of what could be meant by function. The first is Galileo's attempt to map the motion of objects in space. While one can draw a parabolic curve of a thrown rock in flight, this track does not capture the instants of the rock's movement which accelerates from the hand, rises into space, decelerates towards the ground and so on. As the authors conclude from this, 'We say the motion is a "map" (or "function") from time to space.'[28] This category then consists not of the rock itself, but of mapping the movement of an object, could be a rock could be a bird, between when you are measuring it, just thrown, highest point, coming to the ground, its temporal location and its spatial location. The map of this then can be written as

$$TIME \xrightarrow{\text{flight of rock}} Space$$

What is interesting here is that the rock of time is a different object to the rock of space, even though ontologically speaking it is the same rock. This shows the limitation of the term 'object', for here what is really meant is property of an object, what it is doing, and second property of an object, something else it is doing. The function between these two states of the same object allows one to relate the time-rock to the space-rock, preserving the structural relation between the two at all times so that at any point you can say where the rock is *in* time. In category theory an object with two different functions would be two different 'objects' just as two different objects with the same function, rock and bird, for example, would be taken to be the same object. Existential identity is entirely defined by function, not by being *qua* being.

Now let's think of that special form of categories called sets, Lawvere and Schanuel's second example in fact. Our object is now clearly defined as a set, to make it easier a finite set with three elements called [John, Mary, Sam]. We are now going to map this set onto another set by first designating what the three elements like for breakfast. Leaving the first set are three arrows; there are three elements in that set. These arrows arrive in our second set, things one can eat for breakfast. This second set is potentially infinite in size, which means that many of the elements of this set will not participate in the mapping of the preferences of our three initial elements so that this set is partially ordered. Also these initial elements might like the same thing so their arrows can map onto the same element in the set. The function here is liking, the movement is the mapping of preference from element *a* to element *b*.

Interestingly here, again, the content of the two 'objects' which are actually called in category theory domain and codomain, is indifferent by which we mean, does not determine their functional identity. For example, both sets could be made up of the same elements [John, Mary, Sam] with a new function, favourite person, mapping the domain onto the codomain. You can even place our three elements on a raft for four weeks in the middle of the pacific and retain the breakfast preference function in relation to [John, Mary, Sam] if you so wish! The point being here is that the relationality between objects in different domains is an identity-difference function, but the identity between domain and codomain is in terms of the mapping of function, not of being. John can differ from himself in the domain and codomain because in the domain he is a liker, while in the codomain he is the person liked. This can be pushed to the point where John likes himself and himself only, represented by the self-regarding identity arrow we already touched upon.

POSets

At this point we should consider partially ordered sets or POSets as a point of differentiation between sets and categories as regards pairs in functional relation. As we saw, the codomain of things [liked for breakfast] is infinite in that anything in the world called breakfast could be included in it and appear, even if functionally it has no relation to our likers in the initial domain. This is one way of thinking of a POSet. In set theory, the function between two objects is called an ordered pair. This is two objects, one which must come first, the other which must come second or (x, y). This allows us to stipulate that $(x, y) = (z, w)$ if and only if $x = z$ and $y = w$. Ordered pairs obey the transitive laws of symmetry, meaning that as long as you obey the associative order of pair one, x then y, then the relation between pair one and pair two is absolutely symmetrical, enshrined in set theory as the axiom of replacement or substitutability. They are precisely the same set. Categories however do not operate in this fashion. They can capture ordered pairs, but the ordering of pairs of functions in a diagram is not substitutable; rather, the associative nature of the ordered pair extends to include the function between two pairs such that while it may be true to say $(x, y) = (z, w)$, it would not be true to say $(z, w) = (x, y)$ unless you have dual directional functional arrows to show this (example of intuitionist rather than classical logic re: excluded middle). Thus to make an ordered pair categorically, it must be written $(x,y) \underset{\leftarrow}{\overset{\rightarrow}{=}} (z,w)$ showing that the movement from domain to codomain is reciprocal. This process is said to have parallel arrows and has a particular importance to the expression of identity in category theory.

POSets are important because they capture the difference between ontological and logical takes on the same objects or multiples. Ontologically speaking, there are no gaps in the ranking and ordering of multiples which facilitate the axiom of substitutability absolutely essential, for example, for showing actual infinities exist. However, categorically speaking, worlds are not completely ordered: there are gaps which form clumps. Not every multiple is in a successive rank with every other. What this demands is that worlds be made consistent at the transcendental level: all these multiples are part of the same world, even if they are not all related to each other, while ontologically multiples are actually made consistent at the fundamental level, or the naming of the void set [Ø], Ø or number one, from which all other multiples can be successively named. Goldblatt goes further and states that the partial ordering of sets in categories means that the codomain of every categorical function is unique, unless you directly stipulate it is not by adding a reverse function to produce a parallel set of functional arrows. This also means, he says, that the dynamism of the function is better presented: it is what you do that matters and if you want symmetry, rather than in classical logic being able to assume that $\neg\neg A = A$ you have to diagrammatically show this with a number of arrows. The partial ordering of sets in categories is to the philosophical understanding of relation, what the ordered pairs of sets are to belonging.[29]

One final point which is helpful I think is that when you look at sets in terms of set theory, then ordered pairs are assumed and intrinsic. If you look at the same set categorically, it is not and you have to show it, which in miniature is the central function of categories for Badiou. In a categorical world, when a multiple appears as included, you cannot assume that all of the elements of that multiple, all its sub-multiples, will appear in the world unless they are diagrammatically shown to be. What this allows is that an object could appear in two different worlds with two different sets of functions indicating how much of said multiple is being included in this world.

$\leq$

Let us recap, a category is a map, a visual presentation, of a relation between two objects. These objects are not however things, in that they are not defined by what they are but in terms of a dynamic relation between them and another object. Objects then are not defined by what they are but what they do; they are quality indifferent in a classical sense in that what they are composed of is never under consideration; yet, they are quality rich in that what they do, how well they do it, in comparison with other objects and so on, is all significant. The quality of an object in terms of it being part of a category is its functionality or better its functional direction, and the identity of the object is determined as regards which domain you encounter it in and what it is doing. A rock in time is different to a rock in space. John the preferer is different to John the preferred, and so on. There are an infinite number of relational functions, and combinations of them can be mapped by category theory, for example, set theory can be mapped by category theory and its axioms presented therein. That said, in *Logics of Worlds* there is ostensibly only one function, which makes the book's use of categories far more straightforward. Because Badiou is concerned only with existence, with how multiples exist in worlds, he is able to consider only one function, the relational function of an object of existence.

If your question is to what degree does a multiple exist in a world, then the only function you need is one that measures degrees of relational existence, and this function is $\leq$.[30] One object is thought of in relation to another, which is what is meant by existence in a world. If two objects are functionally differential, then one has a greater degree of intensity of existence in a world than another, is closer to the overall category and is then able to envelop the object that is smaller including all of its composable functions. If however two objects are functionally the same, then they are the same object. This is all you need to know about any object in any world when you want to define its existence. It is true for objects with no relations, because they always at least relate to themselves and the categorical world as such: to exist means to be self-present and visible (universally exposed in a world). It is true for objects that compose all relations, the categories themselves. For singleton objects the degree of relation is 1. For categories the degree of relation is All, or ∞, or the category as such. This is very good news for the non-specialist such as myself. Yes, category theory can map infinite mathematical functions, but philosophically speaking, in Badiou's work, only one function matters, the existential function of degrees of relation written as $\leq$.

Arrows or morphisms

It is time to say something more about our objects and their all-important arrows. First, all objects have an arrow that goes out from them, as domain, to another object, a codomain. This makes sense because categories are about functional directionality between at least two objects (at the very least themselves and the category as a whole). Second, this arrow can go out from and return to the same object. This is represented by a circular arrow and all objects have this basic functionality which means they are the objects such as they are in this category. Ontological identity of this kind cannot be presented as a multiple because of the restrictions I mentioned, not least that in category theory objects are non-decomposable in themselves, only in terms of relations and degrees of function, for example, rock as time, rock as space, rock in acceleration, rock in deceleration, and so have to be able to be represented as 'being there' in terms of a functional direction. That said, many elemental properties typified by set theory can be mapped functionally by categories not by breaking open an object to see its elements but by what is called spreading out the functions of an object such that its elements can be seen in terms of their functional traces. One of the central ways this can be done is the means by which exponentiation in sets, multiplying a set by itself or by another set, can be presented in terms of functions, as this opens up the idea of the sub-object which will become important later as we come to terms with categories and indifference.

The next point to develop is that arrows are, as I said, compositional. Simmons calls this partial composition, which means in practice that 'certain arrows are compatible for composition to form another arrow'.[31] Partial composition is another way of capturing POSets. Composability basically links one functional mapping to another if the two functional mappings include the same objects. Take three points or objects. If A maps functionally onto B and B maps functionally onto C, then these two arrows are 'composable': basically you can combine them to form more complex categories which, however, always have to preserve the structural relations of said category. If you name the arrow from A to B, f, and the arrow from B to C, g, then you can write this down as a single composite arrow called $f \bullet g$. What this says is that in mapping a function from B to C, if B is the codomain of the functional mapping of A to B, whatever is mapped between A and B, called f, also has to be mapped from B to C. And if an object comes along that has a functional relation of existence larger than A, call it A', then the relation of A' to A retains all the composable functions A has, with B and with C.

This is the categorical way of showing the idea of recursive deduction or logical heredity. If you have established the composable relations of a group of objects, and then you plot another object which is 'larger', then you can assume all those composable relations and just concentrate on the one new relation. Why is this? Because the definition of A and of B is entirely to do with their functional relation. If you speak of B, what you are talking about is B as a relational target of a function of A. If you want to talk about a rock, you might map the colour of the rock, a red rock: $A \xrightarrow{Red} B$. Now if you want to map the size of the red rock, it is big, then you have to show $B \xrightarrow{Big} C$. The rock was A, a rock with no properties besides existence; then it was B, a rock with the property red; and now it is C, a red rock that also has the property big. If however you wanted to map only the size of the rock, then you would need a new object, D, because you mapped the colour first and, due to the laws of association and composability, if you want to now only map size, then this requires a new function, big without being red or $A \xrightarrow{Big\ but\ not\ necessarily\ red} D$. Again this is ontologically the 'same' rock but it is functionally different. Also, C and D are not the same functional object because C has to associatively preserve its composition, red then big, whereas D has to preserve associatively its composition, big but not necessarily red. Finally, if we now want to make D red we can, but this requires a new object E, and its function would be written as $A \xrightarrow{Big} D \xrightarrow{Red} E$. E and C may look ontologically the same, both rocks, both red, both big, but they are functionally different. C is a rock that is red first and then big. E is a rock that is big first and then red. This matters because we might want to map rocks which are big but orange. We could then map a new object, call it X, to B, but not to C. Yet if we try to map X to E we find we cannot, because while E is big, it is by definition also red. Because X can be mapped to B and not to E, they are functionally different, even if they remain ontologically the same. A note here must be added. When we talk about qualities here, being big or red, we don't mean that in the traditional, class-essence ontological sense. Here being red is actually something the rock does, it functions for us as a red object. Quality then can be part of categories; indeed in Badiou's use of category theory, it seems to be the dominant mode of function, when you accept that colour is something an object does, not what it is or what it possesses. If you prefer a rock is not red (adjective), rather it reds (verb). So from now on when we speak of quality, we mean quality as function between two objects, not as property possessed by an object. To red means, specifically, to share in common redness.

Associative composable commutative (ACC)

While composable association can appear restrictive, it is in fact rather liberal, thanks to its restrictions, something it shares in common with poetry. It is because diagrams are structure-preserving, composable functions that are associative, that you can build very big categories with huge numbers of internal relations and never concern yourself with the world becoming contradictory or chaotic. You can also navigate your way around the world in a clumping, clotting manner. If you have a series of arrows going from one object, through others, to the same object, the direction you choose to travel first is indifferent, as long as the sequence of each functional composition is maintained. For example, you might start with the size of the rock B to C, and then talk about its colour, the result will be the same but the direction of the arrows must be maintained. The value of this associative law will become clearer later; all it tells us is that composability is flexible in that it allows you to speak in many different ways about the same category as long as in each case the structure is preserved, and that structure is the functional direction of all the arrows.

For example, John, A, maps onto breakfast in terms of what he likes, B. Now let us introduce a new piece of functional information, morning, C. C maps onto breakfast through the function of [time of day]. However, John maps onto mornings in terms of [liking]. So John likes breakfast because he likes mornings, and everything included in mornings he likes. You can speak of John liking mornings, $A \to C$, or of John liking breakfast because of mornings $A \to B \to C$. The route you take from John to mornings does not matter. But you cannot speak of John liking mornings but not liking breakfast because breakfast is composable with liking mornings, or C is embedded in the function from A to B. It is because he likes mornings and breakfast is mapped functionally onto mornings that he likes breakfast. The functional liking of breakfast, for John, is entirely enveloped by his liking of morning, not sausages or because he is a foodie. He will like anything else, temporally, mapped onto morning, but he will be unable to dislike anything mapped onto morning.

We can see from this that the choice of the composable functional lines does not matter, but the order of the arrows within each composite set of arrows cannot be reversed. Just because John likes breakfast does not mean breakfast likes John. Just because breakfast occurs in the morning does not mean that morning occurs in breakfast. Just because John likes breakfast because of mornings does not mean he likes breakfast for other reasons. As he likes mornings, anything that can be functionally mapped onto morning he will also like. And so on. This is the basic definition of structure-preservation: all functions are composable and their composability must be associative producing commutative results: liking mornings commute with liking breakfast because it is a compositional part of mornings in this world.

You may have realized that associative composability is why categories are intuitionist in their rejection of the excluded middle.

Diagrams

An important component of categories is irrespective of the kinds or numbers of relations; they must be mappable in diagrammatic form. You have to literally be able to see the functions, their direction, their composable structure and so on. In the first instance these diagrams can be linear, $A \rightarrow B \rightarrow C$, Badiou's favoured algebraic format in *Logics*, but in that a diagram only describes a part of any category; every category has to be represented in the final analysis in a tabular fashion, primarily in the form of a commutative triangle. For example, to be able to show $A \rightarrow B \rightarrow C$ and $A \rightarrow C$ in a form that maintains all the

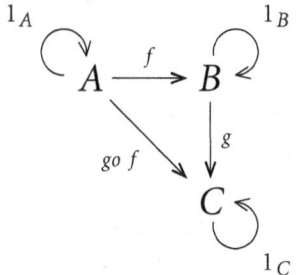

functional relations, compositions and associative orders, you need to image them as a triangle of relations. Again, as we shall see, this is because everything in a category must be visible. You have to be able to see the relations, and the only position in any category of any significant size, categories are primarily simplified ways of looking at large numbers of operations, where you can see all the operations from a vantage point above all diagrams or functions. This vantage point has to be able to see every relational point, so imagine between B and C in this diagram a third position that has to see B, has to see C and has to see their relation, $B \rightarrow C$. The only position that can achieve this is the apex of the triangle A formed with $B \rightarrow C$ as its base. Looking again at our commutative diagram the position A here is the categorical position. It forms a cone, as it is called, from a position of universal exposition; it can see all the diagrams in its world. What A sees here is that it can go to B and then C, or it can go to C, with the same overall functional result. In addition, it can perceive that $g \circ f$ is functionally the same as $A \xrightarrow{f} B \xrightarrow{g} C$. Yet it can also see that while we may functionally take these two objects to be the same, by objects we mean functional relations, in terms of visibility they are different – in a sense giving us a more sophisticated method of understanding $A=B$. Finally, what the cone looks down on is the associative nature of functional equivalence. The two functional objects, from A to C or from A to B to C, are only equivalent if the order of functions is maintained. For example, A to C is not the same as C to B to A which means that A to C cannot be reversed and become C to A. Not unless the functional arrows of the diagram allow this, and as there are no parallel arrows in our diagram, then this is not allowed, giving us diagrammatic representation of the intuitionist demand that $\neg\neg A = A$ be shown. If $A=B$, that does not necessarily mean $B=A$. This is the essential law of asymmetry that differentiates categories from sets.

Categories and communicability

'The procedure that founds set theory is the effect of a *decision regarding the intelligible*. This decision takes the forms of axioms ... The categorical procedure is itself *descriptive*. It proceeds by successive definitions, which enable the specification of possible universes' (*MT* 15). Or, we might say, set theory is intelligibility, category theory communicability, which is why the title of this book is *Badiou and Communicable of Worlds* even if Badiou himself does not use this term. Communicability, rather, is our term to describe the manner by which significance is determined not in terms of the content of a statement, but rather as regards what a statement does, or is allowed to do. Communicability determines the sanction of what is intelligible such that an intelligibility can become a truth in the non-evental sense of being what Badiou calls veridical in *Being and Event*. In that book veridicality, which is always a property of re-presented or worldly multiples, is defined as regards a vague sense of what he calls the encyclopaedia, but which we are now able to formalize in much great detail as a category.[32] Badiou says initially that for a multiple to become veridical, to move from intelligibility to communicability, it has to be discernible and classifiable, that in being discernible it automatically becomes classifiable. We can now say that a multiple is presented, discerned and immediately re-presented, classified, although now classified has to be replaced with another term, for categories do not classify in a traditional sense. In *Being and Event* classification pretty much described the movement of a multiple from an extensional, indifferent set to an intensional, quality-rich set. That, however, has not proven to be the case at all. Now we can say that a discerned multiple is a multiple that can literally be seen by the line of sight of the category itself.

Intelligibility of this order is not that of set theory, although only intelligible multiples can be discerned. Rather, categorical discernment is not the axiomatic formalism of set theory, or better this is only one logic of discernment, becoming a logic not an ontology when it is categorized. Remember that sets are one of the primary modes which can be categorized. A discerned multiple is a multiple that exists in a categorized world, a rock in the world of rocks. A classified object however is not, what kind of rock is this as regards its properties, predicates or qualities as we said, instead 'classification' as a description is replaced by degrees of relation. An object that can be seen in a world is then classified in that world by what relations it has with itself, other objects and the category itself. When an object is discerned, how intense is the object as a full manifestation of its ontological potential in this world? A rock in a world of rocks appears with maximal intensity. A rock in a world of a landscape appears with less intensity. A rock on the street of a demo is out of place. If it is there because it was thrown, then it has some intensity; if it is there at random, then it has nil intensity. Once we have decided how intense the object is as a node of appearance, we can then compare it with other objects that have appeared. Two low-intensity objects combined, for example, could come to have a higher degree of relation. A rock and a bottle in the street at the feet of the police during a demo suggest both are projectiles, and so the incongruity of the rock gains legitimation when functionally bound to a bottle, more congruent with an urban location, and together at the feet of the police they come together to form the function of [projectiles]. What they 'are' in this world is [something thrown] irrespective of the fact that one is a human-made receptacle, the other a natural found object. Finally, if the category is [rocky landscape], then rocks will occur with quite some intensity; they belong there after all, while a bottle does not belong. But if your category is [landscape and the Anthropocene], the bottle's incongruity gives it greater intensity than the rock. In a rocky landscape a rock should be there but is one of a thousand similar objects, so then you might want to discern the rocks, by colour, for example, red rocks standing out in a sandstone desert as examples of the presence of iron. If your landscape category is [exploitation of landscape for resource], red rocks might have a very high degree of intensity now. Thus we have a new sense of classification so crucial to the definition of the event in *Being and Event*, which allows us to let go of this term permanently and requires that we start again with our thinking of events. Instead of classification we now have degree of functional appearing across three indicators: self-intensity, relative intensity, categorical intensity.

What makes discernment and relational intensity communicable rather than intelligible? As ever power, potency, force. An object acts on another object in terms of what it is capable of doing within the strictures of the world it finds itself in. This is the power equation of every existent being. If for now we stick with statements á la Foucault's work on intelligibility and communicability in *The Archaeology of Knowledge*, we can say that a statement, actual infinities exist, appears in a world called mathematics. Within that world the statement should have strong self-identity in that it is a mathematical statement but, in the nineteenth century, the statement had nil intensity of discernment because it was an impossible statement. The statement could be made, but it could not be seen. This is a classic basis for any evental statement. For a statement to become visible, it needs to cluster with other statements. As it does so it becomes larger, more intense, more visible. It may have to lose a sense of itself; however, to do so, make compromises such that it barters off self-intensity against discernible legitimacy. Finally, a statement that was perhaps unacceptable becomes acceptable because it has relational functions with already discerned and relationally intense statements in a particular category. The category then draws a line of sight with the statement and starts to discern it in relation to other statements making associative, composable diagrams. Perhaps this new statement turns out to be able to envelop and thus equalize or cancel out other statements. Perhaps it also allows for new functional relations to be drawn. Maybe over time it comes to be the right-hand woman of the category itself or maybe it becomes the category.

It has become communicable in three ways. First, it appears such as it is. Second, it can be seen by the category through a line of functional communication: you now exist such as you are in this world. Finally, third, it creates lines of functions with other objects in the world. The more it does that, the more intensity it gains, the higher up the triangle it goes, the more sanctioned it becomes. It moves from something looking for sanction at the lowest level to, over time, a force for sanction of other statements below it. We must mention that in this statement, actual infinities exist, is not a being; it does not exist ontologically. There is a world of difference between a multiple that exists but not in this world, that is, all multiples aside from those that appear here and a portion of all those that appear here, and an evental multiple. A multiple is an 'old' object in a new world; an event is a new object in an old, already existing, world.

We are now in a position to innovate our theory of communicability. Instead of statements we can now speak, as Badiou does, of objects. When we consider communication, what we mean is functional relationality. In terms of discernment, we mean can be functionally perceived by a category. In terms of sanction we are saying to what degree can an object remain close to its being, within this world, such that it can gain very intense, for which read larger or higher relations, meaning it is not just sanctioned but becomes a force of sanction. This is no longer classification but categorization. In that categorization includes discernment as well, we can replace discernment and classification with one word, categorization, and we can now speak formally of communicability, the power of sanction of existence due to action rather than meaning, as what categorization does. Yes, we can say logics of worlds but, if we really want to understand the political power of Badiou's work and the differential relation between intelligible sets and functional categories, we are arguing the communicability of worlds is better.

The Preface: The Invariant Exception of Truth

Dialectical vs. democratic materialism

The invariance of exceptions over time and space, spanning disciplines and their conditions, such that you can prove that truths exist, by simply giving examples of them, is the purpose of the extensive 'Preface' – a purpose that is initially occluded however as the book explodes with immense confidence and élan, exposing the entirety of the political landscape of our new millennium through the production of a devastating critique of our liberal, capitalist presuppositions. While my contention is that *Logics of Worlds* is Badiou's most important work of political philosophy, it is not however contrary to these opening segues, a political critique of global capitalism. That said, when he describes our age as 'democratic materialism', captured by the maxim, *'There are only bodies and languages'* (*LW* 1), we find it is an assertion which rings true, albeit by controversially allying the neoliberalism of global capital with its supposedly radical critics, such as theorists of otherness, identity politics and biopolitics. For Badiou, going admirably *á rebours*, the heightened, almost sacred, importance of bodies to our neoliberal and biopolitical culture constitutes the suspect materialism of our age. In order to promulgate the equation existence = individual = body, for example, democratic materialism must call on the animality of the human, equating human rights with simply those of the living. This is, for him, a faux materiality that will be easily superseded by his idea of the materiality of the void and its role in founding the atom of existence as real.

Rejecting biopolitical somatic, animalized materialism, he is equally dismissive when it comes to the democracy of our age with its emphasis on the freedom, diversity and, of course, the digital networking of speech, lamenting that 'the contemporary consensus, in recognizing the plurality of languages, presupposes their juridical equality … everything and everyone deserves to be recognized and protected by law' (*LW* 2). On Badiou's reading at least our democratic materialism, which is neither purely of the right nor of the left, states that we all have life and we all have language and so we all have universal, equal rights. No one life is worth more, no opinion can be judged more true. Within this profound state of linguistic indifference where no language can be said to be better or more true than another, there is, however, a limit: 'A language that does not recognise the universal juridical and normative equality of languages does not deserve to benefit from this equality' (*LW* 2). There is so much here that could be said of our current, political quandary in the West, with the populist right espousing absolute freedom of speech, and the identity politics of the left demanding curtailment of the freedoms of such speech due to its being hateful and likely to incite violence against bodies of diversity; speech freedoms for the right, body freedoms for the left, but regrettably perhaps, Badiou is in no mood to speak of such things here.[1]

Rather, ever the contrarian, as a counter-position to our democratic materialism, he proffers his own theory which he calls, with studied provocation, a *materialist dialectic*. We need not debate here the communist overtones of this designation, Badiou speaks of Althusser, Stalin et al., as this turns out not to be the purpose of the book either, but we ought to consider his justification in terms of the dialectic, as this comes to structure the being-there of truth as exception. Badiou argues that the democracy of the dominant paradigm of our age is conducted around a set of oppositional dualities, Cold War democracy versus totalitarianism, free world versus terrorism and so on, and that indeed the very formula of democratic materialism is a duality: bodies and languages. Finally, he pleads, 'Let's agree that by "dialectic," following Hegel, we are to understand the essence of all difference as the third term that marks the gap between the two others.' If we do so then, 'we understand the following statement, in which the Three supplements the reality of the Two: *There are only bodies and languages, except that there are truths*' (*LW* 4). If this is accepted then the 'there are truths', which 'serve as an objection to the dualist axiomatic of democratic materialism (the law protects all bodies, arranged under all the compatible languages), is for me the initial empirical evidence' (*LW* 4). Such evidence is materialist, 'since it does not require any splitting of worlds, any intelligible place, any "height"'. Instead, and this is the crux of the matter: 'In our worlds, such as they are, truths advance. These truths are incorporeal bodies, languages devoid of meaning, generic infinities, unconditioned supplements. They become and remain suspended ... "between the void and the pure event"' (*LW* 4).

The assertion that our age is dominated by oppositional structures is not, at least since Derrida, a surprising one. Yet central to Derrida, and other thinkers of the metaphysics of opposition, for example, Agamben, is hierarchy. For both Derrida and Agamben, what matters is not two terms placed together but two terms placed together in a difference of 'height' as Badiou calls it, after Mallarmé. After Mallarmé perhaps but, more meaningfully for us, after categories. A truth, in contrast, is materialist because it is not located functionally in a category; because, by definition, a category is tabular, it has height. A truth then occupies the point of suspension that determines Agamben's critique of metaphysics,[2] but that suspension does not produce the negation of dialectic height, for example, between a common and a proper, but between the void as such and the event. What we can glean from these compacted statements is that first, the centrality of a truth is that it is flat, linear, non-hierarchical. As he says, truths advance, step by step, they do not ascend, relation by relation. Second, that truths do have a suspensive function, but they do not, as Agamben would have it, suspend the functional economy between hierarchized diagrams, but rather fail to participate in that economy. Instead, truthful suspension is strung between the void, which does not succeed, and the event, which does not relate. Non-succession of the void is effectively translated into non-relationality of the event by the onto-logical movement from set to category theory. It is between the void of the non-successor multiple and the event of the non-relational object that truths are developed.

On this reading we must, therefore, revise any sense we may have possessed of dialectic materialism inspired by a love of *Theory of the Subject* or Marxism in general.[3] For Badiou, the dialectic of any world, reduced to the simplification of opposing functions, is determined by height or one term lording it over the other. The so-called third of the dialectic, here truth, is not therefore an *Aufhebung* in the strict Hegelian sense because it is not possessive of height. The inter-position of the third has a suspensive function, á la Agamben, but its suspension is not between bodies and languages, or the proper and the common, *zoe* and *bios*. Truth does not suspend the hierarchal, asymmetrical functional potency between a category and its opposed diagram either. Rather, the suspensive function of a truth is that it exists between, rather than above or below, the void, which is a non-successor multiple, and the event, which is a non-relational multiple. An event does not succeed but it also does not relate, so that a truth lacks structuration in terms of ranking *and* relationality. The bare concomitant of this is that truths are real material, because the only real thing in ontology is the precedence of the void which, in being named, is the basis of all subsequent ranking. Therefore, if a truth exists, it has to be real in terms of non-succession, the void is real because it exists before rankable collection, and in terms of non-relation, events are real because they exist but cannot be constructed and that which exists in a non-constructible sense is, by definition, the only real thing.

'except that'

The exceptionalism of truths is of a particular order based on this reading. It is not the exceptionalism of the philosophy of difference, that's for sure, or our contemporary clicktivist moment of digitized identity politics. It is certainly not Brexit and Trump's national exceptionalism. Indeed, coming to terms with the rather wonderful and unique nature of the 'except that' of truths will be one of the joyful tasks of what is to come, but for now we must satisfy ourselves with a series of maxims of exception such as '*A truth affirms the infinite right of its consequences, with no regard for what opposes them*' (LW 7). We might term this Badiou's new ethics of the event, upgrading the ethical injunctions such as 'keep going' with a new kind of ethical right of exceptional consequence.[4] It also reminds us that truth is not language and that its impact on our worlds is in the form of consequences: it is not what a truth says, but what it does, that matters. This is perhaps one of the most important aspects of truth for the book. Another rule of exception is: '*Every world is capable of producing its own truth within itself*' (LW 8). Thus, whatever the 'there is' in question, whatever world you are acting in and speaking of, there is nothing about that world that can stop an event. Truth is non-relation to the world with the wider implication that no world can be better-placed than another to facilitate events. Furthermore, said truths are immanent. They do not come from the outside. While truth may seem 'other' and thus exceptional, it is an immanent otherness determined by a profound non-relationality which makes a nonsense of the late-twentieth-century humanism of the ethics of the other.

Actually we are learning nothing we don't already know after reading *Being and Event* and the challenge now, Badiou admits, is not *that* truths happen inside worlds but *how* they do. How can the indifference of being as facilitator of the truth of an event survive the 'passage' from indifferent non-relationality (multiples) to differentiated relations (bodies as objects) and remain all those things we just celebrated about it? Ironically, democratic materialism helps us in this regard. Having been so vociferous in its attacks on truth, Badiou calls it a war, we liberals have come up with an alternative maxim to 'there are only bodies and language' which is '*There are only individuals and communities*' (LW 8).

This alternative version allows Badiou to muster his quartet – being, appearing, truths and subjects – against the idea of individuals and communities to great effect. We find that truths rest on subjective forms that subtract themselves from communities and destroy individuation. Such a subtraction results in the fact that the war on the politics of the philosophy of difference, what he calls democratic materialism, is waged by the indifference of subjects to truth. Said subjects subtract themselves from the communicability of collective bodies due to common languages by occupying a non-relational indifferent place within the world, but not related to it (thus without the identity-difference oscillation needed for a democratic community). To do this they negate the very basis of all communicability in the modern age at least, the individuation of each body or humanimal life, within the language of what we hold in common. The only way to exceed individuation is to refuse it, without agreeing to some mass culture ideal either. Such a *klesis* behoves upon a subject that she become an indifferent body without relation to a differentiated world of related bodies. In fact, if you choose to be a body without individuation or to live in a non-communicable world without relations, the effect is the same, as in truth the world and the body, as we shall see, are intrinsically linked.

'There are only bodies and languages, except that there are truths' in effect summarizes the totality of the Being and Event project to this point; for bodies read multiples, for languages read logics of worlds. Although it is premature as a summation, because we don't yet speak the language of being-there in the world, the mathematics of the transcendental, it is a mnemonic aid for all that is to come. A truth, thanks to an event, is what exceeds set theory ontology, a truth is not an indifferent multiple, and what is exceptional to category theoretical logical worlds, a truth is not a relational function. The possibility and nature of the 'except that' of truths, cast out of ontology in Volume 1, left to wander unattended to in the worlds of Volume 2, are the purpose of everything else Badiou will now go on to say.

For a didactics of eternal truths: Invariance

In our first volume we worked very hard to ask if events as such could actually be said to be proven to 'exist'. We concluded that Badiou had done enough to deserve that, or at least that he had opened up a space wherein he could 'prove' ontology in such a way as it could not exclude events per se, even if it could exclude them from ontology as such. Now we have to work just as hard to ask if events exist in as much as they can be shown to inexist, the basic conclusion of *Being and Event*. Can they form bodies due to subjects to truths in real worlds? One of the simple tools Badiou proposes to engage to this end is examples of the invariance of truths through time and across conditions. Truths, he explains, defined as existing exceptions to the there-is of bodies plus languages, produce a form of 'primary evidence' by being observably invariant and consistent in the worlds they form consequences within (*LW* 9). This is an example of Badiou's realist materialism: the void's inexistence can be stated empirically and immanently. He then uses this intuition to explain the purpose of this second volume of *Being and Event*: 'the constitution, of the appearing of truths, and therefore of what grounds the evidence of their existence' (*LW* 9). To achieve this Badiou says he will 'demonstrate that the appearing of truths is that of wholly singular bodies (post-event bodies), which compose the multiple materiality wherein special formalisms (subjective formalisms) are set out' (*LW* 9). Truths are what appear in the form of nonrelational points or bodies.

As we saw in our first study, events cannot occur in terms of being even though they occur due to, in a highly complex sense, the indifference of the void that determines being as such. These evental bodies in-exist in a manner related to, but not the same as, the way being in-exists. Bodies cannot be said to have being, but nor can they be said to have existence. Existence is determined by the simple rules of all forms of discourse of constructivist communicability: that the object in question has a consistent, delimited body (being as such) and that this body is meaningful within an already-existent language, the discourse of democracy, or first order predicative logic. Post-evental bodies clearly have the first quality, and there is nothing that cannot be spoken of in language so they will be communicable, but before they become communicable in a language world, or a logics of worlds, their inexistent, because excluded, punctual form begins to thicken and spread its intensity to make a multiple materiality. The void is not a multiple, although it is material; it exists in reality. So one must take this materiality, introduce it into a world of multiples where truths can exist, namely words, and then pursue this inexistent punctuality into existence.

To prove all of the above will be difficult and time-consuming, so Badiou, perhaps rashly, decides to show us that truths do exist 'simply by considering the invariance existing across otherwise disparate worlds … Here it is merely a question of describing, through the mediation of some examples, the sufficient effect of truths, to the extent that, once they have appeared, they compose an a-temporal meta-history' (*LW* 9). First, we show an invariance of existence across disparate worlds, then, he goes on to add, we show they are truths, not just meanings, in that 'subtracted as they may be from the pragmatic opposition of bodies and languages, are nonetheless in the world' (*LW* 9). The outcome is a clear, three-part, dialectic structure. We have multiplicities or bodies: this is what there is the stuff, the fact that there is something, proven by *Being and Event*. Then we have languages: meaning, relations, logic, discourse and so on – the purview of much of *Logics of Worlds*. Finally, we have the 'aleatory third term (subject-truths)' that 'supplements' the other two (*LW* 10). There we have it, the sum total of what is being, how said beings exist in the world and how a third term supplements this.

Mathematical invariance

To provide empirical evidence of the invariance of truths Badiou now speaks of his four conditions on philosophy as the four realms where he can test the invariance of a truth in disparate worlds over time. All of the four examples 'aim to indicate what an eternal truth is through variation of its instances: the multiplicity of its (re)creations in distinct worlds' (*LW* 10). Of these four it is the first mathematical example concerning the invariant truth of numbers which will detain us, which Badiou considers due to the now well-trodden proofs of the fact that not only are there an infinite amount of prime numbers but, using the process of biunivocal correspondence, that there are an equal number of prime numbers as there are numbers. This demonstrates that a subset can be greater than the set itself. The significance here is not the proof, although Badiou gives it, but the point that asserting that there is an infinity of prime numbers and there are the same number of primes as naturals would be 'for an ancient Greek, even a mathematician, to speak in an entirely unintelligible jargon' (*LW* 11). Being a Greek meant having an ontological belief in finitude and an assumption that something contained in something else is necessarily smaller than the object that contains it. Badiou's point is that this issue of unintelligibility means that if there are only languages then yes, if something is non-communicable to a world because sets of belief preclude it, then said 'truth' cannot be made communicable even if it is actually, provably, true. Here Badiou speaks to the most fundamental law of Foucauldian and Agambenian discourse theory: that intelligibility is determined not by what is said but by the fact that it can be said. A statement should not be considered for what it means, but in terms of what structures of meaning, or in Badiou's language what world, it reveals through the communicable sense of its meaning such and such a thing. What a

Greek mathematician will allow to be a meaningful statement in mathematics is determined by what is a communicable mathematical world for the Greeks. A statement becomes communicable first because it has being or a body, then visibility, as a community we see it as the statement we think it is and allow it to speak to us, and finally the sanction of power, said statement is legitimatized by being included in the world of statements allowable at any one time. If a statement is made in that world, such that it has a body, but the community refuses to see it and the state refuses to allow it, then that statement remains invisible or mute, to use Ranciere's terminology,[5] noncommunicable to use our own.

The fact that Greek mathematicians could not comprehend the proof of actual infinity is clearly determined by the fact that they are Greek first and mathematicians second, which

> might lend credence to the notion that anthropological relativism should extend to the purported absolute truth of mathematics. Given that there are only languages, it will be affirmed that in the final analysis 'prime numbers' does not have the same meaning in Euclid's Greek language as it does in ours, since an ancient Greek could not even comprehend what is said about prime numbers in the modern language.
>
> (*LW* 12)

We have here the crux of communicability laid out before Badiou and a problem that will recur many times as we try to apply Badiou's theory of communicable worlds to real-world examples. It is all very well to speak of numbers, horses, rebellions, wars, demonstrations, pillars, colours, climbing plants across ancient buildings and so on as he repeatedly does, and to determine their relations using the same mathematical logic of relation, minimal and terminal limit, but what do you actually mean by these words, given that their relations are easy to determine? Badiou is not insensible to this issue, nor the related Deleuzian point that word and relation co-implicate and co-found each other. For Deleuze, relation precedes objects or at least co-determines them, an issue Badiou is clearly grappling with here. There is then a simple, Quinean non-translatability between Greek thought and our own,[6] which means when we speak of prime numbers we are not speaking of the same 'thing' as the Greeks. This being the case, Foucault and Quine are both right: truths are nothing but linguistically constructed meanings, and all we have to fight over is how they are constructed, what role if any does power play, can we break free and so on.

Badiou, however, now states quite the opposite. First, he explains that it is the very fact that an eternal truth, actual infinity of prime numbers, can be enveloped in different 'conceptual and linguistic contexts' or worlds, that proves they are invariably true. Second, he argues that in each case there is an invariant type of subject who is 'implicated by the demonstrative procedure' whether they are Greek, Arab, Chinese, ancient or modern. If we try to accept this axiom then what we realize is that the truth of the infinity of numbers is not really concerned with infinity itself. Infinity, for all its mystery and glamour, is just a number and a very commonplace one at that. Even Badiou is not really interested in infinity but what infinity reveals about ontology. So here, mathematicians are not debating infinity but the structure of numbers: 'namely, that they are all composed of prime numbers, which are like the atomic (indecomposable) constituents of numericality' (*LW* 12). If then we take numericality as the truth, we can show that modern mathematics for all its complexity is primarily concerned with prime numbers, and we can 'envelop' number in new worlds without ever abolishing the concept of number such as the Greeks also conceived of it. This answers the riddle of how new subjects discover new things, how they can be said to be new and yet how they come to exist in worlds where there is nothing new as such. Which comes down to a key point concerning not so much the fact of a new discovery, but the mode in which that discovery is formalized point by point by a subject to truth. As we already saw in Volume 1, all events are indifferent and inexistent, but what they allow to happen is a subject to truth composing the effects of that truth point by point so that the truth can become communicable in the world, and yet not simply become absorbed into pure communicability as such: just another statement.[7]

Badiou sees that each truth is attached to a body; let's use the works of Archimedes as that is his example. Archimedes isn't the subject, his works are not the subject, many of his works may not be by him, many works he produces are not part of his subjectivity. So how does this subject, which as we know is not psychological or somatic or liberal, operate in relation to an event as truth? They 'link a formalism to a material body (a body of writing in the mathematical case) ... which exhibits and makes explicit an indefinitely subjectivizable constraint relative to the body of writing in question' (*LW* 14). Every subject is not just a subject to truth but a subject to constraint as regards the link of a formalism, which is invariant, to a body of work, which is 'new'. Badiou's thesis, and even he seems to find this surprising, is that 'the subjective type committed to the constraint is invariable' (*LW* 14). Let us be clear at this early stage. Events which 'produce' truths are indifferent and so in this sense, according to our reading, are universal, but they are not, according to Badiou, universally true. A truth must be pursued by a subject to truth for an event, which is indifferent and thus meaningless, to become meaningful for a world. For this to transpire the subject must be differentiated in some degree as they are Greek or modern. Such an identity is determined by their world, but their identity is not their subjectivity. As regards their subjectivity, they are invariant so while they may not be indifferent, they are not differentiated in any normal, identitarian sense. All subjects are the same and they are equivalent because to formalize a body of work which is eventual such that it can be said to exist they must succumb to the same constraints. If this is the case then the debate shifts from the relativity of words and grammar to the reality of a certain set of formal constraints. And our question is not: Is the world communicable or true? But: Are these formal constraints on the truths of events communicable or true? Badiou states firmly that they are.

Badiou sets out the formal invariants of Greek thought about number and finds two central constraints. The first is that in deduction through descent, there must be a halting point. The second is that to prove the existence of something you can use *reductio ad absurdum* and simply say, imagine there were an infinite number of prime numbers, what logical impossibilities would that throw up? Having shown these impossibilities, you don't prove your case, you just show that the opposite cannot be true so your case must be true. Descending deductive reasoning attached to a halting point and the allowance of *reductio ad absurdum* are not only invariant subjective operations across the history of mathematics, but Badiou's ontology through set theory relies on both such that set theory disproves Greek thought in terms of the actual existence of an infinity of prime numbers, it does so using the same invariant procedures as the Greeks themselves used. Are these procedures real or true?

Logic tried very hard to show that mathematical procedures are reducible to an invariant set of procedures which can be called constructivist, but we know very well that Badiou is no constructivist. This being the case, it cannot be the procedures which are true but rather the basis of these procedures on something which is real, in Badiou's case for set theory the void and for category theory the atomic reality of an object, thanks to the void. At the same time here, Badiou also expresses his belief that there is something about subjective behaviour; remember subjects are not people, that is invariant and thus true because it is real. He says:

> This subjective figure too is eternal: examining the situation in accordance with the determinate concept, one perceives a real point in this situation which demands that one choose between the maintenance of the concept and that of the situation. It is true that we thereby presume that a subject does not want

the situation annihilated. It will sacrifice its concept to it. This is indeed what constitutes a subject of truth: it holds that a concept is only valid to the extent that it supports a truth of the situation. When all is said and done, rejecting the *reductio ad absurdum* is an ideological choice with vast consequences. (*LW* 15–16)

Let us try to express this as simply as we can. If given a choice between rejecting the situation or rejecting the concept, when a subject is confronted with an impossible body relative to what is communicable within their world, the subject will always preserve the situation. This is a truth, it is eternal, it is real. It is as real as the void and as real as the categorical atom. If using the same methods of deduction you find that you can prove that actual infinity exists, you could say I don't accept that so my methods of deduction are incorrect. Badiou's gamble, which is based on a discursive data set of a vast size, is that subjects in situations never do that. They always preserve the situation of what is formally acceptable and jettison the concept. This has immense implications. As he says, *reductio ad absurdum* requires that you change your ideology. If you remove it from mathematics, then you are not doing mathematics any more. If you are not allowed to say if not *a* then *b*, then the whole classical basis of mathematics falls.

The following sections pursue the invariants of the other three conditions – the formal intelligibility of art, the necessity of violent change for politics and the power of Two for love – nailing down his point as regards the invariance of exception as firmly as possible, and reminding his readers of the four conditions of universal invariance. After these fascinating case studies, Badiou then presents us with a five-part schema for the formal, point-by-point, mode of appearing of a truth in a world.

- Material traces: in mathematics it is the materiality of the void and the atom, in poetry naturally it is the material mark, in politics the party and so on.
- Subjective break: we know how enamoured Badiou is of the idea of the subject to truth; there can be no appearance of truth in a world without a subject.
- The work of consequences: mathematical consequentiality is ingrained in its deductive method, there can be no political action without consequences and so on.
- Excess over any particular language: this is a crucial point that pertains specifically to the relation of a truth to the constructivism of knowledge, or here the logics of worlds. In the basic formula of bodies and languages we

began with, a truth creates a material body that is in excess of the language which would be able to construct and communicate the meaning of that body. If that body 'exists', even as that which is inexistent, then it does not have meaning and therefore, according to Badiou's dialectic and classical reasoning, it must be a truth.

- Latent eternity: when one is in love, one seeks to access the eternal as is shown by Virgil's sublime poetry in the *Aeneid*, but of course every truth is eternal and universal. The different instances of the truth in question, if they display the invariant features Badiou insists they must, are, he says, by definition eternal. Not because the same idea occurs across vast divisions of time and space, that is not eternal just impressive, but because of what allows them to be invariant across time and space. It comes down to the formal point-by-point testing of the truth against eternal yet intrinsic laws that proves the eternity of any truth. Badiou is well aware this can never be proven by examples, so the examples simply showcase the formal method.

Speaking still of the Aeneid Badiou notes two more 'singular traits through which the discontinuous singularity of truth manifests itself' (*LW* 29). One of these is infinity which, we know, is the driver for Badiou's ontology and so of course is a central part of any truth. The other is 'the transfiguration into the Idea of the most banal, most anonymous aspect of a situation. This is what I called, in *Being and Event*, the genericity of the True' (*LW* 29). This dialectic forms the basis of Badiou's conclusion on the very nature of the Two, speaking of love, and experience of the 'exceptional infinity of existence – creating the caesura of the One through the eventual energy of the encounter – and the ideal becoming of an ordinary emotion, of an anonymous grasp of this existence' (*LW* 32). It would appear, then, that even in the logics of appearing, which are differential and thus not indifferent, there is still the generic nature of anonymous indifference. For example, Badiou says: 'The power of the Two is to carve out an existence, a body, a banal individuality, directly on the sky of ideas' (*LW* 32). Adding, 'Love is this disjunctive synthesis, as Deleuze would put it, between infinite expansion and anonymous stagnation. Ontologically, every truth is an infinite but also generic fragment of the world in which it comes to be' (*LW* 32). The best example of this confounding compound infinity + indifference is, he feels, Aschenbach's passion for Tadzio where the ludicrous somatic decrepitude of the dying writer is still capable of attaining 'the unfettered sight' of his love object. Badiou ruminates: 'Through the separating power of the Two, love illuminates the anonymous existence harboured by this "unfettered sight"' (*LW* 32). The insistence on the indifferent, generic anonymity of the body that, in being separated from the idea, produces the unfettered sight of truth is a warning shot across the bows. As we progress, we will become as enamoured with Badiou's calculated phenomenology as Aschenbach is with Tadzio, albeit with less tragic results;[8] yet, Badiou is warning us that the *Logics of Worlds*, the languages that describe the bodies of appearing, the communicability of all knowledge and meaning, is all in the service of those occasional truths. At some point, if we wish to avoid Aschenbach's fate, we must let them go.

Distinctive features of truths

'Let's sum up the properties which permit us to say that certain productions, in worlds that are otherwise disparate, are marked by this disparateness only to the very extent that they are exceptions to it' (*LW* 33). There, in a nutshell, is the kernel of this immense fruit *Logics of Worlds* and it all hinges on two disparate conceptions of difference. Here it is clear there is a disparateness of exceptionalism. If difference is presented logically, in a classical sense, then a disparateness of exception implies that something is exceptional to disparateness which demands, of course, it is not-disparate, which in turn implies it is the same or an identity. What other way is there of saying disparateness to disparateness? Well, two come to mind. The first is the possible bifurcation of difference into differing kinds of difference, for example, difference of relation versus difference of identity. The other, obviously, is indifference. We favour the second solution because, as I have shown extensively elsewhere, different 'kinds' of difference are component parts of the more consistent and complex indifferential reasoning that comes out of a reading of Badiou's work.[9]

To this summation, disparateness of disparateness is exception due to indifference, we may add that 'though their materiality, their "bodies" as we would say, are composed only of the elements of the world, these truths ... nonetheless exhibit a type of universality that those elements, drawn from worldly particularity, cannot sustain on their own' (*LW* 33). This is the paradox of truth as, what might be called, an emergent phenomenon. Truths are made of bodies found only in the world yet transformed in an almost alchemical fashion into truth-sustaining materialities rather than truth-negating ones. This process, which is rare, consists of seven stages or elements.

1. Produced in measurable time, truths are however eternal so that grasped from another time the 'fact that it constitutes an exception remains fully intelligible' (*LW* 33). The intelligibility of truths depends on the intelligibility of communicability as such. Truths have no direct intelligibility because they are truths due to the fact that they are non-communicable, yet presented, inexistent exceptions.
2. Although always written in a particular language, truths are trans-linguistic. This is one of the most important contentions of *Logics of Worlds* and *Being and Event*. The constructivist project did not fail, indeed *Logics* is dominated by it, but it is incomplete. There are truths that exceed the relativity of language systems. In a sense Carnap's principle of tolerance wedded however to a Fregean Platonism.
3. If every truth 'presupposes a closed set of material traces', these traces are not empirical uses in a world but rather consist of a 'frontal change, which has affected (at least) one object of this world'. Such material traces are traces of an event. A truth composes a consistent closed set of materials, like any constructed language, except that the materials in question pertain to an inexistent element, the event. The innovation here is that a truth is a composite set or concept that does not extend over any objects in the world as it currently is, yet cannot, as would logically have to be the case, be defined as false. Thus in logics of appearance thanks to the ontology of set theory, one can both have a 'concept' that is not yet 'true' in the logical sense of the term (extends over at least one object in the world) but which is not false either. In addition, this composite is always already a set of multiples which means, by definition, it does extend because it has formed a set. It is, in essence, to use a concept foundational to all modern logic, an inextensive extension. That this inextensive event can be materialized is primarily because of the reality of the void, an option available because of the foundational role of set theory to the logics of appearing called category theory. It is the materiality of the void that allows for the halting point which is the atomic materiality of all bodies. This materiality means we can insist on truths, things that exist before languages, and then subsequently we can 'prove' said truths constructively. This, and only this, is the way in which we can speak of something as truthful even though it does not extend over an object, and as extended in terms of being a set, even though it does not extend over object(s). This perhaps makes clear the differentiation between Badiou's truth and the related yet dissimilar conception of truth in extensional philosophers, in particular Frege, Carnap and Quine.

4. All traces are linked to a subject: 'a subject is an operative disposition of traces of the event and of what they deploy in the world' (*LW* 33).
5. Truths articulate and evaluate their components, both terms are carefully chosen here, due to consequences not merely givens. Consequence is not being determined as a form of causation as we said, but as a means of negating the stagnation of all constructivist worlds. (We have already explained consequence in our first study and will come back to it extensively later as well.)[10]
6. Due to the articulation of consequences, 'a truth elicits subjects-forms which are like instances of an invariant matrix of articulation' (*LW* 33).
7. Finally, as we just saw, a truth is infinite and generic meaning that indifference bookends truths. Not only is the event, which is the basis of all truths, indifferent, but the world which the truth bears consequence upon, due to it being profoundly differentiated, that is, a constructivist communicability, is ultimately indifferent or meta-indifferent (localized changes make no difference to it overall).

All of this allows Badiou to sum up by saying of a truth: 'It is a radical exception as well as an elevation of anonymous existence to the Idea' (*LW* 34). It is this combination of exception and indifference, surely, which will determine the eternal truth of Badiou's philosophy.

Book I

Formal Theory of the Subject (Meta-Physics)

Unlike *Being and Event*, where the crucial content of the study – the event and the creation of militant subjects for truths due to the trace of the event in an actual situation – is held in abeyance until the second half, *Logics of Worlds* begins at its endpoint, so to speak. Although Badiou concedes that at this initial stage he cannot do much more than assert his overriding thesis that subjects and truths exist, all the same he takes it as read that they do and proceeds to detail their formal nature. This has strategic importance because it disallows our simply admiring the calculated phenomenology of *Logics of Worlds* without being aware that this is hardly the point. It also has a double methodological justification. The first is that in mathematics, at least, the method of assuming something and then retroactively proving it is not only central to mathematical formalism, but was the means by which Badiou first realized that he could 'prove' the event using retroactive axiomatic reasoning. The second is that, as he says later, you don't have to prove that it is possible to have bodies in worlds, you need but to look around you. This speaks to the particular nature of the extensive use of the example in the book. What follows, therefore, is almost diametrically opposed to how *Being and Event* was composed, clearly a response to complaints that that first volume was too far from actual situations and real-world examples. Across the first chapter Badiou makes an assertion about the subject and its body, he presents a mode of formal notation, then he gives illustrative examples, without providing, at this stage, the rational deductions that make it impossible to question his presupposition. He calls this a method designed 'to show from the outset that which is only fully intelligible at the end' (*LW* 45).

For example, he says, 'It's possible to start speaking of a subject at once, because the theory of the subject is essentially formal' (*LW* 46). By this he is stating that a subject, and remember a subject is not a person or a consciousness, 'formalizes the effects of a body in accordance with a certain logic … It is clear then that a subject is that which imposes the legibility of a unified orientation onto the multiplicity of bodies. The body is a composite element of the world; the subject is what fixes in the body the secret of the effects it produces' (*LW* 46–7). The subject, according to this, creates communicability, here called legibility, vis-à-vis an already-existent body. This communicability or intelligibility can be positive and negative. He gives examples of both productive and counterproductive effects of political events pertaining to communism of the twenties and thirties, and aesthetic events, Austrian music between Schoenberg and Webern that moves between moments of true rupture along with the 'sedimentation of a new sensibility' (*LW* 46). What these examples show is that subjects make legible bodies in varying ways that can be truly evental or actually rather reactionary. You can even become, Badiou's believes, a reactionary revolutionary. Putting these elements together, without yet proving this to be the case, Badiou argues that a theory of the subject is formal because it designates 'a system of forms and operations' (*LW* 47).

As we explained in Volume 1 of our study these are the universally true formal means for a subject to track the consequences of a body point by point.[1] This theoretical formalism is 'indifferent to corporeal particularities' in that, as we saw say in deductive descent to a halting point, said formalisms are universal, indifferent, abstract means that exist between the trace of the event and its actual existence in a situation. It is, as we saw in the case of multiples in set theory, a theory of content-neutral or im-predicative collections or the indifference of bodies to go alongside that of the indifference of multiples. Such an abstract formalism of the subject is supported, materially, in the world by what he is calling a body, which is a collection of elements that, as yet, inconsist. Such an inconsistent body is the equivalent of the generic set of multiples founded in set theory at the level of presentation, re-counted in a worldy situation in terms of re-presentation while remaining, paradoxically, generic – without particularity. Paradoxically because a world is defined as relational differences between objects due to degrees of intensity thanks to 'qualities', although as we shall see it is in fact incorrect to call the properties of objects in worlds qualities as they are, in fact, functions.[2]

Another way of thinking of this is, take our example of the generic in sets, a room full of an infinite number of people whose names (numerical rank) you don't know but you know they all have names (they are all rankable).[3] Now think of this instead as a room full of people who are all there for the same reason but some are more committed to this cause than others and each degree of commitment is determined relationally between any two people at any time. The first is a generic indifference of rank as a relation, the second a generic indifference of relation as rank. In the first instance the element indifferentiated is relation: multiples have a rank, but you don't know where in the rank they are, so their relation is indeterminate. In the second the element indifferentiated is rank: all objects in the room have a determinate relation, in terms of another element, but where they stand overall, their rank in relation to what they all have in common remains indeterminate. This 'ensemble', as Badiou calls it, produces one of three things: a truth, a denial of truth or an occultation of truth. We have already encountered a typology of subjectivities in *Being and Event* where we accepted that a subject is not always a subject to truth. In addition, while we can say that a body only exists due to the formal activity of a subject, a body is not always a truthful body. This opens up the idea of the subject, the body and truths in a fashion that feels intuitively right. We can easily observe that not every radical event results in radical change. There are always reactionaries and powers that try to eradicate the event altogether.

In that Badiou has written two immense studies of the subject, *Theory of the Subject* and *Being and Event*, and has been writing about this topic since 1982; it seems fair that he can now presuppose that the subject exists. Yet, in that by his own admission here and in *Being and Event*, key concepts of *Theory of the Subject* are misguided, in particular the 'splace' and the idea of destruction; one might raise the possibility that the problem is lodged deep within the project itself. Indeed, he begins by conceding that his theory of the subject contravenes what he sees as the three dominant traditions of subjectivity. These he lists as a subject of experience (phenomenology), of morality (neo-Kantian) and of ideology (Althusser). I won't dwell on Badiou's refutation of these traditions but rather draw the reader's attention to the point we have arrived at within Badiou's work which is, as we have not yet presented his theory of the object, all we can say at this point is that the subject is 'pure act: to endow an efficacious body with an appropriate formalism' (*LW* 49). This definition is in keeping with the particularity of his choice of category theory; for categories are made up of 'acts', they are operations not objects per se. It also allows us to see that category theory can broach a subject to truth thanks to an event better than set theory even if, in both instances, events as self-mentioning multiples are, in theory, banned from both kinds of formalism. If a subject can give a body the correct kind of formalism through functional relations, then it should be able to make a self-mentioning object visible logically and, according to the intuitionist logic of categories, if you can see it, it exists.

Badiou's subject is, therefore, defined as this operational process: to give a visible body to an impossible object by making it formally visible through logical procedures. Badiou further promotes such a definitional limpidity by placing the subject between two forces: that of restriction and amplification. 'In sum, we oscillate between a restrictive (or conditioned) construction and an amplifying (or unconditioned exposition)' (*LW* 49). If this is so, the subject inaugurates a truth into communicability due to a set of generic, formal procedures that are the basis of all communicability within that world/condition. Yet at the same time, because these procedures are universal and because truth is a response to the inexistence of an evental trace that as yet is totally noncommunicable within a world where it appears, truths do not simply become forms of knowledge. There is a delay, a modality of exposition, a spectrality, a remnant of indifference, something about the subjective constructive exposition of a truth that means it is not knowledge even as it is treated by the formalism of knowledge. The easy answer here would be to say of course, because of the formal process, the indifference of the void and the materiality of the object as indivisible atom prove that there is a truthful element to every world, but this would not clearly be truthful in the sense that Badiou would have the term.

Anyway, we now have our subject-structure which, Badiou asserts, can be fixed by schematic operations of which he names four: the bar, the consequence or implication, erasure or the diagonal bar, and negation. At this point, Badiou also proposes some basic notation to better express the relationship between the event, the body and the subject. The event is present only in the form of a trace, the event as such as we know inexists and is inaccessible to the subject directly. The trace of the event is represented by ε. Then there is a 'body issued from the event' (*LW* 49) which shall be called C. In simple terms, Badiou says, we have to presuppose that a rupture has occurred in the world. This rupture, the event, leaves a trace, which we are calling ε, and results in a body C, that is 'correlated to ε' (*LW* 50). This body only exists under the condition of the evental trace so all bodies are the consequence of events. The totality of the formal theory can be expressed as due to ε and C, there is a theory of operations of figures, and destinations or acts. This is basically a schematic version of category theory which combines functions (operations) with destinations. We have already met our four functions – the bar, the consequence, erasure and negation – although we do not yet know what they really mean, we now also have our destinations which Badiou calls production, denial, occultation and resurrection. Much of the rest of the first book is a consideration of these four destinations of a body under the condition of the evental trace. In terms of categories we take C, and trace its target or codomain, of which there can only be four, through the arrows or monisms of four types of function. If C can be functionally mapped onto production, multiple times, thanks to the subject, then the eventual trace will start to form a body.

Referents and operations of the faithful subject

Badiou now moves on to clarify some basic qualities of the subject. First, as it does not conform with the three dominant ideas of the subject, he declares that the subject is primarily axiomatic, meaning that there are no deductive processes which can 'prove' the subject. Like the void for set theory, the subject is external to any form of constructivist thought including category theory. In addition, the relation between subject and truth is one of tautology: subject means truth, truth means subject. Just as a subject cannot be deduced, it cannot be found experimentally either. It is not the result of empirical observation; yet, it is to be found on the horizon of an irrefutable empirical truth as can all of Badiou's axioms, which can be expressed as, except that there are truths or the materiality of the real of the void. This is why Badiou insists on calling his work materialist for, however abstract his mathematical and here also logical reasoning can become, his modes of thought are marked out by their realism in terms of the basic axioms upon which the deductive systems are placed. Truth is real, the void is real, as we shall see objects as atoms are real too. There is a halting point, a place outside of every system which for Badiou cannot be proven by the system, Gödel's incompleteness theorems, but which can retroactively be taken as real due to the system, Badiou's extensive use of the mathematical mode of retroactive axiomatic thinking. Set theory is decisionist, and its decisions occur before the logic of its formalism, while category theory is concerned with possible choices, thanks to the formalism (*MT* 57). Another reason why events, remember illegal in both sets and categories, can never present themselves in ontology is because the decisions that ban them have already been made and thus are, in effect, necessary, while the modal logic of categories allows for the 'impossible' to be possible in a world where self-mentioning objects can be shown to exist. If intuitionism disallows the double-negative because it cannot show it, an operation so central to classical logic one might call it banal, then it keeps open the possibility that the event's 'impossibility' is just like that of the double-negative, impossible at the moment in this world.

Now we consider the relation between the event and what Badiou calls the body, a crucial innovation in *Logics* absent from the earlier work. It would appear that the subject is a functional '"subjectivation" of a link between the physics of the body and the name or trace of the event' (*LW* 51).[4] To better capture what functional subjectivation does, Badiou commences with one of the most abiding examples in the book, the uprising of the slaves in Rome in 73 BC under the leadership of Spartacus. The revolt-event is large numbers of slaves coming together to form a body under Spartacus' leadership against the forces of Rome. The trace of this revolt-event, Badiou says, is the phrase 'We slaves, we want to return home'. Apropos of this event, the operation where a new body is made up of these slaves is the subject-form: 'the conjunction that governs the strategies of Spartacus' (*LW* 51). Note that the subject is not Spartacus himself but what happens strategically point by point once the evental trace has been given a name. Also be aware that the subject is a set of operations and strategies, not qualities or components. As we saw in mathematics the formal strategies of *reductio ad absurdum*, so here we see the army goes north, then the armies go south and so on as formal strategies. A central word for the formalism of the subject is: 'then'. The subject-form appears to be resolutely serial and systematically concatenated, tied intimately to the if ... then formulation of logical implication.

Although logical implication appears as a central function for subjectivation, Badiou explains that the movements of the army cannot be said to be subjectivated as a response to the original trace of the event. Rather, he insists that 'the subjective identity which is fashioned in and by these military movements is not identical with them' (*LW* 51). Such a non-identity is because the body of the slaves moves in a 'new present' so that while they were slaves forming a body due to a trace event, as this becomes subjectivated in the formal means by which they actuate the trace-event through their body, they enter into a situation that was not possible before. For example, their initial body made up of slaves is no longer a body of 'slaves' because they are now free. These 'slaves' then reveal that what was impossible previously, when they became a body due to an event, is now possible: it is possible for slaves to become free or at least to be no longer a slave. 'This institution of the possible as present is typically a subjective production. Its materiality is constituted by the consequences drawn day after day from the event's course ... These consequences affect and reorganize the body by treating successive points within the situation' (*LW* 51).

What this also suggests is that the original ontology of the object slave, differentiated from free soldiers, for example, is in this world such that functionally it can be shown that the objects 'slave' and 'free soldier' are identical. Such a state of functional parity is called isomorphism in category theory. Isomorphism is a very common procedure of simplification wherein if two objects have exactly the same functional relations then, however different they may be ontologically, categorically they are said to be identical. This is a parallel I feel to the similar situation in sets due to the axioms of collection and substitutability. If two objects appear in the same rank in two sets of the same cardinality, then they are 'the same' event if in terms of qualities they are radically different. Isomorphism is one of the most wonderfully optimistic of all the properties of categories because it states that you can change what you are, in terms of what you do, in a manner that also changes your world. Slaves can become free by acting free, but this also alters the functions of free soldiers because slaves that are free render the central differentiation freedom/bondage indistinct or indifferent.

We have clearly encountered one of the more exciting innovations of clarity to be found in *Logics of Worlds* as regards the subject. Subjectivation moves in a present of the possible, carrying with it day by day a sort of collective laboratory of what one can do, if one accepts the possibility of the phrase 'We slaves, we want to *and can* return home'. For me this is the most convincing moment in Badiou wherein he is able to break that limit insisted upon by analytical formal reasoning between a constructed system and the real world. The slaves are operating as a body just as mathematicians 'operate'. If we take the example of actual infinity, Cantor behaves as if there were such a thing and then tests this day by day, point by point to see if, in the new present of the possible, 'there are actual infinities', new avenues opening up that, however, are still in accordance with the formalism of the world. This testing of new possibilities point by point is the dialectical heart of Badiou's entire system, namely that at some point, and it is literally a point here, day by day, within the present of the possible, you need to decide either yes or no to something: should we go north, should we attack Rome and so on? It is these points that 'unfold the subjective formalism that this body is capable of bearing. In this sense, a subject exists, as the localization of a truth, *to the extent that it affirms that it holds a certain number of points*' (LW 52).

That these points are determined by simple yes or no answers is significant. It means that even as an event-trace comes to appear in the world as impossible, unlike in terms of ontology, this impossibility can be systematically made more and more possible by each operational choice on the original event coming out positive. While you have to decide on the event, an ontological operation that means you have to exclude the being of the event, subsequently you can choose the event over and over by applying its consequences to a series of real-world situations which slowly come to reveal that the impredicative impossibility of the statement 'there are events' comes to be shown to be less and less impossible. That this requires a complex mix of classical, yes/no and intuitionistic logic, the modality of the possible and necessity, to be able to show this, is perhaps reflective of the incredible difficulty of the task to hand, and Badiou's immense control of the varied resources of modern thought. While the onto-logical combination is still some way from our grasp perhaps, we can say a couple of more obvious things such as, in subjectivation, while there is a yes/no decisive process, this does not mean that a yes is the production of a negation of no, or that in the end of the process this yes is the direct negation of that rejected no, not least because this is an exploratory, heuristic process. In the localized function of the decision, the destination it heads to is not yet determined, and so we decide not knowing if the final result will be positive or negative.

Returning to the text, Badiou is now able to describe the process of subjectivation due to four processes. The first is the event trace (ε). The second is the body (C). Now we also have the present. Subjectivation is a process that takes place almost entirely in the present in that, effectively, all bets are off, so the past does not help and the future is literally impossible to predict. If a slave joins the slave body he is joining an army effectively, but due to the subjectivation of a new present of the possible, names like 'slave', 'army', even 'joining' cease to become communicable terms within our common world. They do not become meaningless or noncommunicable, but rather the basis of their communicability, which is the presupposition of their meaning due to the consistent stability of the world in which they operate, has been suspended. As he says of categories, in contradistinction to sets, they are defined by a restraint that is 'suspended between possible logics by which it treats the ontological material' (*LW* 57). And as it treats the ontological material of names like slave or army, the functions of such material, in this world, can alter even to the point of contradicting the original sense of the meaning of the term. This is possible because, like signatures in Agamben, the term slave is content neutral, both as a set, all sets are property indifferent, and now, more shockingly as an object in the world, because as we saw said objects are not determined by what they are, based on the composition of their predicates, but what they do.[5] It is worth noting that self-contradiction, you can be a slave and yet be free, is banned from classical logic and indeed from all modes of analytical thought. The only reason it is possible here is because categories depend on intuitionist and modal forms of logic, and because the contradiction in question, slaves that are free, is composed point by point rather than in one instant: true or false.

Thus the words in question become indifferentiated in the sense that their denotative function exists, but it becomes indistinct as to what they actually denote. Now the slave is working out point by point what it means to be a slave who can be free, rather than accepting the meaning of the term 'slave' provided to them by the social function of language á la Quine or Wittgenstein. The army in its operations works out point by point what this new model army could be like. Even the idea of allegiance to a military force that has no nation, no binding force, as Badiou will go on to say no transcendental, is being worked out anew. Point-by-point testing not only suspends the denotative function of words, it also results in the production of consequences in a world. For example, the more slaves join the slave army, the more points that army can treat at the same time, the more ambitious the subsequent points and so on. Thus in addition to the third operation of the present, here called π, we have the consequence, represented by the traditional notation for implication: ⇒. The four elements – the event, the subject, the present and the consequence, or ε, C, π, ⇒ – are organized mathematically using subordination, for example, here the body will be subordinate to the evental trace. The symbol for subordination is the bar –, allowing the simple equation $\frac{\varepsilon}{\delta}$.

With the notation in place, if you find the insistence on notation off-putting don't worry Badiou actually does not really use his own notation extensively; now we must contend with an important element of the body, which is that because it is treated point by point in real time, so almost entirely contained within the present, the body is at no point complete as at any one time it is only treating some points. As Badiou says of the body:, 'It is divided into, on the one hand, an efficacious region, an organ appropriate to the point being treated, and, on the other, a vast component which, with regard to this point, is inert or even negative' (LW 52). Thus the body, C, should mostly appear under negation: C̄. Badiou explains by saying that the slave army is made up of a core of trained professionals, and a large fringe of disorderly remainder composing many different languages, the presence of women, rivalrous sub-leaders and so on. If this unit decides to treat the point [attack the Roman cavalry], it may fail due to the remainder. Yet if it decides to set up a slave city, the remainder now becomes essential for forming civic life, while the trained militia find they have no place and fall into a marginal existence.

We now have all the component parts of the subjectivation as functional, heuristic process. We have a body under erasure because not complete: the still-forming slave army that has no coherence. They are subordinate to an event-trace: 'We slaves can go home.' That said, this is due to the incorporation of the body into a point-by-point set of decisions, each of which has consequences. 'These consequences, which treat some of the major points in the Roman historical world, found a new truth in the present: that the fate of the wretched is never a law of nature, and that it can ... be revoked' (*LW* 53), albeit for a relatively short duration. All can be summarized in the following 'matheme' if that is your preferred way of reasoning:

$$\frac{\varepsilon}{\cent} \Rightarrow \pi$$

Badiou's matheme effectively presents a theory of nominative suspension, taking names and suspending them from their denotative function due to real-time contraventions of their conventions of reference – I am a slave and yet here I am acting in a free manner – marking a return to an idea first developed in *Being and Event*. At the end of that text Badiou describes how generic, canonical naming functions can be used to extend the generic multiple made possible by the axiom of choice, into what he then called situations (these are now worlds). In so doing eventual multiples in situations could behave as if they had names whose specificity would be filled in later as the subject to truth completed her yes/no enquiries. This was one example of a naming function wherein the specificity of the name itself, in logic we would call this the concept, is suspended for the canonical fact that as these multiples do have being, then they can be named when eventually they come to be recounted as included as well as belonging. How is the new theory of the event different from this already highly sophisticated, in many aspects totally brilliant, formulation?

First, in logics of appearing, the names in question are not generic because they are canonical naming functions: x, y, z, for example. Rather, the names retain their referential extension; there is a concept set called slaves and I am one of those, but the concept itself is suspended by your inclusion in said set due to your actions: they call me a slave; yet, my behaviour refutes the meaning of that term. What is significant here is that the concept slave does not cease to extend over Spartacus' army; instead, the objects over which the concept extends literally act to change the 'truth' of the concept: you can be called a slave and behave freely. Second, in *Being and Event*, the subject tests whether the new multiple, which has been chosen because the axiom of choice allows one to do so, which cannot be given being because it is inconsistent, you cannot rule it out but you cannot rule it in either, can begin to form an existence out of the quasi-complete rules of constructivist systems. Can it be said to exist even though it is indiscernible? Can it be said to have properties even though it is undecidable? The generic nature of the named multiple means that not only can you speak of an event as if it has a specific name, meaning one can discern it, but also you can then classify other multiples or objects as belonging to it: decidability. All of this occurs through the point-by-point decision making of a subject, who says yes or no to multiples or objects, as regards whether they can be said to belong to the set of the multiple's expressible truth – an inspirational proposal, but not how subjectivation actually works. Instead, the process of point-by-point decision making is not so much, can these objects be said to be part of the evental set, but rather how point-by-point decision making due to the impossible made possible by that initial event, suspends names of sets and multiples in an actual world, through the actions of the slaves here, and the consequences of those as well. In the first system objects are generically included in a set that possessed a generic naming function. In the second, objects are singularly included in the set of the event's consequences due to real time, on the ground decision making of the body, the slave army, such that their denotative function is suspended, rendered generic, so that the enslaving function of being named a slave is not only deactivated, but devastated. We now have the concept slave extending over the objects, free humans.

What I hope is now apparent is that the event described here as the process of subjectivation through the formation of bodies is radically different to the relation of the event to the subject enquiry point by point and its role of suspended nomination, that defines the final chapter of *Being and Event*. It is not just that it modifies it slightly, but is radically at odds with it, and the option here or anywhere else in the second volume of bringing generic enquiry and in-world subjectivation together is not taken up. We might ask at this point which is the better system. As we know there are major problems with the theory of the event in *Being and Event*. These problems are not there in *Logics*. In addition, one can immediately see how much easier it is to understand the event from the perspective of the suspensive deactivation of transcendental names of sets, such as [slaves], as a localized set of political actions and decisions, each of which is damaging to the world, the state and so on which operate through said transcendental functors, as they are later called. An event on this reading does not just do something new, but as it does so it debilitates directly a world of oppression say, by changing the nature of the concept that extends, rather than changing what it extends over. This is profoundly political. Good it is to say [slaves] no longer extends over African Americans in 1865, for example, but much better it is to make it impossible for [slaves] to enslave them because the concept [slaves] is not shown to extend over the free. If I then try to enslave others, I cannot because the concept no longer means that. What Badiou's theory does, which is why it is intuitionist, is allow the concept slave to extend over objects that contradict each other; there are slaves and the free in the same set, such that the truth of the concept [slaves] becomes undecidable. It is not that [slaves] now means the free, but that if you say you are a [slave] I cannot decide if that means you are free or enslaved.

The four subjective destinations

Badiou applies this notation to four different typologies of the subject. We have just considered what he calls the faithful subject. Next, he considers the reactionary subject. The reactionary denies that there has been an event so that we might write this as $\neg \varepsilon$ if we are so inclined, but a reactionary subject is not entirely negative. They, like the faithful subject, claim to produce a present and this production is due to the event, albeit the need to deny the event. If we think of the slaves' revolt for a moment, reactionary slaves are those who were too afraid to join the rebellion. The present produced by the reaction is a 'measured present, a negative present "a little less worse" than the past, if only because it resisted the catastrophic temptation which the reactive subject declares is contained in the event' (*LW* 55). Badiou terms the changes resultant in the reactive present to be small novelties, a kind of amelioration, and defines the present they create as the present under negation or double-bar of extinction '='. In any revolt there are a number of subjects who define the new present due to the trace of the event as under negation. They accept that things have changed, and they react by presenting these changes in terms of violence, terror, chaos and so on, making a case for things to stay pretty much as they are with some changes. One can see here that on the whole this is the modern form of our capitalist, democratic, governmental politics.

In terms of a reactive subject, beneath the bar Badiou places the whole matheme of the event which ultimately negates the present but at least concedes that some thing has to change. In terms of our third kind of subject, the obscure, the present itself is occluded under the bar in favour of a myth of the full body. Badiou says that the reactive subject likes to place the body as far as possible from their concept of the negated present. In contrast, the obscure subject uses the body as a transcendental myth to negate, then hide, the new present entirely. It is not that the new present then is negated, but totally denied. The obscure subject pertains specifically to sovereign power, as you need power to make actual events totally noncommunicable. In the case of ancient Rome, the ruling class would first deny that it is true that the slaves wanted to return home, and second that in any case there is 'no legitimate body that can be the bearer of this false statement' (*LW* 60). The statement is denied but also the body, or rather it is transformed from the divided body of the point-by-point testing of eventual consequences. Instead, 'the obscure subject calls upon an atemporal fetish: the incorruptible and indivisible over-body, be it City, God or Race' (*LW* 60). This results in a paradox of the occlusion of the present in the present itself. This temporal atemporality is a typical operation of all communicable discursive features. It consists of composing from the statements contained in any present world a transcendental term which denies what is actually happening in the present moment, by calling upon a foundational, historically legitimized, always-already completed body. Badiou's theory of the historiography of power resembles Benjaminian *Jeztzeit* where a founding present composes the narrative of its legitimate historical foundation. Discourse works in collusion with so-called history to make and renew this false, completed body which, however, is entirely constructed from within communicable discourse. Badiou's version of this classic view on discursive intelligibility is as follows: 'The fictive transcendent body legitimates the fact that the (visible) destruction of the evental body consigns the pure present which was woven by the faithful subject, point by point, to the invisible and inoperative' (*LW* 61).

We now have three clear destinations for every subject: production (faithful), denial (reactive) and occlusion. More than this we have a linear progression as well: production→ denial→ occlusion, which Badiou has been able to produce by the formalism that he used to define the subject. This progressive mode is important as a strategy for the communicability as such of everything that Badiou is going on to say. He explains, naturally, that if you define, say, the reactive subject as $\neg \varepsilon$ then you need in the first place to have ε. Similarly, if you are occluding the present surely you are accepting that there is a present which needs occlusion. Even, he argues, if you wish to propose a full body, you need the concept of a divided body to support this. Badiou, still using the mode of classical logic at this point, is able to access the inaccessible in the worlds of communicability by arguing that said worlds are the worlds they are because of what they deny, negate, occlude and abuse.

Badiou now proposes a fourth and final kind of subject, that of resurrection. It differs from the other three because its element is not entirely in the present. Rather, a resurrection is the return of a revolutionary name within the context of a new revolutionary event. He calls this supernumerary 'if we no longer consider each figure separately, but rather consider the complexity of the subjective field in its historical scansion' (*LW* 62). Resurrected subjects are trans-evental or trans-subjective moments which consider the history of events if you will, held beneath a recurring nomination, in this case Spartacus. He traces the historical use of the sign Spartacus across numerous revolutionary moments in history so that he can say that while the slaves' revolt ultimately failed, its political truth has become immortal all the same. To demonstrate he returns us to the initial assertion of the eternal nature of truths. In *Being and Event* Badiou shows we are able to concede truths are universal and immortal because they're based on the reality of the void and the indifference of being, such that every truth has a realist base and a generic essence. So yes, whatever truth you speak of is, at root, universal. Then we saw that Badiou wanted to go further than that and suggest that the mode of appearing of truths was also universal. This was more contentious, but he made a strong case for the fact that the form of appearing for each truth was universal to that world, the world of maths, the world of revolt, the world of music, and more than this was also indifferently generic. The deductions used in maths are always the same, irrespective of what they are used for. We were then able to consider some relation between universal formalism and the differentially related nature of worlds. Now he seems to go one step further. He appears to suggest that because the word 'Spartacus' is used repeatedly in the same revolutionary situations that this somehow makes it eternal. Speaking of Spartacus he notes how this resurrected destination 'reactivates a subject in another logic of its appearing-in-truth … Of course, a resurrection presupposes a new world, which generates a context for a new event, a new trace, a new body – in short, a truth-procedure under whose rule the occulted fragment places itself after having been extracted from its occultation' (*LW* 65).

This is a rather complex and perhaps even troubling proposition. If we read this right each time that the name Spartacus is used in a new present, it becomes a resurrected subject which is a different subject to the initial faithful subject of its actual present, ancient Rome. The name Spartacus makes the subject appear in a new logic of its appearing. How can this be so? When we spoke of the original Spartacus, the truth of its appearing was surely the point-by-point treatment of the body of the army as it vied with the Romans for dominance. This cannot be the truth of the new subject as there is no slave army and no ancient Rome in the later appearances of the name. Instead, what must be resurrected is the formal truth of the Spartacus event: that slavery is not natural. This also answers another question: How can Spartacus be the original subject when there are, in Badiou's ontological and logical systems, no origins? What is universal is the non-natural nature of slavery; what is recurrent is the use of the name Spartacus to resurrect this idea. Naturally, Badiou says, the new use of Spartacus, in 1796 in the colony of Cap, in 1919 in Berlin, in 1939 in Koestler's *The Gladiators* and so on, presupposes a new world as the context for a new event. To this new world the old subject must allow itself to succumb if it wishes to extract itself from its centuries-long slumber of occlusion.

The following example pertaining to the work of Archimedes helps us better understand what this resurrected subject consists of. Badiou explains how the work of Archimedes from the third century BC worked in anticipation of differential and integral calculus that will not be discovered until the Newton–Leibniz event of the seventeenth century. For two millennia these foundational works became, in the West, 'unreadable, in a very precise sense: they were in discord with all the subjective formalisms, and it was therefore impossible to articulate them to the present' (*LW* 66). To this fascinating portrait of the nature of the noncommunicable, because this is what Badiou means by becoming unreadable, he adds that the Arab reception was different confirming a simple maxim: truths exist differently in different worlds. He also notes that for Western mathematicians this was because of the rivalry between Aristotle and Plato over Platonic 'mathematicism'. So we also get the sovereign mode by which Aristotelian thought was able to make a set of statements unreadable for 2,000 years. By appealing to other complete bodies, such as substance and division (note that division itself can be a completed body even whilst negating a divided body), Aristotle was able to stifle the appearance of Archimedes' truth for longer than civilizations. Such is the power of communicable sanctions. Finally, in the sixteenth and seventeenth centuries, Archimedes' ideas chime with an evental change in mathematics, the move to abstract formalism typified by calculus, and they are allowed to speak again. For all this time they have existed as statements, they belong to the world of mathematics, but they have never been allowed to be included in that world, they are noncommunicable, due to sanctions of legitimization.

Badiou's reading of this is as follows: 'Every truth is eternal; of no truth can it be said, under the pretext that its historical world has disintegrated, that it is lost forever' (*LW* 66) so that, he says, to suspend the consequences of a truth you can't just change the rules of appearing. You need to act, to deny or to occlude. Returning to the classical *reductio ad absurdum*, once Archimedes' statement is out there, once his truth is given a body to use Badiou's language, or a statement to use Foucault, it has appeared, and to make it disappear you can't alter the rules of appearing as these are fixed as the basis of all communicability. No one is suggesting we negate these rules, no one perhaps except for myself, and so if you want to make a statement non-communicable you need to act to make it no longer readable. This is a side of discourse that perhaps is not given its due. Most discourse theorists represent discourse as relative, constructed, contingent yet stable. If there is a radical moment of discontinuity, Foucault, or suspension, Agamben, it is not due to the return of a repressed truth but the result of internal contradictions always there, momentarily coming to light. In contrast, Badiou thinks that what is always there are truths, and that when a truth becomes communicable it is not through rendering discourse noncommunicable but in re-making a noncommunicable truth body communicable once more. It is a position that explains how a truth can reappear after twenty centuries, and suddenly be seen as true for a second time, even though the original context of its appearing has disappeared entirely.

Typology

Throughout the typology of subjects Badiou has referred repeatedly to the body, in particular the divided body and the mythological full body. Yet he also concedes that at this point the body remains an enigma. If you recall the textual strategy here is to start with the general conclusions re: the subject and the event, and then go on to supply the detail of the 'proofs' later. That said, he is willing to let slip some basic characteristics of the body in this first book, before finally explaining it in Book VII.

The body is a multiple because everything is. Its main capability is that of allowing for the thinking of the true in terms of its visibility in a world. It does this point by point so the body is divided and, I think we can add, never complete so, if it has consistency, it is an actual infinity. For the body to allow a truth to appear it must have the basic qualities of objects in constructible worlds such as separation, cohesion and unity. The dominant idea of the body in our age, democratic materialism, is a red herring and has little or nothing to do with the body we are discussing here. This being the case, almost never do we find ourselves in a situation that when we speak of body we mean the animal body: 'Our idea of the subject is anything but "bio-subjective"' (*LW* 68). Finally, Badiou lists four characteristics that the body must possess or that we must be able to think in relation to the body. First a compatibility between the elements of the body and its being. Or, in Rome in the first century how did the rebellious slaves 'put together an army' (*LW* 68). This is the basic ontological condition of all considerations of worlds. Second, a synthetic unity where the multiple, the body, is both unified in appearing and in its being. Or, what is the new principle so that the army of slaves can be designated Spartacus' army? Once we can say there is such and such a body, ontology, what kind of a body is it, logic, we move on, third, to how appropriate are the parts of the body for treating such and such a point. Or, how are the detachments of the army organized to meet the challenges they encounter. Finally, we have to test the local efficacy of the body's organs or the strength and weaknesses of the slave army point by point.

One issue that must be raised at this juncture is that when we consider the answers to these questions, we are not seeking empirical answers. Empirical answers will always be simply communicable and thus constructible, which is fine for worlds in general, but not for bodies appearing in worlds as noncommunicable, new, impossible, illegal, banned and so on. This being the case, to answer the question as to how bodies appear in worlds, we need a formal, logical set of rules, not a historical analysis, say, informed by knowledge of Roman society and a specialism in military issues. That said, the use of examples is not simply illustrative. As Badiou says, 'The formal character of the theory of the subject entails that it does not qualify its terms, save through the didactic detour of examples' (*LW* 69). Thus the examples are not just exemplary, but nor are they a mode of amassing a convincing set of empirical evidence either. Like the use of the archetype in Agamben, the insistence on didactic examples in the book is a radical questioning of empirical and historical evidence. And again like Agamben, Badiou applies a set of large-scale headings under which archetypes are organized, the problematic conditions of politics, love, art and science, so that whilst we have a four-part typology of subjects, we also have a quadripartite mode of classifying a truth for the figure of subject under consideration: political, artistic, amorous and scientific. The next pages are then taken up with a revision of these conditions, but as we have covered them in our first study, we will leave those pages for the reader to peruse at their leisure and move forward to our conclusions on the all-important process of subjectivation as the formation of a well-pointed body.

Badiou concludes the first book with a table that maps out the various destinations, typologies, bodies and so on of the four kinds or conditions of truths. A truth is political if it involves the unequal relationship between a state and the people. This inequality is based on the excess of the state's representation of the people. The fact that the state, the recount of subsets, is greater than the set of the people it represents leads to the fixation of the superpower of the state or the point where the state's excess exceeds itself. The body that this evental trace composes is that of an organization operating in the new local present of an egalitarian maxim. Each subjectivity has an affective state which is the anthropological element of every subjectivity, he mentions this only in passing, and for politics that affective state is enthusiasm. Finally, all of this results in a global present or the universal formalism to be found in every political event, here, in this instance, sequence. Now to the arts, these concern sensible intensity and the tranquillity of forms. The evental trace here is that what once was formless can become form. The body it composes is the work of art, of course, and the local present it operates in is a new perceptual intensity. Art produces the affect of pleasure and it demonstrates the universal or global mode of configuration or the cut of the line as he calls it. The ontological ground of love is sexed disjunction that pertains to an evental trace of an indeterminate object, the love object u. This forms a body made up of a bi-sexed couple operating in a local present that has a new existential intensity. The affect of love is happiness and its global formal means is enchantment. Last of all we deal with science. Science works upon the ontological ground wherein there is a boundary between the world grasped or not grasped by the letter 'l $(\mathbf{m})$'. This is simply an abstract notation. The event of science is when what was once rebelled against is now submitted to, resulting in a body that is itself a result, a law, a theory. This activates a local present he calls a new enlightenment that brings joy to the subject through the universal pursuit of a theory. This table concludes Badiou's most complete, up-to-date, statement on the subject. All elements of the table have been presented in such a way as they are fairly clear, here or in other works, except, of course, the new enigma of the body. In that the body is not addressed until the final book of *Logics of Worlds*; it is safe to say that the entire trajectory is a means of completing a full description of the body upon which the entirety of the table pivots.

Subjectivation summarized

We can now summarize the process called subjectivation. Something 'new' and thus impossible happens beyond the constructions of ontology or worlds. This event leaves a trace. A subject takes up the trace and decides to live according to its dictates. On a daily basis, point by point, they are forced to make decisions apropos how to live according to the dictates of this event. The decisions are simple; they all have yes or no answers. If the subjectivation process continues to make affirmative responses in relation to the trace of this event, the event as such, which remember has no ontological form, starts to build up relations in a world. As it does so, it thickens, extends, distributes becoming a body. This 'body', we don't yet know what it is actually composed of, is not the same as a multiple becoming an object in a world. That said, like a multiple appearing in a world, it forms relations. However, the mode of its relation differs significantly from other objects in a world, objects which are determined categorically in tabular, triangulated relations under the auspices of a transcendental functor. In contrast, first, evental relations due to subjectivation proceed in a strictly linear form, one after another. Second, worldly relations are degrees of relation, while evental ones are absolute, either yes, the evental trace continues to build a body of truth, or no, the process comes to an end.

In addition, instead of a transcendental functor, a name of the world, the event has a localized subject, the agent of the event. The subject does not sit over the event, but is composed point by point through its faithful pursuit of the consequences of the event. Events can be betrayed, they can fail at the first hurdles, differing kinds of subjective states can negate the event wilfully and so on, but if and when an event is able to build a significant body, locally, point by point, in response to real-world problems and the actual consequences of the actions of the subject-agent, then this highly singular, world-specific event will always be shown to have a generic, universal quality. Said universal quality is dictated by the conditions of the communicable context within which the event is seen to occur. An event can never find relations with objects already present in existent worlds, that is not an event but an occurrence, but it must always find functional commonality within, according to Badiou, one of only four conditions. If these conditions are not generic enough, as the final table shows (*LW* 77), they all appear to share in common six features: an ontological ground, and evental trace, a body, a local present, an affect and a global present. Thus in this sense not only are events indifferent, ontologically speaking, they are generic in terms of actual appearing in a world. Every event must be conditioned, subjectivated, decided on point by point in a classical, yes/no fashion and produce the six features of its appearance.

One central feature of the event as described here is the means by which it avoids one of the traps of classical reasoning. An event cannot self-belong because it then is subject to Russell's paradox which shows that a self-belonging set is a contradiction. As regards subjectivation, this threat is ameliorated by the point-by-point nature of the extension of a concept, 'slaves can be free', into a world, Ancient Rome. Subjectivation operates in a 'hot bath', heuristic mode of investigating its extensionality, which means it can participate in experimental, low-level, contradictions that accrete, rather than single logical decisions in the classical sense.[6] In effect, an event is a false object that extends slowly into the world and begins to discover its potential truthfulness, possibly by changing the world as it goes along. That it does so in a localized classical manner, yes/no, means it adheres to the conditions of logical reasoning. That it is never a closed-off whole means it never has to decide once and for all on its truthfulness. In this way it avoids the absolutism of logicism when it comes to truth. For Frege, when you discover a truth, it becomes a banal entry into the encyclopaedia of what is now known to be true, which is why for him there is only one indifferent truth-object. For Badiou, you never stop discovering a truth, and thus you never tire of the truth, and it never becomes indifferent. And of course, for Badiou, an event is not a new concept extending into an old world, but a new object in a world from which a new concept can extend into an old world. Perhaps I should add that a self-belonging only partially determined object (not entirely true or false) is banned by classical logic and hence by Badiou's ontology. Yet it is perhaps a perfect description of the object in category theory which possesses an identity arrow (self-belonging) and which only ever partially appears in a world.

Much of what I have said is really just a better formulation of the subject already present in the earlier studies, especially the fifth and sixth parts of *Being and Event*, but what has changed is not so much the procedure of fidelity, as the nature of the event that prompts it, and the modality of the world the event occurs within. For example, a localized, point-by-point theory of conceptual extension that is never fully decided and thus occupies a position of getting more truthful in this world is only possible with a combination of intuitionist, modal and classical logics, unavailable to ontology, workaday for categories. However, the idea of a well-pointed body is straight out of the pages of the category theory textbooks. Up to this point then, readers of *Being and Event* will find little novelty to detain them, but from this point on, everything is about to alter, utterly. If radical change is made possible thanks to the ultra-stability of the situation it occurs within, Badiou's fundamental contention, then dramatically changes the background to the event, and how we see the event will also be transformed. This, basically, is the purpose of the extensive description of the Greater Logic that occupies the next three huge sections of the book.

Book II

Greater Logic, 1. The Transcendental

The entirety of the second book of *Logics of Worlds* concerns one single concept: the transcendental. Indeed, the formation of a transcendentalizing effect, the transcendental functor as he comes to call it, that is however not Whole, echoes the way in which the count-as-one function in his ontology operates. If a multiple is a count-as-one, a transcendental is a count-as-whole. If Being is-not then beings taken together do-not, meaning, do no form a closed-off Whole. As can be seen from these observations, the meaning of the term transcendental in Badiou's work is very specific, running counter to the philosophical traditions he operates within, requiring of redefinition accordingly: 'We will call *transcendental* of the situation that which, in any situation, serves as a domain for the evaluation of identities and differences in appearing.' He goes on to explain that a transcendental is a multiple, because everything is a multiple, that is 'endowed with a structure', the logics of appearing is concerned with structure-preserving functional relations, and that this structure has a particular function. Specifically it 'authorizes the arrangement, on its basis, of the values (the degrees) of identity between the multiples which belong to the situation, such that we can fix the value of the function of appearing **Id** (α, β), whatever α and β may be' (*MT* 167–8). The transcendental therefore is a function, not a god-like creature or a universal essence – a function that authorizes a non-Whole yet stable, delimited structure. The greater logic then is a stability from the top-down, in contrast to ontology's bottom-up approach. Furthermore, the greater logic structurates extrinsically, what relates two multiples is a third they share in common, while ontology structurates intrinsically, the entirety of being is determined by the internal interaction of a set and subset, and the localized rank-relation between an ordered pair of multiples.

For a multiple to appear in a world, the function described in *Being and Event* as inclusion, representation or the recount as prerequisite for a multiple to be included in a situation he calls in the earlier work a state, it must do so due to two relations. The first is that multiple α, which is any multiple whatsoever so not only an indifferent multiple but a generically indifferent one,[1] must relate to at least one other multiple, we will call it β. What α and β are, in any traditional sense, for example, two objects in front of you, is the wrong question. The first point being that they are indifferent and generic multiples, not objects possessive of qualities. The second is that when they appear, they appear as relationally different. You can say there are at least two multiples, because you can compare them and say they are two, not one. The role of the third multiple, the transcendental, is to vouchsafe the basic structure of relation which allows multiples to be said to appear, by which is meant to exist in the world or be included in a worldly situation. The transcendental provides a 'domain', a world if you will, within which two radically indeterminate multiples, any two multiples whatsoever reduced to the simple notation of indifferent variables (α, β), can be allowed to appear relationally by its being possible to say these two multiples are related because they both appear in this domain of relation to x degree of intensity.[2] The transcendental, therefore, is the domain of structural relation where the indifferentiation of two co-appearing multiples is established by their being provided with qualities, rather than being only in possession of what he calls 'the flat surface of indifferent multiplicity' (*MT* 166), before going on to assert that: 'existence is nothing if it is not a *quality* of being. But every quality implies variability and nuance. Every quality is modal' (*MT* 166), modality being a quality that an indifferent multiple of being cannot possess as they are or are not their being locally globally or absolutely. There is no degree of belonging, but there is only degree of worldly inclusion.

Having established the centrality and peculiarity of the transcendental in his work, he then notes an important directional change from *Being and Event* which affects, in particular, our own studies of this immense project. 'Previously', Badiou says, 'I identified situations (worlds) with their strict multiple-neutrality ... I assumed the dissemination of the indifferent multiple as the ground of all that there is, and consequently affirmed the ontological non-being of relation' (*LW* 99). It was on the basis of this thesis that we began our consideration of indifferent being. Now, however, the whole point of this second volume is to consider that being-there as 'appearing-in-a-world has a relational consistency' (*LW* 99).[3] We should not assume, however, that relationality negates indifference, for a central dynamic of the logics of appearing is how indifferent existents can be proposed in relational algebra such that the qualitative, modal nuance of existence can be abstracted without losing its specificity (*MT* 168). Indeed, Badiou himself insists that the move from non-relational being to consistently relational beings is not a negation of the non-relational in favour of the relational. Such a move would dramatically destabilize the ontological basis of his entire life's work. As I explained in my first volume, the radical power of *Being and Event* is the indifferent non-relationality it demands we accept as the basis of being. Maintaining that whatever happens in the rest of the second volume the fundamental concept of indifferent non-relationality remains intact is a position we have to endorse.

One last preparation for our journey which Badiou has diffidently delayed for a fifth of the entire book is the three-part method of the study which presents a triple exposition of conceptual exemplifying passages, historical studies of specific 'authors' (philosophers, poets, painters and so on) and formal exposition. Our emphasis will be on the formal as it was in the first study, dipping into the single author studies if and when they add something to our general understanding. The strong presence of examples is new to *Logics*; there was a limited amount of this in *Being and Event*, so we will make use of these examples schematically but leave the reader to pursue the detail in *Logics* itself for that is indeed what examples are there for. The tripartite mode of exposition echoes a tripartite nature of the substance of the second book, resulting in three 'motifs': 'the necessity of a transcendental organization of worlds; the exposition of the transcendental; the question of what negation is within appearing' (*LW* 100). Accordingly we will consider one by one transcendental organization, exposition and negation primarily focusing on the formal proofs, and invite the reader to pursue the exact detail of examples in *Logics* if our formal exposition fails them. We sincerely hope this will not be the case. Badiou now considers the three themes in greater detail and we will go along with him.

Necessity of a transcendental organization of the situations of being

Every world, or every situation of being, not only is reducible to the pure multiple, that is, its being as such, but also contains a transcendental organization, or at least this is a central thesis not only of *Logics of Worlds* but the entirety of the two volumes of Being and Event. Badiou recasts this immense problem, after Kant, in terms of possibility: 'How is it possible that the neutrality, inconsistency and indifferent dissemination of being-qua-being comes to consist as being-there?' (*LW* 101). The answer to this will be found in the basic transcendental organization of every world which means by the end of this study we will also have an answer to what, I contend, is the most significant problem in our discipline: How can ontological indifference be translated and translocated into the logics of appearing? Or, rather, on a more positive note, in what way does ontological indifference affect relational specificity of objects in worlds such that the two main historical problems of a bi-valenced articulation of being, the ontico-ontological relation and the consistency of immanence, cease to be problems?

Badiou's use of the term transcendental, as we said, does not always match the norms of the application of this term and here he points out that unlike Kant's 'subjectivated' transcendentalism, 'the transcendental that is at stake in this book is altogether anterior to every subjective constitution, for it is an immanent given of any situation whatever' (*LW* 101). So while Badiou retains both 'subject' and 'transcendental' as redolent signifiers when it comes to appearing, the subject is a rare and intermittent case, while the transcendental pertains to absolutely every situation. The transcendental's main job is to impose on each 'situated multiplicity the constraint of logic'. Said constraint or binding force is what is meant by being *there* or appearing. When an indifferent multiple is bound in a differential relation due to the transcendental functions of logic, it can be said to be appearing *there*. As said multiple cannot appear in ontology as such, then the mode of the appearing of a multiple, what Badiou importantly calls 'the intelligibility of its manifestation', must consist of a set of immanent procedures that clearly differ from the axioms of being. These operations are what *Badiou* means by the transcendental so that logic and appearing, for him, refer to exactly the same thing. Finally, Badiou concedes that there is an essential disjunction between Being and being-there which his work will 'force', using Cohen's set-theoretical strategy, based on the presupposition of 'the impossibility of determining a being of the Whole, and finally the thesis according to which *there is no whole*' (*LW* 102).

As we have spent an immense amount of time on Badiou's detailed proof of this fundamental thesis, it is practically the first thing he says in *Being and Event*, where Badiou again shows this to be the case we will simply refer the reader to those sections and, for our purposes, assume that Badiou has proven that, in terms of Being, there is no Whole. Here then all you need to accept is that it is also true that in logic, in appearing, in the 'there' of worlds, there is also no Whole. Concomitants of this assertion are that being-there is always local, that the empty concept of an absolute Whole will be called a universe, that a world in contrast is a 'complete situation of being' and by definition there must be several worlds, for if there were only one it would be a universe and, as we have just insisted, there is no universe as there is no Whole.[4] Indeed we will have to eventually come to accept that there is an actual infinity of worlds, each of which is also an actual, indeed cardinal, infinity.

Exposition of the transcendental

Once we have established that being-there is the logic that binds indifferent multiples so that they can appear in one of at least two worlds, then we need to present the operators that can give coherence to the manner by which a multiple appears 'in' a world. 'In' here, he explains, is a metaphor. There is, in fact, no world as empty space which beings then occupy. 'A world is nothing but a logic of being-there, and it is identified with the singularity of this logic. A world articulates the cohesion of multiples around a structured operator' (*LW* 102). This is a not-insignificant point. Worlds only exist due to relational, ordering operations. Logic does not order and explain the world around us, as its mode of organization *is* the world around us. There is no brute nature then logical meaning, there is just logical meaning. When things are in a world they are not in it then ordered around in it by operators, they are in the world already ordered. This means of course there is no world origin, no pre-ordered world and no world-destination. These assertions appear to render Badiou powerfully constructivist, a position he strongly rejects in *Being and Event*. He will modify this constructivism with a radical materialism as we go along.

Now we come to the very heart of the matter. The central tenet of the transcendental is 'the evaluation of the degrees of identity or difference between a multiple and itself, or between a being-there and other beings. The transcendental must therefore make possible the "more" and the "less"' (*LW* 102). Given that there is a world, a multiple is in that world due to what degree it is identical to itself, and what degree it is identical to other elements in that world, based on a simple more or less. This is a statement impossible to make of a multiple ontologically. If a multiple has little self-identity in such and such a world, it is likely to be a marginal presence there, or it has had to compromise on its 'essence' so as to even be able to appear. If it has strong relational identity to other weakly present multiples however, then perhaps their overall presence could be seen to be quite strong. If a multiple is strongly present to itself but weakly related to every other element in that world, then it will have a very different nature and so on. This, in a nutshell, is the sum total of what *Logics of Worlds* investigates and is the great difference between the two volumes of the project. Ontology requires nine axioms, whereas logics of appearing really only demands one function: ≤.

Our opening comments were designed to highlight the distinction between the logics of appearing and the mathematics of the transcendental, thanks to category theory. This division becomes immediately important for it is not the case that category theory per se is encapsulated by a single, over-arching function: ≤. Indeed, in that the function of relation is one of a comparison of 'properties'; Badiou regularly considers the existential intensity of objects in terms of what they are like, not so much in terms of what they are doing, in a sense one could argue that relationality is not a property that needs category theory to capture it in a structure. Badiou, because he is considering the categorization of being in worlds, has reduced the actual infinity of functions that can be treated by categories to one single, existential function, that of relationality. This is a decision on his part; he at no point justifies it or even refers to the fact that he is doing this. At the same time, we need to accept that relation is due to functions of relation, not properties. Two elements in a world relate, thanks to the relational function of intensity, which may be that one pillar in a painting is more in shade than another to use one of Badiou's favourite examples, but that what matters here is not the shaded quality of the pillar, but the functionality of said shading relative to how they appear in the overall world of the painting; not what the pillar looks like, but how its appearance does something through its visual quality so that if we accept that Badiou's is a logic of appearing, then appearing is not what something looks like say or what qualities it possesses when it appears, but the function of appearance, or what does appearing in a world do? One final point is that because the logic of category theory is intuitionist, which means you need to be able to show relations, which in category theory means presenting them as diagrams, then of course the visual field is foregrounded. Appearance does literally mean being able to be seen by the logic of categories or being capturable by diagrams.

Accepting these provisos on appearance as function we can say that consistently Badiou demands: Given such and such a multiple, how much, literally, does it appear in a particular world due to its degree of self-identity (we will explain this shortly) within that world? And given that degree of appearing – weak, average, strong, maximal, minimum – to what degree does its appearing measure up against other multiples that also appear? As Badiou says: 'There must exist values of identity which indicate, for a given world, to what extent a multiple-being is identical to itself or some other being of the same world' (*LW* 103).

The questions we need to ask of a multiple of being-thereness then are pretty simple. Is this multiple in this world? If so, to what degree is it in the world, and to what degree is its presence in the world comparable to other multiples that also appear in this world? Again, sticking with simplicity, the relational operators <, >, = are all we need to determine this. That said, we also need two bracketing operators to bind this world and make it coherent. Primary of these is a 'minimum phenomenology of abstract appearing, by which we mean what is conceptually required for appearing to be bound' (*LW* 103). This determines what he calls the 'wordliness of a world, or the logic of the localization for the being-there of any being whatever' (*LW* 103). You might prefer to think of this as the fact that there is a multiple that appears, at least one, in one of at least two worlds, or thereness as such.

Note the term 'whatever' here. The careful reader will realize that while there can be no indifference in a world, because everything which appears in a world is differentiated due to a quality of intensity of relation, it is more or less like itself or something else, the rules of difference are themselves abstract and indifferent, reducible as we saw to the simple algebra of indifferent appearing **Id** (α, β). More than that, we are still talking of indifferent quantity as we were in regards to sets. Just as in sets it was not what qualities the multiples had but their quantitative nature, here what determines the quality of a multiple in a world is the degree of quantity that multiple possesses in relation to other multiples and itself. This multiple is more or less like this other multiple given that both multiples are more or less like themselves when found in this particular world. In sets quantity is absolute, in categories the quanta are relative.

We now suddenly have a complete phenomenology of appearing, devoid of the traditional logical aporias, impasses, onto-theological propositions or historic intuitions! It is composed of three operations:

- The minimum of appearance is given.
- The possibility of 'conjoining' the values of appearance of at least two multiples.
- The possibility of 'globally synthesising the values of appearance of any number of multiples' even up to infinity.

It is literally as easy as 1, 2, 3 multiples coming into relation. A world is such that there are multiples that appear in it to some degree (1), that at least two multiples can be joined through comparing their value of appearing in the same world (2) and finally the coherent sense of 'globally' which world they appear in (3).

This last global value however is not a totality. The world as such, what we will come to call the transcendental functor, is composed only of what it contains, and there is no limit to that. At no point is said world closed or complete. It is, if you will, an open closure that operates in a locally global fashion. Or more accurately, an actual infinity.[5]

Badiou remarks on the nature of the 'economy of means' represented by these three operators of existence by simply saying of course appearing is bound (not chaotic) if I can 'set out degrees of appearance on the basis of non-appearance (minimum); second, know what two multiples do or do not have in common when they co-appear (conjunction); and finally, if I am capable of globalising appearance in such a way that it makes sense to speak, in a given world, of a region of appearing (envelope)' (*LW* 103). Again, using 1, 2, 3 we can say the minimum determines the one, conjunction the pair and the envelope triangulation. These thee rules, he calls them minimum, conjunction and envelope, are all we need for an objective, calculated phenomenology, but Badiou also appreciates that the causal bond of existence is important, so he closes by supplementing these three with a fourth that can be derived from these other three. This he calls 'dependence' which measures the correlation in a world between the appearing of one multiple and another. In other words, we don't just comparatively measure two multiples, but we also measure to what degree the appearance of one depends on the appearance of another; this is another name for the logical relation of implication. If the first three rules show that things appear in the world, the fourth explains why, perhaps replacing the Husserlian value of intention, with the more logical value of implication.

The origin of negation

To assert the being-there of a multiple, you need of course a concept of the not-being-there or perhaps the being not-there. Badiou concedes that, historically, the topic of negation has been a thorny one to say the least. Sticking with Kant he presents the dense and complex circumlocutions the *First Critique* takes the reader through, before Kant arrives at a formulation of objects empty of concept. Badiou is naturally drawn to the conception of 'objects designated by their lack alone' (*LW* 105). That said, he admits to being profoundly disappointed with Kant's examples of shadow as the negation of light, cold as the negation of heat and so on. As he rightly points out, nothing about darkness is negative; cold is not in some sense worse than heat to the degree that you could call it the

Greater Logic, 1. The Transcendental 73

privation or negation of heat. He says in conclusion: 'For real lack cannot be illustrated by cold or shadow, which are themselves nothing but transcendental degrees applied to neutral objects' (*LW* 105). More than this, as regards negation in appearing, which is what we are concerned with, appearing as such is always an affirmation of being-there so how can you affirm a negation from within appearing? One issue we can address is the first transcendental operator, the minimum. This allows us to 'think the non-apparent in a determinate world' so that you can speak affirmatively of a multiple whose degree of appearance in a world 'has nil transcendental value' (*LW* 105). Nil transcendentalism means we can think of the negation of the appearing of a being of a multiple. 'The negation of being-there rests in the affirmative identification of being qua being' (*LW* 105). Fair enough, but the problem remains that the non-apparent is not the apparent negation of the apparent. Instead, what we want is to make negation as such 'appear'. Badiou pursues this problem from Kant, back to Plato and forward to Sartre before concluding that no one has really made negation appear thus far in the tradition.

At this point of desperation Badiou brings in to play a concept from category theory called the reverse, perhaps the first moment in the book where an intractable from philosophy is resolved by mathematics. We will return to the detail of reversal, which is an important operation, but for now we have to be satisfied with a three-part, schematic presentation of this rather complex means of treating negation affirmatively, because this is the only way negation can be said to appear. The first point states that the reverse of being-there is another being-there in the same world, not some externally located extra-worldy other. This is facilitated by the ease by which categories permit all kinds of functional and diagrammatic reversals meaning that the reversal of a function of appearing is absolutely routine.[6] You measure the intensity of the appearance of a multiple in the world, its being-there, then you reverse it by providing a different measure of intensity which shares nothing in common with the first except that both appear in the same world. The second explains that the reverse is similar to negation proper in that you are able to state that being-there and its reverse have nothing in common in this world or 'the conjunction of their degrees of intensity is nil' (*LW* 107). Finally, three, mostly the reverse has little else in common with negation. Most pointedly the reverse of a reverse of an appearance does not necessarily equal that original appearance. This is perhaps the crucial difference as regards the classical nature of negation, if you negate not-A you get A, and the intuitionist nature of the reverse, if you reverse a reverse you do not necessarily return back to the original position.

In miniature this encapsulates the non-classical nature of category theory and its influence on the logic of appearing in general. Because we are treating degrees of appearing, the classical presentation of the dialectic of same and other does not pertain. Instead, we always consider degrees of identity, degrees of conjunction and, in the case of the reverse, degrees of dis-identity and non-conjunction. Overall, Badiou concludes that as regards the transcendental, mostly, classical negation and thus deduction by double negation are not available. This is a notable statement. Just as in sets where we found that what we consider is not quality, so now we discover in terms of worlds there is no legitimate same-other dialectic of how something exists in a world. In other words, our age of alterity and otherness, apparent across so many disciplines, originating in Hegel, promulgated by Derrida's influential, Levinasian turn and a thousand studies in otherness that followed, can come to a close, as yet another concept from the philosophy of difference that Badiou's work renders inoperative. In worlds, there is no identity nor any difference, there is only one simple value: degrees of relation. Worlds are, by definition, non-dialectical, non-correlational and, thus in a basic sense, non-metaphysical. Or, due to the replacement of negation with reversal, there is no other.

One final note on this early discussion of the remarkable function of the reverse is its proximity to the ideas of nonrelation that dominate *Being and Event*. The reverse is not the contradiction of something, as we saw. Thus the traditional, dialectical, correlational nature of our tradition, including modern philosophy of difference, is suspended. In categories, when you negate something, you do not speak of its opposite, the difference to its identity. The reverse of an object has so little in common with this object that you cannot even establish a dialectic between the two; the reverse is not the antithesis to your thesis and between them can there be no synthesis. The reverse, then, is a profound example of nonrelational difference, thanks to the relational laws of comparative difference that define the logics of appearing. A remarkable result.

Section 1: The concept of transcendental. Inexistence of the whole

These opening, schematic comments prepare us for the detailed, step-by-step consideration of the transcendental that makes up the first section of this chapter. We need to move slowly through this formal exposition as it contains the large part of the totality of what the transcendental is, informed by both set theory precepts and those we are developing relative to category theory. Badiou commences with what must be taken to be his foundational statement in totality: the inexistence of the whole. All we need to say on this topic is that there is no multiple of multiples and because there is not, and because worlds measure the degree of appearing of multiples, there is no existential universe either or a world of all worlds. The reader, it would seem to me, cannot easily quibble with the statement there is no whole. Nor can they fault the simple implication that if a world is composed of degrees of appearing of multiples, then the inexistence of the whole is carried over into worlds. So they are left with asserting that worlds are nothing more than degrees of appearing of multiples. The rest of the book being is a profound presentation of this new, and yet also familiar, concept.

Derivation of the thinking of a multiple on the basis of that of another multiple

A multiple can only be thought in terms of its composition or the elements that belong to it. This is a fundamental law of set theory and ontology explored at length in *Being and Event*. Any multiple that has no elements is immediately determined as the void set, the singleton, the number 1. All other multiples, aside from the void, 'are determined in a mediated way, by considering the provenance of their elements' (*LW* 111). This is the universal formalism of descending deduction which is one of the central conditions of mathematics. Every multiple can be thought due to the think-ability of the multiple that is before them, down to a halting point which is the void set. The only difference between this mode of reasoning and that say of Aristotle or infinitesimals is that there is a halting point, a moment of indivisibility, which can be proven. So in short, the inconsistency of the whole means you can consider multiples up to the point of actual infinity without having recourse to some onto-theological One. Now you can also consider the divisibility of any set of multiples, determine it absolutely and simply by the multiple that came before, without entering into endless divisibility of the bad infinity of proliferation of the smallest, by being able to prove a halting point: the void. Again, the proofs of this are extensive and, to our mind, irrefutable and take up a large part of *Being and Event*.

From this second axiom we can deduce two classic positions. Take a multiple, it is consistent to think of another multiple whose elements are the elements of the elements of the first multiple. This is the immanent dissemination of multiples. Second, given a multiple, one can easily think of another multiple the elements of which are parts of this first multiple. This is the mode of the recount or representation central to Badiou's politics of the state, or in more technical terms it proves that given the belonging of elements to a multiple, all multiples are sets, all sets are multiples down to the void, there are also those elements which are included as subsets of this multiple. What we are left with is a totally determinant chain of hierarchically ordered multiples. However complex the chain of multiples, they can all be traced back, multiple by multiple, to their first multiple, the void, if you so wish. The void is the only multiple that cannot be deduced from another multiple but, thanks to set theory, it can now be 'proven'. If there were a whole, one could determine a multiple in terms of qualities it possesses that make it singular relative to that whole; there would be a universal place of all beings from which the relation between specific beings could be presented, so that 'predicative separation would uniformly determine multiplicities through their identification and differentiation from the Whole' (*LW* 112). These modes of determining the being of a being are more familiar perhaps to a reader, perhaps the more intuitive but, since the Greeks, right up to and including Heidegger, the determination of the Whole has always depended on an onto-theological intervention. Even Cantor's set theory ultimately calls upon God to resolve the issue of the continuum, a position finally negated by Gödel's incompleteness theorems. Put simply, if one determines a being due to a conception of a Whole, one will never be able to determine the being of beings without God, nor the difference between beings, without bad, infinite proliferation. As Badiou has shown here, there is no consistent Whole so that there is 'no uniform procedure of identification and differentiation of what is' (*LW* 112). This being the case, when you think of a multiple it is always local, derived from singular multiples that come before this multiple. It is 'not inscribed in any multiple whose referential value would be absolutely general' (*LW* 112). There is no horse-ness in other words, nor for that matter is there an external Other.

A Being is thinkable only insofar as it belongs to a world

Having blithely negated the entire ethics and politics of alterity, now it is time to speak of beings. Beings, not Being as such, have their identity determined locally due to their relation to other multiples. This relation is hierarchical, deductive and descends down to the void. A local site for the identification of beings is what Badiou means by a world. It is to be noted that a world is not precisely a set, although categories can look like sets. As Badiou makes very clear in *Mathematics of the Transcendental*, categories differ radically from sets in that what concerns category theory is the relations between things, while for set theory it is the composition of things. Categories never break open sets, although they can spread them open if they wish. That said, staying for now within set theory, beings are multiples determined by their relation to other multiples composed within a single world which is simply 'the multiple-place in which these operations operate' (*LW* 113).

Any being aside from the void, in order to be thinkable, present in the formal procedures of deductive thought, has to fulfil two conditions. It must be thought of relative to at least one other being, and there must be at least one operation that allows one to pass from this other being to the one whose identity you wish to establish, the monism or arrow that moves between a domain and a codomain (John and his breakfast to use Lawvere and Schanuel's example). This space is always presentable. By this Badiou means it must never depend on an absolute Other, an unknowable onto-theological Whole. This point actually explains why he needs a logic of appearing. If there is no Whole, then there needs to be an axiomatic insistence that every multiple aside from the void must be presentable, local, knowable, deducible. By the way, all of this is possible because the void itself is non-presentable. This is a more profound way of stating a centrally important concept for all communicable systems: they are entirely surface located. They contain no hidden depths, no inconceivable heights. Everything that is presentable is without depth. This is what is meant by the local which is no longer defined dialectically in terms of the global, although Badiou still uses this opposition, but rather in terms of being 'where an operation operates'. The local is not a place at all really, but simply the locality of a specific operation. As regards this operation, which can be expressed in non-technical terms as simply how do we determine this thing in relation to some other thing which it is not, this other thing is not truly other, it is simply not this thing. Nor is this other thing different from this thing we are talking about, rather it is indifferent in terms of its being. We determine a being as local by the operation that allows us not to say it is not that other thing, but to deduce that it is this being due to that other being. By the same gesture this being we are using to determine our being itself has been determined by another being and so on, all the way down to the void, all the way up to an actual infinity that exists even if we can never count it. Locally, between these two points 'lies an operational passage, with the place as such as its background' (*LW* 113).

In our first study we noted that this place is the communicability of communicability as such or better the communicability function. In actual fact, there is no neutral place waiting to be inscribed, the idea of the place as the neutral medium or the blank sheet or tablet, rather, and we spoke of this at length in Book I: 'what indicates the place is the operation' (*LW* 113).[7] The place is not a place then unless it is first an operation. Now Badiou asks simply, what localizes an operation, and answers, it is a world. 'The place where operation happens without leaving it is the place where a being attains its identity – its relative consistency' (*LW* 113). This functional place is where the indifferent, non-relational being described by set theory is determined by an operation such that it ceases to be indifferent and now attains an identity due to a consistency determined relative to other beings within that locale. Allowing us to think precisely what a situation of being is, which of course also means what a world is, '*we call "situation of being" for a singular being, the world in which it inscribes a local procedure of access to its identity on the basis of other beings*' (*LW* 114) Clearly this is an immanentist position that usually would call up the problem of the origins of the other being, or the means by which the transcendental whole of a being can be determined from the local. However, we do not have to address either problem. If there is a provable halting point and no whole only an actual infinity then yes, quite simply, the existence of every single being can be proven only by relation to one other being. This is, for me, an astonishing moment in the history of not only philosophy but thought in general. Two simple axioms, the inconsistency of the whole and the reality of the void, mean that we can define everything else as localized due to an operation of one other being.

If it is clear that a being, if it exists, appears in a world, it is not true to speak of *the* world of a being. As a being is an abstract, pure multiplicity, it can appear in different worlds. If there were something about being that pre-destined it for a particular kind of world, then that would not be a pure multiple. Similarly, if there were types of worlds that in some way call up certain sorts of being, then the foundational nature of being in relation to a world would be negated. I would like to quote Badiou on this point as I feel, in the past, critical studies in questioning the fundamental nonrelational nature of being may have led readers to think that there could be a link between certain worlds and certain types of being, in particular that type of inexistent being we call the event. Badiou now lays this ghost to rest: 'It would be absurd to think that there is an intrinsic link between a given multiple and a given world. The "worlding" of a (formal) being, which is its being-there or appearing, is ultimately a logical operation: the access to a local guarantee of its identity' (*LW* 114).

Here then we could add one more point as regards this essential nonrelationality. Because a being is indifferent and a world is a logical operation, if a being appears in a world all we are saying is that an indifferent being is now subject to a logical operation pertaining to relationality due to measure of intensity of that being within this world. We already know that the being in question here is radically without quality, so nothing about it recommends it to the world or other beings in it per se. Similarly, although one might think of the world of relations as measuring quality, which it certainly does, the logical operation that we are considering here is the simple abstraction of relational measure. In that every world is composed of relational measure we can, at this stage, say that said operation is effectively neutral, totally abstract and so in this sense indifferent. I believe this is the only means by which being and worlds can be brought into any mode of articulation. Returning to Badiou's point, which is of a different order, he explains that just as there is a plurality of worlds, the same multiple (same in the ontological sense) 'co-belongs to different worlds' (*LW* 114).

We now encounter a significant moment in a movement from ontology to the logic of appearing that is the real purpose of the book. Badiou describes this theme as 'the worldly multiplicity of a unity of being' (*LW* 114) and admits it composes an immense difficulty for thought. He explains that when we speak of a pure being only in terms of ontology (mathematics), we do not take into consideration at all how it may appear to different worlds. We only think of its being, and this being is mediated by its relation within the hierarchy of deduction down to the void. One being is derived from another being whose overall being is derived from a set of axioms. This derived form of being, so crucial to the ontological sphere, is not determined by, or indeed related to, the derived nature of every assertion about its being. In particular, those assertions derived logically rather than mathematically. He uses two examples here to illustrate this.

The first is Messiaen's little-performed opera *Ariadne and Bluebeard*. In the opera the proper names of Ariadne and Bluebeard 'convey the capacity for appearing in altogether discontinuous narrative, musical or scenic situations' (*LW* 116). We meet Ariadne before she meets Bluebeard, Ariadne with Bluebeard, Ariadne fleeing the castle and so on. He declares that there is no genealogical construction that allows us to say each time we read or hear or see 'Ariadne', who is after all a fictional construct being played by an actor-singer, that this is the 'same' Ariadne. While it is true that said genealogy is assumed as 'Ariadne' appears in various disparate situations, this genealogy never appears on stage. Although a 'genealogical invariance authorizes the thinking of the same ... this "same" does not appear; it is strictly reduced to names. Appearing is always the transit of a world; in turn, the world logically regulates that which shows itself within it qua being-there' (*LW* 116).

You may object that the reason the genealogy of the same does not appear on stage is simply because there is no genealogy. Ariadne does not exist, the person on stage is an actress and so on. To counter this Badiou recomposes the same example using the set N of whole natural numbers. This is a long way from an obscure opera, and for most people it is indubitable that whole numbers do exist. One can use prime numbers in a variety of complex ways, or simply as a means of numbering pages in the book or which candidate won the vote. In each case the 'same' whole natural numbers appear but in each case the set N of these natural numbers never does. We can then say that it is not simply the fictive nature of Ariadne's genealogy that means it can never appear, as a whole, that which we take to be the same in a world, the being of that world, can never be made to appear in that world; yet, it can operate within a world as a means of identifying stability across names. If this is the case then when one grasps the identity of a being in a world one must be grasping something else besides its being because, while the being regulates the fact that said being in the world can appear, it itself can never appear. Some other regulatory force must be in operation here. Badiou names this force logic.

The question he poses is as follows: What does it mean for a being which is defined as singular to be-there, if its being as such, its mathematical multiplicity, 'does not prescribe anything about this "there" to which it is consigned' (*LW* 117)? This is, effectively, the controversial question of nonrelationality. We need not belabour this point as regards the history of philosophy but instead we should concentrate on Badiou's innovation which is not to create a philosophy out of the impossible relationality of being and beings, but to fashion philosophy that thinks non-relationality as a thing in itself if you will, rather than an impossible aporia for thought. With this in mind, he presents two basic implications as regards the simple position of accepting the impossibility of relation between indifferent being and communicable worlds and tries to think through said impossibility. The first is that a singular being differs from itself. Being-there is not the same as being-qua-being because thinking being-qua-being does not 'envelop the thinking of being-there' (*LW* 117). The second point is that this singular being differs from other beings of the same world. This is an important stop on the influence of such thinkers of virtual becoming such as Deleuze, for it insists that being-there is this being which is not another being and there is nothing about its 'inscription' with other beings in this world that can negate this. Badiou then leaves us in the traditional paradox of Western thought. He says it is true that the differentiated identity of being as such cannot determine how said being appears in a world, we know this. Yet at the same time the identity of a world is not sufficient alone for the 'differentiated being of what appears' (*LW* 117). We know this too. What we do not know is how this problem can be resolved in such a way as we can say that there is such a thing as being as such, and there is a mode of determining the consistency of multiple worlds due to this being.

Badiou replies with the following 'solution' to the problem:

> The key to thinking appearing, when it comes to a singular being, lies in being able to determine at one and the same time, the self-difference which makes it so that being-there is not being-qua-being, and the difference from others which makes it so that being-there, or the law of the world which is shared by these others, does not abolish being-qua-being.
>
> (*LW* 117)

If there is such a thing as a singular being as such, a thing such as it is, actual being of some order, then you need simultaneously to be able to accept that said being differs from itself without this resulting in the deconstruction of being and that said being differs from other beings so that it has in common with these beings that they all appear in the same world, but that this world-sharing does not negate the basic singularity of this being. How can being exist whilst differing from itself and at the same time being the 'same' as other beings in that they all appear in the same world?

Returning to our examples, Ariadne, on this reading, must differ from herself as 'Ariadne' so that she can appear in different worlds. She must also be different from Bluebeard's other wives even though it is central to the tale and indeed Bluebeard's misogynistic psychology that these wives are all the same. The whole story world, Badiou insists, has consistency only if we know Ariadne is herself, against the other wives she is not, and that she is not herself when she is placed within the disparate situations of the story. He then follows the same logic with the number 327 which is both the whole natural number it is, but when it is a page number, it also isn't the whole natural number 327 but page number 327. Then, how does 327 differ from 328 in that both are the same, both are page numbers and both differ from themselves as regards their being as a natural number; yet, it is essential to their appearance in the world of the book that we see them as different? We can simplify this by saying once a being is worlded 'it is and is not what it is' (*LW* 117), in a totally consistent fashion. In other words, yes a being differs from itself (Heidegger, Derrida) and yes beings only exist in terms of being part of a series of other beings all of which hold their relationality in common (Deleuze), but this is simply not a problem for ontology, indeed is the very proof of its efficacy.

Badiou ends this rather important section for the history of philosophy with an explanation as to how this formula, by necessity, means that beings must appear in worlds only by dint of measurement of differences. If 327 and 328 appear in the world of book pages in the same way, then to differentiate them we need to simply say to what degree 327 appears that is different from 328, for example. Here then we have a second law of difference. Our first law states that as regards ontology, all differences are indifferent. Now our second law states that as regards logic of worlds, all differences 'are a matter of more or less' (*LW* 118): 'The logic of appearing necessarily regulates degrees of difference, of a being with respect to itself and of the same with respect of others' (*LW* 118). The important point here is that when beings appear in worlds, they are as consistent as when we speak of them ontologically. In ontology every multiple has a rank and so its order is determined vertically. In logic every multiple has a degree in relation to the other multiples in that world. This is determined horizontally and vertically in a two-dimensional planal space of more and less relative to each other under the overall transcendental field they find themselves in. Or x relates to y because as regards T, the world they have in common, x has a greater degree of relation than y does even though both x and y can be said to have a degree of relation to T (the classic commutative diagrammatic definition of a category). Badiou confirms this by just reminding the reader that as regards pure multiples as such, said multiple cannot differ from itself nor take up a degree of difference from another being. All pure multiples are indifferently singular by which we mean they are indivisible with themselves, and they differ from another multiple absolutely. Indifferent being means that within a being there is no difference, no otherness, no alterity. And that as regards placing multiples together, they all differ in exactly the same degree, which is totally. We have spent a whole volume on this problem so we will move on after noting that Badiou ends this section by restating the thesis that we also hold to and which he now feels he has proven: 'The ontological determination of beings and the logic of being-there … are profoundly distinct. QED' (*LW* 118).

Appearing and the transcendental

We now turn our attention to the precise nature of Badiou's use of the term transcendental. If we take appearing to mean the way in which a mathematical multiple is made intelligible by being placed in a relational network of local consistency, or a world, it then becomes possible to say of this being, which is appearing, that it is 'more or less different from another being belonging to the same world' (*LW* 118). The transcendental is the 'set' that allows us to understand 'the "more or less" of identities and differences in a determinate world' (*LW* 118). This is all that the logic of appearing, the transcendental algebra as he calls it here, or later category theory, does. It evaluates the identities and differences that make up the worldy place of the being-there portion of any being. Badiou's justification for this logic is that it is apparent that the world of appearing is not chaotic because of the strictly ordered nature of being as such which underpins this world.

After a diversion into the swamps of prehistory, Quentin Melliassoux and dinosaurs, we proceed with the stipulation that beings always appear locally without any recollection, as he calls it, of the innumerable instances or worlds pertaining to this appearance. While a being appears in a world it never composes the totality of this world, this is impossible. That a being appears always locally, never globally, means that this appearing is regulated by the logic which determines a variable degree of identity and thus difference to the other beings of the same world. The same issue returns again and again: how can beings appear differently in different worlds and yet be the same being, and how can two beings appear as the same in that they are in the same world, and yet retain their singular difference?[8] The solution, and this is the most important point here, is that there must be a scale of these degrees of appearance, a scale against which the measure of their intensity of appearance can be gauged. The scale of these degrees is what Badiou means by the transcendental.

Accepting that the local appearance of this being does not negate the indivisibility of its being, and that the comparative relation of two beings as being the same but different allows for different beings to exist on the same level or in the same context, all you need is a transcendental measure. This mode of indexing a being to its transcendental requires what Badiou calls the double difference of a being to another being and the appearance of a being relative to its mathematical being as such. This is not particularly news; the problem was never the knowledge that such a measure was needed, as ever the problem was that it could never be attained at a transcendental level without recourse to the One and infinite divisibility. The transcendental organization of any world is what Badiou calls 'the protocol of response' to the basic questions, how does this being differ from others and how does it differ from itself? Or the transcendental 'fixes the moving singularity of the being-there of a being in a determinate world' (*LW* 119).

Let's go back to our examples, Ariadne and Bluebeard and the page numbers 327 and 328. If we look at Ariadne we would say that while she is a wife-victim, and so appears in the world of all the wife-victims in the various versions of the story, she is different to the other victims. She is aware of her potential status as wife-victim and so responds accordingly. In the various versions of the Bluebeard myth one must be able to 'respond with an evaluative nuance' to her difference relative to the version or world you are looking at. This might mean variations in the narrative or language, in the music if it is an opera 'considered as the transcendental of the (aesthetic situation)' (*LW* 119). Ariadne is one of the wives; yet, she is different from all the others. Then we must add in the transcendental nature of the aesthetic world, story, poem, music, opera and look at how her difference appears in terms of the form. In contrast, all the other wives are ostensibly the same, forming a substitutable series. They are, on this reading, transcendentally identical; they are all just wives. This identity can be extended further if one thinks of the story as a comment on misogyny then the wives being all the same extends to all women being the same that is, without the possibility of agency and subjectivity.

If we now consider Bluebeard we can say that his love for Ariadne is represented in what Badiou calls 'his lag with respect to himself' (*LW* 120). He wants to treat her with the same hatred he treats all women, he wants to index her as the same and push her into the chorus of death made up by his other wives, all women to him are his wives, but he cannot. Because of this inability his degree of identity to himself fades and diminishes in relation to Ariadne. In the opera this lag, this fundamentally psychoanalytical moment when the subject Bluebeard is other to himself, is represented by what Badiou calls an extravagant cipher. For the last act he stays on stage but never speaks or sings: 'This is truly the limit value (which is in fact exactly minimal) of an operatic transcendental: Bluebeard is absent from himself' (*LW* 120). Here Bluebeard appears on stage as a multiple that is empty of value. He appears in this way as the empty set of himself or what a multiple looks like when it appears, he is on stage, as empty, he does not speak. Any less than this would mean he does not appear, any more would mean he appears as a positive charge as regards his relation to himself. One point to be made in passing here is how much the appearing of a being relative to itself depends on its relation to other beings. It is not just that beings appear to some degree relative to the transcendental; their degree of appearing may be determined by their relation to another being: here Bluebeard appears as minimal due to his love for Ariadne. This is what Badiou means by dependence.

In contrast to the minimal value of appearing, on stage and silent, in terms of our two numbers 327 and 328 as regards their degree of appearing in the world of being page numbers, Badiou speaks of the maximal value. In terms of their being, 327 and 328 are absolutely different. But when it comes to reading a book they are almost identical, let's say this book is page-turner not a work of philosophy. This then is as close to being the same as two numbers can get without being the same number. If you later return to this book and you wanted to read a section from 327 which particularly impressed you, suddenly 327 has a greater degree of appearing within the world of the book or reading the book, and 328 now differs from 327 greatly. Badiou summarizes: 'The value of the identities and differences of a being to itself and of a being to others varies transcendentally between an almost nil identity and a total identity, between absolute difference and indifference' (*LW* 120). Obviously we cite this because of the use of indifference in a world made up entirely of differences. Two beings which appear as the same in the same world are indifferent even if they are actually two different beings.

It must be possible to think, in a world, what does not appear in that world

This proposition basically concerns the nature of the minimum whose importance we have already attested to. So far we have put our weight behind the assertion that there can be a minimum, both in terms of ontology and now as regards logic. This halting point, we argued, is one of the foundation stones of a revitalization of the traditional problems of Western thought which now, thanks to Badiou, have been, for all intents and purposes, resolved. This however is not quite the same point as arguing that worlds should have a minimum, although if we are speaking of this particular form of non-intentional primarily desubjectivized phenomenology (subjects only pertain to certain moments within certain worlds) then the only way it would make sense is to accept the minimum as a halting point. All the same, Badiou gives three proofs pertaining to the possibility of the minimum relating to there not being a Whole, then the necessity of there being a not-being-there as part of the being-there construct; otherwise, being-there and being-qua-being would be identical. Finally he notes that if being-there is determined by evaluation of identity and difference between two beings, then the measure of larger or smaller is meaningless unless there is always a less large which ends at nil, the halting point. All three proofs are considered in *Being and Event* relevant to being as such and all we need to show here is that Badiou is founding the laws of being-there repeatedly on the axioms of being as such, even if being-there itself is non-axiomatic.

The conclusion is that 'there exists, for every world, a transcendental measure of the not-apparent-in-this-world, which is obviously a minimum (a sort of zero)' (*LW* 123). The minimum is what 'zero' means in the logic of appearing, which is not the same as zero in set theory, but which depends on said zero for its own relational minimality. Here, by way of clarification, he states that while we are speaking of the degrees of appearing of a being, we must never consider a being in a world in isolation. In that being-there is a logic and logic is relational; every being that appears must appear in relation to at least one other being. The detail of this we will consider as we progress, but for now the point is clear. Every being that appears does so in relation to at least one other being within the same transcendental field that is itself bounded at one end by a minimum of appearing which we are calling nil appearing.

One final point is, just because we say such and such a being does not appear in this world and hence, in this world, it does not exist, this does not mean that it actually does not exist as a being as such or that it doesn't exist in another world. If, he says, a book has 700 pages then page 721 does not appear in it as none of the numbers in the book can be said to be 721. This does not mean 721 has no being, or that 721 is incapable of appearing; it can appear in a longer book, for example. Badiou then says that it is not possible for one to force 721 to appear in this world, as it would have to be 'co-thinkable in and for the world that this book is' (*LW* 123). He says this is not possible as you could find no transcendental measure between the other numbers of the book and 721. This is because you are not building a world out of numbers or even pages, but pages of this particular book. If you were to force 721 then you would have to either have a world book where pagination is not successively consecutive, which one could have but that would be a different world book, or page 721 would not be the same as an actual page.

Finally, Badiou concludes on what he calls the delicate point which is that the non-apparent must always be determined in a world in relation to an evaluation of its minimal identity in this world. This does not mean that such and such a being is not there ontologically as not-being-there has no being as such. All it tells us is that such and such is not there in this world. As we are speaking here of appearing in terms of logic not as regards mathematical ontology, then all the properties of being-there *have to be relational*, which also means they can never be indifferent. So nil appearing simply means minimal relation.

The conjunction of two apparents in a world

Consistency of a world depends on the fact that what sustains or allows for the co-appearance of two beings in that world should be 'immediately legible' (*LW* 125), absolutely intelligible, instantly communicable. This legibility is based on the fact that the intensity of the appearance of the part that the two beings hold in common is itself available for evaluation. 'This part is what these two beings have in common to the extent that they are there, in this world' (*LW* 125). This common element is made apparent in one of three ways or three cases as Badiou calls them. Case 1 is when two beings appear in a world due to a necessary 'connection of their appearance' (*LW* 125). The example here is a being which is an identifying part of another. At this point Badiou brings in a new world as an example, the autumnal scene of foliage on the wall of a house. If we take the red leafage of the ivy on a wall in autumn, we can say that this leafage is constitutive in this autumn world of the being-there of 'ivy'. Ivy appears because of the foliage of the ivy seen against the wall such that the measure of the being-there of the ivy and the 'red-leafage-unfurled' in terms of what they have in common in this world is the value of the appearance of the red leafage because it is the red leafage which identifies the ivy in terms of its appearing. He says, 'The operation of the "common" is in fact a sort of inclusive corroboration. A being, insofar as it is there, carries with it the apparent identity of another, which deploys it in the world as its part, but whose identifying intensity it in turn realizes' (*LW* 125). He goes on to call this first relation inclusive 'because the appearance of one entails that of the other' (*LW* 126).

There is, as regards the appearing of something in the world, a relation called the common or inclusion. In this relation the being-there of one element totally includes the being-there of another. The first being can then be said to be larger than the second because it includes it. Yet at the same time the being-there of the larger item is determined by what it includes because, if the leafage can include the ivy because it is larger or appears more dominantly in the world (presumably because there are a variety of red-leaves and ivy can only appear as being one of them), we can only say it is larger and thus able to include the smaller item, because it includes a smaller item against which its relative grandeur is determined. This is perfectly in accord with the set-theoretical basis of these arguments for a multiple is the multiple that it is by being the next largest all the way down to the halting point of the void, and that this basic structure is carried over into the logic of worlds. One element is larger than another to the degree that it includes it entirely; yet, its size is determined by the smaller element it includes and so there is a co-mutual corroborative function here.

The second case determines the appearance of two beings in terms of their relation to a third. Once two beings co-appear in a world, this third element is the most apparent, the largest, that the two beings have a common reference to once they have both appeared. If we speak of the appearing of the house in the world of autumn and the appearance of blood-red ivy leaves, then there is an element which conjoins these two disparate elements which is, he argues, the wall which is both a part of the house and 'the intermittent ground for that plant that creeps upon it' (*LW* 126). The wall then is proposed as 'what maximally conjoins the general appearing of the ivy with the appearing ... of the house' (*LW* 126). Here, as regards the ivy and the house, neither includes the other but they are in common in that both have a third element which 'maximally underlies the other two in the stability of the world' (*LW* 126). It is not that the wall is larger than either the ivy or the house, for example, the wall is larger than the ivy but it is clearly smaller than the house; rather, it is the largest single element that the two beings have in common. Badiou calls this intercalary or intercalation meaning an extra element which is inserted or interposed between the elements of a sequence.

The final case treats two beings appearing in a world 'without the "common" of their appearance itself being identifiable within appearing' (*LW* 126). Or, the intensity of the appearance of what two beings have in common is nil. Here, into the scene of the ivy and the setting light of day, Badiou introduces the sound of a passing motorbike. This noise does not destroy or divide the autumnal world; it just means there is no common part between the leafage and the motorbike. This raises an important point. The motorbike does appear in the world, the autumnal scene, so its degree of intensity of appearing in that world is not nil. It is just that the intensity of the appearing of the noise of the bike relative to our ivy, the common element in all three considerations, is nil. Something can appear in the same world as something else and yet they share absolutely nothing in common in terms of their relation within this world, suggesting that having something in common in a world is not just because we are both in this world. Worlds are more capacious and perhaps capricious than that. So we can say that the degree of conjunction between two beings can be inclusive, intercalary or, in the case of the last example, disjunctive. These are the three modes of conjunction, and the only three, that exist in the logic of appearing in a world.

Badiou now moves on to consider the modes of conjunction relative to transcendental measure of the intensities of the beings involved. Speaking of the wall which, if you recall, was an example of intercalation, said wall appears through the support provided by both the house in total and the ivy. Thus when we come to measure the intensity of its appearance, we can say the wall is comparable to the house and the ivy. By comparable we mean that all the differential intensities under consideration here are measured within the transcendental. Specifically, the appearance of the wall is less than or equal to that of the house and that of the ivy. It depends on them to appear. More than this it is the largest or greatest visible surface to present this common relation with the two other beings. Speaking more generally if there are two beings in a world, then each of them has a value of appearance indexed in the transcendental of the world in question (here the Autumnal scene). The conjunction of these two beings which is defined as the 'maximal common part of their being-there' is also measured due to the transcendental by the greatest value that is less than or equal to those two initial measurements. If the greatest measure between the two is nil, which it can be, then there is no conjunction and the two beings are both in the same world in a disjoint manner. The closer the measure of appearance of the common part of these two is to the values of the two beings in question we can say the more that conjunction is in the world. Yet however strong the intercalary intensity becomes, it can never be more than the intensities of those two initial beings. If the intercalary value becomes equal to one of the two beings, then it ceases to be intercalary and becomes instead inclusion and the common part instead is entirely borne by one of the two beings in question. The simplest way of saying this is that if this third common part that has something in common with two other parts has so much in common with part 1 that you cannot tell them apart, then in fact it is included in part 1 because it is the same as part 1 and so it no longer operates as a third intercalary element. Instead it is just the same as part 1 and so the conjunction of the two parts is determined by the law of inclusion. This would state that some of the elements of part 2 are included in part 1, namely those elements of part 1 that are also to be found in part 2.

One final point needs to be made here which is when we speak of the intensity of appearing of any being; what we are actually describing are the intensities of difference between at least two beings. All these values are determined relationally and not in themselves. Everything that is said of being in the world is said due to an identity achieved through the measure of the intensity of difference between at least two beings. Badiou sums up by saying that the logical stability of any world 'deploys conjoined identifying (or differential) networks' (*LW* 128). The conjunctions are deployed from the minimal or disjunction, up to the maximal or inclusion, through a spectrum of intermediate values of which there is an effectively infinite number but all of which are indexed to the transcendental. This accounts for, in its entirety, the logical structure of any world. Take any world, within said world are any number of beings which appear in that world. If a being appears in a world and you compare it to another being and find they are the same relative to the world, then you are at the maximal value of inclusion. If said being however is incomparable to this other being, then they appear together at the minimum value of disjunction. Two beings that are the same in this world need not be the same in another world and similarly two beings with nothing in common in this world may indeed be taken to be the same in another. In between the maximal and minimum cases are the large majority of all relations between at least two beings as you consider what they have in common relative to the transcendental. This is the basis of what Badiou calls his 'objective phenomenology' or a phenomenology divested of intention and thus the problematics of consciousness and universal subjectivity.

Regional stability of worlds: The envelope

Yet at the same time, when Badiou now returns to our problem of disjunction, it is primarily the language of intentional horizons that he uses. The problem is how can a being appear as disjoint in a world and not as a form of dislocation of said world. In this mediation Badiou is re-engaging with Husserlian–Heideggerian and Deleuzian phenomenology although he is primarily simply talking about that pesky, noisy motorbike we have already encountered. We are in our autumnal scene in which Badiou says he is lost in contemplation. He hears the noise of the engine and the wheels on the gravel. This noise is now there in the world but is 'conjoined to my vision only by the nil value of appearing' (*LW* 128–9). This noise however does not dislocate the world or make me reform another world. The transcendental of the autumnal scene is able to accommodate new elements and remain stable. In this case, 'the world deploys the inappearance in a world of some One of the two beings-there, and not the appearance of a being (the motorcycle) in a world other than the one which is already there' (*LW* 129). This second point is clearly an option. If the motorcycle exists already in the world say of the mechanized and the philosopher-poet is lost in contemplation of nature and more artisanal forms of techné, then instead of saying the noise appears in the world of the ivy-house with the value of nil, one could just as easily say that the world of the ivy-house is negated by the arrival of another world. This threat being very real, how does

Badiou accommodate the noise into the stability of the world? Primarily, as I said, through the phenomenology of intentionality, reaching out to the horizon of experience of a central, subjective consciousness.

The world as such here, Badiou explains, is not composed of the intensity of his attention on the ivy-house. These two beings are a part of a larger space which 'envelops' the ivy-house. This would include a path leading to the house, a border of trees and so on. This scene envelops not only the ivy-house but also Badiou's body or gaze and an 'entire invisible background which nevertheless leads towards it' and also the sound of the bike (*LW* 129). To access this, as yet, invisible aspect of the same world Badiou simply needs to turn his body when he hears the skidding sound. As he does so, 'it's not because I imagine, between the world and the incongruous noise that disjoins itself from the red of autumn, a sort of abyss between the two worlds. No, I simply situate my attention … in a wider correlation, which includes the house … the crunch of the gravel, the motorcycle' (*LW* 129). As Badiou's attention, here dictated by the movement of his body which controls the horizon of his gaze, is taken up by the sound of the bike, then at this point the nil conjunction of the bike to what he has been looking at so far is presented. Yet although this conjunction is nil, 'it takes place in an infinite fragment of this world which dominates the two terms, as well as many others' (*LW* 129). In this world he mentions various elements ending with hills and the sky 'which the disjunction between the motor and the pure red is powerless to separate out from the clouds' (*LW* 129). In other words, there is a higher unity that nil disjunction cannot dispel because nil disjunction only appears as such due to the stability of said world. Nothing appears in a world that is not relational to it except events in the form of truths tested point by point due to consequences by a subject to truth. Aside from these special cases, such appearances in worlds which appear in said world as disjoint are not nonrelational true events. Badiou says that, in the end, the world of the sky, clouds, path and house is 'superior to that of all the disjunctive ingredients: ivy, house, motorcycle, gravel. This is why the synthesis of these ingredients, as carried out by the being-there of the corner of the world in which the nil conjunction is signalled, prevents this nullity from amounting to a scission of the world, that is a decomposition of the world's logic' (*LW* 129).

It is clear that Badiou is working hard here to resist Deleuze's point as regards multiple, indeed infinite events. Yet Badiou is just as keen to say no to Husserl and Heidegger as he is to refuse Deleuze. He immediately states that the synthesis in question has no need for his gaze, his consciousness or the movement of his body. Instead, the regional stability of the world is dependent on the fact that if you take a random fragment of a world, then the beings which appear therein are there not because someone sees them or thinks about them but because they possess 'differential degrees of appearance indexed to the transcendental order of this world' (*LW* 129). In that nothing which appears in this world including an infinite number of disjunctions can affect the unity of this world 'means that the logic of the world guarantees the existence of a synthetic value subsuming all the degree of appearance of the beings that co-appear in this fragment. *We call "envelope" of a part of the world that being whose differential value of appearance is the synthetic value adequate to that part*' (*LW* 130).

The envelope is a significant innovation in the phenomenology of appearing. The envelope assumes that from any collection of degrees of appearance of beings in a part of a world, the transcendental order 'contains a degree superior or equal to all the degrees in the collection (it subsumes them all), which is also the smallest degree to enjoy this property (it "grips," as closely as possible, the collection of degrees assigned to the different beings-there of the part in question)' (*LW* 130). The envelope is like a world within a world or perhaps a country within the world, sometimes a continent, at times even an island. It contains all the other elements of the world. No being that is currently appearing is bigger than the envelope that is the fragment of their appearing. By the same gesture, although the envelope is bigger than all the other elements, it includes as regards the relation of its belonging to the world and its relation to the collection of beings in question, it is only just bigger. If the envelope were enormously bigger, it would not function as the local synthesis of the beings in question. So an envelope is bigger than all the elements it contains, but no bigger than all the elements contained therein.

Returning to our example, at the moment that Badiou's reverie is interrupted by the noise of the engine and he turns around to see what the cause is, he says he does not need to invoke the entire planet or even the local horizon of hills. Instead it is sufficient to 'integrate the dominant of wordly fragment' (*LW* 130) that can absorb this new piece of information as disjunction between noise and ivy still within the consistency of appearing. There is, he says, enough in the fragment of avenue, a few trees, the front of the house that can guarantee that the two disjoined beings still co-appear in the same world. This fragment, which is now big enough to encapsulate at least one disjoint element relative to at least one element in the world, the disjuncture between engine and ivy, is the envelope of these beings. Said envelope is the smallest value of appearing in the world that is able to encapsulate or dominate the values of the beings in question. Presumably the size and scope, to use a logical term, of the envelope are not determined by a predetermined horizon of experience, an actual horizon, or subjective consciousness located in an ambulatory being, but is rather defined by how big it needs to be, to fulfil the dictates of the least largest envelopment of the elements in question.

The conjunction between a being-there and a region of its world

The envelope, a categorical function, is an important component of the structure of appearing. Aside from the minimum and the modes of conjunction of two or more elements moving towards the maximum which, we might say, is the world at large, there are of course localized fragmentary subsets producing interim structures of some complexity within the world. This is what Badiou alludes to when he speaks of the conjunction between being-there and a *region* of its world. For example, considering the sounds of the motorcycle instead of the conjunction of an alien noise with an already-existing apparent, say the red ivy, I am now rather asking how does this disparate noise fit into the fragmentary world of the autumnal scene, including the house, the sky and so on. To work out how this element fits into the larger region, we need to ask, as ever, as to the value of the conjunction. In this case it is the value of the conjunction between the noise and all the other elements already appearing in the region. Badiou calls this the 'conjunction between this noise and the global apparent, the pre-existing envelope which is this fragment of the autumnal world' (*LW* 131). To measure this conjunction you need to consider this noise in relation to every element in the envelope. So while we said that the noise is not conjoined with the other elements of the envelope, we were considering, and so was disjoint because its value of relation was nil, now we think of the noise more widely as part of the overall scene. Opening up the scene, Badiou speculates, elements such as other distant noises, hearing the motorbike before and so on start to increase the degree of relation of the new noise to parts of the envelope as a whole. This is possible because of the nature of the envelope which 'designates the value of appearance of a region of the world as being superior to all the degrees of appearance it contains. As superior, in particular, to all the conjunctions it contains' (*LW* 132). Ergo when we think of the noise of the bike, we compare it one by one to all the other single elements we have taken so far to be part of the autumnal scene and while we find no value of relation between the bike and certain elements, we find some value of relation between the bike and other elements, which means we now have to enlarge the envelope to include the bike.

Our new envelope has to be suited to all the elements within, which means its overall value has to be more than the minimum of the value between the noise and the ivy, because the value between the noise and other conjunctions, other noises, previous bike noises and so on is not nil. This then gives us a simple law. An envelope is that subset which dominates all local conjunctions. Or, in more detail: 'the value of the conjunction between an apparent and an envelope is the value of the envelope of all the local conjunctions between this apparent and all the apparents of the envelope in question, taken one by one' (*LW* 132).

Dependence: The measure of the link between two beings in a world

Badiou's system of objective, calculated phenomenology is based on three simple elements all of which we have now detailed: the minimum, the conjunction and the envelope. He calls this a principle of completeness and admits that it assumes that every mode of being-there can be derived from these three basic operations. At the same time, if you recall, he also admits to the need for a law of causality or implication, which he calls dependence. Within objective phenomenology we might have various forms of causal relation such as if a certain apparent exists in a world strongly, then a certain other apparent equally exists within the world. Or, conversely if said apparent appears, it forbids the appearance of another apparent. Finally, of course, we must admit to basic syllogistic logic of the type which proves that if Socrates is a man then he is mortal. We arrive at three orders of dependence: total dependence, non-dependence and partial implication of the kind if A and B then C. If there is implication in worlds or physical causality, can this still be deduced from our three basic operators? The answer is yes, if we admit to a fourth operation which Badiou calls dependence.

Dependence is always defined as regards an apparent A in relation to another apparent we shall call B. If we were to define the degree to which B depends on A, we need to identify the apparent with the greatest intensity that can be conjoined with A yet whilst still being beneath the intensity of B. This means that dependence, here the degree to which B depends on A, as the 'envelope of those beings-there whose conjunction with A remains lesser in value than their conjunction with B' (*LW* 134). Naturally, if B is to depend on A, then B as a whole must be larger or in this case the elements which depend on A which appear in B must be smaller than B. One cannot have, for example, an apparent that depends on A which is 'smaller' than A as in that case B is not the envelope of this element. Badiou notes in relation to this basic logical principle that 'the stronger the dependence of B with regard to A, the greater the envelope' (*LW* 134). This allows for the fact that there exist beings with a very high degree of appearance in the world at large; yet, in terms of their conjunction with A they remain inferior to B by which we mean in terms of dependence, these other elements depend less on A than B does.

Dependency plus envelopment allow us to present a stratified set of envelopes within a larger world. For example, speaking of the ivy and the house façade we can say that conjoined these two remain less intense than the house as a whole. Therefore, the wall enters into the dependence of the house as regards its conjunction with the ivy. Yet one could also consider the tiles on the roof in relation to the ivy and determine a second dependency which totally excludes the wall. To work out the dependence of the house in relation to the ivy however you would need to include both the wall and the roof because we included the roof in relation to the ivy by comparing the differences in their colours. In this instance while you might think of the house depending on the wall and the roof, instead the house depends on the ivy as it is the colour of the ivy that is our means of relation, not simply that a house is literally bigger than ivy and by definition has walls and a roof.

Badiou ends with a couple of formal clarifications of this slightly tricky formulation. If in considering how B strongly depends on A, you can say it is possible to conjoin almost the entire world to A whilst staying beneath the value of the appearance of B so that if something generally is the case for A, then *a fortiori* it holds for B. This dependence means that the description of the predicative situation of A holds 'almost entirely for B' if the value of dependence is high. If B depends on A then it stands to reason that what holds for A will most likely hold for B. The more B depends on A the more this is the case, although B cannot entirely depend on A because then it would be A. Indeed, this is one of the properties that result from dependency. The dependence of a degree of intensity of an apparent with regards to itself is maximal; 'since the predicative situation of a being A is *absolutely* its own' (*LW* 135). What this implies is that the tautology of self-dependence is maximal and is another way of generating the idea of self-identity.

The reverse of an apparent in the world

To add to dependence we have one more derived operation which pertains to negation. Thus far we have already spoken of how to measure the inapparent, which we called the minimum, but now we are concerned with, given the appearance of a being-there in a world can we negate that appearance? This mode of negation, as we have already said, is called in category theory the *reverse* and, like dependence, it can be defined using our three basic operators: minimum, conjunction and envelope. We start by taking all the elements which are external to a given apparent, in this case the ivy. All the elements that appear in a world but which have a degree of conjunction with the ivy set at nil or minimum form a set. This composes the 'disparate set of beings that are there in the world but which in terms of their appearing have nothing in common with the scarlet ivy' (*LW*135). The envelope of this disparate set is what synthesizes all these external elements defined as a being whose appearance is greater than or equal to all the beings that are 'phenomenologically alien to the initial being' (*LW* 136). Such an envelope is made up of the conjunction of all elements that have a degree of relation to the ivy that is nil, is what we call the reverse of the ivy in the world called autumnal scene. The region called the reverse is made up of all the elements in a world which have no relation to the element in question you are 'negating'. Badiou concludes by reminding us how it is more than notable that negation, here in the form of the reverse, is not a basic condition of appearing but is derived from appearing. As soon as you consider the appearance of beings in a world, by definition you can consider the existence of the set of elements that composes their negation; yet, you do not *need* negation to make a being appear. When some thing 'is', it does not emerge out of the is-not and it is not directly defined in terms of the other beings that it is-not in a world. Yet for a being to exist in a world it must have a direct relation with the minimum, a kind of quasi-negative inappearance, *and* of course its appearance is relational.

There exists a maximal degree of appearance in the world

If you place together the axiom of the existence of the minimum with the derived value of the reverse, you naturally come to the question: What is the reverse of the minimum? This value would be the reverse (negation) of the inapparent which, by definition, must be the value of the 'apparent as such, the indubitable apparent; in short, the apparent whose being-there is attested absolutely' (*LW* 138). For Badiou this has to be the maximal because it is not possible to have an appearance greater than that which validates appearance as such. Such a meta-appearance would take us into the realm of traditional transcendental ideas of the whole which are absolutely disallowed by Badiou's ontology. The example of pagination is particularly instructive here. Badiou selects the number 1,033 in terms of how it appears in his fictional book. If we take the book to have 650 pages, then the degree of appearance of 1,033 is nil. If 1,033 is inapparent in the book, then what is its reverse? That must be the maximum page number that can be found in the book namely 650. So 650 marks the number of the book and any number smaller than that down to the minimum of nil appears in the book. Every other number is inapparent in the book and thus is the minimum even though numerically 1,033 is larger than 650.

Badiou points out that the existence of the maximum taken as the reverse of the minimum is the basis of all worldy stability: 'Appearance is never endlessly amendable; there is no infinite ascension towards the light of being-there. The maximum of appearance distributes, until the beings indexed to it, the calm and equitable certainty of their worldiness' (*LW* 139). The reason for this is because there do not exist universes, only worlds, and so in every world the maximal value of the transcendental degree speaks to this world but never to *the* world. 'A world's power of localization is determinate: if a multiple appears in this world, there is an absolute degree of this appearance' (*LW* 139). One clarification, we said earlier that the reverse did not accord with classical logic and the law of the excluded middle. That you cannot assume that the negation of a thing is its opposite, that negating its extensional truth will necessarily show extensional falsity. This law remains in place except, as we can see here, when it comes the reverse of the minimum which has to return its opposite, the maximum. The reasoning behind this is surely that in order for a world of immanent relations to be stable, it has to have modes of delimitation that avoid bad infinity and infinite regress. These modes of delimitation are ontological, and ontology is strictly classical.

What is the reverse of the maximal degree of appearance?

Badiou says it is obvious that the reverse of the maximum is the minimum or the reverse of appearance as such of a world must be what does not appear in that world which is the minimum. Yet he also says that this result is derived from another interesting point which is that the conjunction between the maximum of a world and any degree of appearing in that world is equal to that degree of appearing. If we take the scene 'end of an autumn afternoon in the country', then the degree of appearing of the maximum of this scene is the 'there' of its entire being-there: 'its absolute appearing, without the cut provided by any kind of witness' (*LW* 139). Now we might ask what does this enveloping generality have in common with a singular being that is there in this world? The answer is 'precisely that this being is there with the intensity proper to its appearing' (*LW* 139–40) so that if we take say the intense red of ivy as the sun hits it and we relate it to the total scene, all that is returned from this conjunction is that the red ivy is there: 'It is simply identified, repeated and restored to itself ... conjoined to the autumn, the ivy is its red, already-there as "ivy-in-autumn"' (*LW* 140). This law, which Badiou calls phenomenologically limpid, says that the degree of conjunction between any being and the world in which it appears is equal simply to the appearance of that being in that world. All that the maximum returns in terms of degree is the intensity of the appearing of some thing in this world. The world as a whole then is simply made up of all the beings it can return to themselves as beings there in this world. This being the case, the fact that the reverse of the maximum is the minimum is a derived function from this fact. The reverse has to have nothing in common with what it reverses. If it reverses the maximum, then it cannot have any relation to the maximum. In that as it appears everything in that world has something in common with the maximum; otherwise, it doesn't appear; ergo, the minimum must be everything that does not appear in the word which, by definition, is the minimum: 'It is the reverse that inappears in that world' (*LW* 140). This reiterates our earlier point that the reverse is a mode of negation that is gifted with an additional degree of nonrelationality to that of traditional, oppositional or logical concepts of the function. The reverse is an object that *has nothing in common* with the world in question, defined by the transcendental functor of its maximal, here [autumnal scene].

We are now mid-way through the immense second book of *Logics of Worlds*. What it has asked us to consider is what Badiou calls the transcendental of what in category theory is called the category as a whole. Said category is what Badiou means by a world. As we have seen, the term transcendental is problematic in that little about the categorical transcendental shares anything in common with the philosophical history of the term, which is why later Badiou will speak more often of the transcendental functor. What this allows us to perceive is that the transcendental is not a set of things or a thing itself, although it is bound by some of the basic axioms of set theory, for example, that it is an inexistent whole, but a function. What the transcendental does is allow for us to construct worlds that are consistent, non-closed, immanent and inter-relational, and it achieves this because of category theory. In the simplest of terms, category theory does for existence what set theory does for being. Which also means that in exchange for a consistency of worlds, to match the consistency of being, we have to accept the laws of categories, just as we had to adopt the axioms of set theory. These functions explain how one can construct radically immanent, relational worlds based on functional relations rather than old-fashioned ontological ones like, for example, two beings of the same kind, or two beings with the same predicates. Now when we consider two beings in the same world, it is not what they share in common that matters, although they both have to share in common two functional relations, with themselves and with the categorical world or transcendental as a whole, nor what they do not have in common. Rather, beings in the same world relate or do not relate in degrees of intensity from minimum (nil nonrelation) to maximum (they are then effectively the same object).

What this requires of the reader is that they put aside the entire tradition of existential beings and start again with a categorical set of propositions along the lines of, if you want an immanent theory of possible worlds that is totally consistent and founded on the irrefutable formalism of sets, so in this sense doubly consistent, then you have to think again as to what you mean by *objects in a world*. This being the proposition let us try to summarize what an object in a world thanks to categories actually is. The whole of the world is inexistent meaning all existential worlds, not all worlds, are actual infinities. It is not anything that can appear in said world but there is no way of saying what will appear to any world remains radically impossible to close. Internal to the world, as was the case with sets, the structure is based on localized relations between multiples, although the modality of relation is very different. For a being to be in a world, it has to belong to that world which means it has to appear in it. Belonging in terms of worlds means self-relation, you are the thing such as you are. Inclusion is all other kinds of relation, for example, by necessity relation to the transcendental of the world at large. Non-appearance in a world is not an absolute other, an outside of the world or outside of all worlds, but a derived function of appearing such that inexistence is world specific; to inexist means a being that cannot be shown to appear in this particular world.

If you appear in the world, this is defined solely by degrees of relation with other apparents due to functional relations taken from category theory. The primary functions of relation are inclusion, two beings that share something in common, one of which will be larger than the other; intercalation, two beings share in common relations to a third; and disjunction, two beings appear but share nothing in common. These functions of conjunction are further regulated by others such as the envelope, dependence and the reverse. Said functions have to systematically replace your assumptions about existence based, I would imagine, primarily on an ontology of something like classes with properties and commonalities of predicates and essences. If, however, you come here straight out of the pages of *Being and Event* or my own consideration of that text, then you may have a new assemblage of ideas about being taken from sets. Apparents are not the same as multiples from sets, for example, by definition they cannot be content indifferent because their relational appearance is due to degrees of comparative difference.

While multiples do appear, or are included as Badiou used to say, in worlds, and this is thanks to some of the central axioms of set theory, when they appear they are no longer multiples of that order. For example, their basic relational rankability up to infinity and down to zero is replaced by an interrelational degree of rank, greater than, equal to or lesser than. This is founded on a minimum but that minimum is not defined by deduction down to the void set or 1. And they are gathered together into an actual infinity, but this infinity is not of the same order as in sets, for example, because it does not result from the qualities of rankable sets as Cantor's examples of actual infinities do. All worlds have to be cardinal infinities, but you cannot prove that they are from within worlds themselves. Finally, although worlds cannot be closed, they do have a maximum, which is the transcendental functor, and something can appear maximally in that world, indeed infinite things can; although when they do appear, they are all the same maximal object. Finally, the reverse of the world in question, all that does not appear in said world is not some negative-theology of absence or negation, some universal Other or anything of that kind, but again is just a derived function of reversal. A reversal of the maximal is basically within the category of [autumnal scene], everything that cannot possibly appear in that scene which is, practically speaking, as in reality nothing can be truly excluded from any world, everything at any one time that is not appearing there.

Worlds are categories or headings of relationality. When a being has existence, it means it appears in a world under a category. This being will then have to appear as the being it is, have more than a zero degree of self-relation and this appearance will have to have at minimum a degree of relation to the category itself at the very least. If multiple beings appear in our world, and we want to speak of their structure, this will be determined locally in terms of degrees of conjunction, and regionally as regards say envelopes or the least largest unit that envelops all the other beings. An envelope being something akin to a localized transcendental functor. These modes of functional relation do not have the benefit of ordinality and cardinality, as in sets, so they have to determine structural consistency using localized rank, larger than, which is less consistent than saying, this is the fifth member of a set of eight. That said, what it does mean is the difference in a world is neither absolute nor indifferent. Things can be partially different. They can also be totally different yet be in the same collection, which is inadmissible in sets. They can, in other words, express partiality or degree in a way that multiples of being cannot. Also, a multiple can be added to the collection of the category and it remains the category it is, because the functional operator of the transcendental functor has nothing to do with the size of the set, but with a shared common quality, we are all members of this world because we all have some mode of relation to the categorical heading because if we did not, we would not be appearing in it.

Section 3: Algebra of the transcendental

Logics of Worlds is composed using a three-part mode of consideration and analysis, a model also used in *Being and Event*. Once the basic ideas, here as regards the transcendental, are presented, then Badiou reconsiders them first from the basis of the history of philosophy and then again in terms of the role that mathematics has to play. It is not our aim to base our analysis either on the role of the history of metaphysics or category theory except where these two aspects further illuminate the central questions to hand. Thus when Badiou turns to Hegel in the previous section, we will leave the detail of this interaction to others and remind the reader of a sustained consideration of Badiou and Hegel in *Being and Event* and more widely our own work.[9] That said, in contrast, when Badiou now returns to the twelve elements of his concept of the transcendental from the perspective of algebraic category theory, as he does in the final section, we find much here that should detain us. The final part of this chapter reconsiders the concepts of the first section providing the formal basis for these ideas as regards set theory, category theory and certain core concepts in the history of constructivist logic. One could 'skip' this section as they primarily prove the concepts we have already explained using more mathematical detail and notation. However, as the concepts of appearing are so foundational and, if accepted, have such an intense potential for reconfiguring how we consider worlds that have meanings, let us go over these proofs to really secure everything else that Badiou will build atop of them.

The inexistence of the whole: To affirm the existence of a set of all sets is intrinsically contradictory

Badiou makes it clear that the whole inexists because the affirmation of a set of all sets, which is what Badiou means by the Whole, is intrinsically contradictory. To place this into a wider context, the proof of the inexistence of the whole is provided by Russell's paradox. This paradox concerns sets that are members of themselves. It was communicated to Frege in 1902 in a famous letter and it is this communication that concerns Badiou. For him, the self-predication paradox proves the inexistence of a whole as an after-effect, in the same way that negation is a derived function and not fundamental. Instead, he believes that what self-predication really shows is that Frege's basic assumption, which founds modern analytic philosophy, is fundamentally untrue. Frege insists that for every well-defined concept there corresponds a 'set of the objects that fall under this concept' (*LW* 153). What this insists on is that language, the well-defined concept, controls the world such as it is, the concepts that fall under its definition. This is the basis of first-order predictive logic namely that nothing exists except that it is a predicate of a concept and said concept is, by definition, logical and thus linguistic. For Badiou, in contrast, some things pre-exist the language we use to describe them, for example, the void. From his perspective, which is also that of set theory, it may be possible that to a well-defined predicate which is consistent in language, 'there may only correspond a real inconsistency (a deficit of multiple-being)' (*LW* 153). In other words, there exists an object in the world that is not predicate-dependent, that of the actual existence of the inconsistent, the void or the inapparent. This is not only central to his idea of a materialist ontology, it is also, as we have noted in the previous chapter, the means by which eventual traces can, through a process of subjectivation in response worldy consequences to yes/no decisions, thanks to simple yes/no decisions, come to be assigned a well-pointed body such that their inexistence as impossible starts to become possible. This process is not possible, as I said, if you insist that truth is entirely limited to concepts that extend over objects.

Badiou uses a simple logical procedure to show that if you take the predicate 'not being an element of oneself', the basis of Russell's paradox, you cannot find a single set which manifests this concept. There exists, therefore, a predicate without concept or an object that exists external to the language of logic, provable by the basic premise of modern predicative logic: Russell's paradox. Once we have this, we then can disprove the whole using Zermelo's central axiom of separation which states that well-constructedness alone is not enough to infer the existence of the presentation of sets. If sets exist, they pre-exist logic, and it is indeed only by presupposing that the presentation of at least one set occurs that you can prove the well-ordered nature of sets. This 'first set' is the void, and the void, based on this axiom, is real. Thus, for Badiou, all thought is materialist at root and the well-ordered logical systems we use to construct worlds can only be constructed in a well-ordered fashion if we assume that at least one set exists that cannot be proven by logic but upon which logic depends. Badiou uses this axiom now to show that the inexistence of the whole is a derived feature of the real existence of at least one multiple prior to language (logic). If, for example, the whole exists then there must exist the set of those elements which are not members of themselves within that whole. The whole after all contains all elements, all multiples that there are. If this were to be the case then the whole would contain, within itself, what it does not contain. The logical impossibility of this is profoundly felt in Russell's paradox, Derrida's paradox of margins and centre and Agamben's indifferentiation of inclusion and exclusion. It is, basically, one of the foundational ideas of our age.

Badiou has proven this before so our question is rather why does he emphasize the derived nature of the inexistence of the whole? The answer is pretty simple. Increasingly we will be leaving behind the ontological axioms of set theory and allowing ourselves to be seduced by the well-ordered linguistic systems of classical and intuitionist logic. At no point, Badiou is saying, should we forget however that there is no well-ordered logic without the presupposition of the real material existence of at least one set, the void, which is present in every single well-constructed set as the element which is present as that which does not belong. This is a tour de force. He takes the Frege and Russell debate over self-predication as the basis for predicative logic, the cornerstone of the strong argument for constructivism throughout the last century, and uses it to prove that something pre-exists logical linguistic construction, confirmed by the very rule that predicative logic depends on the paradox of self-predication. This is an axiomatic trick, I suppose, in that it combines retrospective thinking and an insistence of the proof of something impossible based on the very laws of what is possible within the particular rational system, here logic, but a very fine, totally beguiling one.

Function of appearing and formal definition of the transcendental

We now turn to the difference, ontologically and logically, as regards identity and difference, in particular how this determines the formal definition of appearing indexed to the transcendental. As regards multiples ontologically speaking, one multiple cannot differ more or less from another. If two multiples contain the same number of elements, they are totally identical and also self-identical. They are the same multiple. If one contains an element that the other does not, they are absolutely, not just slightly, different. The difference between the two is as absolute as any difference between any two multiples of different size. This is the law of the set as radically indifferent which demands that every ontological difference between one multiple and another is global, they are absolutely different, and local, they differ in this particular way, at the same time. In terms of ontological difference, every difference is global-local and so radically indifferent as regards their being different only in quantity with no reference to qualities. It perhaps goes without saying that no global difference is totally global as that would result in the Whole which, we have accepted, inexists. We might also say that each difference is, therefore, the same and in this way indifferently different. Every multiple differs from every other multiple at a local level, the specific difference between α and β, that is always global, the difference between any two multiples whatsoever. As Badiou puts it, 'The ontological theory of difference circulates univocally between the local and the global. Every difference in point entails the absolute difference of two beings. And every absolute difference implies that there exists at least one difference in point' (*LW* 155).

When it comes to appearing this is not the case at all and marks the central divergence between the ontology of indifferent being and the logic of communicable worlds we are reaching after. Instead, multiples in a world *can* differ more or less. They can resemble each other, be closer, more distant and so on. What determines their identity in this world is their relational difference to another being, rather than their absolute difference to all other beings, as is the case ontologically. These relational differences are determined by the logic of the world they are appearing in. Each world has its own logic, and that will determine the nature of the 'there' of any being's being-there. One cannot stress this distinction enough; it is the key to the entire Being and Event project. Ontologically multiples are indifferently, radically non-relational in terms of their 'difference' from each other. Logically they are differentially and relationally existent in terms of their *degree* of difference from each other relative to their overall identity as beings in this specific world.

For a multiple to appear in a world it is enough that it fulfils the basic law of communicability which is also the only real law of communicability. The being must be there, for it to be compared to another being; yet, the being is only there because you have compared it to another being. Existence due to communicability is profoundly different to 'existence' due to ontological indifference. The function of appearing is brilliantly simple. 'The minimal requirement of every localization is being able to determine a degree of identity (or non-identity) between an element α and an element β, when both are deemed to belong to the same world' (*LW* 156). This allows us to present the simple *function of appearing* which measures the degree of identity between two beings in one world. This function is **Id**(α,β). The function tells us the degree to which α and β are identical, from being totally identical, through partially identical, to not at all identical.

This basic functionality of appearing is true for every single appearing or existent being except that pertaining to an event. In this very real sense the law of identity, existence as the thing such as it is in this world, which is always a law of difference, due to the degree of difference between this being and at least one other, is indifferent. It is indifferently so for every single being. Difference then appears in the system due to the singularity of the world in question. It is the transcendental indexing of the appearances in play that determines the specific nature of their differential identity in terms of degrees of quality they possess. A pure multiple can appear differently in two different worlds and still be the same multiple. This is the complete opposite of the ontology of the multiple. In ontology, due to indifference, all local differences are global. In logic due to communicability, all global differences are local including the transcendental index itself which is, of course, a multiple in its own world and not a Whole or a participant in self-predicating paradoxes. The mathematics of this particular multiple, that of the transcendental as such, will need further work.

To sum up, in every world, if you take two beings, there always exists a value of their identity. This value is determined by the transcendental index of the world they are both appearing in. If you wish, taking our two beings α and β and writing their degree of value of appearing as p, then **Id**(α,β) = p or they are identical to the p degree, p being the index of their common world. For this formula to be functional it must make sense that the degree of identity, which is also their degree of difference, has a scale on which you can assign one of three values: more than >, less then <, or equal to =. This allows you then to put forward the next basic step as regards the constructible communicability of any world which is to say in the same world α is more identical to β than to γ. If **Id**(α,β) = p and **Id**(α,γ) = q then $p>q$, or taking two sets, the degree of relation between α and β is greater than that of α and γ. Another way to put his is once you have the degree of identity between two multiples, this allows you to compare that value to the degree of identity between one of these multiples and another multiple. From this, every single structure of communicable relation from nil through to maximal can be easily measured as the local level.

Equivalence-structure and order-structure

We now have to contend with the precise nature of order. Order is being able to say that a given element is greater or lesser than another. This is the primitive relation of all logical worlds. Greater or lesser, by the way, are not absolute measurements of size. To say that $\leq$ means lesser than or equal to and $\geq$ greater than or equal to does not exhaust the entire field of order-relation. Badiou says: 'These are merely ways of reading the symbolism; the essence of the order-relation is comparison "in itself"' (*LW* 159). Over time we will have to come to terms with the fact that bigger and smaller than are almost metaphoric ways of thinking about pure comparison as such, just as in set theory actually quantity is really a metaphoric means of thinking about the pure presentation of sets as such. Keeping this in mind Badiou tries to help our understanding of order by comparing it to the axiomatically primitive relational state of equivalence, central to set theory.

Take two elements, α and β. You can say that they are identical or equivalent if:

- the elements are identical to themselves (reflexivity),
- $\alpha = \beta$ and $\beta = \gamma$ then $\alpha = \gamma$ (transitivity) and
- $\alpha = \beta$ then $\beta = \alpha$ (symmetry).

Equivalence argues for an extremely strict symmetry and is often called the axiom of symmetry. What it results is the value of pure substitutability which states that a relation of pure equivalence between two elements exists when using α in an equation or β makes no difference. If they can be 'said' to be different by using two different symbols, this is in truth a radically indifferent difference, as effectively they are equivalent or the same, even if symbolically they can be represented as different.

In contrast to equivalence, order-structure's comparative differences cannot be captured by these three axioms because it is precisely α is not the same as β that they can be said to exist or 'a comparative evaluation always presumes that we are able to contrast really distinct elements, which is to say non-substitutable elements' (*LW* 158). This is not possible with the axiom of symmetry as I hope is now clear. Order-structure is defined by reflexivity and transitivity, but *not* by symmetry: 'Antisymmetry is what distinguishes order from equivalence, and what allows us to truly enter the domain of the relation between non-substitutable singularities' (*LW* 158).

One final point is that the order-relation alone is not enough to account for all the elements of a base set A. In general, in ordered worlds, you have three options of relation: $x \leq y$ or $y \leq x$ or neither $x \leq y$ nor $y \leq x$. This third case speaks of a multiple that exists that is incomparable to the other two. That worlds contain incomparable elements as we have already touched upon means that most worlds are partially ordered sets or POSets (Badiou tends to write this as POS). Basically every transcendental T of a given world is a partially ordered set except for certain special cases meaning we can say that the ontology of the transcendental is 'the existence, in every world, of a POS' (*LW* 159).

This is our most primitive point then, equivalent to saying that in terms of ontology, every multiple is indifferent. If ontologically every multiple is indifferent, then the 'ontology' of the transcendental, or the field of being-there, is a POSet. These two points at first seem to have no direct relation but, in fact, it is because ontological sets are totally ordered that one can allow multiples to be indifferentiated, say in terms of content. It doesn't matter what the multiple contains, only that its cardinality is totally ordered in terms of ranked succession. Ranked succession then allows for indifferent being. In a way the ontology of the transcendental, that there must be a POSet, is just approaching the matter in the opposite direction. Because the order of worlds is partial, multiples therein cannot be indifferent, because they lack rankable succession, so order must come from local comparison, and that requires degrees of difference between multiples, which is only possible if they are not property or quality indifferent. POSets are to relation what ranking is to indifference.

First transcendental operation: The minimum or zero

In relation to the transcendental set in possession of the simple order relation ≤, which is in accord with the three axioms of reflexivity, transitivity and antisymmetry, said T, which is the basis for all evaluations of intensity, is capable of presenting a nil intensity. Such a degree-zero intensity is of course necessary to stop the logic of presentation, which is an immanentist philosophy, succumbing to the infinite regress of endless divisibility. We don't need to prove this via category theory, as its proof comes from the basis of appearing on the ontology of the multiple, set theory, for which we can prove the halting point of every descending-deduced set tied to the void. In doing this we must be clear that in a world there is no void. The void is an entirely ontological proposition. Rather, as regards worlds, when we speak of zero we mean simply nil intensity of appearing, which is not the void but a multiple that could appear, but does not. In contrast the void can never belong to a set, but can always 'appear' through inclusion. Nil intensity operating as that all-important minimum for category theory leads to the deduction of a strange property which is that relative to a specific world, the minimum is unique or there is only one minimum for that world. If we write the minimum as μ and we take a second minimum μ', then as these elements are both minimum they must be the smallest element possible. This means that μ has to be smaller than or equal to μ' which in turn has to be smaller than or equal to μ. As it is not possible for either to exist as smaller than the other, and as the law of symmetry for equivalence does not work for order-relations then, due to the law of antisymmetry the only possible conclusion is that both elements are the same element. Badiou declares, while there exist 'an infinity of measures of appearance' there is 'only one for non-appearance' (*LW* 160). This is just another way of writing that nil-intensity is the minimum and echoes the unicity of the void argument he presents in *Being and Event*.

Second transcendental operation: Conjunction

The basis of conjunction as you might imagine is to show what two beings have in common appearing in the same world. It is a problem that has troubled Western thought all the way back to Aristotle's theory of classes. Set theory as a theory of collection shows what two multiples have in common in terms of being multiples in the same set, but only by refusing to speak of what they have in common. This then is the law of extensional sets. But sometimes in sets you want to speak intensionally, and that means thinking what they have in common in terms of properties. Set theory ontology avoids this because, historically, this has been where the whole idea of comparative identity-difference collapses. One of the most important discoveries of *Logics of Worlds* is that you can treat the state of in-common consistently when speaking intensionally of multiples, in other words when they are quality-rich multiples in worldly situations. To achieve this, not-inconsiderable, result Badiou says it is not that you are looking for what two things have in common but more specifically, it is 'the question of what appears as being common to two apparents' (*LW* 160), which is a slightly different emphasis.

With this in hand we can say that having something in common means, specifically, the comparison of intensities between two beings on the basis of the order-structure, all of which of course is relevant only to the world we are considering. Using the vocabulary of order we can say that taking two degrees of order, two appearing beings, 'there always exists a degree that is immediately "enveloped" by the two others; that is, the greatest degree that the two others simultaneously dominate' (*LW* 161). Immediate here refers to the absolute envelopment with no remainder; like set theory, category theory is intolerant of gaps between two locally related multiples, even if category theory does allow them across the world at large. This is an important part of order and envelopment, category theory being concerned primarily with values such as the least greatest or the largest smaller value. It allows us to take any conjunction as a degree of order, which means it is also a being appearing in a world, that is always immediately smaller or equal to the two other orders that it conjoins. The envelope effectively makes mini-worlds within worlds, or subsets, wherein the envelope is a world immediately smaller than the two objects which dominate it. However, unlike a world as such, the transcendental function here is fulfilled by the comparative relation of two objects at a local level. It is, if you will, a localized transcendental function.

We can now say that in any POSet, which is nearly all of them, considering the transcendental which is always T, and taking two elements of T, here p and q, then there is always an element 'which is the greatest of all those which are lesser than both p and q' (*LW* 161). Although we will not overdo the use of notation in this guide, out of interest this is written $p \cap q$, a pretty important formalization of a previously often confounding property: What do two things which are different have in common? I won't waste the reader's time by listing all the philosophers since at least Aristotle who have struggled with this problem, but special mention should be given to Hegel because the development of the dialectic is precisely to solve this conceptual bind.

Badiou revisits his three examples of conjunction relative to the [autumnal scene] but we will pass over that and instead just register that the transcendental order which allows us to compare intensities of appearing in the world with the notation $\leq$ and the law of conjunction which shows what degree of appearance two elements have in common, shown by the notation $p \cap q$, are equivalent. So if we say $p \leq q$ this is the same as writing $p \cap q = p$. In both cases p being smaller than q is the largest element the two apparents have in common or the envelope. This cannot be q because it is larger than p, so it must contain elements that are not included in p. These are elements it does not have in common with p and so they cannot feature in the conjunction. Badiou ends by saying this means we could proceed in terms of the notation of conjunction and neglect that of order-relation, which would actually make our description of worlds quite similar to that provided by set theory relative to beings as such. We could make all our observations at this local, quasi-rankable level, because this is what $p \leq q$ actually means, q is the immediate successor of p. Proceeding in this fashion then the envelope is always the smaller of the two units. It has the great benefit of simplicity but, for Badiou, this means missing out on the central logical nature of order, which is that of relation and thus is real meaning of the term 'envelope' or why he differentiates conjunction, which can envelop, from the envelope function per se. Or, the conjunction is what joins two elements at the base level, while the envelope is what joins them at the next highest level.

Third transcendental operation: The envelope

Conjunction concerns the largest element held in common by two elements, the element just below those two. In category theory this is usually called the greatest least. In contrast, when it comes to the envelope, we are looking for the least largest element that envelopes or includes the two elements in question. This is the global appearance of this conjoined fragment appearing in this world. It is pretty obvious that given two elements, if you can hem them in terms of their conjunction and their overall envelopment to a degree of absolute accuracy, basically one below and one above, then you have a very tightly ordered system indeed. This desire for tight order leads to several useful distinctions relative to the envelope which is probably the most complex of the three axioms of order. First, Badiou's formal consideration of the envelope reminds us of the difference between a world and the transcendental of that world. A world is all the elements that appear in that world. A fragment of this world however is not the same as an envelope because there is no order of relation insisted upon a fragment. In any world T indicates an order of relation. In some senses this is tautological because nothing can appear in a world unless it is related, but T formalizes this relation in terms of measure of degree. T then, as opposed to the world or its fragment, must show an order relation, admit to a minimum and allow for envelopes.

The demands on T then take us into a more subtle configuration of order relative to an envelope. Remember our [autumnal scene]? He now asks that we take S to be a part of the countryside in autumn. It is a fragment of the world of autumn in nature say, but a disordered one. To order it we invoke B which is the subset of all the intensities of appearing in our fragment relative to the transcendental of that fragment which is their overall ability to be ordered. So B

is basically S plus order, or plus ≤. This means we speak of ivy, wall, house, red, motorbike and gravel, all elements of the scene, in terms of how they relate to each other in an ordered way. If we want to now designate the envelope of this fragment, that is basically all these relational values taken together or rather the intensity of all elements taken together. This, by definition, is larger than or equal to every element it envelops, all of which are subordinate to it and so smaller than it. Taking the world of autumn, B would be the envelope of a fragment of autumn in an ordered fashion.

Within the envelope we can also consider an element that is included in T, which is the ordering of the world autumn or, if you will, the largest possible envelope of this world, but which is bigger than B, our local fragment. Badiou says think of the overall atmosphere of the autumn evening in this regard. This is called an upper bound of B. The upper bound as the name suggests ties down the envelope with even greater accuracy. If our envelope B has an upper bound, then relative to all the other elements larger than B found in our ordered world, we know which ones are larger. It is a measure of order that very much helps us to further confirm what is contained in our envelope B. However, we can go even further by defining what is the least of all the upper bounds of B. So if t was one upper bound and μ is another, by designating $\mu \leq t$ we can say that μ is the least largest element after B. What this permits us to do, as the golden light fades and the atmosphere becomes tinged with mist, is tie down that evanescent atmosphere to its specific effect as regards the play of light on the parts of B caused by the specific atmospheric conditions. We now have a precise definition of the envelope: 'a degree of intensity which dominates all the degrees belonging to B, but as closely as possible' (*LW* 164).

In category theory one would say that B is the 'territory' of μ or all the apparents that μ dominates by enveloping them. Again, as was the case with the minimum and with the element of conjunction, the envelope μ of the territory B is, due to the axiom of antisymmetry, unique. Badiou concludes by calling this property an example of 'phenomenal completeness. We are capable of thinking (or measuring) the enveloped (the intensive synthesis) of every phenomenal presentation, whatever its ontological character may be' (*LW* 164). Nothing that exists, which is tantamount to saying nothing that appears, is immeasurable. Everything that appears in a world can be determined as regards its relation to other elements, enveloped in a stable set relative to the T of the world, its order. This set is fixed by three unique elements. It has a unique minimum, internally it has a unique set of conjunctions and overall it has a unique smallest upper bound, which is its envelope. This is true of every world. There is no world that is not ordered in this way, and nothing can appear in our worlds unless they appear according to these three basic conditions of category theory.

Conjunction of a being-there and an envelope: Distributivity

The final value of the transcendental is distributivity. Distributivity really just confirms the stability and total spread, if you will, of the conjunctions held within an envelope. So if we take the relation between a local conjunction and the global envelope then what the element and the envelope have in common is 'the envelope of what this element and all the elements that the envelope envelops have in common' (*LW* 166). This is equal to declaring that there are no gaps in the envelope because the elements conjoined therein make up, in their totality, that envelope. As in set theory, it is not that you have an envelope that is filled later but rather the envelope is formed from the conjunctions of the elements it envelops, all of which have the same relation to the envelope irrespective of their internal relations. With distributivity in place to make sure there are no gaps between conjunction and envelopment, we can confirm that a crucial element of mapping sets in general onto sets in category theory is that there are no gaps. All the elements included in the envelope are all the elements included in the envelope. Include more elements, remove others, it is a different envelope. In a way this maps the absolute global-local difference of set theory onto sets that compose worlds in that as regards the envelope in question, there is a move from local to global in that if you modify a local relation, by introducing a new conjunction, then you produce a new envelope, which has, of course, a relatively global property.

Transcendental algebra

The purpose of these reiterations for Badiou is to spell out what he calls the algebra of the transcendental, although mostly I have held off using the algebraic notation in play here because it is not particularly necessary. This algebra is the algebraic presentation of the topological diagrammatic presentation that tends to dominate category theory but which, over the years, Badiou decides to sideline, perhaps because algebra is more widely communicable than diagrammatic forms. So when he summarizes this algebra for us, it is more useful to pause yet again to consider the basic rules of ordering worlds.

Greater Logic, 1. The Transcendental 113

- We have a world, **m**.
- In this world there is always a being which belongs to **m** which is its degree of order or T, the transcendental.
- T is ordered based on the simple relation of $\leq$.
- As such it is determined axiomatically in terms of reflexivity, transitivity and, crucially, antisymmetry.
- For every T there exists a minimum, written μ.
- While given two degrees of T, p and q, there always exists a degree of their conjunction written $\cap$. The envelope of B is any set of degrees of T. This is written $\subseteq$.
- Furthermore, there always exists in T, a degree which represents the smallest of all the elements that are greater than or equal to B. This is the envelope of B and is written Σ.
- A side point is that if B is made up of only two elements, then the envelope of B is called the union of those two elements written $\cup$.
- Finally, all the elements enveloped obey the law of distributivity. Whatever the degree of the conjunction of an element to its envelope, this is equal to the envelope of the conjunctions of that element and each of the other elements in B. Otherwise, by definition, they are not in B.

This is the complete logic of being-there to be found through Badiou's radical employment of the mathematics of category theory, which is also called, in category theory, a complete Heyting algebra.[10]

This complete algebra of the transcendental due to category theory provides unshakeable support for our philosophical consideration of the same resulting in the following triple-tripartite summary of the greater logic of appearing/existing.

- Inexistence of the Whole
- The transcendental as the function of appearing of one being in relation to another
- The order relation of $\leq$ and how this works with the three axioms of reflexivity, transitivity and, importantly, antisymmetry
- First transcendental operation: the minimum
- Second transcendental operation: the conjunction
- Third transcendental operation: the envelope
- Distributivity
- The reverse
- Dependency

One can see from this list that there are three levels of transcendental logic. The first level concerns the fundamental conditions of appearing in terms of our saying that this is transcendental. Saying something is transcendental means saying it has no Whole, it is entirely relational and that relation is ordered in terms of 'size'. The second level gives the detail of how order-relation actually works. There must be a minimum just as there must not be a Whole. In terms of relationality there are three different degrees of conjunction, and then we have the envelope which determines localized set composition indexed to the transcendental of the world under consideration. Finally, the last three functions are derived. They are significant components of ordered worlds, but they are derived from the other functions. In the case of the reverse and dependency, this disallows constructing a philosophy of worlds based on the precedence of difference or causal relations. You might say that taking the three operations of minimum, conjunction and envelope, the first level tells you how you are able to have these axiomatic operations and the last three tells you what you do once you have them, namely, pretty much everything. This means that our greater logic of worlds is basically complete and all further comments are effectively derived from this second book.

Book III

Greater Logic, 2. The Object

Although we may have at times referred to the apparent as a thing, suggesting it has some kind of objectal existence, in truth, so far, in terms of the transcendental, what appears in a world is merely a relation of order between two abstract points: α and β. At the same time, we have regularly emphasized that certain key components of the ontological basis of appearing, for example, the minimum, have allowed us to say things in relation to the immanence of appearing, such as the Whole inexists. Finally, we have stated that appearance is when a being as such appears in the world in such-and-such a fashion. But none of this is quite the same as showing that pure, indifferent multiples appear as relational objects in an actual world. We are, clearly, missing a component that links ontological materiality and logical order. This component is what Badiou calls the object.

Calling it the object is problematic to some degree because, as is the case with subject and transcendental, Badiou's conception of the basic vocabulary of our philosophical tradition is filtered through the mechanisms of a certain estrangement. At the same time 'object' makes some semantic sense, as it is true that we *are* dealing with a conception of the one, for example, 'by "object" we must understand that which counts as one within appearing, or that which authorizes us to speak of *this* being-there' (*LW* 193). In this sense yes, the object is pretty object-like. It is defined basically as the 'this' of the 'there'. If a consistent being-there is a logical possibility, then the object is the specific 'thing', the actual 'this' that conforms to this consistency. On the other hand, this object is totally adrift from familiar moorings such as the subject. We are already well aware of the fact that the subject, in Badiou, is nothing like any subject that has existed thus far in the history of thought. So naturally it does not need to cohere to the tradition of thinking subject in relation to object. Indeed, the subject depends on laws of change not laws of appearing, and in the same way, Badiou argues, the object relates to being-there and does not presuppose any subject. We have already seen the truth of this in his definition of objective phenomenology as being without consciousness and again in what is to follow he will further stress the decoupling of object from subject by showing that objects appear to different degrees in a scene, as they do in any phenomenology but, because they do not depend on an intentional consciousness, this appearing is in part atemporal.[1]

Eventually there will be a relation, of sorts, between object and subject in terms of the way in which the subject appears in the world by virtue of the step-by-step construction of a body. This allows us to think more generally of the whole of *Logics of Worlds* as object-less subjective formalism, subject-less object and finally objectivity of the subject which Badiou calls bodies. Again the point can be made that the object is to be constructed primarily so that it can offer a form of material appearing to truths which otherwise inexist in worlds. This is perhaps rather odd because, as Badiou himself admits, one of the central themes of this chapter is the way in which it establishes a difference between the Kantian concept of the '*immediate* subject-object correlation as the unsurpassable horizon of every cognition' (*LW* 194) and his own position which is simply that object and subject have no direct relation.[2] This is radical indeed; yet, it is worth remembering that being radical for its own sake is not Badiou's intention. In a kind of philosophical periplus he wishes to decouple the subject from the object only so that when it comes to the subject's objectal existence in a world, he can construct for the subject a 'body' that means the subject can 'exist' in worlds precisely due to the fact that the truths they embody inexist.

But we run ahead of ourselves. This chapter is primarily concerned with the transcendental indexing of multiple beings. Having shown that multiple beings as such exist, *Being and Event*, and having provided a greater logic of appearance as existence, the transcendental of Book II, we are now in a position at last to say how multiples appear in worlds. This is achieved by indexing or 'a function which links every difference immanent to the multiple to its intensity of appearance in the world' (*LW* 194). As a functional process, indexing is dependent on a simple evaluation of differences, which is what Badiou means by the *phenomenon*. We are very comfortable now, I hope, with this basic function which is as follows. Take x and y as two elements of a collection called A. Then as ever take T to be the transcendental of a world. Indexing is the identity-function of relation **Id**(x, y) which measures in the transcendental of said world, the 'degree of "apparent" identity between x and y'. If then the **Id**(x, y) can be termed P, we can say that x and y are identical to the p degree in terms of their appearance in the world in question. The only difference between the indexing of an object as a phenomenon in the world and the basic function of conjunction is that, strictly speaking, transcendental algebra considers the differences within a world, in the abstract. It is not concerned with actual objects. This means that the question of existence is 'entirely distinct from that of being' (*LW* 194).

Thus far we have been able to show the degree of identity between two elements without having to prove the objectal consistency of those elements in themselves. Rather, and this is what is remarkable about transcendental algebra, the identity of x can be entirely determined in relation to the identity of y relative to the transcendental T in question without any need for actual objects. For Badiou this is not enough however, so that you can say of a multiple, a being as such, that it objectivates in a world, not just register an existence within that world, you need to establish 'an effective link' between multiple-being and transcendental appearance. If you recall, the transcendental differed from the world because it took the elements of a world and placed them in a totally consistent order. Now we can say that given such an order, it is meaningless unless said order is the order of specific beings within a world. Beings have no qualities as such; they are indifferent. By the same logic if we deal with abstract appearance as such, then the elements that appear in that world have no qualities either, even if they are differentially relational. Transcendental algebra is remarkable because it is a mode of indifferential degrees of relationality, something impossible in set theory and in general always assumed to be based on objects in a state of relational difference to each other, thanks to their qualities or properties. We need to populate the indifferent formulae of appearing with actual beings, just as we need to consider actual beings in terms of how they appear in a world, to be able to talk about specific qualities of those beings as distinct from others. This requires making indifferent beings differentiated through relational degree through transcendental logic. At the same time the fact that we are dealing with actual, indeed at times singular beings, demands that the greater logic ceases to be neutral and indifferent, and instead becomes an indexing of actual beings in specific worlds. At this stage these beings which appear become objects. Badiou's question is: 'At the end of the logical process of the worldly regulation of differences, under what condition can we affirm that it is indeed this ontologically determinate multiple which is there as an object-of-the-world?' (*LW* 195).

If we take a being as such, grasped in its being, then we know we are dealing with a pure multiple. There is no multiple which is not made up of at least two components. Every multiple then is determined by the elements which belong to it. If the object is the localization of a multiple but is not its determination, then there has to be a means of linking the object to the elements of the multiple which it objectivates. This demands that we take the object, analyse it as regards its components, pushed to the point where this is attached to the analysis of the multiple in question into its elements. Now when we speak of an object as appearing, we have three elements to take into consideration:

1. We have to identify, as regards appearing, what a component or part of the transcendental indexing of being actually is.
2. We have to, as ever, show the minimal form of these components; these will be called atoms.
3. We need to find an 'intelligible intersection' between an atom of appearing and an atom of being or between a 'minimal component of what is given as localized in a world, and the elementary composition of the multiple-being which underlies this givenness' (*LW* 195–6).

The tripartite conditioning of appearing is due to the materialist axiom of ontology according to Badiou and so depends on both whether you can show that being is material and if you desire to do so. Badiou's position on this, as ever, is clear: 'No world is such that its transcendental power can entirely de-realize the ontology of the multiple' (*LW* 196). Due to this, the articulation between the transcendental and the ontological is this one, this object, this atom.[3]

It is clear that we are heading back from appearing to being as such to show that objectivization is a 'transcendental marking of beings' (*LW* 196), not just 'words', the position re: language that he rejects in the 'Preface'. This allows us to think which beings lie beneath the appearance of objects in a world. It is clear, thanks to this, that ontology forms the foundation of all appearing, even if no being as such can ever fully appear in a world and be fully intelligible. This may, to some degree, curtail or even undermine the object as appearing because it is relational; yet, at the same time in order for a being to underlie the appearance of its elements in the world, the pure multiple is also tainted in its pristine indifference. For a multiple to appear as an object first it must admit to being localized due to the transcendental ordering of degree, an ordering that makes no sense to the indifferent pure multiple. Then it must allow itself to be inscribed in a relation of compatibility between two elements of multiple-being that is entirely at odds with the means by which two multiples or two elements of a multiple are combined ontologically. Finally, the elements of a being must allow themselves to be captured in an order relation which 'amounts to the projection onto being of the fundamental feature of the transcendental (the partial order structure)' (*LW* 196). As we saw, indifferent being as such admits to no partiality: there are no POSets in ontology. The implication to be drawn from this is that if a multiple is there in a world by virtue of the object, 'it exposes itself "in person" to a singular intelligibility, which is not conveyed by its pure ontological composition' (*LW* 196). For a being to be communicable as a being, it must renounce the very quality of indifference that makes it radically noncommunicable. This is something of a sacrifice, although you can present it the other way: 'It happens to that which appears that it is otherwise thinkable in its being' (*LW* 196). Yes, a multiple must become intelligible as differentially relational rather than indifferent and nonrelational, but at the same time as it does so what is differentially relational can benefit from the axioms of indifferent nonrelationality, for example, materiality, the minimum and the consistent inexistence of the Whole. This interaction can arrive at an intense point where the intelligibility or communicability of a pure being, which means of course that it can appear in a world as differentially relational, can, at certain points, allow a pure multiple to be enveloped. Envelopment gives to the pure being a homogeneity or unity that is other than that ascribed to it by its being a pure multiple. At this stage appearing has infected being so that being appears to take place in a world and not in ontology.

Transcendental indexing: The phenomenon[4]

Phenomenon describes for Badiou the nature of a being in terms of the total system of evaluating that being transcendentally, as regards its relational identity to all other beings that co-appear in the same world. He explains the phenomenon with reference to a wonderfully detailed and humorous depiction of the various parties involved in the slow accumulation of people and sensations in preparation for a demonstration on the Place de la République which leads up to beautifully simple summation of the entire problem of existence and phenomena: 'to the extent that these multiple-beings partake in the world, they differ more or less' (*LW* 200). Going on, more expressively:

> When all is said and done, the innumerable joy of their strong identities (loudspeakers, steps, clapping, ranks ...) and that of their equally pronounced differences (the red or black flags, the snaking cops, the cadence of the African djembe drums over against the miserabilist slogans of the threadbare unions, and so on) is what constitutes the world as the being-there of the people and things which are incessantly intermingled within it.
>
> (*LW* 200)

It is one of his most perspicacious and lyrical moments thus far in the book, preparing for the thesis of this section which is 'We call *function of appearing* that which measures the identity of appearance of two beings in a world' (*LW* 200). Badiou's objective phenomenology therefore wishes to capture the functional interplay between phenomena that appear in terms of where they appear, and what else appears in said world. It is this degree of relational appearance that differentiates logics of worlds from the ontology of being.

Returning to our demo we can see precisely how functional interplay between phenomena operates. He first describes two different groups of students. Although they differ, coming from two different schools, he argues they are 'sufficiently indistinct' that their identity 'is equal to the maximum of the transcendental order' (*LW* 200). This is a breakthrough moment, actually, in the history of thought that Badiou is able to present, thanks to category theory's particular way of determining identity and difference. Thus here, two ontologically different multiples, when they co-appear in the world of the demo, share so much in common that the index of their identity is close to maximum. This is in accord with the categorical definition of functional identity such that if two objects share absolutely the same functional relations, regardless of their ontological difference, they are categorically speaking identical. What this argues is, take two groups that are distinct ontologically meaning that they differ absolutely as multiples. Place them within a common transcendental order, [demo], wherein you discover relative to this specific worldly situation, it is hard to tell them apart. Their initial absolute distinction now becomes a degree of indistinction. If this degree of indistinction arrives at maximal level, for example, during the demo they join up and then perhaps the police intervene and groups from both are arrested and treated the same, as pesky students, then the world has removed all their difference and they become, functionally, identical.

Badiou now considers the opposite case which is that of radical distinction represented by two violently opposed revolutionary groups, the post-Bolsheviks and the post-Krondstadt groups, which sport red and black flags, respectively. These two groups, he tells us, hate each other so absolutely that 'the function of appearing evaluates their identity to be the zero of the transcendental' (*LW* 200). Yet in terms of both being on the demo together and the fact that often these groups are lumped together as say extreme lefties, he concludes, 'It would be prudent to suppose their identity has a weak but non-nil value' (*LW* 200). While if we take their flags, they are, naturally, incompatible as *political* banners but absolutely compatible as political *banners*, such that they form a relational grouping with all emblems and placards on the march. This grouping of banners of protest then is able to form a relation with another banner, a closed shutter that Badiou sees as a banner or emblem of non-protest. We can then place the shuttered window alongside the red flag and find nil transcendental value between the two, yet say they both appear in this world: one as symbol of participation, the other its 'reverse'. If we trace the relational indexing of the red flag here, we can say it has a strong index as a symbol of bolshevism, it forms a diametric opposition to the flag of the opposing movement, it is in this sense its reverse represented by the function of colour difference. Yet as regards being on the demo the two flags become relational, we tend to group together extreme movements so that red and black flags become, say in the eyes of the bourgeois observer, one symbol. These two flags also become part of a wider relational grouping, banners of protest, so the red flag is now relationally determined not by who holds it or its colour but being one banner among many. Symbols of participation then allow us to fail to index another 'banner' or symbol, the closed shutter, which becomes their reverse, symbol of non-participation. What we learn from this is that the modality of distinction and indistinction is a constantly shifting one, so that radical distinction, red and black flags, can become indistinction, banners of protest. While at the same time multiples that are fundamentally distinct, shutters, rely on their becoming apparents of nil intensity, for their indifferential multiple status to become a differentially, non-relational one in this world.

This process of transcendental indexing is of great importance when treating the phenomenon 'as the infinite system of differential identifications' (*LW* 201). Naturally, the nature of the phenomenon needs rules to keep it consistent. These rules determine to what degree a phenomenon is indexed relative to another. This takes the form of partial, total or inexistent identity. These are the only three degrees of relational identity necessary, which may seem limited, but if you consider that previously it was more the case that a being either was or was not in a world and it either was or was not the same as another being, the addition of degrees of relation is a significant expansion. While in general the transcendental rule is that of anti-symmetry, when it comes to the most basic relation of phenomenon it is symmetrical: 'The value of identity between two beings-there is the same, whatever the order in which they are ascribed' (*LW* 201). This law of symmetry teaches us something about our indifferent formula of appearing which is **Id** (α, β) = **Id** (β, α); a law of symmetry that is, in fact, a hindrance in the formal translation of the logics of appearing into the mathematics of the transcendental for the very basic rule of all category theory is that all functional relations are associative, not symmetrical.

This is demonstrated when Badiou considers the indexing of a third object in relation to the first pairing. He now speaks of three groups of apparents indexed to each other. First we have Kurds and Anarchists who share in common a degree of wanting to appear literally untamed. This introduces a high degree of relational intensity approaching a transcendental maximum. But it cannot be a maximum as then you would not be able to differentiate Kurds from Anarchists. He now introduces a third group, Postmen on strike, which forms a triplet of relations formative of a differential network. Yet each of these apparents, to appear, must be indexically related to one other apparent. Is there, Badiou asks, a method wherein the ordered pair of transcendental appearing can then be found to be consistent with a triplet of appearings? There most certainly is which is, in every appearing, there is the question of what two apparents have in common, which will be called the law of conjunction. The Kurds and the Anarchists share in common fierceness; the Kurds and the Postmen share in common sartorial elegance, according to Badiou, and the Anarchists and the Postmen masculine Frenchyness.

It is at this juncture that Badiou chooses to move from the law of symmetry which defines the basic algebra of relational appearing as co-indeictic, indexed on each other, to that of triangulation, which is the first time that Badiou openly considers the mainstream definition of a category in the book. Still within the realms of the transcendental greater logic, take two beings indexed to each other based on their degree of identity: **Id** (α, β). Now introduce a third being. Badiou says that taking what is in common between one being and another, then moving to what is in common between a third being and the second being you can never end up with a degree of intensity less than that which exists between the first and the third. This is because the appearance of a relation c to the conjunction a and b must always be subordinate to or equal to the conjunction of a and b. Adding an element to a conjunction can never surpass the degree of identity between those two elements or 'the intervention of a third term cannot augment the intensity of co-appearance because it exposes the first two elements to the differential filter of a supplementary singularity' (*LW* 203). A stipulation which results in what Badiou calls 'triangular inequality of the transcendental conjunction' (*LW* 203), which states that the degree of identity between x and y, conjoined to the degree of identity between y and z, remains bound by the identity between x and z. This forms a triangle of asymmetrical identity between x and y, y and z and x and z which states that if you want to consider the relation between y and z and you already have a transcendental indexing between x and z, this additional relation cannot in any way supersede that initial identity but must be what is called a composable part. If you are x and you want to relate to z, you have to go through y but, as relations with y are presupposed within those of z, because of z's conjunction with y, you can go straight to x and the relationality with y can be assumed. This type of asymmetrical diagram where you can go in one of two directions, and end up at the same target, is called a commutative diagram and is the very essence of category theory. This is basically another way of expressing the commutative triangle which forms the basic, descriptive definition of a category.

Keeping this triangle in mind, we can now put together symmetry and triangular inequality to give us a consistent definition of the phenomenon in terms of its transcendentally indexed degrees of identity. As regards symmetry, we can think of Badiou's comparison of a black flag to a red at the demo. Here what differentiates the black flag from the red is the same as that which differentiates the red from the black. Now, if instead we evaluate the relation between two beings in terms of a third which participates in the construction of the phenomenon of the second being in question, this evaluation must remain lesser than or equal to the evaluation of the relation between the first and the third which is part of the construction of the phenomenon of the first being. Now we have a triangle of relations. Badiou's example is those three sets of protestors: Kurds, Anarchists and Postmen. We can see that in terms of the linear relation conjoining two beings we have symmetry, but in the triangular or tabular relation conjoining three beings we have associative inequality. As we explained in our introduction the dynamic interplay of composability and associativity, or between symmetry and asymmetry, is the functional equivalent as that between belonging and inclusion in set theory. It is the very essence of a categorical means of presenting the world or as Badiou concludes rather simply: 'Symmetry and triangular inequality are the necessary laws for evert transcendental indexing' (*LW* 204).

Existence

Having defined the phenomenon we now move to its actual existence. Every phenomenon exists relative to at least one other within a world indexed transcendentally through the order relation ≤. But what does existence actually mean? Badiou turns to Hubert Robert's painting *The Bathing Pool* to help develop an answer. The painting shows women from the classical age in various states of disrobing, watched over by a statue and placed within an idyllic natural setting. Badiou considers the presentation of the foliage. In the image the central scene concerns the temple and the bathers. The foliage therefore might seem tangential. Yet the more we look at the foliage the more we see how much of what appears in the temple is framed by it. As Badiou peers, indeed, the identity he finds between elements of the foliage and the bathing scene increases in intensity, and as he maintains his gaze he finds that the self-identity of the foliage increases. A common experience when looking at a work of art, all the same ontologically speaking this is impossible. A being is the being it is absolutely. However, in terms of appearing, beings are not present absolutely but *to a degree*. The foliage as being is only partially present as the foliage in the painting. The question then is how can one being exist more than another based on its own self-identity, and how does this self-identity get to be measured?

Badiou's answer is to link the two elements together. The self-identity of a phenomenon is based on the transcendental elevation of the phenomenon in question. In other words, a phenomenon exists more the greater number of conjunctions it has within the world which means the higher up the transcendental index it is. This makes clear sense. An element that has no relations is minimally present, or does not appear. An element that has maximal relations is the maximum taken as an envelope or, eventually, the world as a non-closed 'whole' or transcendental. The more a being is transcendentally elevated, 'the more this being affirms its belonging to the world in question, and the more it testifies to the force of its being-there-in-this-world. The more, in brief, it exists-in-the-world, which is to say it appears more intensely within it' (*LW* 208). Encouraged by this formulation we can present the law that the existence of x in a world is 'the transcendental degree assigned to the self-identity of x' (*LW* 208).

The implication is that to exist per se does not actually mean anything. Existence is always relative to a world and is defined as nothing other than the transcendental degree of the appearance of a multiple in a determinate world. If we accept that existence is self-identity, in terms of appearing, said self-identity is entirely determined by the transcendental index of that being in relation to at least one other being relative to a determinate world. Self-identity, on this reading, is actually a degree of relation relative to a transcendental index. Again the maximal and minimum help. If x takes the maximal value of T, 'it means it exists absolutely in the world in question' (*LW* 209). And if it takes the minimum, it inexists absolutely. Remember, as we have shown, as regards maximal and minimum, these values are unique, so a being cannot inexist more than another or maximally exist more. We are gifted now with a central law of existence: 'In a given world, a being cannot appear to be more identical to another being than it is to itself. Existence governs difference'; or 'one exists as least as much as one is identical to another' (*LW* 210).[5] We can draw from this that although relation determines existence, a relation between *x* and another element cannot be more intense than the degree of the appearance of the thing itself. It can equal it, but it cannot surpass it. What matters first is the degree of self-identity and, as that is determined by the degree of identity of one being to at least one other, if that other being overwhelms our initial being, then clearly that first being is nothing other than an aspect of that other being or a subset. A being must exist in order to be related, even if its relation is the basis of its existence. While existence subsumes difference, this does not make existence 'the One of appearing' (*LW* 211). It is not an ontological entity; it is a logical one demanding that it is, by definition, relational, and if it is relational then it conforms to the basic idea of the stable inexistence of the whole or actual infinity.

What we can glean from these deductions is that a thing must exist before you can compare it to another being, which makes intuitive sense. Yet the existence of the being is always a comparison of a being to at least one other so that you can say it exists in this world, so that while a specific difference is determined by self-identity, you can't compare two elements if only one exists in the world, said existence is by definition or abstractly relational. All identity is differential and all difference second to identity, without this being an aporia, due to the axioms of set theory that underwrite appearance.

Analytic of phenomena: Component and atom of appearing

Having established the degree to which a multiple appears in the world in terms of how we fix its self-identity, its existence, relative to the self-identity of at least one other existent being, it seems logical to ruminate on how this degree of appearance relates to the composite nature of every multiple. As we know, every set is composed of subsets. Badiou now asks if the components of subsets find their equivalence in terms of appearing or can we be certain of the being-there of parts of a set. Speaking again of Robert's painting he says that the columns in the work appear to be a part of the temple but wonders if there is a rigorous proof of this. In actual fact this question, could there be a rigorous concept of an analytic of parts in terms of existence as there-is in terms of being, really sets up Badiou's more pressing concern. If there can be an analytic of components, does this lead to a proof of the halting point within being-there? We have already been working on the basis that there is a halting point in terms of the proof of the minimum of appearance, but this is not actually quite the same as the smallest element of an existent being. The minimum determines the degree of relation between two beings, whilst now we are thinking in terms of the basic, atomic structure of each being such as it is.

In ontology there are two very strong halting points. There is the empty set which is an included part of every multiple but which does not allow any other part than itself (it is empty). And then there is the singleton which is the set, A, whose sole element is a or more accurately $\{a\}$. If you recall from our first book, the singleton of the empty set $\{\Phi\}$ is not only the halting point of all sets, but allows us to then construct from this halting point every single set that there is. Can we then carry this over not just as the halting point for the stability of a world due to the minimum or inexistent, but as regards the make-up of the elements which appear? Is there what Badiou calls a law of the one-at-most or 'a minimal threshold of appearing on the hither side of which there is nothing there?' (LW 212).

On the issue of parsing an element into its components, as regards appearing, our only option is to proceed in terms of degrees of relation. For example, thinking again about Robert's temple Badiou notes a total of fourteen columns each equally spaced or at least perspective is used to make this appear to be the case in three dimensions. Some are brightly lit, the ones in the background are dissolving into blue, foregrounded columns on the right are black, in shadow but discernible. Then there is a column in the background on the right that is almost obscured by the one in front and a column in the background on the right which is totally obscured. This is surely the most minimal column: it is in the shade of the right, it is in the distance of the background and you cannot see it because there is another column in front. This obscure column is the minimal element of the scene defined as an element that is lesser than or equal to every element of T, here the painting. Nothing can exist less than these dark columns which literally inappear in the scene. If we now shift attention to the demonstration, specifically the set of [anarchos], Badiou says this set is defined by Badiou as having five properties, things such as dressed in black or carrying a black flag. If an element has all five parts, then it appears with maximal intensity. For each element it does not have, it is less intensely a part up to having none of the five or having a quality which directly contradicts a person's being an anarcho, for example, having a red flag which symbolizes that they are in fact the anarchos' deadliest enemy. This should be taken as our minimum which is not the possession of only one of the five properties, but actually not possessing any of them or possessing their reverse and yet still appearing in the demonstration scene.

The point of these examples is to illustrate Badiou's contentious principle that there can be an atomic component of every set or transcendental index of appearing. Not least because according to Badiou the atomic component is not the smallest possible unit that belongs to the set, that is the smallest part larger than the minimum (possessing one element out of five). Instead, the atomic particle is the maximal element of any set which seems initially counter-intuitive. Let me explain. Given a set and an element x, if x belongs to the set absolutely and another element y belongs to the set absolutely, then $x = y$. If x does not equal y, then that is because one of them does not belong absolutely. This means that the atomic component is based on the law that 'the component can "absolutely" contain at most one element' (*LW* 214). Badiou cordially invites us to think about this 'at most' because it clearly distinguishes the idea of part of a set ontologically and logically. As we are aware, ontologically, there are no degrees of belonging. All multiples are indifferently differentiated without quality. In contrast, when we ask after phenomenal components of the world, we are asking 'what can come to the world ... under this component' (*LW* 214). If two apparents come to appear in this component only 'in exchange for their strict intra-worldly identity', then we know this is an atomic component.

As I said, confusingly, the atomic component is not, as the name suggests, the smallest possible element but the largest possible, how can that be? Take an atom of appearing. Its phenomenal component is such that 'if an apparent absolutely establishes itself within it in the world, then every other apparent which comes under this case will be identical to the first ("identical" in the sense of appearing, that is of transcendental indexing)' (*LW* 214). As was the case with set theory, the rules of category theory mean we have to behave counter-intuitively in relation to certain qualities we took for granted. First, an atom is something which is largest not smallest. Second, if other elements appear which are identical to it, they are not actually identical. No other element can appear that is identical to the atomic, maximal component. If they are, then they are the same element because, as we have shown, the maximal, like the minimum, is unique. Identical therefore means smaller than the atom, larger than the minimum. Badiou summarizes this by saying when you speak of an atom of appearing, you are not talking of the 'one and only one' as you would in ontology, but instead you are conceding to the 'if one, not more than one and if not none' (*LW* 214).

Returning to the painting, Badiou asks us to consider the component 'applying the colour red to an important surface'. There are many instances of red in the painting but only one instance of applying red to an important surface, the dress of a woman leaning on a column. Red applied to a surface is atomic, as one element does belong to it, if only one. Now let's take 'displaying the masculine sex'. There are no men in the painting but there is a statue of a man. This statue is hazy; the penis veiled by drapery. One cannot say that the statue itself is maximally a part of this component, but if you asked for the component 'not displaying the masculine sex' you could not say this is 'phenomenally applicable in the same manner to all the apparents in the painting' as the statue partially suggests a sculpted penis which, Badiou says in all seriousness, can be said to appear to the p-degree of intensity. In contrast to the red dress, which was the only element of the component but which was maximal, the statue is also the only element of the new component; yet, it is not maximal. This does not mean that the red example is more atomic than the male sex example. Both are just as atomic because they both admit to at least one element which, if it is not one, is not more than one and is not none. For the red dress the part fills the component, for the male sex the part does not, but because at least one element appears in the painting that is equal to or smaller than the component, then we can say that this component is atomic; it just does not have a part in the painting that totally coincides with it.

If we now return to our earlier example of columns, we can see that the atomic component is 'pillars of the temple'. While we may dicker over what is the smallest part of this component, the component itself remains unchanged. It is atomic. It is the largest possible intensity of this example, it has at least one member and it has a minimum as well. This then helps us make it clear that the atomic component, which allows for subsets, is not the smallest part but, as we said, the largest. It is not the minimum but that which is larger than the minimum. And all elements that belong to it are identical to it because they take their identity of appearing from their degree of relational intensity not because they are the same. Each column is 'different' in that they display a different degree of intensity; yet, they are all identical because they all depend on the atomic component for their identity. If instead we said we were looking for things in hazy blue, then still some of these columns would belong to that set, but now they would be said to be identical to the statue, in terms of their belonging to this different set. And so on. These observations push us very close to saying that the difference of elements relative to their transcendental index is again indifferent. A column is the same as another column because it is different to it relative to their shared atomic component. This is backed up by Badiou admitting that two ontologically different multiples can appear as a single unique element.

The conception of the atomic adds a degree of complexity to our demonstration example. If we take being an anarcho as an atom, it disallows us from differentiating hard-core anarchos from ultra-hard core ones, or anarchos from one region or another. If the logic of appearing is 'political visibility', unless these two groups adopt different clothing, for example, then we end up with the '"worldly" inseparability of hard anarchists from Montreuil and those of Saint-Denis' (*LW* 215). These groups are two different beings as such, but when they appear in the world, they are identical. Now, if we think of the columns in terms of typical Roman columns, a number of these columns that are identical in the way they are portrayed mean they appear as the same, even if you can see that they are different. The result is that 'an atom of appearing can be an ontologically multiple phenomenal component' (*LW* 216). A stronger proof perhaps you do not need to show the distinct nature of the laws of being and those of appearing.

We can conclude this fascinating, at times troubling, but ultimately successful section with the following basic principles. An atom of appearing is the largest element not the smallest. The minimum of any set does not appear and has nothing to do with atomicity. Identity is relationality under the atom. Two elements which are said to be identical can be different, but their difference is their degree of identity relative to the atom of their appearing. Two ontologically distinct multiples, which, you recall, are always absolutely different, can appear as the same due to the law of the atom. If you assess two apparents in the world such as they are absolutely different, meaning one is the minimum or reverse of the other, then if one apparent belongs to an atomic component, the other absolutely does not belong and never can. This finally demands that if in terms of an atom of appearing two components both belong absolutely, they are identical. If they are not absolutely identical and one element belongs absolutely, then the other simply cannot.

Real atoms

We have now arrived at the central assertion of Badiou's materialist philosophy in relation to existence or the appearance of beings. What it states is that the atomic principle which we have just described proves that atoms are real. What does this mean in truth? Badiou has been happy thus far to accept that, in terms of logic, all worlds are constructible. They are not real but linguistic constructs or discursive elements. There is no object that does not manifest a concept so that, in Fregean and Russellian terms, every thing in the world is linguistically constructed, bears meaning, is communicable. If an atom is real, therefore, its reality cannot be generated or in any way determined by logic. Nor is the real something empirically determined for all the obvious reasons. Instead, the real must come from ontology where elements exist which pre-exist logic and which can be said in this way to be real.[6] Most important of these is being-qua-being as the void. As *Being and Event* shows, the void is real. It comes before mathematics which precedes in turn logic, according to Badiou. To build any theory of sets you must accept the presence of the inexistent void set. And therefore, for Badiou who is, in terms of maths, a Platonic realist, it comes before logic. To be clear, as there are atoms, if we say these atoms are real, their materiality must be generated by pure being and not by existence. This, by implication, means that no world is constructible without the influence of an ontology in which at least one element is not constructible, that of the void multiple.

Badiou asserts that, as regards the existence of real atoms, 'it attests to the appearance, in appearing, of the being of appearing. For every pure multiplicity A led to be there in the world, we are certain that to the ontological composition of A (the elementary belonging of the multiple a to the multiple A) there corresponds its logical composition (an atomic component of its being-there-in-this-world)' (*LW* 218). Furthermore, this relationship is, he argues, reciprocal. If every pure multiple of a worldly being results in an atom of appearing, then every atom that appears is determined by a pure multiple. We can deduce, thus far, not that every pure multiple must appear but, if it does appear, it does so as an atom of appearing. On the other hand, this does mean that every atom of appearing is proscribed by a pure multiple. There is a dissymmetry here which is fairly usual between the virtual fund of possible appearances of the infinity of multiples that make up the realm of pure being and the limiting dependency of the actual presence of this infinite fund of the virtual. So far so phenomenological.

That said, Badiou is very clear that he does not see these issues in any way as reflective of, say, the Deleuzian terms virtual and actual. To make this point however he has to depend on a speculative decision, as he does in *Being and Event* on occasion, which he cannot prove using transcendental deduction. This decision 'excludes that appearing may be rooted in something virtual' (*LW* 219). On the contrary, every one that appears, call that actual if you will, is based on a one that already exists ontologically to the degree that the ontological One can be said to be real, and so the part of the One, the one that appears, at the atomic level, in other words its nondecomposable element, is also real. If we take c to be an atomic component, here the set [temple] in the painting, then the existence of c is determined relationally as regards the degrees of intensity of the elements which belong to it, the columns, but also atomically 'since in the phenomenon c we will have the degree that measures the identity of c to itself, a degree which is nothing other than the existence of c' (*LW* 217). Now we can go further and say this atomic element, which means c is entirely self-identical, is real because it depends on a pure multiple to appear. This pure multiple is real before it appears, while c cannot appear unless it is real. Thus the actuality of c does not co-found or co-cause the multiple it is founded on, as it does to some degree in Deleuzian quasi-causal co-belonging. As we said, Badiou has to assert this at this point as he cannot deductively prove it in a transcendental fashion. But this does not mean he cannot deductively prove it in an immanent, axiomatic and retrospective fashion, a method which is not of less value than straightforward deduction. 'The significance of the axiom of materialism is evident: it demands that which is atomically counted as one in appearing already have been counted as one in being ... The one of appearing is the being-one of one which appears' (*LW* 219–20).

Definition of an object

We are now in a position to say what an object is. In a world, an object of the world is the combination of a multiple and its transcendental indexing.[7] Such a state of affairs is based on the assumption that all the atoms of appearing related to the multiple in question are its real atoms. Let us consider this first in relation to the Anarchists as an object in the world [demonstration]. The group is an object: first, because its visibility is supported by a transcendental indexing 'adequate to the world in question (that is by collective indices)' (*LW* 220). And second, because every atomic component of the group is identifiable by an individual of the group '(it is prescribed by a transcendental identity to this individual)' (*LW* 220). By the same reasoning in Robert's painting, the round temple is an object because its consistency is guaranteed by the pictorial operations that make it appear such as it does (form, perspective, colour) and also because every instance of the One of its appearing there, for example, its verticality, is tied to 'the elementary composition of the apparent multiplicities (one of the fourteen or fifteen columns for instance)' (*LW* 220). Put in abstract formulation: 'An object is jointly given by a conceptual couple (a multiple and a transcendental indexing) and a materialist prescription about the One (every atom is real)' (*LW* 220). It is not sufficient that a multiple appear in a world due to the logic or laws of that world, the collective or pictorialism, but more than this every atom of this world needs to be provably real, that is, directly tied to a pure multiple. This means that an object is not simply a substantial given, because how it appears differs wildly depending on which world it is appearing in. Yet it is not purely fictional as, for example, in all constructivist formulations, 'since every one-effect in appearing is prescribed by a real element of what appears' (*LW* 220). This means 'the object is the ontological category par excellence' (*LW* 220) because it is totally logical. Appearing in fact means nothing more than becoming-object. Yet at the same time it is fully ontological 'in that it only composes its atoms of appearing – or stopping-points-according-to-the-One of the there-multiple – in accordance with the mathematical law of belonging or of pure presentation' (*LW* 221). The object is both a fiction and a real thing, a *fixion* as Badiou terms it here.

Atomic logic 1: The localization of the one

Having defined an object, Badiou tries to firm up the terminology so that when we use the term object we know precisely what we are speaking about. In particular, he wants us to consider carefully what an element of an object actually consists of. Necessarily this will be an ontological determination as it concerns a real element of a multiple to the degree that identifies an atom of appearing. More than this we need to be able to think the relation between elements of an object, and this of course will mean that the transcendental nature of appearing be located in relation to multiple-being itself (so in this sense will again be ontological). Put together these stipulations present what he calls 'the retroaction of appearing on being' (*LW* 221). What retroaction entails, simply enough, is tracing back the logic of appearing, via the atomic nature of the object, to its real basis on a pure multiple. Such a genealogy provides foundational security for the object which is invaluable, but it raises complicated questions for being as such, for example: What actually happens to being when it is there in the world? 'What happens to a being in its being, insofar as it becomes an object, the material form of localization in a world? What of being thought in the feedback-effect of its appearing? Or, what are the ontological consequences of logical apprehension?' (*LW* 221). For example, once an individual is identified in a world as an anarchist, how can that individual, that pure multiple, appear in the same world through other registers?

This question concerns Badiou in particular because of the nature of the event. The event alters the transcendental conditions of a particular world which changes the conditions of appearing in that world accordingly. These modifications can be seen as a change in objectivity in that world, as objects appear due to the transcendental index of that world. If you change the nature of an object, which depends on its being a real atom, can that change being retroactively? We know that this is what a subject is or does: 'The precondition for becoming a subject in a determinate world is that the logic of the object be unsettled' (*LW* 222). Is this disquiet transmittable all the way to the pure multiple itself upon which the real atom of the object is based? Badiou provides us now with a specific focus. When we speak of a change in the object being transmitted to its being, if that can be the case, we need to concern ourselves with that component of the object that is real, because that is the only component that touches, if you will, the pure being of the multiple. All well and good but that of course raises a question as regards the atom of appearing and what it precisely means for an atom, which is real, to be there in a world, which is fictive.

Let us revise once more what an atom is or what is specifically atomic about it. All an atom in fact is, is 'a certain rule-governed relationship between an element a of a multiple A and the transcendental of a world' (*LW* 222). Given a, our atom, if you take x then the transcendental of x is identical to the degree of identity between this x and a, not, for example, between x and another element, call it b. What one can see here is that the atom makes sure that if you are considering a relational part of a, say the temple or being an anarchist, it is a relational part of a that you are considering, not a relational part of something similar but not identical to a. This is very important because a Deleuzian might argue that each 'new' element of a changes the being of a, or at least potentially can. Badiou insists that due to the law of the atom, a is a real component that can suffer an infinite number of transcendental appearances, and yet always remain a real part of the multiple A. When we speak of an object appearing, therefore, we are really considering a correlation between elements of a fixed multiple A and transcendental degrees of appearing of these elements which are also fixed in terms of being indexed to the same transcendental T. To think a as regards a correlation between A and T is what you do when you speak of an object.

Badiou says that the essence of this correlation, a complex one because pure being remains untouched by its appearance and yet affects said appearance, is 'the localization of A in a world, conceived as the logical capture of its being' (*LW* 222–3). The atom then is shared between the multiple composition of a being individuals in the group [anarchists], columns of the group [temple] and the transcendental values assigned to them which are those of localization and intensity. This could be very typical of Anarchists or indexing the vertical in a painting.

The following section is rather dense. The basic premise is given an atom, and a localization, the degree to which an element transcendentally indexed in a world relates to that atom; whilst before we spoke of the atom as the maximum degree of intensity of relation between the atom and its parts, in terms of the relation of an atom to that degree, we discover that said degree of localization is also an atom. Unless of course the degree of relation is maximal in which case the localization is the atom, as only one unique element can ever fulfil this function. Putting aside the maximum, every atom appears as a localization due to its transcendental degree. This associates to every being in the same world, a conjunction of the degree of belonging of this being to the atom and of the assigned degree. It is not enough to say that a being belongs to an atom; you need to also say how much it belongs. This means further that 'an atom relativized to a particular location gives us a new atom' (*LW* 224). And an atom relativized to a particular location of that atom is an atom and so on. Important to remember is that this degree of relation must be lower than maximal as in that case the conjunction between the two degrees of intensity means they have the same intensity and so are the same thing. And again while you can subdivide atoms due to lesser and lesser degrees of local intensity, this is not infinite regress at it ends at the minimum. In a sense this is just another way of saying that relationality is controlled in every world by having two halting points. First the nature of order is less than or equal to. If you speak of the atom of column in relation to temple, no column can have a greater intensity of identity to the temple than the temple itself. If it did, the temple would be an atom of the column. Within that you can subdivide degrees of intensity as much as you wish, but if you reach a state of local intensity that is minimum, then that element is not an object of this atom. In addition, using the reality of the atom we can say there is a minimum for every atom which is the pure multiple itself and its foundation on the singleton of the void set. Just as we can say there is a maximal of every atomic localization which is the world as such considered as T which is, however, not the Whole. This means that 'every localization of an atom on a transcendental degree is an atom' (*LW* 225). And every atom is real.

Let us take a to be an element of the multiple A, as it appears in the world due to T, its transcendental degree of appearing. If we localize this element to a degree, that is, not maximal and not minimum, then we have a new element b. This b is a localization of a or an object conjoined with a to a degree smaller than a yet larger than zero. This means that 'through the mediation of the transcendental, we define a relation that is immanent to the multiple. We thus have a sketch of a retroaction of appearing onto being' (*LW* 225). Why is this so? Simply because if A appears in the world then some of the elements of A are localizations of other elements of the same multiple. This is always true because every multiple contains at least two elements right down to the halting point of the singleton of the void set, which is the number 1. Ergo, we can say first that the transcendental can return to us ontological truths such as parts that belong to the multiple. One can see these parts appearing in the world and deduce from that the nature of the being in question. Also, we can say that every relation between an atom and another element in the same world is also an atom as long as it exists, it is not minimum or maximal. These atoms themselves are real so they have the same halting point validity as pure multiples. Indeed, they are obviously all parts of a pure multiple. If they are not parts of a multiple, they cannot appear because beings are merely parts of a multiple that appear. If they appear then however you subdivide them relative to an actual localization of relation, the parts you end up with are always real, are always parts of a multiple, even if you don't know which multiple when you are comparing two elements relative to T – a truth that is, by the way, essentially determined by the indifference of the generic central to Cohen's modification of set theory.

Atomic logic 2: Compatibility and order

An important feature of the object is the means by which it performs, logically, a retroactive function on the pure multiple as such. All localizations on A, such as we have been considering, are atoms which means that said localization concerns a relation between elements of the being of a multiple. Said relation depends on the logic of appearing not least because multiples are quality-indifferent and absolutely classical, so degrees of belonging or degrees of inclusion make no sense ontologically. When we speak of the localization of objects relative to other objects, we are speaking of parts of real multiples, but said multiples can only 'partially' appear due to the logic of appearing and so it is clear that, as in *Being and Event*, the proof of the object's reality will have to be a retroactive process. Another familiar element from the earlier study is indifference. Badiou says that in each example he has used to develop the specificity of a localization of one atom relative to another, in each case the logic considered, say pictorial logic 'feeds back on the neutrality of what is there' (*LW* 225). A formalized proof of the intuition of the *Il y a* of Levinas and the neuter in Blanchot which are central statements in the move towards philosophical indifference in the last century. Or what, in the case of the demonstration, is 'a relation between such and such and individual and such and such another' (*LW* 226)?

Moving on, Badiou concedes the complexity of the dual relation between pure multiples and existent beings or, in my terminology, indifferent beings in communicable worlds. He also sets out the desire to present 'a *relational form of being-there* capable of lending consistency to the multiple in the space of its appearing, so that ultimately there is a solidarity between ontological count as one of a given region and the logical synthesis of the same region' (*LW* 226). To achieve the relation between nonrelation and relationality which has eluded even the finest minds, he mentions as ever Kant in this regard, we have to think first in terms of the One, or the multiple, that even the smallest element of being-there 'is prescribed by a real element of the multiple that appears'. While globally, through logical retroaction, we can say that immanent to every multiple are relations perceptible only when it appears in a world. This means we can speak of a synthetic unity between indifferent pure multiples and communicable relational objects that is simultaneously dependent on the multiple-composition of such and such a being and the transcendental laws of its appearing. This synthesis is possible due to a relation, or meta-relation perhaps, between 'the structure of the transcendental and the structure that is retroactively assignable to the multiple insofar as it appears in such and such a world' (*LW* 226). Badiou calls this global relation the *transcendental functor*, a term we will grapple with when that bout is announced in due time by Badiou himself. The transcendental functor results in 'regional ontological consistency' (*LW* 226), or how pure, indifferent being as such, can retain its consistency when it appears as a localization, and more than this if it can do so, how it can communicate its profound consistency and reality to constructible worlds.

To introduce us to the transcendental functor or if you prefer regional ontological consistency, remember ontologically all consistency is immediately global-local so in theory disallows regional localization. Badiou declares this quality to be existence as such, remember existence means simply relation. This says that for every element x of an object there is always a transcendental degree p which evaluates its existence. Existence then is always the p of x, the relationality of the object localized on another object. We should then add that the p of x is always the relation of x, the object, to y, another object, which is itself localized. This means that every p of x is always at least the p of y. Badiou says, 'Given two real elements of the appearing-world, we can localize the one on the existence of the other' (*LW* 227). This results in an atom which we can say is real. That said, the order of localization matters; it is a central difference between the logic of category theory and the mathematics of set theory and goes back to our previous comments on the asymmetrical nature of the logics of appearing.

For example, Badiou ruminates on a column and then a tree in Robert's painting. We look at the column and we relate it to the leaning tree. The column is transcendental, we have taken it to be maximal, but if we now localize it, basically take a part of it, relative to the tree we make a new atom. Said atom considers the verticality of the column, which itself was a part of the vertical axis of the pictorial space as a whole, relative to the diagonality of the tree due to the shadow it casts on the temple. For Badiou the tree thought of in terms of the column is subject to the power of the column because the column is the atom localized on the tree. In this way the tree is 'straightened' by the vertical column and we are asked to measure the precarity of tree-time versus the stability of temple-time. However, if we reverse the process and localize the column on the atom of the tree, we return a different atom. Now the temple verticality is subject to the diagonality of the tree returning a sense of the time of the ruin versus the precarity of the leaning tree; we now measure the temple-time relative to the tree. This is a different atom, not tree localization measured by temple atom, but temple localization measured by tree atom, but the result is the same. The interrelation between the column and the tree shows what Badiou calls transcendental compatibility: you can easily speak of one in terms of the other and vice versa. This leads him to say that

> if two symmetrical localizations are equal, one will say that the real elements are transcendentally compatible ... *given an object that appears in a world, we will say that two (real) elements of this object are "compatible" if the localization of the one on the existence of the other is equal to the localization of the latter on the existence of the former.*
>
> (*LW* 227)

The opposite is also true. If you try to localize the atom of one object on the existence of another and fail, then you can say that in terms of their real elements this is definable by inequality. Here he uses the example of the typical anarchist object failing to be localized on a 'stray postman'. These two real elements, two actual individuals, prove to be incompatible in their common world. This is simply reiterating degrees of relationality that we are already familiar with; only now in this instance they directly affect the reality of multiples. How parts of multiples appear in worlds allows us to think of them in terms of their compatibility and non-compatibility in a manner absolutely disallowed ontologically. Badiou then defines atomic incompatibility as 'existential disjunction which is internal to the co-appearance in the world' while compatibility means 'not only that two beings co-appear in the same world, but moreover that they enjoy a kind of existential kinship which in it, since if each operates atomically in its conjunction with the existence of the other, the result of the two operations is exactly the same atom' (*LW* 228).

What this shows is that the 'operator of similarity' can act retroactively on the basic composition of a multiplicity, giving shade and degree to an ontological 'universe' where no such sense of quality comparison is possible. In so doing, in presenting an operator of synthesis, we must bring the relations internal to beings closer to the transcendental by developing a middle ground which is the envelope. For example, the relation [temple] [column-tree] is enveloped by say [temple-tree time], indexed to the transcendental of their appearance in the world of the picture. Another envelope could be [appearance of columns] or [vertical axes]. And if we have a degree of internal synthesis, which is what we speak of when we say two beings are compatible, enveloped or incompatible, not-enveloped, then of course we need the order relation $\leq$. Simply put, when considering an element of an object of the world possessed by a type of being-there, in other words when coming at relational existence from the perspective of real objects in the world or from ontological rather than simply transcendental order, if two objects are in a relation of less than or equal to, they can be enveloped and thus be said to be compatible. If they are not, then they are both in the world but they cannot be enveloped so they are incompatible. We are then, thanks to the potent combination of category and set theory, in possession of a complex sense of relation relative to equality and inequality of a non-absolute or non-ontological sort, applied to real parts of a multiple. The order relation is a degree of inequality on the whole. Two objects are compared relative to their degree of intensity to another, enveloping object. Yet there is also equality. They can only be thus compared if they both share a relation to their common enveloping object. A column and a tree can be compared relative to verticality or sense of time.

What this shows first is that 'the envelope of an objective zone for the order relation sustains the unity of the being-there, or of the object, beyond the inequalities in its appearing' (*LW* 230). If we take the set made up of the objects, columns in the background, we can identify a real object, the central most visible and still yet blue and hazy column as the least upper bound of all the rest. Its degree of existence is 'immediately superior' to all the others and so proves their 'real synthesis' or actual objects that are real that are ordered under the same transcendental envelope or heading. Second, this permits under certain strict but very common conditions that we can make a unity for the being of an object or certain objective zones. 'The key point of the retroaction of appearing on being is that it is possible in this way to reunify the multiple composition of a being. What was counted as one in being, disseminating this One in the nuances of appearing, may come to be unitarily recounted to the extent that its relational consistency is averred' (*LW* 230). Over time I suspect this may come to stand as one of the most profound statements on absolute consistent stability ever made. Not only does it found relational stability on ontological stability, but it retroactively allows us to go from relational stability back to the component parts of an actual, real multiple being and see their relational specificity in a manner absolutely forbidden within ontology. The blithe manner by which Badiou moves between ontological being and existential beings is, perhaps it goes without saying, also a remarkable high point in the history of modern thought, generally inaccessible to all other thinkers who have tried to do the same, say from Kant to Deleuze.

Atomic logic

The reader will now recognize a certain rhythm to our analysis which dances closely to the rhythm of *Logics of Worlds* itself. We have laid out in detail what the object is. We have skipped over Badiou's comments in relation to the metaphysical tradition, in this instance Kant, and now we are left with the reiterative formalization. In this instance, what Badiou calls atomic logic or the logic of the object. In the very brief introduction to this section Badiou explains the benefit of this approach which allows one to move forward following a line of reasoning which imposes materialist restrictions on general logic. Then one is able to 'reascend' from the logic of appearing back 'up' to being through the consideration of how atomic compositions affect pure multiple-being. This method is especially robust. It easily answers the question as to the relation between multiples and existence, without the complexity of say quasi-causal co-belonging and its insistence on vitalism in Deleuze. It also echoes the rational and powerfully communicable methods of mathematical reasoning via axiomatic speculation in that it has this element of retroaction which allows one to reascend from a speculative position, all atoms of appearing are also real, back to a firmly accepted axiomatic position, set theory's basic axioms. Finally, it negates the long tradition of separating the intuitionist from the empirical, which finds its strongest proponent in Kant. The ontological and the logical are articulated constantly by the dual-directionality of the object, which Badiou calls onto-logical. As Badiou sees fit to return to atomic logic using more formal means, we should follow his lead up to a point and formally present the fundamental concepts of this logic.

Function of appearing

A is a set or pure multiple. This multiple appears in a world **m** with a transcendental T. This will be called the function of appearing; category theory concerns itself entirely with functions. A function is the same as a relation and, as in the case of the relation, a function is itself an object in the world. Our function can be written as **Id**(x, y) or degree of identity of x and y when they appear as this pairing in our world relative to T. We saw already that the degree of appearing in T is called the p of T. The measure of the p of T for this **Id** is facilitated and guaranteed by the order relation $\leq$. If **Id**$(x, y) = M$, we will say that x and y are as identical as two elements can be, which means inside the world for which T is the transcendental, x and y, although they are different elements ontologically, are logically absolutely the same. If we write **Id**$(x, y) = \mu$, then the two elements are absolutely different with nothing in common even though they both appear in T. This is another significant difference to set theory where belonging determines equality. In category theory instead, appearing in a world does not mean two elements appearing in the same world have anything relational in common. Finally, we have **Id**$(x, y) = p$ or there is a degree of identity between maximal and minimum. We end up with a simple model for the totality of relations in every world, and for every world, $\mu < p < M$. This is the formula for communicability across all worlds. It determines degrees of identity beneath T relative to at least two elements. Every element which appears in relation to another is captured by the formula which also gives, in miniature, the image of a world, however complex. It does not matter how many elements a world makes appear, an infinite number in actual fact, the DNA of the world, so to speak, is determined by combinations of identitarian relations under the auspices of $\mu < p < M$. Either an element shares no identity with another, they share some, or they are effectively the same in terms of their appearing.

The coherence of **Id** depends on those two axioms similar to the equivalence-relation. This says the degree of identity of x and y is the same as that of y and x. This is the axiom of symmetry. To which we would add the conjunction of degree of identity between x and y, and that of y and z remains less than or equal to that of x and z. This we called triangular inequality and we can write it as **Id** $(x, y) \cap$ **Id** $(y, z) \leq$ **Id** (x, z). Missing from the equivalence-relation axioms is reflexivity. Reflexivity in the absolute would state that $(x, x) = M$ or that an element x is always and totally identical to itself. What is truly radical about category theory is that identity does not mean total self-identity as we saw, but degrees of relation that determined degrees of appearing. This allows x to appear in the world as 'identical' to itself or as an identity, to a degree, so that x does not always return itself absolutely. This means that $\mathbf{Id}(x, x)$ is not always and perhaps rarely M in the world, but it is always M ontologically.

The phenomenon

If we have A then we can speak of a as belonging to A and call this the phenomenon of a relative to A in our world in question. This phenomenon is the set of the values of the function of appearing $\mathbf{Id}(a, x)$ for all the x's that co-appear with a in the set A. So, for every x that co-appears with a indexed on A, we can establish a degree of identity between a and that x. This allows us to relationally differentiate different elements of A as being the different elements of A alone, due to the fact that these elements have in common that they are indexed on A and yet are not, necessarily, the same elements. So, if we take a to be young anarchist indexed on A, {group of Anarchists}, the singularity of the young anarchist is based on their comparison to other 'kinds' of Anarchists in the group, old ones for example. The phenomenon is important as it is a couple formed of pure multiples, this individual appearing in our group, and transcendental degrees, they appear in the group in a severely restricted fashion as in terms of all the ways they could appear in a world, they are restricted to age and political affiliation. The phenomenon is then an 'ontologico-transcendental notion' (*LW* 246).

Existence

A degree of existence of x in our set A and thus the world **m** is the value of the function $\mathbf{Id}(x, x)$ in T or the transcendental of the world, as we have just said. For a given multiple 'existence is the degree according to which it is identical to itself *to the extent that it appears in the world*' (*LW* 246). This is perhaps the most important statement of the book so far. It encapsulates the idea that a multiple-being x has more existence in the world the more it affirms its identity within it. This is a formal intuition that has, surely, profound ethical and political implications. Now we can differentiate the relation between x and y and that between x and itself. If (x, x) is M (maximal), then x exists absolutely in the world. This does not mean it is the same size as the world, but that in this world x is allowed to exist in all of its elements. In contrast, if $(x, x) = \mu$ this means that x inexists in this world. It does not mean it is present but inexists in relation to other elements; rather, it says that no element of the multiple *x* appears in said world so as to be related to other elements. This can come from the direction of the multiple, no elements of this multiple will appear in this world, or from the direction of the world, as no elements of the multiple *x* are related to any other elements in this world then *x* does not appear in this world. In reality, the two elements co-belong or co-cause as we have been emphasizing. A concomitant effect of this is that if *x* appears in a world in relation to *y*, the degree of identity between *x* and *y* can never be greater than the degree of identity of *x* to itself or *y* to itself. This means that if *x* and *y* share a maximal degree of identity, they are the same phenomenon of existence. Badiou says, 'The force of a relation cannot trump the degree of existence of the related terms' (*LW* 246). It perhaps is pointless to point out that the obverse is also true. If *x* inexists in a world, then its degree of relation to all elements in the world is nil; otherwise, it would exist. Existence then needs a multiple composed of parts, which they all are except for the void, some or all of which appear in a world such that they can be compared to themselves and we can say how much of the multiple appears, and such that they can be compared to another element, no element can appear in a world and not relate to any other element for, at the very least, the element *x* relates to the world **m**, which is itself of course an element in the world as there is no Whole.

Phenomenal component and atom of appearing

The formal definition of an atom in terms of it being a phenomenal component is as follows. Start again with set *A* appearing in world **m** with a transcendental *T*. A phenomenal component of *A* is the function that links a transcendental degree of *p* to every element *x* of *A*. This function is called π by Badiou so that for every *x* of *A* or every part of *A*, there is a degree *p* so that $\pi(x) = p$. Or a component is a means of linking parts, called *x*'s here, under the degree of their relation called *p*. The component of all such *x*'s is the degree of relation they all share in common. If you recall, this implies that the atom is not the smallest element of a world, but the least upper bound of a set of elements which can all be said to be part of the same subset of *A*. Badiou says that $\pi(x) = p$ measures the degree by which an element, say *x*, belongs to the component of *A* whose characteristic operator is π. If $\pi(x) = M$, then we can say *x* belongs absolutely to the component constructed by π. If $\pi(x) = \mu$, then *x* does not belong to this component at all. And if we have $\pi(x) = p$, then *x* *p*-belongs or belongs to our component, our atom, to some degree.

We can now reiterate and develop aspects of the minimal components for the set A. This component as regards the order relation of how it appears in the world is the One, below which appearance is not possible. The One allows us to define this component as an atom when it has at most one element. If we say there is an element of A which can be said to belong absolutely to the component, there is only one such element. As we saw all maximal degrees are unique. Any other component that appears as maximal in this way, in other words, is the atom and is identical to this component. Therefore if several multiples all appear maximally in a world, then as regards their appearance in that world they are identical. Badiou explains that all components will now be written as $a(x)$ as our main concern is atomic components. This helps us with our first axiom of the object: A.1: $a(x) \cap Id(x, y) \leq a(y)$. What this demonstrates is that as regards the belonging of y to an object-component, it cannot be less than its degree of identity to x plus its degree of belonging to this x. Or, if x belongs strongly to the component $a(x)$, and y is very identical to x, then y must belong strongly to $a(x)$ as well. We can see then that there is a transitivity here which you would expect. The degree of relation between an x and its atomic component $a(x)$ means that if x has a degree of identity to y, then y shares that same degree of relation with $a(x)$. If a column in the painting has a strong degree of relation to the atomic unit of columns of the temple, if you remember this was a column in the foreground, and another column is very similar to this column, it also has a strong degree of relation to the atom columns of the temple. There are two simple points to make here. The first is that the atomic subset determines the degree of relation between two elements in terms of their appearing. Two elements appear as related in terms of the degree of their relation to the atom of their common appearing. The second is that if two multiples maximally appear relative to the atom, then even if they are different multiples, they are the same. In the same way two multiples you might think are similar can be totally unrelated in the world in which they appear if in terms of their shared degree of relation to the atom, this degree is μ.

Badiou now gives us a second formal axiom: Ax.a.2: $a(x) \cap a(y) \leq Id(x, y)$. This shows that the conjoined degree of belonging of x and y to the atomic component a depends on the degree of identity of x to y. This is the atomizing axiom. What it says is that it is impossible for two different elements to belong absolutely to the same atom. So, if x and y are absolutely distinct from each other, this means the degree of the identity is μ. If then x belongs absolutely to the component a, y cannot belong to it at all. Again this is logically obvious. The atomic function and the degree of relation between two elements beneath an atomic heading must be related. Badiou draws a second conclusion from this. The second axiom says that two totally different elements can't belong absolutely to the same atomic component. 'In this sense, an atom is indeed a simple component (or marked by the One)' (LW 249). An atom is any subset which is maximal such that only one element can ever belong to it. It is, in other words, the least upper bound of any particular group.

Real atom and postulate of materialism

Badiou ties the ontological side of a component to its degree of appearing such that he can say that for every atom that appears, this atom is real. This relates to forms of notation. If we say that a belongs to A we are speaking of its ontological reality and when we do so we are also saying that it appears in a due to x. Thus $a(x)$ is the transcendental degree of appearing leaving us with a more formal example of a point we already made. Any multiple which appears is an $a(x)$, and any atomic component of A is due to a multiple which belongs to A and so is $x \in A$. Badiou now uses the formal verification of the first two axioms to prove this, an eight-step process that we will skip. He sums up with the formula $a(x) = \mathbf{Id}(a, x)$ which shows that if an x belongs to A, it belongs to a relative to the atom of a. If an x appears in a world and it has no identity with a, then it is not a component part of that atom. Said atom is definable as real if you take an atom, defined by the function $a(x)$, and it is such that it is identical to a single atom of the type $a(x)$, then you can say that there exists a single $a \in A$ so that for every $x \in A$, you can say that $a(x) = a(x) = \mathbf{Id}(a, x)$. And if you can propose that, then you know that this is a unique atom and therefore real. Badiou says: 'A real atom is a phenomenal component, that is a kind of sub-apparent of the referential apparent which, on the one hand, is an atomic component (it is simple, or non-decomposable), and on the other, is strictly determined by an underlying element $a \in A$, which is its ontological substructure' (LW 250). This is the basis of the postulate of materialism that, contra Bergson and Deleuze, every atom is real.

Definition of the object

The formal definition of the object states that an object is the couple composed by a multiple A and a transcendental indexing $\mathbf{Id}$. This is under the condition that, every atom of which A is the support is real. Such an ontological basis however should not confuse us into thinking that an atom is ontological. Two distinct multiples can appear as the same atom in a world as we saw, so that although an atom is always real, it is primarily 'a concept of objectivity, hence of appearing, and its laws of difference are not the same as those of ontological difference' (*LW* 251). Specifically, ontological difference is determined by indifference while logical difference is determined by local relationality. The radical nature of this difference of differences, absolute to the point of indifference, local to the point of an identity of difference, means, for example, that two 'people' appearing under the same atom of typical Anarchists are therefore not two distinct people as regards their communicability in the world in question. Say the Anarchists in question commit a crime and this is reported on the news; it is very likely that they will speak of 'the anarchists' or 'a hard-core few' within the anarchist grouping, proving that the communicability of these real people is based on the relationality of their identities measured against the degree of their appearing in the world in question. Communicability determines how beings appear in worlds not what said beings ontologically are. Yes, they must have an ontological basis, they must be real in this way, but they appear in the world in terms of the sanction of the transcendental.

If we take our Anarchists to be two multiples, then the ontological differences between them, which one might term their real being, are negated in relation to their relationality relative to T. If they have no relation in T, they don't appear. If their relation is maximal in terms of the atom of their appearing, then their actual difference is negated in terms of their atomic or primitive, generic nature. What we discover then is in order for beings to participate in a system of real, local, comparable, predicative differences, or difference in terms of comparative qualities rather than absolute quantity (as we have in terms of ontological difference), we have to allow for a disturbing degree of genericity. Two people will appear as one single, generic anarchist as the sanction of their appearing, T, dictates that that is the only way these pure beings can exist in terms of appearing. In the end, what atomicity dictates is that all beings in terms of their appearing are generic. It is impossible to preclude the possibility that real beings who differ ontologically, that is absolutely, will simply be lumped together as typical examples of x or y relative to this world. So that for real difference to occur in a world, it must occur under the communicable sanction of the T of this world, such that the atomic nature of their appearing will always be generic even if all of the multiple appears. Even if all of a multiple appears under the atom, any other multiple can also do so at which point its real ontological difference is negated in favour of communicable indifference. Even if we state that in terms of communicable worlds, there can be no indifference, as all existence is relational, if one ties the atom to the real one discovers that every object which exists does so generically. No object exists absolutely as the object it is, not because no multiple can appear in its totality, but because even if it does, another multiple could appear partially which could be taken to be identical to it.

Take two multiples, one with four subsets and another with five. If all four elements of the first appear, all it needs is for the other multiple to share four of its five components with it, and have all four appear, for the two multiples which are absolutely different ontologically, to be the same generic examples in the world at large. Badiou explains this differently but the conclusion to be drawn is the same. He says, speaking of two Anarchists they are the same if 'the degree of their identity is precisely the degree of their existence. This result is profoundly significant. It indicates that our two Anarchists are both typical if their intensity of existence is the same ... and if this intensity of existence regulates their identity' (*LW* 251). We will not detail the formal proof of this, but leave the reader pondering over this major incursion of the generic, into the realm of pure differences that is the world.

Localizations

I digress, I wandered abroad, lost in abstruser musings. I need to re-localize my mind. The next section pushes our analysis away from qualitative metaphor, x has a p degree of similarity to y, in favour of spatial considerations which are rightly topological and thus categorical. These will allow us to consider the appearance of an object specifically in terms of its 'there-ness', not its qualities. Localization is one way in which this move to the *there* is pronounced. In particular, Badiou considers the localization of an atom on p. So far when we considered $\pi(x)$, we thought of it globally in terms of its being a function of a multiple A in a transcendental of the world. Now we want to move from the global, the atom indexed on T, to the local relative to p, so that we are asking: What is $\pi(x)$ worth relative to a p in this world? Another way of asking this is 'what appears in common between the degree according to which x belongs to the component in question and the degree p?' (*LW* 253). This localization on p of an objective region means we can consider the object-components 'in terms of a local decomposition of the spectrum of intensities' and may also allow us to reconstruct the object as a whole from these local parts (*LW* 253). The most important comment to make in relation to this is that every localization of an atom is also an atom. Using two new axioms he demonstrates this, again in more detail than is needed in this study, before concluding that as regards the global analysis of objects, atoms, you can move into local analysis, degrees of an atom localized on another atom, without 'losing the guiding thread' which is that all these objects, global to local, are atoms (*LW* 254). Again we find ourselves 'retrogressing from the transcendental constitution of appearing towards the ontological constitution of what appears' (*LW* 254). The notation for localization is ∫.

Compatibility

We now progress to looking at the degree of proximity between elements of an object and their order relation. The first of these which we encountered was compatibility. Formally we will now say that two elements of *A* are compatible if the localization of *a* on the degree of the existence of *b* is equal to the localization of *b* on the degree of existence of *a*. If you recall, our example here concerned the localization of columns on trees and trees on columns returning the same value as regards mythic and natural temporality. Compatibility shows us that two elements are transcendentally of the same kind, although this only states one can be localized on the other and vice versa. This introduces a new form of notation, ‡, which designates compatibility. What is of precise interest to Badiou here is the manner by which compatibility between two elements can be shown using two equivalent definitions. You can speak of compatibility in terms of localization, which is topological, or in terms of the algebraic nature of the measurement of the co-existence of the two elements being equal to their degree of identity. The proof of this second way of presenting compatibility occupies the majority of this session. 'We may thus conclude that compatibility is a kind of affinity in appearing, borne by the underlying relations between the atoms' power of the One, on the one hand, and the intensity of the real elements that prescribe these atoms in the world in question, on the other' (*LW* 257). Again all this is really doing is strengthening the tie between the ontological basis of the appearance of every atom, and the transcendental nature of the existence of an atom relative to another on the other.

Order

Order can be defined in terms of compatibility or thanks to the basic ontological order. As regards compatibility, we can say that order is the being-there of compatibility 'by defining it as the inequality of degrees of existence between two compatible elements (grasped as atoms)' (*LW* 257). If the degrees of existence between two compatible elements were the same, they would be the same elements. Instead, we have two different elements relative to a third atom or envelope that, however, share a significant degree of identity relative to their localization. At the same time, we can define order more simply in terms of existence and appearing. Speaking of the relation of a to b, we say that the existence of a is equal to the degree of its identity with b. This compatibility can then be shown simply by the order relation, so that we can say that $a < b$ if a exists to the same degree as it is identical to b. More formally, we would write **Ea** = **Id** (a, b) showing that 'the structuration of the multiple here takes place through an immediate retroaction of what legislates over appearing' (*LW* 257). Once more we highlight the retroactive reasoning here. Badiou spends some time formally proving this but as ever the issue for us is not the proof, but the means by which one can prove compatibility in terms of localization or in terms of transcendental logic as regards the basic order relation. The other key point is that the order relation itself can be retroactively projected onto the elements of the multiple that appear in the world.

The relation between relations

We find ourselves in possession of three forms of relation: compatibility (‡), order relations (<) and localization ∫. Compatibility shows that what two elements have in common is equal to the degree of their identity. In other words, they both appear in the world due to their co-relation to a third atom or element. This also helps us to understand localization. The localization of an atom is the relation of an atom to a smaller atom, also an atom, which is a local degree of intensity of said atom less than the atom itself. Quite often you prove compatibility through the relation of two elements to a third they have in common which is localized on the two atoms in question. For example, the atom of temporality in the painting localized on the verticals of column and tree. As for the order relation, at this stage that needs no further clarification. Badiou now says that any theory of intra-objective relations must also be able to think of the relation between these three different yet related relations: two elements that share an atom in common, one element defined in relation to another beneath an atomic in common and simple order. Badiou defines the three orders as being topological (localization), algebraic (compatibility) and transcendental (order relations).

Speaking of compatibility and order Badiou now shows how compatibility is a more general subsuming of this most primitive of relations. The example is important not least because it reveals a fundamental and classical law of relation that will become increasingly important as we move towards the triangular, topological proofs of category theory. This law insists on the following relation: 'the similarity between two terms placed in an identical dependence with regard to a third' (*LW* 260). If two objects 'undergo the same domination, they are related' (*LW* 260). Here then we are identifying a basic order relation, $a < b$, for example, not in terms of the relation between a and b but in terms of their co-relation to c. Obviously here we are not trying to define the order of a in relation to b but the compatibility of a and b in terms of their co-relation to c. Badiou's example is two isolated workers in the demo, a postman and a worker from Renault. Both are loosely attached to the demo and are considering leaving it in fact. In terms of objective traits, these two multiples have little in common. But they share in common their weak identity to a third. Badiou chooses a firebrand anarchist leading the procession whose commitment to the demo is clearly very strong. So if our atomic predicate is 'bellowing somewhat lewd slogans', which is the atomicity of the anarchist leading the protestors, one finds an 'identical subordination of the postman and the worker according to the ontological order' (*LW* 260). These two multiples share in common that they both share little in common with the anarchist. This is what is meant by compatibility. The two multiples may have little in common in terms of degrees of identity presented by a simple order relation, but in terms of what they share in common relative to a third atomic presence, they are identically weak which means the degree of their compatibility relative to their common atom is very strong.

Not only does this further embroil us in the remarkable logic of what it means to appear and be communicable and intelligible and thus existing in a world, it also suggests ethical and political implications for every degree of appearing. When two atoms appear as compatible relative to a third, what they share in common is the degree of their subordination. Is not this the basis of all political action, indeed of politics per se? Regrettably Badiou does not openly state this and indeed the language of this section appears almost designed to avoid such conclusions. For example, Badiou coldly calls the concept of subordination proposition 5: if a and b are dominated by c, so that it is both true that $a < c$ and $b < c$, then a and b are compatible. For him, the importance of proposition 5 is not political but rather that if in a multiple that appears one of the elements of its appearing dominates a part in that it is the upper bound of all the elements belonging to this part (<), then all these dominated elements can be paired off and proven to be compatible due to this shared subordination. Once more this is further proof of the retroactive synthesis of multiple-beings due to transcendental logic or the order relation.

We exit this section by showing that the formula for localization can also be found to be tied to that of the order relation. If b is localized on the existence of a, then by definition a is less than b. This allows Badiou to state that the formulae for localization, the algebraic and the transcendental are equivalent, a fact he goes on to show vigorously in an appendix.[8] This observation then knots together 'the intimate identity between being and being-there' (*LW* 261), through the equivalence of topology, algebra and the transcendental. What this allows him to state is that the relation between three orientations of thought is proven by the relation between ontology and transcendental logic, and the relation between ontology and transcendental logic is confirmed by the relation of these three orientations of thought.

Real synthesis

Real synthesis, you may remember, was a means by which we moved from multiple composition to transcendental order using the retroaction of the transcendental on the multiple, so that once we have achieved transcendental synthesis, compatibility, we can reapply that synthesis back on to real multiples. As Badiou says: 'What was counted as one in being, disseminating this One in the nuances of appearing, may come to be unitarily recounted to the extent that its relational consistency is averred.' If so, then it becomes possible to 'reunify the multiple composition of a being' (*LW* 230). We know that a being is composite but that the composition of the parts of a multiple is not determined by relationality but by pure being as such. We are also aware that this material reality of every being can then found the reality of the atoms of their appearing. We can state that atoms can only appear as real due to pure multiple being and also that said being can only exist if it exists and if it exists it does so relationally. Finally, we can assert that as a pure multiple is indifferent it is non-relational; yet, once it has appeared in terms of its components and their relation to others under a condition of compatibility which forms an object which is real, or an envelope, real synthesis means we can speak of the sub-parts of any multiple in terms of their inequalities of appearance in the world such that we can speak of the relation between these parts. An operational totally banned in the ontological. In this way we could summarize *Logics of Worlds* as nothing other than a process whereby we can show that the relational world is real to the degree that the real can be shown to be relational within it. This is an immense achievement, to say the least, but it is not Badiou's aim. Rather, for him, this formula is necessary to allow for events to exist as truths that have real effects, in other words that affect the ontological as well as the logical. For this to happen he needs to formalize very tightly the relation between the ontological and the logical as a process of interaction and retroaction. Only then can beings which come to exist in worlds due to subject-truths be said to be beings, for all beings in the world must be pure multiple being as we saw, to such a degree that their existence can be defined as actual forms of change with universal effect.

Badiou says that to prove a real synthesis you have to apply the rules of the envelope to those of objective order. Readers may already have noticed that this is all the atom is: the envelope tied to the real of a multiple being in terms of its appearing. He now lays this out formally by saying that there exists an envelope participating in the order relation of course that operates as the least upper bound for this order relation. This envelope assigns to the object, conceived as composed of atoms, a different kind of unity which is the retroaction of the logic of appearing onto the multiple. This being the case, this unity which is relational is also real because it is ontological. Proposition 5 is the precondition for this real synthesis leading to a new proposition, proposition 6, which neatly shows that if we have two compatible elements of one set and we define those elements as atoms, then the conjunction of these two atoms will always be less than or equal to the identity of the two atoms. From the relational value of two objects we can define their relation at the real or ontological level such that if the identity between the two elements in terms of their transcendental relation is nil, then the two real components of two multiples cannot be compatible. 'This means that if the atomic components b and b' are compatible, they cannot accept into their composition totally non-identical elements' (*LW* 262). In contrast, if the identity is fixed at M, then the absolute identity of the two elements due to their compatibility means they 'can "absolutely" accept into their composition (ontologically) different elements x and y, provided these elements are "absolutely" identical in appearing' (*LW* 262). These facts then embolden Badiou to give the *Fundamental theorem of atomic logic*: 'Given an objective region B of the support-set A of an object $(A, \mathbf{Id})$, if the elements of B are compatible in pairs there exists an envelope ε of B for the ontological order relation $<$ defined on the object' (*LW* 263).

This theorem will become the basis for one of the most complex and far-reaching of all the concepts in the book, the transcendental functor, which

Badiou devotes a whole section to at the end of the third book. Yet before we can move to that we need to accept what Badiou calls a lemma, which shows that if the elements of B are compatible in pairs, then the function of A in the transcendental is itself an atom. In a way this goes without saying, but in saying it Badiou is encouraged to make a series of profound observations on this lemma. First we can say that this function of A, which is an atom, has to consider all degrees of identity between an x of B and all the other elements of B. What this shows is that any envelope has to fix the maximum degrees of the identity we are considering so that any object, any $\pi(x)$, means nothing other than 'the greatest identitarian proximity between x and the elements of B' (LW 263). So any object of B, indexed to the atom of A, is defined in terms of its relation to every other element of B. It must share identity in common with each of those relative to B to be a part of B. This facilitates the measurement of any isolated element relative to a subset based on the measure of identity between this element and the elements of the subset in question such that no element is truly isolated. Each object is measurable in terms of identity; otherwise, it does not appear in A. However, the precondition for this is that all the elements of B are compatible in pairs. This is because their compatibility is based on a function of commonality with B as a subset of A. If this is the case, and it must be, then a concomitant effect is that taken in pairs, the degree of existence of elements can't be more than their degree of identity. An element cannot exist more than its identity with another element relative to their atomic common. 'We may accordingly affirm that B is an existentially homogenous subset, to the extent that within it existential disparities cannot outstrip differences. Nothing exists within B whose existence is not regulated by its networking of identity to the other elements' (LW 264).

The transcendental functor

The final section of this chapter is entitled, charmingly, 'A Scholium as Impressive as It Is Subtle', and concerns the transcendental functor defined as an operator which links every degree of the transcendental to the set of elements 'of the object whose common characteristic is that their existence is measured by this degree' (LW 278). This function is simply that which links the degrees of existence of parts of an object as it appears to the real multiple or multiples which form its atomic basis. This is what Badiou terms reascending from the transcendental backup to the ontological, in a confusing topology in that it feels more intuitive to think of the ontological as the real foundation and the transcendental as that which is on top. All the same, the transcendental functor simply matches the parts of appearing to their multiple basis making every atom a real atom. The other name for this is the global analysis of an object or the regrouping of parts of an object such that we can subdivide the elements of the object 'into rigorously existential data' (*LW* 277). This will prove to be very important and not a little vexed as a procedure and thus requires a little summing up. First, we can say that we understood the transcendental order relation. Then we showed how we could consider the elements that appear as atoms such that we could show that they were real. Accordingly we could also retroactively divide multiples due to their appearing such that we could relate real parts in such a manner as is not possible ontologically. Now, we are looking at this local mode of division in terms of its being global such that the subdivisions within an object are real subdivisions. Having applied the transcendental to the ontological to get relational parts at an ontological level due to how they appear, we can now reascend and show that the parts that appear are real parts of an actual multiple so that the parts of an object can have the vigour of being homogeneous parts of the same multiple, which is, after all, what being as such is supposed to provide for us.

Badiou adds more detail. Initially we began thinking the local through the localization of an atom, the compatibility between two elements and the ontological order I just outlined. Then we moved to regions resulting in the real synthesis, due to the envelope of a region of appearing. Using compatibility, we were able to describe how a real element guarantees the cohesion of the objective region which, as I said, is the whole point of ontology. When we speak of parts of a whole, we can say that the whole as such is 'real' and that its parts are real parts of a real whole, not simply the fictive result of their constructability. This is the main innovation of Badiou's greater logic after all. We have, therefore, looked at an object locally, then regionally, such that we are left with the global section and this is what the transcendental functor supplies for us.

Although this functor describes a process that we are already pretty familiar with, we cannot simply skip over it because it actually relates the local to the regional via the global in such a fashion as we finally have a sophisticated tool for analysing the complexities of worlds as they are, in terms of the means by which most of us experience them. This being the case before we leave the object we should work through one or two of the examples Badiou gives us of the transcendental functor.

Let us reconsider the transcendental functor 'group of postmen at the demonstration'. This group can be broken up into levels or strata based on clothing, slogans, level of commitment and so on, so that subgroups can be given anything from a high degree of existence to existing on the edge of inexistence. This functor, so-called, is not actually a function per se, Badiou reminds us, as it does not assign transcendental degrees to elements of objects but to subsets. The point being that before you analyse an object completely, the functor allows you to speak in general about an element of the object that is '"representative" of its existential class' (*LW* 278). In other words, the transcendental functor is a summary of an object based on its comparative typical-ness, sort of assigning it a general place in the order of things, literally, before you break it down into atoms and fix it due to localizations. Badiou says that crucial to this functor is that the transcendental degrees correspond to a clearly defined envelope such that the functor is a synthesis of elements to the point that it can be called a real synthesis. If we take columns in the temple, we could assign four different degrees of typicality to those columns from the typical, through two degrees of typicality to almost atypical. For each degree of typicality however there exists at least one column which is exemplary in its way. This envelope obviously works at a transcendental level, but the functor's job is to make this also a real synthesis 'that structures the elements of an object in the retroaction of their appearing' (*LW* 278). If we can assert this to be the case, then we have a rather remarkable result. Badiou says that based on a set of transcendental degrees, one can select typical elements. These elements can be placed together in a single envelope so that we can project the laws of the transcendental onto the real analysis of the object.

This is the same procedure of retroaction that we have encountered numerous times so why is the functor so special? First, it guarantees that any synthesis at the transcendental level, the envelope, is a synthesis at the real level as well. More than this it permits one to talk of representative elements, summaries as we called them, as both transcendentally ordered and existentially real. The group of postmen hardly committed exist in the constructible set of postmen, but they also exist as a real group, not just real because they are there, but real because they are there as examples of hardly being committed. What this allows is that the quality of the subset is a *real* quality. This somewhat changes the direction of modern thought.

The generalized terms which we use to speak of groups of objects rather than constantly talking of them in their complex singularity are not fictions; they are real. If we return to our postmen, Badiou notes that for each degree of existence we have selected a typical representative. This gives us 'an internal metonymy of the object' (*LW* 279) composed of the maximal existent, the minimum and at least one intermediary. We end up with an average existent for 'every nuanced existential stratum of this average' (*LW* 279). If nothing else, this is a really important mode of simplification. Given a demonstration of a hundred postmen, we can speak of a limited selection of types of postmen, assign this average to at least one actual postman and thus combine degrees of relation at a purely transcendental level to actual objects in terms of their reality. Such a process halts the tendency to singularize, which can be controlled by greater logic as regards the halting point of the minimum, but which is still dangerous, time-consuming and complex. One needs a system in a constructible word of mid-order subheadings if one wants to speak of x in terms of T or of y in terms of T. By the same gesture it stops one moving to T too rapidly. All postmen are not the same, just as some postmen are effectively the same relative to this world. Again, greater logic's axiom of the inexistence of the whole means the archetypal postman is actually only a subset enveloped to the maximal degree. There is no transcendental pure postman as such (no essence of postman, no postman-ness). This solves a traditional problem when it comes to the essence of the object which is the need for that essence to define an actual object yet never be reducible to it. Hegel in particular struggles with this prospect. Now we can speak of our maximal postman as a typically committed postman and point to at least one of him, and we can also point to those postmen very committed but not totally and so on. One ends up with a stratified world made up of real atoms that can be localized in compatible pairs relative to a coherent T of a specific world within which there are clearly defined strata that are both real and purely relational. This is a profoundly coherent, flexible yet workable world of existential metonymy where parts of the world can stand in for real elements of that world in a philosophically unproblematic way. All of this is possible, however, only if the functor is 'faithful'. If we take our postmen, we need a functor who provides the real synthetic unity of the metonymic group. This could be the leader, for example, whose degree of existence presupposes that of all the others because he leads them. If this functor, leader, who is real and metonymic, he stands in for the whole at a maximal degree, can be shown to envelope all the transcendental degrees of relation in this group, then he is a faithful functor.

We now need to ask if faithful functors exist, for they may not. The leader may not exemplify the relations of all those she leads. The leader may not be metonymic. The leader may not be real and so on. If the leader does exemplify the relations of those she leads, and Badiou gives us the formal proof of this in relation to the complex idea from category theory of sheaves (even he does not attempt to define them), then they do so in a manner which is both restrictive and overabundant. The restrictive side of the faithful functor, our leader remembers, is based on the formalism that the selective metonymy of the object, typical representatives of classes of existence, 'gives us a subset of the object all of whose elements are compatible in pairs' (*LW* 279). This means we must be able to localize our leader on each element of the subset and vice versa. If the leader cannot be localized on all the elements of the subset or one element cannot be localized on him, then they cannot be a faithful functor. This is actually a rather subtle version of the democratic processes of proxy selection and leadership in general. If a leader is appointed who clearly shares nothing in common with a defined subset of the group they lead, then they will not be a faithful leader and either will be toppled or the subset will be expelled from the group.

If every functor is restricted to pairing, which is the basic formalism of all localization within an object, at the same time they have access to overabundance at the level of each object of the group. If the leader is restricted by compatible pairing, each element of the group is liberated by their being a part of the group due to their being compatible with every other element in the group including the leader. Badiou speaks of the fugitive running from the postmen group as having the least visible presence yet, because the functor needs to pair with every object in its group to metonymically stand for them all 'if you localize the great ruddy postman who leads the group on the degree of existence of the fugitive running along the gutters, you will get, as the resulting atom, the fugitive himself (the function that assigns to every x of the group its degree of identity to this fugitive)' (*LW* 280). Again there are profound political implications here. Because the leader must represent absolutely every object in the group to be 'faithful', even the most marginal members of the group who are weakest in terms of identity are metonymically of the same value as every other member up to and including the leader. Thus the transcendental functor ties down the power of the leader, due to compatible pairing, and disseminates totally the power of even the most despised or weakest member of the group.

After an extended and brilliant illustration of the functor through a reading of the battle of Gaugamela, which sadly we do not have space to consider here, the final section of this chapter proves the functor formally, concluding by calling it the sheaf resulting in the topos called the 'Grothendieck topos' (*LW* 295). We need not linger on that except to say that like Badiou we call this sheaved topos 'remarkable'. It has the potential to completely change the landscape of philosophy, in particular constructible thought and discourse theory. We end up with a world made up of atoms, compatible pairings, envelopes, real syntheses, projective representations of territories under the control of a single transcendental functor which is marked by two astonishing qualities never before proven to be the case. The first is that the functor is a part of the set it composes, contravening Russell's paradox. The second is that this functor is real, negating any need for an onto-theological absolute Other.

If the reader has been able to trace our argument from the first page of the first volume of our study to here, and they have looked at the formal consistency of each section as we have tried to do, then they must now know they stand on the threshold of a new universe of communicable worlds. We can now assert that there exist worlds which are communicable in sheaf form, in other words in terms of archetypes held under the control of a single held-in-common term, which do not succumb to infinite regress because they are real, and which conform to the inexistence of the Whole whilst still having a maximal upper bound. For most thinkers this would be more than sufficient, but for Badiou it is not. The whole point of this hyper-stable world formation, of communicability which is real and actually infinite, is to be able to destabilize it, to defeat death and to create life in the form of an actual change. The logic is as simple as it is disturbing. Why has there never been an adequate theory of real change in Western thought? Because there has never been an adequate theory of absolute stability. If we can vouchsafe this theory, then actual change will follow. The fourth book, on relation, is then the last part of the stability of communicable worlds such that actual change can finally be proved.

Book IV

Greater Logic, 3: Relation

Badiou is explicit in the opening remarks of this chapter that the construction of a greater logic is to facilitate the theory of real change to come in Book V. Summarizing the process up to this point he explains how we defined the laws of any world whatever such that a multiple can appear therein. This was the transcendental logic of being-there due to the order relation. Then we looked at the object in a world such that it articulates the logical and the ontological, linking intensity of appearance to pure multiplicity. From this we proceeded to consider the more complex make-up of the atomic components of an object. This final analysis promotes Badiou to push out four statements in this regard. Anything that exists in a world is a pure multiple. Yet the existence of the multiple, its existence in the world not its pure being, is dependent on its 'contingent indexing' on the transcendental (*LW* 300). (Contingency will be a term with a more pronounced usage in this chapter.) From this we say that existence is-not, by which is meant it has no pure being as such; rather, it is the appearance of a pure being or parts of a pure being. Although existence is-not, it isn't ontological. It has the power to retroactively present to pure being a consistency 'which is distinct from its own multiple dissemination' (*LW* 300). This is a proposition that is entirely unpredictable from reading *Being and Event* on its own. The result is that we can say of the non-being of existence that 'it is otherwise than according to its being that being is' which is what is suggested by the idea of the being of an object. We now have a complete definition of the object as it appears in the world such that its relation to pure being means that existence 'is not' to such a degree that it affects pure being as such in terms of how we see its consistency. The only problem left then is how to consider the relation between objects in a world.

It should already be clear that there is no object in the world without relation. As we said the identity of an object to itself such that it appears is dependent on the relation between this object and at least one other. Furthermore, much of the consideration of the atomic make-up of an object, so crucial for Badiou's overall vision of the onto-logical combined, is determined by the localization of one object on another, the enveloping of several objects and finally the exemplary or archetypal object relative to the group it defines. All of these functions are relational, obviously, so the relation between objects is far from mysterious to us. Specifically, in the fourth book Badiou wants to address two fundamental problems pertinent to all these relations. The first is strictly ontological: How many objects are there in a world? This has been a question that has troubled the greatest minds of our civilization. Badiou begins with Aristotle and ends with Kant, to whom Badiou's response is unequivocal and decisive. He will show that every world is infinite, and he will also define the 'type' of infinity this is, namely an inaccessible cardinal. We will explain this very shortly by reiterating some of the central ideas of *Being and Event*.

The second question he asks is simply: What is a relation? This is a purely logical question but posed at the most fundamental level. If a world is made up of relations between objects and we now know what an object is formally, what do we take a relation to be, relative to this infinite world of objects? The central problem here is that as relations exist between objects that appear in a world, if objects are-not, so relations cannot possess any being at all. Here Badiou agrees with early Wittgenstein by saying that any relation between two objects must be intrinsic to the objects which therefore must come 'first' so to speak.[1] This necessitates the following definition: 'A relation is a connection between objective multiplicities – a function – that creates nothing in the register of intensities of existence, or in that of atomic localizations, which is not already prescribed by the regime of the appearance of these multiplicities' (*LW* 301). This is an important stipulation. First, although we have stated that no object appears in a world that is not immediately relational, this does not mean the relationality is the 'cause' of an object's appearance. In that objects appear they relate, but they appear due to pure multiples and these multiples are themselves radically nonrelational. Thus one could say that appearance is the means by which multiples can relate through their being objects. Relation, which does not exist ontologically, is a derived function. The second point is therefore that any system that depends on the privileging of relationality is, according to Badiou, incorrect.

As we proceed to consider the nature of relations between objects, we will make extensive use, for the first time, of the classic triangular diagrams that are central to the operations of category theory. These triangular diagrams are a means of visualizing a basic concept for all of category theory which is universal exposure. What this says is that all relations within a world are visible in this world. There can be no definition of a relation in a world that makes use of any sense of exteriority either below or above the world in question. This takes us back yet again to the self-predicative paradox and Gödel's incompleteness theorems, which both state that there can be no exterior universality of a system. We have already seen how Badiou is not tied to these posits due to the peculiar nature of indifferent extensional set theory. So it is perhaps no surprise to see that Badiou also believes in the universality of relation that is immanent to a world. More than this, he argues all relations are universal. In particular, he will show that the infinity of worlds, the ontological basis of worlds, 'entails the universality of relations' or their logical basis (*LW* 302).

This argument results in a second, derived law of materialism. If, he argues, every object is real then we can show that every relation between every object is universal. By this is meant that for each relation it is 'universal if its intra-worldly visibility is itself visible' (*LW* 302). When you describe the relation of one object to another, there is nothing hidden below this world that determines this relation and nothing above. All relations are constructed but these constructions are determined by the reality of the objects related. Relation is thus relegated to a derived function, but in doing so it means that in every world every relation between every object can be seen by every other object. There is no going in and out of intentional focus of any order. The result of this is that we can conceive of the nature of the contingency of being-there. In every object there is an element 'beneath' it whose degree of appearance in the world is nil. This is because every atom is real, but no real multiple can appear in a world as a pure multiple as such. When a multiple appears in the world, it appears as an object; yet, the being as such remains pure multiplicity. As this is so, every relation between every object links the inexistence of one with the inexistence of the other to the point where 'relations, which conserve existence, also conserve inexistence' (*LW* 302). It is this troubling, apparently paradoxical maxim that the whole of this chapter is moving towards.

Section 1: Worlds and relations. The double determination of a world: Ontology and logic

Badiou draws on one single, geopolitical, colonial example for the entirety of his consideration of worlds and relations: the history of the French-speaking area of Canada centred on Quebec, the colonial history of the foundation of

Quebec and the nationalist movement that pushed for independence from Canada resulting in a no vote in 1980. Quebec therefore is a world, founded in 1534 and coming to a point of crisis in 1980. As a world it has what we call a double determination, as do all worlds. First, there are the intrinsic elements of this world: French language use, territory, population and so on. There is an actual infinity of possible predicates that can appear in the world [Quebec]. Then there is the network of relations, for example, antagonism between Anglophone elite and Francophone mass, neo-colonial conflicts between European settlers and indigenous 'Indian' population and so on. As is the case with Quebec so with every world we can say it is composed of 'a configuration of multiple-beings who appear "there"' (*LW* 305) and the relations between them which are regulated by the transcendental laws of order relation. What appears in a world is an ontological assignation; the relation between what appears is entirely logical so we can say that every apparent or object is both ontologically and logically determined, hence the double determination.

Now we can think of the fundamental nature of all relationality in a world which, due to the nonrelational nature of indifferent being, is all relationality as such. Badiou presents relation with admirable clarity: 'If an object is of the world and another object entertains with it the relation in question, then the second object is also of the world' (*LW* 305). For Badiou, if an object appears in a world related to an already-existent object, and this object also appears in another world, then it is a different object whose stability is determined by it being the same being with two object modes of appearing. Thus we become beneficiaries of our advertised double determination of relations. We have to consider 'the constitutive relations (or operations) of the theory of the pure multiple' (*LW* 305). If every world is based on pure multiples, we need to know how these multiples 'are globally exposed to constituting the being of a world' (*LW* 305). Or, what is the stuff of this world? Once determined, the relation between this stuff is self-evident, one might call it tautological: they are all of this world or they compose this world. This is an ontological relation only in as much as it relates multiples together in a single set due to something they all share in common: the quality of each that appears in the same world. The second form of relation? What is the relation between the objects that appear in this world due to pure multiples? A usefully provocative example given here is how to think of our galaxy as a world. Take our galaxy with its immense span and unbearable yet limited numeracy, 100 billion stars. First, we can say which stars are in our galaxy, so they share this ontological relationality. Second, we can describe what certain stars and clusters have in common within the galaxy: star types, localizations, planet types, gas clouds and so on. These second relations result in both degrees of consistency and difference. For example, the galaxy has a centre, it has outer arms and so on. If we take a certain planet, we can consistently categorize it as being in this world like these other types of planets and differentiate it; these types of planets are different to these other types which are all still in this galaxy.

Every world is infinite and its type of infinity is inaccessible

The double determination, although profound in its implications, is, at this stage in our analysis, I hope, clear enough. Moving on, we have to grapple with the more complex problem of how big a given world is or can be. Badiou defines it as an infinite of an inaccessible type, which is absolutely not the same as infinity as simply uncountable, and I assume readers are well aware of the idea of actual infinity that is central to *Being and Event*. The point here is simply the observation Cantor and others have made which is that there are more subsets in every set than the size of the set per se. If we have a set with four elements in it, each subset of those elements is also in the set, and there are more than four of these. We spent a good deal of time on this in Volume 1 so I won't go any further with my definition but instead ask, as does Badiou, what this means in terms of worlds? If we return to Quebec, then the basic territories of Quebec make up Quebec, but each territory is itself made up of elements, say neighbourhoods, and each neighbourhood of streets, decomposable to houses and so on. We already know that infinite decomposability has a halting point so the infinity of the world is not due precisely to that, even if it is determined by that. The central issue here is rather that of transitivity. If an object belongs to a world, all the sub-objects that belong to that object also belong to that world. This is how set theory controls infinite regress and bad infinity by determining a minimum and stating that the Whole inexists. What this process delimits is precisely the fact that while any world is infinitely decomposable, all the decompositions of objects in the world are sub-elements that are disseminated in that world such that however 'small' you go you will hit zero and there is nothing smaller than that. As Badiou says, 'The world does not have a "beneath" that would be external to it, a sort of preworldly matter' (*LW* 307). Everything that composes the composition of a world is to be found within said composition. As we said, all relations are universal. Nothing lies beneath. Every world that exists, exists entirely at the surface level.

Another way of saying this is that all worlds are totally communicable due to relation, just as all beings are indifferent due to nonrelation.

The second important point, of course, is that no world has a 'heterogeneous above either' (*LW* 307). We can cut to the chase here and say that we began our analysis by proving that the Whole inexists for a world so here we don't need to prove this yet again. Instead, we can just assert that if you add up all the elements of a world, that total is still an element of this world, contravening of course the self-predication paradox. Badiou says: 'A world makes immanent every local totalization of the parts of that which composes it' (*LW* 308). Just as there is no formless matter beneath, there is no overall state of affairs (God) above either. Now we come to the point where we prove the interrelation of halting point plus inexistence of the whole, and infinity. For a world to be immanent in the manner just described, it has to be an actual infinity. If it were finite then all the beings that compose it would have to be finite. If any of those beings had an actual infinity of parts, then this element would have more parts than the world and so the world would have to be infinite because it includes an infinity within it. And we know of course that in terms of beings, they are all composed in an infinity of infinite sets. This is one of the primary messages of *Being and Event*. First that actual infinity exists. Second that more than one exists. Third that different types of infinity exist. Fourth, infinity is the norm, finitude the exception.

If a world is determined by pure multiples and pure multiples exist in terms of actual infinity due to Cantor's theorem that the parts always exceed the whole number of any set, then, by definition, no world can be finite. Every world, because composed of multiples, is transitive to the basic condition of all multiples relative to their subparts such that every world is an actual infinity. Badiou says the following: 'The principle "neither sub-sistence nor transcendence" ultimately results in the necessity that every world be ontologically infinite' (*LW* 309). Although worlds are infinite, the operations that make them so are ontological and worlds are instead logical. The infinity of every world is not to do with the operations of relation. The operations that determine dissemination and totalization in the world due to transitivity are those of the ontology of sets. This being the case, 'the extension of a world remains inaccessible to the operations that open up its multiple-being and allow it to radiate' (*LW* 309). While Gödel's incompleteness theorems remain pertinent to ontology, even if ultimately for many including Badiou they are resolved, incompleteness is simply not a problem for worlds at large. The operations that allow a world to be infinite, immanent and consistent are not to be found in the world. This results in a neat formulation which echoes that of the role of the void relative to pure being.

Because the functions which determine the nature of the world are not to be found in the world, as they are ontological not logical, then said world is closed 'without it thereby being representable as a Whole from the interior of the scene of appearance that is constitutes. A world is closed for the operations that set out the being-qua-being of what appears within it: transitivity, dissemination, totalization of parts' (*LW* 309).

The definition of inaccessible infinity is an important development in his work on infinity in general. Badiou says that when I am in a world and I apply the laws of 'expansive construction' to it by determining subparts of objects I am always in that world. If I were then to make that world very small and carefully composed, it should not be infinite. But because the laws of the world in question are external to the world I compose, I can never close the world from within. No world is totalizable because 'the "number of the world" – its type of infinity, and therefore this world itself, as thought in its multiple being – remains inaccessible to the operations of ontology' (*LW* 310). We define worlds as being 'globally open for every local figure of its immanent composition' or better that paradox of their ontology means all worlds have 'operational closure and immanent opening'. This is the truth of their infinity which Badiou sums up by saying 'every world is affected by an inaccessible closure' (*LW* 310).

What is a relation between objects?

Badiou calls the axiom of relation the statement that 'relation draws its being from what it binds together ... a relation creates neither existence nor difference' (*LW* 310). Here he reconfirms the basic point that relation per se does not exist but is, according to Badiou at least, a derived function. If an object is the coupling of multiple-being and transcendental indexing, then the relation between two such objects is 'every function of the elements of the one towards the elements of the other, such that it preserves existences and safeguards or augments identities (that is, maintains or diminishes differences)' (*LW* 310). From this we can propose that a relation between objects comes after and is subordinate to the existential make-up of those objects. It is absolutely not possible to draw a relation between two objects in the same world such that said relation either exceeds the identities of those objects in that world, or in some way disrupts the world in question due to the relation itself. Every relation has the job of confirming difference. These two objects are related but different. Then it has the job of establishing identities. If these two objects are different objects in the same world, this is the degree to which they are similar in this world from not at all, through partially, all the way up to maximally. Relation on this reading, contrary to what other philosophers might insist, is derived from difference and identity, and no relationality of any order can disrupt a world from within. This is because no relation can exist except as a means of preserving the specific kinds of difference and repetition that objects participate in.

Badiou's example of this assertion is carefully selected as it concerns a rebellion in Quebec of the Indian community in the 1990s called the 'Oka Incident'. During the incident two objects in the world, the remains of the indigenous population and the machine of government, meet in a clash over the proposed siting of a golf course on ancestral ground. Thinking about this very specific clash, Badiou raises the increasingly pertinent question as to whether the new intensity of the Indian community relative to the government, resulting in armed battles, is a new relation or one that was already latent. As we already know, for Badiou there can be a new event in a world, which will result in new relations but, as he makes clear here, a relation can never be an event itself. 'It does not transform the transcendental evaluations; it presupposes them' (LW 311). The fact that a new relation can never be an event means that at each stage in the conflict, he is forced to concede, the 'new' fraught relation between Indian community and government is secondary, effectively already there, and always follows on after the objects in question appear. He then sounds a warning. Even when considering the complexity and centrality of relation within any world, we should not forget that the object precedes the relation which contravenes the basic law of his own tradition that difference, relationality, precedes identity, the object such as it is.

Badiou's radical re-reading that objects precede relation, which also contravenes the analytical position that every object is the predicate of a concept, solves many deep-seated problems, but Badiou is aware that the initial definition of a relation is a negative one. As he presents it first a relation is an *'oriented connection from one object towards another'* (LW 312). However, this is on the condition that the existential value of the first object cannot be less than the value which causes it to correspond to the second object due to the connection. Furthermore, the transcendental measure of the identity of the first object, how much it appears in this world, has a correspondence to the transcendental measure of the other object, which also cannot be inferior. The relation between two objects can never be larger or more intense than either the components they share in common or their overall degree of value as regards transcendental indexing. A relation can never overturn the atomic logic of objects in other words. This point can then be used to present a more positive definition of the relation if you so wish. Of the relation it can be said that it always conserves the atomic logic of the objects that are related, or what Badiou calls the law of the 'conservation of invariants' (*LW* 312). Not 'difference precedes identity' or 'every object is a predicate of a concept' but *every relation preserves the material reality of its objects* is the footing we need to set our future philosophy upon.

Logical completeness of a world

If we establish that the world is marked by an ontological closure due to the inaccessibility, in the world, of the axiomatic procedures which define the very existence of that world, meaning a world is literally unintelligible to itself, can we also argue that a world as such is also closed, in this instance as regards the ontological realm? This closing principle would allow that there is an operational system in place such that we can assert that we can speak of the world without ever leaving the world and thus trespassing on the ontological in any way. Naturally, this value is relationality as such because a central aspect of the ontological is that it is indifferent and nonrelational. To achieve this requires that we think the relation between any world as such and the relation per se. Thinking relation in this foundational manner results in the astonishing conclusion that 'broadly speaking, the logical completeness of the world will obtain if it makes sense to say that the Relation between relations is itself the world' (*LW* 313). Within a world all relations are universal by which we mean every relation between an object is visible from every object in the world. If nonrelationality then is the defining point of closure for indifferent being, then Relationality as such is the same for communicable worlds, communicable meaning total and universal communicability between each object within a world or universal exposition. And finally, we enter into the diagrammatic triangulation that is the very essence of the innovation of category theory.

Let us proceed with care. Triangulation is fairly simple, its effects will change your world, literally, but it is also unfamiliar territory for most of us used to thinking in a linear fashion, who will now be asked to instead operate in a tabularized manner. Following again Badiou's example of the world of Quebec and the Oka incident, we now take our basic relation, Mohawk Indians and Quebecois State, and add two further objects. First, a liberal citizen whose support for the Mohawks increases as the violence of state increases such that their degree of support for the state decreases. In contrast, we have the conservative citizen who mourns the death of the law enforcement agencies and whose degree of support for them over the days matches an increased dislike for the Mohawks. What we will see is that each of these citizen objects has a degree of relation to our first two objects, Mohawks and state. Yet this also means that they have a relation to the relation that links Mohawks and state under the heading [Oka incident]. They have what can be called a relation to this initial relation.

This complex begins with a triangle called a diagram of the world which is basically our standard commutative diagram (*LW* 314). At position A is the progressive citizen, at B he places the Mohawks and at C the administration. The function f between A and B is [support]. The composite function $g \circ f$ is [vituperation]; usually you would call this composite function h. Finally the function between the Mohawks and the administration is represented by the function g or [Oka incident]. The diagram shows that in terms of the citizen, A, we can see a clear relation between the degree of support for the Mohawks, B, and that of vituperation for the state authorities, C. The equation $f \to g$ or [support] → [Oka incident] is the same as the intensity of vituperation $h[g \circ f]$. The same degree of identity exists between the two sides of the triangle making the political tensions appear as commutative and allowing us to see a direct relation between the support a citizen feels for the Mohawks and the vituperation they feel for the authorities due to the scandal of the Oka incident. In breaking open the function h, we find embedded inside the cause of [vituperation], which is the composite $g \circ f$. Badiou calls the commutative nature of the triangular diagram: 'The fundamental abstract expression for a relation to a relation on the basis of an object. In the end, the commutative triangle ... is the clear-cut expression of the subjective implication of the Quebecois citizen in the conjunctural relation which the Oka incident constituted' (*LW* 314). What the diagram shows is a subjective, political position wherein the ordinary citizen and the marginalized Mohawks become politically conjoined due to functions rather than shared identities, an important result because culturally and politically these two communities might normally be said to share no identity, for example, in terms of identity politics. Functional relations allow groups to sidestep this knotty issue and come together over what they think should be done, rather than who they think they are.

Based on the simple presupposition of the commutative diagram, we can now build up a complex of diagrams. We can overlay the diagram of the liberal and that of the conservative, for example, and realize that for the liberal, support for Mohawks equals vituperation of police, while for the conservative the opposite is true, support for the administration is the same as their vituperation of the Mohawks' reaction to the administration. Then we can link the two citizens as objects as well. The more the progressive vituperates the police, the more the reactionary supports the police and vice versa. This inevitably leads to a situation where the progressive citizen will find themselves unable to support the views of the progressive and support the actions of the administration for the diagram to remain commutative and thus structured. If it loses its structure, then it loses other values attendant on that, for example, a point of universal visibility which is also, structurally, consistent. One final point in this regard is that the triangles in question remain commutative only if they preserve that first, primitive relation of vituperation derivative from the relation between progressive and conservative citizen. If the conservative supports the progressive who in turn supports the Mohawks, then the structural integrity of the diagram, its commutativity, fails.

The commutative triangle permits us to speak metaphorically to better understand what is the nature of a complete world. Badiou says, '*Given a relation between two objects of a world, we say that this relation is "exposed" if there exists an object of the world such that it composes a commutative triangular diagram with the two initial objects*' (*LW* 316). The diagram resultant from this assertion is called the exposition of a relation, and the third object, at the triangular apex, is the exponent (*LW* 317 & *MT* 45–9). We can now return to our idea of universal relations and say that such a relation exists when, '*given two distinct expositions of the same object, there exists between the two expositions one and only one relation such that the diagram remains commutative*' (*LW* 317). What this relation demonstrates is the same balance of degree of all relations. It is large enough to see all the objects, but it is the smallest largest relation that can do so. In our Quebec world the universally exposed is the Oka incident which is the base of our triangles. The combination of universality of exposition and uniqueness of relation is the basis of all logically complete worlds. Badiou sums this up with the simple maxim: 'Every relation is universally exposed' (*LW* 317).

The second constitutive thesis of materialism: Subordination of logical completeness to ontological closure

Although the metaphor of visibility is useful, it must be remembered that relations do not depend on some external viewing subject or consciousness.

In reality all the laws of appearing are intrinsic to the worlds which appear as we have stressed. That said, we can still pursue the metaphor of seeing in more detail, in particular, the quality of universal expositions relative to being as close as possible. Badiou invites us to consider the relation between the earth and the sun in the world of our galaxy from the perspective of the next closest star which is far enough away to see this relation in its entirety but close enough to be the next nearest object from which this relation is visible. This star is Proxima Centuari which is proximate enough to the earth–sun relational orbit that it can be seen from both points of the relation that it can also see. We can then go further and say that while Proxima Centauri is the closest point from which the relation earth–sun is entirely visible, this relation is visible in fact from every single star in our galaxy. This being so, Proxima Centauri universally exposes the relation earth–sun on the proviso that its position is visible to every other point in the galaxy. Badiou, for example, mentions the Spica of Virgo as able to see Proxima Centauri as the next nearest point related to the earth–sun relation (*LW* 319). We can then say that universal exposition is as follows: 'A relation is universally exposed means that this relation is always, at a point in the world (for an object of the world), "given to see," such that this given-to-see is itself visible from every other givenness-to-the-visible of the relation. An exposition is universal if it is itself exposed' (*LW* 318). There is no exteriority necessary at all for a world to be 'complete' in itself.

Badiou now comes to the part of this section which is that logical completeness such as we have described is always due to ontological closure. He explains initially that because worlds are infinite, they can be closed. This of course sounds counter-intuitive, but to prove it all we have to do is remind the reader that worlds can only be logically closed in the manner we have detailed and avoid the aporias of regress and bad infinity if they succumb to the axioms of set theory. If we do that, and we must as the rewards are too great to ignore, then we also have to accept the axioms of set theory that also show that all multiples are infinite multiples of multiples. This has the benefit, as Badiou neatly puts it as regards the logical completeness of appearing, that 'since we can establish that this logic is complete – in the sense of the universal exposition of every relation – simply due to the inaccessible infinity of a world, we can affirm here too the subordination of the main properties of appearing to the deepest determinations of multiple-being' (*LW* 320). The infinity of multiples determines not only the atomic, local nature of objects, but also the universal, global nature of their interrelations.

The inexistent

Consider an object such that it appears in a world. Once it appears in a world, it must appear based on the logic of appearing, that much is clear. Yet it need not appear or, if it appears, it may appear in another world entirely. If this is true then we can determine the appearance of any object in any world as being indifferent to its worldly site. The site itself does not determine the necessity of any appearance. Therefore, it must be the case that as regards the logic of appearing, the contingency of every object in terms of its composition has to be present within the objects themselves. Put another way, whenever an object appears, some element of that object cannot appear, for if all elements of the object appeared this would mean that object could no longer appear anywhere else or indeed retain the possibility of not appearing. This is another way of saying that all objects have a material, atomic base, but thought from the perspective of the object not its multiple. For Badiou the important point here is that 'there is a reserve of being which, subtracted from appearing, traces within this appearing the fact that it is always contingent for such a being to appear there' (*LW* 322). If not, logical worlds, which can be closed, could also be completed; yet in order for them to be closed, as we saw, they must admit to being infinite. This is what Badiou calls a 'real point of inexistence' that can be traced in existence as such. What this trace shows is that no object as a whole ever existed or ever will, an important proviso, because it is the inexistence of the Whole that is the central contention of greater logic such that it does not submit to the aporias of traditional transcendental thinking.

We can then define the inexistent of any and indeed every world as follows: 'Given a world, *we will call "proper inexistent of an object" an element of the underlying multiple whose value of existence is minimal. Or again, an element of an apparent which, relative to the transcendental indexing of this apparent, inexists in the world*' (*LW* 322). The conclusion we draw from this is that every object has among its elements an inexistent just as, ontologically, every multiple has within its set the void. Just as if there were no void there could be no being, if there were no inexistent there could be no existence which means, by a simple deduction, if there were no void there would be no existence.

This does appear to contravene my point that within a world there is nothing hidden. Surely the inexistent is hidden from the world? This is perhaps where the metaphor of sight breaks down. The inexistent is not hidden from the world, not least because that presupposes it could be revealed. The inexistent cannot be seen in a world because, by definition, an object in a world is that which appears and thus exists, and the inexistent does not. Nor can the inexistent be said to be an element per se. The inexistent is surely closer to a function. It is that about being that means multiples can appear in the way they can appear, that is, with a minimum and a maximal within an infinity of possible relations. One could say then that inexistence is just something one has to accept if one wants existence to function in a structurally coherent way. It is not some part missing from the world which is, as we saw, structurally sound, but rather a component that will never appear as such because if it did, then the logic of appearing would fail to make sense. In that this component is an inaccessible element of pure being as such, inaccessible because it is indifferent and nonrelational, and that spoken of in this way every object that appears does so in a material indifferent fashion, the inexistent is an indifferent multiple with an indifferent index of appearance and so, in this sense, is so profoundly neutral that it is devoid of any differentiation at all that would allow one to conceive of it in any case.

Our interest in the inexistent is, naturally, by virtue of its indifference. For Badiou, however, it is the means by which it allows us to conceive of how elements inexist in states with political consequences. He asks that we think of the transcendental value of objects in the Quebec world in terms of voting rights. Let us imagine that a totalitarian regime takes over and bans all voting rights for all citizens. The effect this would have is that of relating all citizens to those who already had no rights in that state. Between 1918 and 1950 'Indians' were not allowed to vote. First, we can say that having no rights is an atom in this state. In a state defined by having rights, not having rights is non-decomposable in that it is 'transcendental without parts' (*LW* 323). As he says, 'Within right, "to have no rights," or more precisely "to be outside of any right," establishes a juridically non-differentiable category' (*LW* 323). The second point is that this atom is real. There was a population in the world of Quebec who existed by having no rights, the Indian population from 1918 to 1950.

Why set up this thought experiment? First, because what it means to be included, excluded and here included as excluded is one of the most important political, ontological and philosophical debates of our time. Translating this ongoing discussion into Badiou's terms results in speaking of an atom of real existence which appears in a world as that which, transcendentally, inexists. What is more, it is clear that for the idea of having rights, the inexistence of an object 'those who have no rights' is essential for simple, logical reasons. It is not even that the juridical needs the anomic to exist because it is the juridical. It needs the anomic simply because the juridical is an object in a world which must, by definition, admit to that which inexists. For Badiou, what is of crucial importance is the means by which that which inexists can come to exist and how it specifically relates to what exists, because included exclusions will be the basis of his revision as to how real change due to events can come about.

Badiou asks us to think about the situation in reverse. If we take the Indians during the time period stipulated for their exclusion, we can say that in the world Quebec relative to the referential object civic rights, the degree of identity of the Indians is the minimum for this transcendental. The term 'Indian' names a real atom representative of the function loss of rights. Now while the term 'Indian' refers to a real object, albeit one whose degree of identity when it comes to civic rights is nil, the being in question exists very much on the 'edge of the void of appearance itself' (*LW* 324). The 'Indian' is ontologically of the world but 'is not absolutely in the world according to the strict logic of appearing' (*LW* 324). Indians are not Quebecois as they do not possess the rights of this group; yet, it is obvious that Quebec is the transcendental site of their appearing. Badiou says significantly for our perspective: 'The inexistent of an object is suspended between (ontological) being and a certain form of (logical) non-being' (*LW* 324). This point of suspension brings our attention back to the role of indifference as regards the event, for it is indeed the event that this comment is urging us towards. What Badiou believes he has discovered here is that every world has an inexistent element. He has proven this beyond doubt based on the ontological axioms needed to found a truly consistent, constructed and communicable world. This inexistent element is to be found in terms of every single world. In that it is indifferent; it must be seen as in the singular, backed up by the fact that it exists as nil and, as we saw, the minimum is always unique. What this does not mean, however, is if the inexistent in question, here Indians without rights, comes to exist, that the inexistent is exhausted. So we can say the inexistent is unique yet plural, indeed infinite. This is by virtue of its being indifferent twice over, ontologically and, as regards the world it appears in, materially as well. Accepting this proposition then we are now in a position to show that an event can appear in the world as a truly new thing and thus a universal truth or as he puts it: 'A truth appears in the world as the surnumerary connection of chance and eternity.'[2] It can do so at the moment of suspension mentioned between ontology and logical non-being. This is a kind of two-way valve. As a being cannot exist without appearing, if events have no place in ontology, which they do not as there is nothing new in nature, then if they exist they have to exist in existence as such. Yet if they simply exist, then they are not events but objects. For what else is the value of unique universal exposition than the fact that there is nothing new under the sun, for if there were there would be an object that is either not unique, it has two elements to it, the determined relation and the nondetermined 'new' relation, or there is an object which exists which cannot be seen, the new object. This is not possible. An object needs to exist in the world to be an event as there are no events ontologically, yet not appear as existent because if it did then the qualities of unique universal exposition mean as soon as it exists it is totally transparent, absolutely and immediately communicable and, thus, not novel in any way. The inexistent then allows for a being to be thought which is not quite being, but which is not existent either.

Now we can think of this in the other direction. If a being exists as inexistent, then this logical non-being is both relational, in actual fact the relation of the non-relation, and ontological, it is precisely because pure being is inaccessible that logical worlds exist. Thus to exist you must admit of a relational non-relationality, not an absolute one but a possible one, and a being that will never appear. If you then apply the retroactive logic of the atomic to this one particular atom, it means you can transpose the qualities of the world back onto the components of a pure being. Pure being allows for the presence of the inexistent, so that the inexistent can carve out this almost existence such that it can then look back at a pure multiple and find it in possession of a component part. This component part is not, however, a part with a quality but something equally as impossible, a part without relation or non-relation. It is an indifferentiated indifferent part of pure neutrality which is what is meant by the event. Between pure being and logical-non-being we open up an impossible space from which a doubly impossible object can be conjured, one which is allowed to exist as relationally nil due to the ontological, and one which can be found in being as totally new due to the logical. It is from this that Badiou is finally able to state that events occur to such a degree that they can be said to appear in a world as something totally, truly new. This real change, as he calls it, is the subject of Book V.

Diagrams

The second section of this chapter concerns the similarities and differences between Leibniz and Badiou when it comes to the issue of best of all possible worlds. If you recall, the thirtieth meditation of *Being and Event* was handed over to Leibniz and the commentary concerning their relation is pretty strong, so we will leave Leibniz with the observation that like him we do conceive of an infinite multiplicity of possible worlds, but unlike him we cannot choose one 'world' above all other, and move on to the next section which composes the formal proofs of the various modes of relationality we have been describing. The first proof is that pertaining to inaccessible closure. This demonstrates that the axioms that determine the closure of a world are not themselves interior to that world. A version of Gödel's incompleteness theorems, but one which holds back from saying all sets are constructible. What Badiou allows is that all worlds are constructible on the basis of sets. In set theory the size of a set is called its cardinal number. Finite cardinals are composed of one, two, three elements and so on. Cantor's great breakthrough was to show that infinite cardinals also exist. Infinite cardinals tell us how many elements there are in infinite sets not through counting them, they are innumerable in that way, but through a number of means of using infinite cardinals as numbers in deductive operations which are widely communicable amongst mathematicians. You can, therefore, use infinite cardinals, they exist, but you cannot count them; thus, their closure is inaccessible. This is the basis of Badiou's transposition of the inaccessible closure to the logics of worlds.

We now turn to the inaccessible nature of the cardinal which operates as the mode of closure for any world. What we see for each world is that 'in effect it is impossible to "construct" (or attain) the cardinality *of* the world on the basis of the cardinalities available *in* the world' (*LW* 334). This is because the dissemination of the parts belonging to our world and the totalization of its parts are both made up of elements of the world in question meaning one cannot close said world internally, as there is always the plus one effect that every count in the world is a part of the world which it counts. This results in the cardinality of the world, its numerical size, being always smaller than the parts contained in that world, Cantor's paradoxical proof of actual infinite multiples. Badiou says, 'It is clearly impossible to construct a world, either from below (dissemination) or from above (totalization), anything whatsoever that may attain the numerical power of that world' (*LW* 334). If this is true, he concludes that the magnitude of any world can be measured only by an inaccessible, infinite cardinal revealing that the principle of inaccessible closure determines the ontology of all worlds.

Next we come to the formal definition of the relation between objects in a world. The proofs here add very little if anything to the ideas we have already considered logically but what this section does contain is a six-part summary of the principle characteristics of a world which is a perfect opportunity for us to digest the rich meal he has so graciously served up.

1. A collection of multiples or sets all belong to the world. This is the stable being of every situation. The quantitative measure of this world called **m**, the number of multiples appearing on the world, is an inaccessible, cardinal infinite.
2. In the midst of the multiples of **m** we have T or the transcendental. T has a uniform structure determined by partial order with minimum, conjunction of each pair of elements, the envelope and distributivity of the conjunction with regard to the envelope.
3. Every multiple that appears in the world is indexed on the transcendental through the function of appearing **Id**. The result of this indexing determines an object which has the atomic components of a type **Id** (a, x) where a is a real element of the multiple in question.
4. Each real element of an object has a degree of existence which is the value of the function of its appearing or **Id** (a, a). This is localizable by an element of T through its being an atom defined as the localization of this object on another object in $T >$.
5. Between two objects there are relations. Relations are functions of A to B that 'conserve the initial givens of appearing' (*LW* 339).
6. Multiples of a situation are 'retroactively structured by their observation in appearing: compatibility, order, envelope' (*LW* 339). There is a real synthesis of every part of a being in terms of their elements being compatible in pairs and all relations conserve this structure.

Finally we can say: 'A world is ultimately a system of objects and relations which makes an infinite collection of pure multiples appear, and prescribes for them an atomic composition which relations leave invariant' (*LW* 339). This is the definition of the communicability of worlds which, historically and in the popular imagination, has been called the Meaning of Existence!

The following two sections place the second thesis of materialism, that every relation is universally exposed, and the idea of the inexistent, on a more formal footing. Nothing substantive is added here however so we can move on to Badiou's final reiteration of the inexistent. It now suffices to just confirm some elements of the inexistent before we travel to consider the implications of said inexistent namely the fact that there is such a thing as real change. We can first say that the 'existence' of the inexistent is to be found in every object because the minimum exists in every transcendental. In addition, we can say that for every multiple A of the world, there is the real atom prescribed by $\emptyset_A$ or that the inexistence of an object in terms of the minimum is matched by a real atom, just as the existence of an object is matched by a real atom. This is because when we speak of the inexistent we do not mean the void, but that which appears in the world as the minimum allowing us to functionally differentiate the inexistent from the empty set. The empty set is being as non-being and is global. The inexistent is the minimum existence of a being within a local world. Some concomitant results of this stipulation include the fact the inexistent insists within each apparent that its appearance is contingent. We can add that as regards $\emptyset_A$ that it 'is', ontologically, as it belongs to the multiple A, and that it 'is-not', logically, since the degree of its existence in the world is nil. This suggests, and Badiou ropes in Heidegger here, that $\emptyset_A$ is a being whose very being is 'attested, but whose existence is not' (*LW* 343). In this way, although fundamentally different from the void, the inexistent operates in the world in a manner structurally similar to the way the void operates in regards to sets. To get a better sense of this complex operator we can also say it is a being whose being-ness is nil, or a being 'who happens "there" as nothingness' (*LW* 343). Finally, Badiou confirms what we have already been stating 'that the "sublation" of this nothingness, that is the tipping-over of a nil intensity of existence into a maximal intensity, characterizes real change … such a sublation is in effect the signature of what we call an event' (*LW* 343). We simply say that the totality of the determination of the logic of appearing is designed to arrive at the point called the inexistent such that the 'sublation' of the inexistent, and we will consider what this means precisely in the following section, allows for real change due to the event. With this in hand, we can close on the greater logic of worlds, confirm its hyper-consistent stability and turn our attentions to the new, complete, radically altered theory of the event which is the entire purpose of the book.

Book V

The Four Forms of Change

Badiou's project from this point of the work onwards is the possibility of thinking 'real change', as he calls it. This kind of change 'imposes an effective discontinuity on the world where it takes place' (*LW* 357). From this we can glean that change has a kind of force, that this force results in discontinuity, as one might expect from change, and further that this is an 'effective' form of discontinuity. For Badiou it is not enough for there to be something new; it must have consequences that are significant. If such a form of change occurs at all, then it can only do so in a world. Finally, such a change affects the world where it takes place, but not worlds as such, such that transcendental logic as a whole is not negated by real change but rather change must be accommodated in some way to that logic. This is what Badiou means by change being thinkable. If change exists, then it must be thought either ontologically or logically as, for him, these are the only two legitimate forms of thought to hand. Thus we might add real change is defined in relation to our two systems of thought; it is change relative to being or to worlds or both which takes us to a concomitant value of change which is singularity. A singularity, for Badiou, is a being the thought of which is not reduced to worldly context. At the same time a singularity, although a being, cannot be thought ontologically, so a singularity is a being which appears yet which is not thinkable as a being ontologically or reducible to the world as such as we saw: 'The thinking of change or of singularity is neither ontological nor transcendental' (*LW* 357).

At this point we might then ask what is the point of trying to think change at all? The ontological and logical systems Badiou has composed pertaining to indifference and communicability are far-reaching and consistent enough on their own to totally change philosophy and more widely how we think. If there is an element which cannot be thought in either system, then one could say that this element, philosophically, does not exist. Badiou goes on to show that pure being as such and objective worlds as such are immobile, consistent and unchanging. True, ontologically there is always excess, but excess itself is part of the axiomatic stability of set theory, such that in a sense it changes nothing and simply confirms the stability of being qua void. Again within each world there are an infinite amount of permutations but the world as such within which the permutations occur is totally stable as is the greater logic of all worlds. In particular, arguing from Wittgenstein, Badiou is keen to show that worlds themselves are actually definable as becoming due to constant modifications so that one can say that 'the appearing of a being in a world is the same thing as its modifications in that world, without any discontinuity and thus any singularity being required for the deployment of these modifications' (*LW* 358).[1] Moving away from Wittgenstein, who only admits to one world, Badiou says that if one accepts the greater logical proposition of multiple worlds, then you don't have to assume that you are thinking of a fixed world in which there occur changes, what he calls here modifications. Instead, an object is in the process of becoming or modification as it appears in the world: 'We are dealing with modifications themselves, situating the object as a multiplicity – including a temporal one – in the world and setting out the relations of this object with all others' (*LW* 359).[2]

We can say, therefore, that first any object is a modification of a being. No being appears in its entirety in the world as we have shown, so every object is a modified being. Then we can say that the mode of appearing of an object in the world is temporal as well as spatial, so that it is not just where a being appears but when. Accept this and appearing is shown to be a process of constant becoming temporally as well as spatially to such a degree that change itself is the law of the stability of all appearing. This idea of existence as becoming means that modification can never be a real change in the world because it is the world. One can admit to a world which is dominated by rapid and almost confounding modifications, indeed a world such as modernist aesthetics, which is defined by radical modification, but this does not mean one is dealing with singularities. More than this, even worlds that are determined by modifications to an extreme degree are still just as stable as say the opinions of the average *Daily Mail* reader. This then is the first point on change the reader needs to accept. What most of us call change is not, in truth, change in any real sense of the word; rather, it is what Badiou calls modification: '*We will call "modification" the rule-governed appearing of intensive variations which a transcendental authorizes in the world of which it is the transcendental*. Modification is not change. Or better, it is only the transcendental absorption of change' (*LW* 359).

This clarifies things quite considerably. In simple terms a singularity as real change is a being which appears in a world and yet is not authorized by the transcendental of that world. Defining real change then, on the back of the work we have done to vouchsafe the stability of transcendental logic, is easy. Proving that such change exists however is far more difficult and is indeed, in the end, as we saw in *Being and Event*, an act of faith or belief. As thinking being or appearing cannot witness change, there must be another source for real change. As Badiou says, 'an exception is required', an exception to the axioms of ontology and the logic of appearing, but an exception whose exceptional singularity is only possible because of ontology and logic. Philosophy can think this exception, only if it is sutured to the formalist conditions of mathematics.

Subversion of appearing by being: The site

Badiou gets caught up in all sorts of circumlocutions in Volume 1 when he tries to define the event as emergent from ontology alone due to the problematic term evental site. By his own admission this failure of definition was due to his lack of a logic of appearing at that point. We have already treated the problem of the evental site in the first volume of our study, so now we can simply say we do have a logic of appearing and so we are in stronger position to define what the evental site is. From this point on however the evental site will be called simply the site. The site is Badiou's construction to solve the basic problem that the two volumes of Being and Event present to us: 'That "pure-being" and "being-there" embody the absolute partition of the "there is" as such' (*LW* 360). If a singularity is to be thought, the site of its appearance must be governed by this absolute partition. There is, for Badiou, no thought of change, no third mode of rational behaviour. Instead, the site of a change must involve a being which appears. How can this come about? One simple way is the mixing of being and appearing such as occurs if 'a multiple lays claim to appearing in such a way that it refers to itself, to its own transcendental indexing' (*LW* 360). Again we have already considered, at length, the idea of a self-predicating multiple and the affect it can have on appearing in our first volume but it is such a complex and important point that we will spend more time on it here.[3] For example, a multiple that refers to itself is a multiple that appears in a world as such with no modification. This multiple does not appear in part, in the world as its referentiality is entirely to itself so it is not bound by the logic of relation; yet, it can appear because it does relate to an object, to itself. From the other side, this multiple can appear because it is indexed transcendentally, the only rule of appearing; yet, as the index is to itself as its own transcendental, it appears in a world without being indexed, at least initially, to the transcendental of *that* world. If such a multiple exists, then certainly it appears in a world in such a fashion that it is not subject to any of the means of modification intrinsic to appearing there. Badiou speaks of the double role of such a multiple: 'First, it is objectivated by the transcendental indexing of its elements' (*LW* 360). This is important as Badiou is very clear that singularity is absolutely impossible within ontology. When it comes to sacrificing the laws of ontology or logic, he must always protect ontology because it is those axioms which allow for the greater logic to be so remarkably stable and yet real. 'Second, it (self-) objectivates, by figuring among its own elements and by thus being caught up in the transcendental indexing of which it is the ontological support' (*LW* 360). This is the concession that has to be made. A multiple can be objectivated if it brings together the mode of its objectivation and the resultant objectivated entity. A multiple whose elements appear in the world such that they can be indexed can be thought of if, paradoxically, the multiple itself is one of those objects, such that the elements of the object in question can be indexed transcendentally, and thus appear, without their being a modification of the being in question under the sign of an already-existent transcendental order. This self-belonging or self-predicating multiple is what Badiou means by the site. Note here he does not yet call this the event as he was wont to do in the earlier work. At the moment all he wants is for it to be possible for a being to come into existence that is not the modification of a multiple in relation to an existent transcendental index. To do so he needs a self-predicating multiple.

A multiple which is an object in the world due to the fact that its elements are indexed in the transcendental of a world can be called a site if it 'counts itself in the referential field of its own indexing' (*LW* 363). If it can do so, then the elements of a multiple themselves are possible, not singular, in that they are indexed due to a transcendental. However, included in the set of this multiple is the multiple itself which appears both because it is part of a multiple which appears and because it indexes itself on itself. This appears to be what Badiou is contending. Such a multiple behaves in that world in terms of itself as it does in terms of its elements 'so that it is the ontological support of its own appearance' (*LW* 363). Accepting this allows a site to produce a singularity by making itself the being-there of its own being. In so doing it 'endows itself with an intensity of existence' (*LW* 363). We can sum up the nature of the site, if it exists, as follows: 'A site is a being to which it happens that it exists by itself' (*LW* 363). What we can deduct from this is that if a self-predicative being exists, then a site can be said to exist which allows for the fact that a being can exist in the world by itself, that 'is' nonrelationally in terms of the transcendental and, initially, in terms of all the other elements in that world. This is a perfect definition of an actual singularity. Of course, self-predicative sets are said not to exist by most modern philosophers but, as we have already seen in Volume 1, axiomatic set theory has novel ways of circumventing the self-predicative paradox so that the insistence on their existence is less problematic.[4]

Admitting that, we are not talking of self-predicative beings but of beings that operate self-predicatively when they appear. This is a crucial distinction. Badiou is adamant in *Being and Event* and, as we saw, here that change, which we now see is due to self-predication, is absolutely impossible in the ontological field. Yet self-predication can *exist*, even if said multiple cannot be said to have self-predicative being. In that a being is not exactly itself in the world where it appears, because it can never appear in full; if a being can, however, take itself as a component part of its being-there, its appearing, its existence, then it can be self-predicative in the world, whilst remaining resolutely not so ontologically. This is not the same as saying this can or will happen, but it should at least clarify why the greater logic is a necessary part of Badiou's overall system. There can be no true self-predication ontologically; thus, there can be no change, but there can be, he believes, logically, which means in the logical world there can be change. Because in the greater logic multiples can partially appear so that this part can be self-predicative without affecting being as such, because all objects self-refer anyway when they appear represented in categories by the identity arrow and because a singularity of appearing can be a world in itself because it possesses (self)-relation and (self)-transcendental indexing. This is not outlandish. If we can accept that the entirety of the natural of ontology can be generated from the internal subdivisions of an empty set, then surely we can concede self-mentioning portions of beings in worlds – not least because the articulation of being, the movement between belonging and inclusion, which is structurally replicated in worlds in the dynamic articulation between commutative symmetry and asymmetrical composability, seems to also be the case with the site. A site is in part a multiple and in part an object of appearing. It is in part self-enclosed, and yet in such a way that it can generate the functions of extrinsic being-there from within itself: relation and indexing. If ontology can be generated from an internally dividing void set, then eventuent sites can certainly be generated from internally relating, nil-intensity worlds.

Some examples please. The first is a specific date during the 1871 insurrection of the communards on the streets of Paris, one of Badiou's most cherished historical moments. Having detailed the events surrounding the revolution he decides that a specific date, 18 March 1871, is a site. If we take our transcendental index of this world as Paris, Spring 1871, then everything that appeared on 18 March is indexed to this transcendental; yet, 'it too appears, as the fulminant and entirely unpredictable beginning of a break with the very thing that regulates its appearance' (*LW* 365). This is because 18 March 1871 is the first day of the birth of the Paris commune or 'the exercise of power, in Paris, by republican or socialist political militants' (*LW* 364–5). Before this date there was no such thing as a commune in this world; after this date, for a period of months, with lasting consequence, there was. Why is this not just a modification of the distribution of power? Anyone involved in any small way with political organizations knows that however novel and radical their origins they rarely if ever mark a break with the discursive world that is politics itself. A new commune, a newly named political entity, is not real change in other words. Badiou argues here rather that it is because when the people of Paris rose up and refused a governmental decree, the seizing of Prussian cannons the rebels had in their possession, at this point there appeared 'an unknown capacity, an unprecedented power … In effect, from the stand-point of rule-bound appearing, the possibility of a proletarian and popular governmental power purely and simply does not exist' (*LW* 366).

On 18 March 1871 everything in that world of Paris was the same as everything that was in the world of Paris the day before and years before. By this we don't mean the same people, the same buildings, the same activities, but the same transcendental index. Anything that rocks up to the city gates of Paris is able to appear there. The commune, however, made up of elements that already exist in the world, makes appear a truly new thing simply because the transcendental index of political power absolutely does not recognize it. In categorical terms, the transcendental functor is unable to sanction its universal exposition. Badiou gives various examples from the period of how truly inconceivable proletarian governance was to the powers that be. It is, in this world, inexistent that the commune can be communicable, yet it comes to exist, and thus it is an example of a real change. Real change on this reading is not something that did not exist in a world then it does, that is modification and is the meat and potatoes of what appearing as becoming actually is. Rather, it is something that appears which, due to the nature of the indexing of this particular world, absolutely should not appear. It is a new thing that cannot gain a communicable sanction. March 18 is a site first because it 'imposes itself on all the elements that contribute to its own existence' (*LW* 366). It does this by forcibly demanding 'on the indistinct background of worker-being, an entirely new transcendental evaluation of the latter's intensity' (*LW* 366).

Badiou concludes with the perhaps confusing formulation: 'Thought as an object, the site "March 18" subverts the rules of political appearing (that is, the logic of power) by means of the support-being "March 18", in which the impossible possibility of worker-being is shared out' (LW 366). A few comments ought to be broached at this juncture I feel. March 18 is an object in the world of Paris. This object is a site because it subverts the logic of power. This is a formulation we have seen across all the four named conditions of Badiou's work, for example, aesthetic event [seriality] and mathematical event [Cantor]. The conditions then operate as indifferent modes of communicability for the world in question. While there are infinite worlds, there are, at present, only four types of world for Badiou. Here you can see the importance of the idea of condition to the theory of the event. It is because every world is composed according to the same one of four 'logics' that sites can appear. Sites do not subvert the logic of appearing as such, but the logic of appearing in a world conditioned by politics, science, aesthetics or love. This is allowed to work because there is such a thing as the support-being 18 March. Ontologically speaking, 18 March is totally indifferent to what appears under its auspices so long as whatever appears is a component part of it. This is the crux. Nothing about being can be an event, but something about being can be eventual if it is forced to appear against the logic of the conditioned world it appears in – in this instance that of institutional power. Once the impossible possibility of the worker-being as political agent comes to exist, it is then shared out across all the elements of 18 March due to the axiom of distributivity. This is to say once it can be shown to appear amongst the legitimate existents of the world, it can set up relations of intensity with them and begin to infect this possible world with the relation to impossibility that it represents *to that conditioned world.*

Ontology of the site

Badiou proceeds to remind us that reflective sets were the basis of his refutation of the existence of the whole, which was the foundational statement for the development of the greater logic upon the tenets of set theory, along with the halting point. There he proved the inexistence of the whole by showing fundamentally that self-reflexive sets do not exist, Russell's paradox. If a site is a self-reflective set, therefore, it must have an ontology which is impossible 'since it is, by reflexive violence, an exception to the laws of being' (LW 368). If this is so, then a site is an exceptional One, 'the form of what dwells in itself as whole and as element of whole' (*LW* 368), producing a momentary violation of the laws of being which, in an instant, then closes up on again. We can now say that the thought of a reflexive set, which must begin with being because as we saw as regards appearing, real change is impossible, is somehow posed ontologically in the manner in which, in mathematics, all concepts are developed as speculative what-ifs. It is immediately rejected as impossible; yet, the moment of its proposition somehow takes on a lasting effect, not on being but on the world that depends on being.

Still unable to prove that sites exist, Badiou is at least now able to present a three-part description of their 'ontology', which must be described as the ontology of impossibility:

1. A site is a reflective multiplicity. It belongs to itself. It transgresses the laws of being.
2. As it presents a momentary cancellation of the gap between being and being-there, the site reveals the void that 'haunts' multiplicities. This point, it must be said, is not treated properly here or developed in any satisfactory manner.
3. The site is ontological figure of the instant that appears only to disappear.

Badiou's strategy seems to be empirical. Events exist, he assumes, real change is possible and desirable. That said, they cannot be thought in terms of ontology or logic alone. This being so, one has to assume that events exist, first, and then reconcile this fact to thought, second. This is the same strategy that is the basis for his contention that the void is real and exists before any formal thought process. More than this, the void and the event are linked. For example, the event reveals the void to the world, which otherwise has no conception of the void, even though it is the void that is the basis of both its stability and its materiality. Like the void, the event is an article of faith or belief. It cannot be proven within the system of set theory or category theory. This also means it is real.

Logic of the site 1: Consequences and existence

Another way of determining the existence of the site as self-reflexive set, again taken from axiomatic modes of reasoning, is to consider its effects due to consequences. More importantly for Badiou this allows him to develop a four-part typology of change: modification, fact, weak singularity and strong singularity. This typology is crucial to his insistence that events do exist as real change, but only rarely. The typology also echoes that we which considered when we spoke of the eventual site in the first volume.[5] The difference between Volume 1 and Volume 2 as regards the consequence of an event is that now we have a fully developed, formal sense of what consequence actually means in the world.

The first point to be made is that if a self-reflective site flares up, that is not enough because its light will be instantaneously snuffed out by the ban on self-reflexivity in ontology. For it to stand a chance of having any lasting life, it must have some form of consequence. Indeed, as we saw in Volume 1, the means by which a subject to truth pursues with militant faith the consequences of an event is the basis of the means by which the truth of the event becomes communicable and effective in a world, although Badiou lacked a developed sense of what a world was when he made that statement in 1988. If you recall, we struggled to come to terms with the exact nature of an eventual consequence in our first volume, but now we can return to that section and be fully confident in the nature of what a worldly consequence is. If I can take you back to our first attempt at this, a consequence is the relation between transcendental degrees. This relation is one of dependence. So the dependence of q as regards p is the envelope of all the degrees (t) whose conjunction with p is less than or equal to q. Put more simply, q depends on p by it being larger than or equal to all the elements that it shares in common with p. This then allows us to measure the entailment of q by p as being equal to the envelope of all the degrees whose conjunction with p remains inferior to q. 'Broadly speaking, it is the degree which, conjoined with the "entailing" degree, lies as close as possible to the entailed degree' (*LW* 370). We see here two classic operations of greater logic. First q is bigger than or equal to p, because the set of the elements of p are all less than or equal to q. That said, q is only just bigger than p; it is the largest object that is closest to p. This then allows us to say what a consequence is. If we take element a of an object such that its existence has the value p, and if element b of the same object exists to the degree q, then we can say that b is the consequence to a to the exact degree of the value of the entailment of q by p. First we say that b is the consequence of a. By this we mean that it contains or envelopes the elements of a which are all smaller than b. Thus b can contain a, meaning it is the consequence of a, allowing us to formally determine how one object can be the consequence of another transcendentally. Then we can also add that b is the next largest consequence of a, that is, it is not only a consequence of a but is a direct consequence of it. If we are to say that b is the consequence of a, we can say this demands that it contains all the elements of a, and thus is larger than a, but it is the next largest object in relation to a and so it is the direct consequence of a.

The formal means for establishing a consequence demands that if a site can be defined according to its consequences, we not only now have a formal method of describing this, but this method is one of transcendental indexing, and even if the measure of the consequence of a site or an event is tiny, because this is a measure of its degree, it by definition exists in a world. Badiou further says that 'a consequence is a (strong or weak) relation between existences' (*LW* 371). What this suggests is that the measure of the degree to which one thing is a consequence of another can't be separated from 'the intensity of existence of these things in the world in question' (*LW* 371).

Logic of the site 2: Fact and singularity

We now have a formal means of determining the consequences of a site. This allows us to start with an event, and from that event trace the commonality of elements between that event and the objects which follow due to consequence formally defined. In each case the next object needs to be a direct consequence of the event itself or a consequence of that event, and at each stage the degree of intensity between the two needs to remain high. If the next object is not a direct consequence of the event, we have stopped dealing with the consequence of the event, and we are back considering simple modification due to relation. Again, if the degree of intensity is low, it means that increasingly the elements of the new object are not direct consequences of the initial event, only some are and, eventually, none will be. Maintaining the sequence in terms of direct *and* intense relation is the art of subjectivated event making, and leads Badiou to a new differentiation in terms of site or evental consequence, fact versus singularity. Badiou rightly points out that a site may possess the marks of true change, self-belonging, indication of the void and instantaneous disappearance, but because it suffers from existential insignificance, it self-refers to a negligible degree, it possesses little more in terms of singularity than a simple modification.

He gives the example of the Central Committee's Manifesto, posted on the walls of Paris, 23 May 1871, as the army are busy slaughtering the communards in the streets. The misplaced confidence of its being designated a 'proclamation of victors' as said victors are dying all around it is sad, but the conviction it shows, for Badiou, is still a consequence of the evental site, such that in terms of consequence and succession it is part of the site. Yet it now becomes clear that immediate consequence is not enough; there also has to be intensity of existence as well. As, for Badiou, the misplaced nature of the manifesto shows it to be a sign of decomposition of the commune, due to its powerlessness against the forces of the state, 'it leads singularity back to the edges of the pure and simple "normal" modification of the world' (*LW* 372). In formal terms, we would say that the elements it contains have a lack of intensity relative to the elements it is the consequence of, and if this is the case then these other elements, by definition, must be relations with objects already in the world, each leaching away the singular exception of the initial event. If elements in a world lack intensity of relation with other elements, here eventalized elements, yet they are in the world, then they must have relations with other elements in the world, ones which do not pertain to the event, and so rapidly become absorbed into the immense machine of the becoming of modifications that defines all logics of worlds. Worlds embrace, indeed expect, new components; thus, components of what we will come to call the body of the event must be consequences of the event, to a high degree of intensity by which is surely meant maximal.

How can we stop disillusionment in politics from happening? Badiou says hope is to be found if the 'force of the existence in the appearing of the site would have to compensate for its vanishing. Only a site whose values of existence is maximal is potentially an event' (*LW* 372). Formally, this means that as regards the parts of an element which is a site, all the elements of that site must remain in relation to the site itself. Initially, this includes the site itself, source of its paradox, but as this becomes instantly untenable, all the remaining elements must stay in a relational identity to the site only. This is feasible in categorical worlds because they admit POSet clumps of this nature. As Badiou goes on to say, 'Only a complete power of existing differentiates a site from the simple network of modifications in which the law of the world persists' (*LW* 372). Logically this must be the case. Each object which is a consequence of that initial site, to be a consequence as we said, must depend on the previous parts maximally and immediately. If this is not the case, then the parts of the site, of this new object in the world, will determine their degree of existence, increasingly, in relation to those objects which already exist. This is the nature of communicability. What Badiou proposes then is that for an event to result in real change, its consequences must be direct, sequential and maximal for as long as possible. If parts of the new object are compared to already-existing objects immediately or too soon, then what is new is swamped by what is not.

Badiou's main point here is that a site that rapidly loses its maximal identity by finding relations of its parts to already-existent political objects can never become a true singularity. Instead, he calls it a fact increasing our terminological distinctions. We have a modification, which is the simple becoming of the world seen from the position of an object of that world – a fact, which is a site, not of this world, whose intensity of existence however is not maximal, so it is slowly watered down by relations to objects already of this world. And then finally a singularity or 'a site whose intensity of existence is maximal' (*LW* 372). On the back of this Badiou can highlight three of his four forms of change:

- Modification: ontologically neutral and transcendentally regular.
- Fact: ontologically supernumerary but existentially, thus logically, weak.
- Singularity: ontologically supernumerary and whose value of appearance is maximal.

At this stage Badiou's attention wanders to another example that he has been discussing which is the love-triangle at the heart of Rousseau's *Julie* picking up on the manner by which the character Wolmar negates the singularity of his wife's love for Saint-Preux. Wolmar accepts the site or the event of their love, but instead of trying to negate them, denying them even factual existence, he decides to regulate those elements of the affair which he deems 'praiseworthy'. Badiou notes that if you regulate a singularity, this 'requires treating its consequences as though they were of the order of fact, and hence appropriate to the transcendental measure of modifications' (*LW* 373). Wolmar, on this reading, establishes relations between the site of the illicit, evental love affair, and already-existent objects of amorous and emotional relation that are acceptable and already existent in his world and the world at large. If regulation can be resisted, then a site is able to place itself between singularity and fact, rather than between fact and modification; then 'it is then up to the network of consequences to decide' (*LW* 374). It is perhaps lamentable that even at this advanced stage, even when an object is intelligible in a world but not communicable, it is not a given that this site, which is singular, will be an event. The final issue to be decided is the degree of intensity of this singularity: weak or strong.

Logic of the site 2: Weak and strong singularity

For the record Badiou states that all singularities have to be maximal, but in terms of their subsequent consequences, they can have a different force. To establish the force of a singularity, 'it is in terms of the links of consequences which the vanished site establishes with the other elements of the object that had presented it in the world' (*LW* 374), so that the '*force* of a singularity lies in making its consequences, and not just itself, exist maximally' (*LW* 374). This very forceful singularity is what Badiou calls the event. At this point he presents the diagrammatic typology of the event which we can perhaps better describe in words. All objects in worlds are in a state of becoming. If this becoming results in no real change which, by far the large majority of the time, is the case, then this is mere modification. It is important not to mistake modification either for change as such or suggest that the immanent becoming of the world means it is based on the possible instability of singularities which can erupt from this becoming. For Badiou the opposite is true and the reader might do well to linger on this point. It is because the world is in a state of infinite, immanent becoming *that* it is stable, absolutely stable. Events, if they occur, do not occur because of becoming, but in spite of it. A site is instead a place where real change could occur, but if this results in non-maximal existence, then this new element, newer than a modification because supernumerary, is instead just a fact. This is how worlds negate most novelties, by immediately regulating them by taking the larger part of the elements of this new object and relating them to already-existent elements. A singularity then must be such that all of its parts relate only to the object including the object itself. Impossible though this is to conceive of ontologically or logically, Badiou is an extensional materialist. If events occur but cannot be thought in normal terms, then the modes of thought are at fault, not his belief in the fact that there are events. Finally, if a maximally singular object is presented, it must retain a maximal degree of identity relation with the initial object in terms of all its consequences up to a certain point he does not name for it to be determined strong. If it is strong, it is an event. These then are our four forms of change: modification, fact, weak singularity and strong singularity, only the last can be termed an event.

Logic of the site 4: Existence of the inexistent

'There is no stronger transcendental consequence than the one which makes what did not exist in a world appear within it' (*LW* 376). Consider this statement for a moment. All of Badiou's work is summarized therein. It is not a statement that he could have made in 1988 when he published *Being and Event*, by his own admission. It is not a statement that makes any sense without a deep understanding of the logics of worlds. It is hardly a statement that pertains to ontology; it is just that this statement cannot be made at all without ontology. All of *Being and Event* then is embedded within it, although none of the terms in the statement are ontological. An event, he is finally conceding, can be entirely considered in terms of its existence in a world. Going further, all of Badiou's philosophy, designed to 'prove' the existence of events resulting in subjects and universal truths, is encapsulated in the second volume of Being and Event, not the first as we all once thought. *Logics of Worlds* is not a supplement; it is a major conclusion, a fact most sustained readers of Badiou seem reluctant to accept, so let us then break the statement down and try to convince them.

Events have transcendental consequences only. Ontologically speaking, there are no events. Thus an event is not a new being but a new object in an existent world. This object is new in this world but, ontologically speaking, there is nothing novel about it. Ontologically nothing is created even if, in that there is an infinite number of types of infinities of infinite multiplicities, it is humanly impossible to 'count' everything that is a being, it is perfectly possible to calculate the presence of every single one. The event then is what happens in a world, due to the appearance of a being which did not exist in that world before. However, it is not so straightforward, as we saw. In that there is an infinity of beings; there is also nothing stopping all elements of all those beings appearing in one single world. This would not mean that all beings appear, because as we saw there is always a part of the being which never appears, nor does it mean that said world has reached a maximum size. Because there is always part of a being which never appears in a world, this means there is always an infinite number of parts that do not appear which could. The point being that inexistence is not simply that which did not appear, now suddenly appearing. This is because the world is in state of constant, immanent, infinite becoming without wholeness spatially or temporally, by which we mean the world's logic, is that of things which did not appear, and thus did not exist, now appearing and now existing. These are modifications. The problem then is not just the existence of previously inexistent objects but the existence in a world of an object that appears in a world and still does not exist in it. These impossible objects exist in a world as impossible-to-exist objects. Such paradoxical objects, less paradoxical than self-predicating multiples at the ontological level but paradoxical all the same, are what Badiou means by events.

What are these objects like? In Paris in 1871, the Central Committee of the revolutionaries makes a proclamation. Present at the proclamation are twenty people, most of whom are simple worker-beings. At the time a governmental paper dismisses the group by rubbishing the status of its members. The workers who, a day before, were not politically existent, come now to exist politically. Badiou says of this that 'its consequence in the world is to make exist within it the proper inexistent of the object-site' (*LW* 377). How precisely does it do this? Who designates that what the workers did and wrote is a political gesture? In part it must be their own self-awareness. They are, after all, a self-predicating set so if they come together and say from now on we have a political existence, as simple workers, this is a political act, certainly in the terms presented by Ranciere's work, for example.[6] Then there is the political logic which determines the kind of conditioned world they exist in. If they met and wrote a manifesto but in terms of aesthetics, then this would be the same 'event' and it may result in an event, but with different consequences because they are operating in a differently conditioned world, not just a different world. One of these workers could also be an avant-garde writer, but that is another story, so that is the second point. The third and final point is that the manner in which the government sources dismiss the political validity of the workers by simply negating their possibility of having a political existence, paradoxically, confers upon them the most political of all existences, revolutionary inexistence.

The inexistence of the workers then is designated at three levels in terms of their existence being noncommunicable in the world yet intelligible. They are making statements in that world, and that world is reading them, but while the statements are intelligible they communicate no possible meaning to the world at large because they lack the communicable sanction of power. This is because first, the group is self-designating or self-predicating. They have decided to be the political group they are, without relational sanction from already-existing groups. Second, the group contravenes the conditioning logic of the political that determines the indifferent ground rules of the world they would wish to exist within. Finally third, statements that are communicable within that world actively seek to make the group's revolutionary statements noncommunicable through questioning not their content but the very communicable basis of their existence.[7]

Badiou formalizes this in different terms. If you take an evental site marked by its self-belonging, which is also a singularity, its intensity of existence is maximal, you can then determine if it is an event or not. This is an event 'if the value of the entailment of the (nil) value of its proper inexistent by the (maximal) value of the site itself is maximal' (*LW* 377). This is rather torturous syntactically but one will do one's best to loosen its thumb-screws a little. In more straightforward language the entailment of the event retains both a nil value as regards the world and a maximal value in terms of its relation to the initial event. As Badiou says, this only appears intricate. In fact, every object includes a proper inexistent as an element, that is what we have called the minimum. So all Badiou is saying is that '*the maximally true consequences of an event's (maximal) intensity of existence is the existence of the inexistent*' (*LW* 377). Take any object. That object has an inexistent element, which exists with minimum intensity. This element is unique. It has only one. The consequence of the sudden, maximal intensity of the appearance of this inexistent element is that the inexistent now exists. It must exist maximally for at least two reasons. First, if the inexistent and its consequence do not match absolutely, then another element must be present and, as the inexistent is unique, that must be an already-existent element. If this is the case then before we have even started, our site has started to be regulated. The other reason is that the only consequence of the inexistent is an inexistent element, if it is a true consequence of the inexistent. As there is only one unique minimum, this demands that the consequence of inexistence must be the inexistent, maximally. The maximal, you recall, is also unique.

Badiou pulls us back from the brink at this point by highlighting what he calls a 'violent paradox': 'If an implication is maximally true, and its antecedent is too, its consequences must also be maximally true: this leads to the untenable conclusion according to which, under the effect of an event, the inexistent of the site exists absolutely' (*LW* 378). This is not possible within a world. First of all, the event and its consequence are the same object. This means that yes, a being can appear in a world as maximally inexistent to such a degree that it is both part and whole or implication and antecedent, but how can this be intelligible yet alone communicable in a world? More than this, what can happen after that? If the consequence of an event is the event, then more than saying there may have been an event, what real-world consequences can this have? Finally, in a world, no object exists absolutely; it only exists maximally. Here one runs the risk of installing inexistence as the Whole, which in fact is true. Badiou never says there is no Whole; rather, he says that the Whole inexists. All the same, absolutism is noncommunicable within a world so the same problem remains: How can events which are the consequence of themselves break out of this absolute circularity such that they can affect the world in which we live in? Badiou gives three solutions.

First, he says yes; at the moment of the event, it consumes the world of those involved absolutely so that 'the unknowns of the Central Committee, politically inexistent in the world of the eve of the insurrection, exist absolutely on the very day of their appearance' (*LW* 378). But this is only an evanescent moment. He explains further: 'The event consumes its own power in its existential transfiguration' (*LW* 378). Such events have no stability so their paradoxical nature is instantaneous and naturally impossible to maintain. Second, he makes the point that the site is itself not the event but the mark of the event after the event has occurred such that the maximality in question 'is the subsisting mark of the event itself in the world' (*LW* 378). What this means in practice is that the absolute nature of the site's inexistence is not a comment on the event as such, but is 'the outline or statement, in the world, of the disappeared event' (*LW* 378). That these statements, by the way inexistence is entirely an issue of Foucauldian communicable statements here, are absolute is impossible in the world for a purpose, Badiou argues. The separation between being and existence as regards inexistence is crucial, not least because, as he says. 'It is through the existence of the inexistent that the subversion of appearing by being, which underlies it, unfolds within appearing itself' (*LW* 378). What he appears to be reaching for here is that the impossible existence of the inexistent in the world, at the absolute level, also impossible, forces the logic of appearance to accept that being as such, on which it is based, will never exist in the world as such. This is for a simple, logical reason. In terms of every object there always exists the minimum which is a component of being which is relationally nil. Speaking of the proclamations of the commune in this light, he says of them that 'these are existents whose absoluteness manifests that an entirely new arrangement of its appearing, a mutation of its logic, has befallen the world' (*LW* 378). They are, in simple terms, statements made in terms of their being statements of a departed impossibility, which can be made, and yet which should not be possible to make. These impossible statements then force the logic of the world to accommodate these new statements through a mutated logic. Badiou does not say if this is a mutation of the logic of appearing, of the conditioned world, or the specific world per se.

Finally third, Badiou argues that 'where existence now stands, the inexistent must return. The worldly logic is not subverted to the point of being able to demand that a logical law of worlds be abolished' (*LW* 379). After all, he reminds us, every object has an inexistent, the minimum. He then applies a phenomenological logic by saying that if the inexistent sublimates itself in absolute existence, albeit for a moment and only as a trace, 'another element of the site must cease to exist, in order for the law to be safeguarded' (*LW* 379). This last point is less clear. Certainly if a minimum becomes maximum and thus inexistence suddenly exists, it does not mean it takes the place of another object in the world as this would imply a finite, closed world. Worlds are not finite. So instead what this has to mean is that no world can be coherent without a minimum. If an object in the world ceases to be a minimum, then another object must become the minimum. There must be a minimum, this minimum is unique, and if the unique minimum has become maximally existent, then by definition whatever takes its place must be different to it.

Logic of the site 5: Destruction

And so we are brought to the last element of the logic of the site, destruction, a term first broached in *Theory of the Subject*[8] and that again seems to be based on empirical observation rather than logical deduction. Speaking of the Paris commune, the creation of the commune, he says, meant the negation of political subordination of the workers, even if the commune as such failed. This is observably but also logically true. If two objects have a relation to a third in that the relation of one object to the third absolutely differentiates it from the other, as we saw in terms of liberals and conservatives in the Oka crisis in Quebec, and the relation between the first object and the third, which was nil, now becomes maximal, then the other object can itself have no relation now to that third without submitting to the envelopment of its opposite.

> What we can say is that there where an inexistent lay, the destruction of what legitimated this inexistence came to be ... if what was worth nothing comes, in the guise of an evental consequence, to be worth everything, then an established given of appearing is destroyed. What seemed to support the cohesion of the world is abruptly turned to nothing.
>
> (*LW* 379–80)

If you think of this formally, if the minimum becomes the maximum first the world now needs a new minimum. From whence will you take this minimum? Well, if the minimum is now maximal, we know that every world also only has one maximal. If then the inexistent has now risen, if only briefly, to the position of maximality, then that which denied the existence of this inexistence before must now be negated. What is this except the transcendental maximal of the whole world? This is because everything that exists exists because it has at least one relation to the maximal object of any world just as it has at least one nonrelation, to the minimum. If the minimum takes on maximal intensity, then the transcendental law of that world is negated and becomes the minimum. It becomes the minimum simply because, it is now minimum and the minimum is unique.

Badiou closes with a simple logical point. If an inexistent is able to rise up in a world to the maximal degree, that world has two choices to make. It can sacrifice the stability of its conditioned logic, or it can sacrifice the stability of the greater logic as such. Naturally it chooses the former option so that the world can live to fight another day. In this way an evental site simply forces the world to abandon its untenable position which is such and such a situation which exists cannot exist. As it does suddenly come to exist, either existence as such is to blame, or the transcendental law of this particular world is at fault. Like Agamben, Badiou's work comes down to a consistent communicable system being forced to accept within the terms of its own logic the inclusion or existence of something which, by their logic, cannot exist, to such a degree that its communicability is rendered noncommunicable. As Badiou says in closing: 'Under the pressure that being exerts on its own appearing, the world may be accorded the chance – mixing existence and destruction – of an other world. It is of this other world that the subject ... is eternally the prince' (*LW* 380).

Beings and events

Something happens – an impossible occurrence, in this world at least. It is real because it predates and exceeds the languages of the possible, and yet still it took place. This event is possible only because the logics of worlds are all constructible, but the consistency of their constructability depends on the possession of the halting point, the void, which is real, because it exists before the notation of its intelligible existence (the axioms of set theory). All axioms of ontological set theory are retroactive; they make legible what already is, for example, actual infinities, so naturally the logical modes of appraising an event are retroactive also. In logic, it is assumed that all objects are predicates of a concept, but an event is impredicative and real. Thus an event is not a logical object; it cannot be captured extensionally by extending a concept into a world and testing its truthfulness vis-à-vis an object. Yet the logic of extension makes sense to some degree. Frege cannot hide the tedium of truth objects, relegating them to a database of known-knowns, leaving the philosopher to pursue not-yet intensional truths which, if proven to be true extensionally, return to the philosopher cognitive value. Yet these are not impossible objects. An impossible extensional truth object is one that exists, and yet is in contradiction, specifically here in contradiction with itself in that it is self-predicating. The reason this is tenable in a logics of words is that while the event is punctual, and worlds are tabular, eventual consequences are linear. Extension is, as the term suggests, a stretching out, a process of growth, a series of local testing of small-scale truth-components of this impossible object in a possible world scenario.

Worlds allow multiples to partially exist and to self-refer to a degree. They also demand a halting point founded on the real of a void, and a maximal delimitation or named actual infinity. Thus an impossible being can be partially possible in a world, thanks to its minimum, all the parts of a being that do not exist in this world, and its self-predication to some degree accepted. No new being can be created, but a part of a being can appear because of its minimum, in this stable world because of the maximal. And if it appears impredicatively, then as that object is impossible, it cannot be absorbed into the becomings of modifications or explained away as fact. Yet does Badiou want events to exist, because he believes in events, or does he want them to exist, because of the destructive effects they have on our worlds? For an object composed of the consequences of a self-mentioned event to develop, point by point, every consequence has to have maximal relation to the initial event. This event, forming a site, is a permanent minimum; it is that part of being that can never appear here in this world because it is an impossible component. If, however, the event relates to this minimum maximally, first it robs the world of its minimum. As there is only one minimum for an object in a world, indeed for a world, then the world in question becomes ill-founded. It needs a unique element to replace the minimum that the event has appropriated, the only one to hand is the maximal. Yet the event has also negated the maximal. An event makes an object's minimum maximal in intensity; it has to by definition because the site can contain only one impossible object, the minimum, and thus every element of a site, there can only ever be one, must be universally exposed and related, meaning the minimum, the only component, is also the maximal. This is weird, but no weirder, as I said, than the generation of literally everything from one, intrinsically self-dividing void set. If the entirety of everything can be generated in this manner, then the possibility of one impossible thing suddenly becomes, well, not so unacceptable.

Yet just as there is only one minimum, and the event has taken possession of it, there is only one maximal, and the event has made the minimum maximal. Thus a world finds itself, due to the event, ill-founded, it has no minimum as halting point, and ill-described, it has no categorical name for the universal exposition of its elements. Suddenly, an ultra-consistent world is, for a moment at least, not consistent. A nonrelation in a world, due to a minimum intensity of relation between two objects, sat left and right, is called into question, and a relation, say between the right and statist interventions, collapses. Simply put, the world at large no longer makes sense, by which we mean its communicable sanctions, in terms of inclusions due to the maximal, and exclusions of the minimum. The logics of worlds breaks. And into the breach, as Badiou says, steps the subject. This, then, finally, is how events function and why, I think, Badiou pursues them relentlessly. Events break worlds whose consistency is founded on being, precisely because of how worlds are founded on being. If it is true to say, due to his committed to the real of the void, Badiou is not a constructivist thinker; I believe we can go one step further and say Badiou is a positivist, destructivist. Logics of worlds is about how to make worlds, so that event can demonstrate the possibility of breaking them.

Book VI

Theory of Points

The theory of points treats the manner by which the step-by-step consequences of an event develop. In particular, it is concerned with the reduction of the infinite number of objects that can be affected by an evental site to a simple yes/no decision. By insisting that the consequences of an event site be dealt with step by step through a simple binary choice procedure, Badiou is able to regiment and control the effective chaos that an event introduces into the order of any world. Yet in truth, his fear is not the chaos of the new but the rapidity by which the new becomes regulated or modified. Points allow for the event to develop slowly and systematically at a local level such that each consequence of the event has a maximal relation to the event through a sequential string of points each of which is tied to its predecessor in terms of maximal relation to the event site:

> While the essence of a generic multiplicity is a *negative* universality (the absence of any predicative identity) the essence of a body of truth resides in certain capacities – in particular, the capacity to deal with a whole series of *points* in the real.[1]

However, if the theory of points vouchsafes the maximal relation between a self-predicating multiple which cannot exist in a world and the objectal consequences of the multiple which can but which are always under threat from becoming simply more modifications, it also explains why there are so few events. At each stage of the development of the consequence of an event, a decision is made, yes or no. If at any stage the wrong decision is chosen, then the event, from this point on, can have no further consequences. This decision also has to be, well, decisive. A weak affirmation is not sufficient as we saw on the previous chapter. The sequential nature of points then has advantages but it is absolutely decisionist and classical. If an incorrect decision is made, then the history of an event's consequences is at an end and it must stand or fall on how 'far' into the world it has progressed from its initial, impossible, existing inexistence.

Yet the existence of an event is not actually a simple yes/no dualism as it is for most, if not all, thinkers of the event. The event happens, so that is always yes. That the event happens as an event in a world however takes time and is in this way a heuristic process. If an event is intervallic, the treatment of its points in contrast is continuous. This is a very important modification in our overall theory of the philosophy of the new. For most theories the new itself is relatively easy to bring about, but its novelty is posed against the background of the already existent and the history of the new is simply how rapidly its impure singularity is betrayed. In contrast, for Badiou the process of treating an event's points is not a depressing set of betrayals but an exciting narrative of new effects. In that for him the event as such is not the absolute moment of the event; what happens after, if handled correctly, can be a long set of subsequent new results. In contrast, if the event as such is taken to be the moment of novelty with no theory of points, of testing or treatment, then it is really only a matter of time before invention becomes convention to use Derrida's terms, or a line of flight becomes territorialized, to use Deleuze's.

A second issue to consider in terms of the theory of points is that it allows Badiou to take an algebraic formulation and convert it into topological considerations, one of the central functional advantages of category theory. For the most part, as we saw, the formal theory of the greater logic emanates from category theory and in particular what is called the Heyting algebra. However, in addition we have been moving ever closer to topological theories which pertain to being-there that are derived mostly from the work of Grothendieck. These two strands of mathematics come together in the idea of the sheaf which is a key concept in algebraic geometry and categories. We could spend a deal of time on the sheaf, but Badiou himself decides not to so we will follow suit. The point is not the technical nature of the sheaf but what the sheaf, in category theory, represents.

Specifically, in treating objects algebraically, in terms of order relation, and spatially, in terms of localization, the theory of points marks the articulation between ontology and logic that is Badiou's ontological innovation. An object can be seen in terms of order relation and in this way maintain its direct basis on several of the foundational tenets of set theory, *and* it can be seen in terms of place, location and localization and so be thought of entirely in terms of worlds. This, as we saw, remains a central pillar in the edifice of Badiou's entire philosophical palace fit for his prince. If an object in the world cannot be shown to have a direct relation of some order to set theory, then objects cannot be called real, the world as a whole cannot be a non-whole consistent set of infinite, immanent becomings and there can be no events. This is why the theory of points is so important. Alone, it merely redescribes what we already know about the relation of objects beneath a transcendental. In this sense the reader need not be dismayed at the change of register because they will soon recognize the same ideas presented slightly differently. In addition, we began in the first chapter with the theory of points. Finally, Badiou explains that in the ultimate sections of the book, formal notation is no longer fundamental to the proof of ideas as it was, but is rather intended as a form of clarity. Thus points are not essential unless they are seen as the means by which an object is both a relation and a localization such that an event site can move from ontology as such to a logic of place or a topology. This then is the final element. You don't necessarily need a theory of points to understand the logics of worlds, but you do need one if you want to develop the possibility of the event confirming our contention that to understand the event is impossible without the addition of category theory.

If I may take you back to the earliest pages of this book, we spent a lot of time on the theory of points in terms of the military decisions of Spartacus. The cavalry of the Roman army operates as a point upon which the rebellious slaves work. They are confronted with the cavalry, and they have to decide what to do about that. If the new body, slave-army, impossible to exist before in the Roman world, wants to carry on existing, it must treat each point in the correct way so that the battle continues and they are not destroyed. Treat this point correctly and there will be others. Each will need to be treated and each treatment will come down to a yes/no decision. Thus we can say that 'in the form of an alternative, a point is transcendental testing-ground for the appearing of a truth' (*LW* 399). Although we call this point a decision, this is but a metaphor. For example, it does not depend on a conscious subject actually deciding something. In fact, the point is topological. It is the 'corporeal localization with regard to the transcendental – which simultaneously spaces out and conjoins the subjective (a truth-procedure) and the objective (the multiplicities that appear in a world)' (*LW* 399).[2]

We can now think of the radical essence of what a point does: 'In brief, a point is the crystallization of the infinite in the figure ... of the either/or, what can also be called a choice or a decision' (*LW* 400). In particular, a point makes all the nuances of a world appear before an instance of the Two which is the yes/no process. This is specifically why a world is not indifferent. Points demand a choice and the choice is classical. Each point takes an infinity of nuance, which can move towards the indifference of chaotic non-differentiation, and ties it down to a determinant difference. At this juncture it must be noted that points are not the exclusive preserve of event sites. On the contrary, all worlds are composed of bodies made up of points making yes/no decisions. This is just another way of saying all worlds are made up of objects in terms of the intensity of their relation. For while relationality sounds modal, and is indeed intuitionistic not classical, the strict ordering of relation tied into the idea of the least great and the largest lesser when relating two objects demands that when it comes to determining the relation between two objects you ask if one is larger than the other or not. So all relations are yes/no and therefore treatable as points of localization if you wish. This, as we said, is the nature of the point, that it allows algebraic relation to be thought of in terms of topology as well. Worlds have to be well-pointed.

A point, and all worlds are made up of objects and points, is the 'correlation of the infinite and the Two' (*LW* 400). Indeed, the whole logics of worlds is encapsulated in this simple formula. As we said choice is a metaphor. There is no decider, no consciousness or agency of choice. Badiou says one should think that the point allows us to think about worlds in terms of choice. Leaving to one side the role of the point as choice in the world as a whole, when it comes to the choice of an event, even though we speak of a subject in terms of the event, there is no actual subject-chooser controlling the point in relation to the world. Instead a point 'is that which the transcendental of a world imposes on a subject-body, as the test on which depends the continuation in the world of the truth-process that transits through that body' (*LW* 400). This then leads to a neat, three-part point-by-point process for the subject-body which perpetually finds itself, in that it is true to the event, 'with its back to the wall' (*LW* 400). First, only two possibilities are presented for the articulation of subject (militant for the event) and the world through an object of the world which is a body. Second, you must choose. Choosing not to choose is possible but it will kill truth immediately. That Badiou references Bartleby the Scrivener here has to be a direct nod to both Agamben's and Deleuze's interest in the suspensive state of impotentiality that Bartleby represents.[3] Finally, once the choice is made, yes or no, one will find that only one of the two choices 'allows for the unfolding of the subjective truth process' (*LW* 400). Thus treating points as consequences of an event site comes down to there being only two choices, having to opt for one or the other, and making the right choice, time and time again. This can be presented as a subject metaphor, one must decide, or an objective one, there are only two possible choices, but in fact the point 'indiscerns' this traditional operation. Yes choice involves subjects choosing in an objective world but after all this time together we know that a subject is not the seat of some coherent agency and that objects are always to be thought of in terms of the logics of worlds based on the reality of being and retroactively applying their differential elements to the indifferent being upon which they depend.

The scene of the points: Three examples

Badiou returns to the ongoing demonstration at the Place de la République. He wants to ask a global question about the demo as a whole to which he can return a binary, yes/no answer. The question is: Does the demo support the current government or not? He says that to do this one would have to 'filter' the complexity of the transcendental 'demonstration' through 'a binary device and reduce the nuances of evaluation to the simplicity that characterizes every choice' (*LW* 403). He seems aware of the dangers of this. Filtration, reduction of nuance and simplicity are all the sacrifices that every scientific mode of reading the world has to contend with. These are opposed to ideas of the frame or filter as being a communicable ideology, the emphasis on nuance and complexity that characterize the non-scientific method that would normally be applied to such questions. He goes further. He believes a yes/no answer would be possible if we moved in a coherent way 'without needing to force or modify the operations of appearing' (*LW* 403). There is a Habermasian 'naivety' here to a degree in the emphasis on a non-violence mode of assessment, but at least the coherence is possible due to the profound consistency of the greater logic. In addition, this logic does not depend on some kind of mutual goodwill; in fact, many of Badiou's examples involve violent confrontation; all the same there is a feeling that one is cramming all the details of the demo into a limited number of reductions. This however is just a feeling or impression. If one wished then one could systematically reduce all the elements that appear to their order relation within the transcendental. The difference being that for other thinkers there would be no end to this process at the lower limits and a theological limit to the process at the upper. Instead, there is a halting point for Badiou, and the infinity of the world and its maximal are both actual, avoiding the onto-theological restrictions of infinity as absolute Whole as Other. Finally, one has to see what can be achieved from all of this. All you would be able to say is that the demonstration, presented as a yes or no answer to a question, 'is a point of that world' (*LW* 403–4). This point 'enacts a kind of abstract regrouping of the multiplicities that appear in the world. Their complex composition is subsumed under a binary simplification' (*LW* 404). Points, effectively, mathematize real-world complexity.

Badiou is willing to sacrifice complexity to simplicity but only inasmuch as you can simplify a point of a world. You have not reduced the world as a whole; rather, you have focused on a point of that world. The world is made up of points. If you wished you could reduce all the objects in it to points, to beings that are there, through the process of localization of one object on another. The addition here is that Badiou is asking for a global point but, logically and mathematically at least, if you accept the premise of the order relation, if you agree with the simple but absolutely revolutionary parameters of the world, then you accept that there can be a global point, just as there can be a truly local point for every appearing object. What are the alternatives?

Badiou now moves to a new example, the plays of Sartre and in particular the means by which they all pivot on a moment of existential choice. In the play *Dirty Hands* the protagonist Hugo must accept to either act on principle or accept that he, like all political beings, has dirty hands through a day-to-day pragmatic acceptance of how things are and the political activity of trying to manage that situation. Traditionally Badiou presents all politics in this reductive binary. The politics of management is that of modifications in the system; the politics of the event or of revolution changes the system. Speaking of politics as management, as governmentality, he says: 'It is the variation of occasions, polymorphous impurity, the sacrifice of everything secondary to everything that is (provisionally) primary' (*LW* 405). The play hinges around the word *recuperation* or salvaging. Can Hugo be salvaged and return to the party by accepting compromise and living with his dirty hands? Hugo forces a point on the party and the whole political situation by reducing the entire play to the simple opposition between that which is salvageable (dirty) and that which is unsalvageable (pure). The result of this is that 'the labyrinth of appearing is thus rectified, re-activated by its projection onto an implacable duality ... a simple choice – a maximal intensity – is obtained through the simple designation of one of the terms' (*LW* 406).

Hugo reduces the complexity of his situation to a single point which is a yes/no answer. He does this by classifying the world under two mutually exclusive predicates, salvageable or not. He then orders these two predicates through the addition of a positive value. Formally was can say of a point that it 'is a type of function which associates, to every intensity of appearing in a world, one of the values of a set with two elements, a maximal element and a minimal element' (*LW* 407). Actually a point is an object viewed from a different angle, not in terms of its relational order but as regards its localization. The issue is not that the point is political, but that if all political activity occurs in the world, then it conforms to the logics of that world, which means we can treat political action in terms of points. What a point does is take an object in the world and define its precise localization such that one can only say yes that object is there or no it is not. If the object is there, because this is an object reduced to its precise point of localization, it is there maximally. If the object is not there, then it has no point of localization and its degree of self-identity at this point is at the minimum. It is not there. What Badiou is able to do then is to force political decisions to conform to a classical logic of true or false; albeit using the intuitionist logic of worlds, these are true or false in this world but they are not absolutely true or false because an object true in this world can be false in another. If choice is of this order, then it is consistent, relational and binary. It also conforms to all the operations of the logic of appearing because actually all it is is an object that appears there. Thus it is party to the envelope, conjunction and so on.

Point and the power of localization

Every point, operating as the Two in relation to the infinite, is localized. This is both its definition, what makes the Two non-abstract (it decides on a specific place) and what differentiates points from objects. This puts meat on the bones of our earlier observation that topology is an alternative way of seeing worlds to that encountered in algebra with certain important methodological implications for Badiou's overall system. If we speak of the logic of appearing, we emphasize certain elements of the algebra of the greater logic, envelopes, degrees of relation of appearing and so on. If, instead, we talk about the form of being-there, we are emphasizing other aspects such as the localization of the multiple, 'that which wrests it away from its simple mathematical absoluteness, inscribing it in the singularity of a worldy place' (*LW* 410). The first thing we can glean from this winnowing process is that localization is more differentiated, more specific, more singular than the order of pure relation. The second, more important in its way, is that the point allows us to think the co-existence of both formal systems, ontology and logic, because the point marks the transition from multiple as abstract mode of relational comparison (object) to point as a localization of a multiple in a place in a world due to its relation to at least one other multiple (place). The point then can think of multiples as both objects and places. 'In other words, the transition between ontology and logic I made visible when we consider the points of the world' (*LW* 410). The theory of points then is a metaphor for the articulation of indifferent being and communicable beings in a world. A second issue is that because points force a decision by which the infinite is dualized due to a specific location in a world, points as decision give a clear indication as to how truths can occur in a world as decision made on an inexistent object.

Interior and topological space

If a point is another term for an object, seen from a different angle, then to localize is another way of saying that you are locating one object in the interior of another. The process of localization consists of taking a multiple or object whose place in the world is already set up and then delimiting the space of the 'new' multiple relative to that multiple. Not really new of course as primarily this is the process we are calling modification. It only becomes new if the object in question is being localized on itself, an event site, or localized on that inexistent multiple, a consequence of an event site. Either way, the issue is that now Badiou asks us to stop thinking in terms of transcendental degrees of intensity and to work instead with the concept of interior and point. With this in mind Badiou educates us as to what is actually meant, mathematically, by topology.

Topology works by distinguishing subsets of a multiple in terms of the subset and its interior. This interior is a subset of the subset. So when you say an object is there, in terms of localization, you mean it is inside the other. Let us clarify this. If you take two subsets of a transcendental of a world and compare them, you will find the following outcomes. They are the same, in which case the degree of intensity of their relation is maximum. They are absolutely unrelated, in which case their relation is minimum, or they have a degree of similarity. If they are the same, then in terms of their existence in the world, although ontologically they are different, logically they are the same, so there is no localization. If their relation is nil, then you are not localizing one on the other. So the final option is that one is bigger than the other. When you localize one multiple on the other, you determine the largest object and you see that all the elements of the other object are a part of the larger object plus at least one other element. This means the first element, being smaller than the second, is a subset of the second larger element which includes it and another element. In this way, you can say that the smaller multiple is inside the larger as everything in the smaller multiple is included in the larger.

This is a crucial distinction, and it requires some formal processes to explain it especially as, in terms of our previous experience of counting multiples in set theory, there was no such theory of interiorization or relational comparison, and as regards category theory, we already argued it is extrinsic not intrinsic. In ontological terms if one object is of a different size than another, it is not 'inside'; it is simply not the other at the local-global level. They are absolutely different in a non-comparative way. The number 5 may contain four elements but it does not contain the number 4. Instead, in the world, the opposite is the case. If an element contains all the elements of the smaller element, it contains that element as we saw. If then we are to think of the world as regards interiorization, then the first axiom we have to agree on is that if we speak of an object as a place, then the interior of that place is identical to itself.

Badiou chooses the new city of Brasilia, founded in 1960, to express how if we want to say Brasilia is a place then the interior of Brasilia *is* Brasilia. An object is determined by the components; it contains, nothing more nothing less. If we establish this, then we might ask can you work out what the interiors of these two interior parts have in common? And further if we have one interior, can we work out what is the interior of the interior? These are just different ways of saying things about objects that we already know. The common part of two interiors is nothing other than conjunction: 'The interior of a conjunction is the conjunction of the interiors' (*LW* 413). His example is Brasilia's south lake and the villas which border it. He says that the gardens of the villa which border the lake are what the two interiors have in common. The garden represents freshness and gentleness as opposed to the thorny limit of the garden at the street level, which signifies hostility. By the same gesture, the lake recalls freshness, as do the cool villas situated on its edge which rest there with an aura of gentility and calm. Thus in reality the garden is not exactly what the two locations have in common. The interior of the garden is actually what the two interiors of lake and villa have in common, which is not the garden itself but what the garden represents: calmness and cool repose. The garden then belongs to the lake as it is its shore, and it belongs to the villa, as it is the garden of the villa, but in terms of the conjunction of lake and villa it brings together these two elements because its interior, coolness, is the same as the interior of the lake and the villa. In contrast, the other edge of the garden, which is hostile, is not shared in common with the lake even if the hedge is part of the garden. Badiou says that if the interiors of two interiors can be said to have the relation of conjunction, then they both share the same interior. Whereas if they share nothing in common, then their interiors can have nothing in common either.

The second question is: Does an interior have an interior? This is actually questioning if an object in a world can have a halting point posed in a different way. He speaks of the Ministry of Foreign Affairs in Brasilia of whose interior space he gives a lovely evocation. Travelling through the different spaces of the building he arrives at a central hall which gives out onto a wonderfully tropical inner garden. This garden is hidden from any external view and from there you can go no further into the building so to speak. He concludes, entering the garden that has almost mythical overtones, 'I can only interiorize this interior and enjoy it from within. When it localises me, the interior has no other interior than itself, reiterated. The interior of the interior is the interior' (*LW* 414).

Badiou summarizes the four features of interiorization:

1. The interior of the set is itself.
2. The interior of a part is included in the part.
3. The interior of the conjunction of two parts is the conjunction of their interiors.
4. The interior of the interior of a part is its interior, not to the point of infinite regress but to the halting point.

These four axioms allow us to map the topology of a multiple, its being there as a point, onto the consistency of defining an object in terms of the order relation. Interior is to space what order relation is to objects in space. More importantly, topology helps Badiou give substance to the complex, paradoxical abstraction of truths in worlds by virtue of points: 'The expression "being-there" takes on its full value. Exposed to points, a truth which finds its support in a body veritably appears in a world as though the latter had always been its place' (*LW* 414). Here Badiou is taking the city to be an event whose truth is found in the body of its architecture and organization of space. Wandering the city at night he says: 'Everything told me that Brasilia's fragments … had incorporated me into the birth of a new world' (*LW* 414). Brasilia is a city that did not exist and then in four years it did. It was the result of only two minds: the town planner, Costa, and the architect, Niemeyer. From the infinity of Brazil's territory a decision was made that forced a truth, a city that did not exist was then made to exist. Niemeyer's great architecture then is a series of points true to that initial site; they are all a consequence of that site. More than this their architectural relations are the site and each other. Each building shares with every other building the same interior and the entirety of the city is its interior. Brasilia then is a strong example of an event, not least because it is an event of space, site, points, decisions and interiors.

The space of points, 1: Positivation of a transcendental degree

We have already seen that greater logic is mappable onto classical logic, just as it works alongside most axioms of set theory, so here we are simply extending that point to present the possibility of a decision in a world of pure communicability such that we can say that decision is true, positive or right, indicated by a 1 as yes, or the opposite, indicated by the 0 as no. In short, 'a point is essentially the binary dramatization of the nuances of appearing' (*LW* 437). For this to function the transcendental of a point, written as T_0, must be homomorphic with the transcendental of the world which it is an interior point of, written T. This makes logical sense but is worth reiterating. Badiou notes in the final section of the book that any reduction of a world to a 1, 0 point must 'conserve the order-relations of the initial transcendental' (*LW* 437). In this way a point must have a traceable relation to the transcendental world it is deciding on and in this sense is local-global. At the same time, because a point is the decision between existing, yes, or not, no, every point has a direct relation to the ontological. The point is an ontological decider after all, the smallest point or object of relation where a being comes to exist in a world. Not only does every point conserve the global of the transcendental, it also preserves the global-local of the ontological whose essence, local-global, it preserves. What this implies is that, as regards the point or T_0, it cannot be the case that a single value of T is assigned to them all, either they are all 1 or they are all 0. Rather, there is always the case that there is one degree that is 1 and another that is 0; otherwise, the Two is dissolved into the infinite communicability of the One or it all being the same relative to the world as such. The complex and nuanced world of communicability is exposed to a yes or no decision by the point, this is its function. 'A point is a kind of analytic mediation between the transcendental complexity of a world (its often non-classical logic) and the (always classical) imperative of binarity or decision' (*LW* 439). Thus a point cannot be indifferent in the intuitionist sense of not yet decided either way. It is decision as such, it is classical and it marks a clear difference.

Our law states that we must find a homomorphism between T and T_0 such that T_0 presents a clear choice between two options of existence. Yet if T is a very complex world full of nuance, then T is simply 'too different' from T_0 and the decision becomes obfuscated or indeed inundated. If, as Badiou claims, the point of the choice is 'that by which a global decision can divide a world, we can see how the question of knowing whether a transcendental world has many points or a few, or even no points at all, carries considerable consequences' (*LW* 440). Specifically, it tells us the kind of world we live in, which Badiou calls atonal or a world so nuanced it has no apparent points. And the kind of world we might live in if we wish to create truths, a tensed world where every object appears to be a point, a life or death decision, which may also be the world in which we are forced to live due to our belief in our atonality.

The decision affects the nature of the interior which defines the topological space of every world thought of in terms of place rather than relational value. One fundamental thing that can be said of any object that is localized is that this object is not the same as the object which localizes it right up to and including the transcendental of the world as such. The interior of A, say Brasilia, is not the same as A, so that while the interior of Brasilia is Brasilia, this does not quite mean what you might take that to mean. Yes Brasilia is made up of everything that is interior to it, but to determine any interior there must be one object larger. This also means that Brasilia is not an absolute whole. If a new town is built close to Brasilia and the two towns expand to such a degree that that they merge, then there is now something interior to Brasilia that was not Brasilia and which is now bigger than Brasilia. Either this new entity is a new transcendental sense of Brasilia, or it is a different object which has interiorized Brasilia. The point here is that being the interior of a T is not simply the same as belonging to T. 'A topological space is a multiplicity such that the predicate "being in", in the sense of "being there", is separate from the predicate "being an element of"' (*LW* 441). The significance is that this being the case, localization is very different from just appearing. Localization ties one object to the interior of another. If you then want to find the interior of this interior, you can, all the way down to the halting point, which is, of course, always a point: Does this object appear in this world or not? Localization in the world works like deduction works in ontology. At any point, if you wish, you can trace the descent of this object all the way down to the zero point where you can be absolutely sure that the object exists and you can trace how it does so.

To recap, a point designates a choice between two mutually exclusive objects, and it does so by saying the choice of one object is the good one or the true, meaning the choice of the other must be false. As we saw in the case of Quebec's politics, however complex a situation is, all can be reducible to a commutative triangle of relations such that the support say of liberals for the Indians means that their opposition to those opposed to the Indians must reduce in direct proportion. Specifically, Badiou considers Brasilia in this regard. The city has a north/south and east/west axis. The north and the south are mainly made up of residences and while some government buildings and I suppose different levels of residence exist, the difference between north and south, dramatized by the planning of the city, is weak. In contrast, the west of the city contains industry, the rail system, military settlements and so on, while the east contains the lovely villas of the despicable rich presenting a very strong contrast or a strong point, as might be the point between the villas and the dwellings of the poor, for example. For Badiou the points of the interior of the world summarize that world in terms of its being-there, in particular along lines of conflict or contradictions. This is a profoundly Marxist reading that I will leave others to contend with but, suffice it to say, if one can reduce the complexity of a world to a series of interior points which are formally decisive then yes, one can provide a formal basis for the post-Marxist philosophy of Badiou and others. This is by far the more convincing path than the one proposed, say, by *Being and Event* such as it is presented in the work of Norris, for example.[4] Here, conflict is formally enshrined in the logic of every world, if you go looking for it.

More than this the points, which are summaries of the world, present points within the whole world that 'space out' this world. They provide, in other words, that missing level in Badiou's consideration of the world. As we said when addressing a world in Badiou's terms, within the confines of the minimal and the maximum, everything else, which is almost everything else necessarily, is relationally present in the same way. Yes envelopes allow us to group objects together, but envelopes of envelopes of envelopes in an infinite world in the end present us with the same problem of conception. The issue is that worlds can be logically deduced but they cannot be conceptually held in our consciousness. Points instead allow us to gather together moments in a world around a commonality of choice or opposition. Summarizing points of conflict in a world results in a précis of the world due to headings pertaining to conflictual points. In the large majority of all of Badiou's examples, points of conflict that can be resolved through complex negotiation, compromise and so on or Sartre's dirty hands are presented as negative, while those resulting in radical or violent change, war, suicide and so on are presented as positive. That said, here he is clear that low subjective intensity through negotiation opposed to the rage of violent refusal can only be fully evaluated based on context: 'To know which of the two terms of the Two is positive depends on the context' (*LW* 417).

The space of points, 2: The interior of a group of points

Badiou moves on to combine the theory of points with that of topological interior in a simple way. He argues that a subgroup of elements or points which all 'positivate a degree of intensity of appearing' can be said to be an interior that is postivated: 'the union of all the positivizations which are parts (or subgroups) of the group in question' (*LW* 418). The interior of a group of points is made up of what the group contains 'in terms of an integral affirmative resource in the world' (*LW* 418). One can perhaps see where he is going with this. A normal group, or subgroup, does not have to contend with binarism to be in possession of an interior. In this instance, the interior of any group is relatively free. It consists simply of those elements that conform to the generalized relational law. In the case of points they also conform to the < symbol, but in this instance the symbol is strictly curtailed so that it always reads $0 < 1$. If you want to group together a number of points, it must be strictly regulated in that every point must conform to the transcendental positive decision, yet of course not be the same as that decision in terms of identity. This is a peculiar stipulation as it determines not only degree of relation but absolute degree: the point must agree absolutely with the localization that is imposed upon it. Badiou now returns us to the four axioms of interiorization which he applies to prove that a group of positivizations conform to the same laws of the interior as any group. Although we will not consider the proofs here, the point is important for Badiou as he is using points as a means of developing the topography of an object that is the consequence of the event. What positivization does, in short, is allow on one side the progress of subjective testing of the event site point by point through a simple judgement; yes, this is a consequence of the event or no it is not. At the same time however this reductive mode of relationality still conforms to the general laws of being-there in terms of interiority and so, step by step, the event-group, if we can call it that, or the group of truth, can expand, point by point, with each point being an object in the world which, however, is postivized and thus conforms to the original decision of the event.

Atonic and tensed worlds

Atonic worlds are worlds of indifference. They are a significant development in the theory of communicability and more widely the importance of Badiou's work, even if he spends little time on them. The atonic world is the world of democratic materialism that we live in. It is defined, as we saw, by a constructivist commitment to truthless consistent logical worlds and, paradoxically, a deconstructivist (in broad terms) commitment to the destabilizing of said worlds by the philosophy of difference. Badiou says, 'A world is said to be *atonic* when its transcendental is devoid of points' (*LW* 420). He believes that there are degrees of atonality I suppose in that he defines our world as markedly atonic. In that atonic worlds are simply all communicable worlds; however, I would contend that no world is more atonic than any other, except for worlds which are tensed. Tensed worlds are where every degree in the world is a point. Naturally these are the opposite of atonic worlds but other than that it seems to be a defining feature of all worlds that they are atonic in their entirety until they are not. This would be in keeping with what Badiou has said so far. Atonic worlds then are totally communicable. This does not mean they are delimited. There is an infinite amount of modification available to an atonic world in fact so that if we follow Badiou's theorem that there are degrees of atonality, we can see that a world which emphasizes the communicability of change to the degree that our world does, along with communication, choice and the technological pursuit of novelty, will be more powerfully atonic because it has taken the values of change and augmented them to such a degree that change becomes the stable basis of this world. While I cannot say our world is more atonic than other worlds therefore, I can accept that if a world takes change as its transcendental, as ours has done since the onset of modernity, then this is a world where real change is harder to see, because there is so much general change around.

In these worlds without points there are no possibilities for subjects to take up truths because there are no decisions to be made: everything is equally as valid as anything else. Thus it makes sense, Badiou says, for the world of democratic materialism to have dissolved the idea of truth into the dual forms of bodies and languages. Bodies become our 'truth' or right to life; languages are reduced to our right to express ourselves, however we see fit. The combination of bodies as subjective possession and languages as universally equal means that democratic materialism has been able to transform difference into the indifference of equivalence. As regards life, we all own our own life but the singularity of this life is indifferent of course, both as neutral principle and as a means of imposing non-relationality onto our existence: we exist in our bodies but our bodies do not exist together in a larger body. As regards language, the paradoxical result of absolute differential relativism is, as we have seen, bad indifference.[5] Without points, a world which takes change as its transcendental becomes, paradoxically, a world in which change stops being different and all our differences become indifferent, just as all our concepts of identity become indifferent too. In this world, Badiou says, nothing happens, everything is managed, except death which we do our best to immunize and defer, Foucault's definition of the imperative of the biopolitical to make live, or which we export to our many deathworlds and bloodshops that we have established through post-colonial exclusion throughout the developed world. Badiou says, 'Atonic worlds are simply worlds which are so ramified and nuanced – or so quiescent and homogenous – that no instance of the Two, and consequently no figure of decision, is capable of evaluating them' (*LW* 420). The millennial dilemma: in a world where everything can be opted for, nothing can be chosen.

We now move on to an important aspect of the theory atonal worlds, that of the isolate. Badiou comes up against the relation between atony 'and the impossibility of solitude (universal "communication")' (*LW* 421). In an atonal world every object is communicable with every other object, and any new object that appears in that world is instantly ramified across the whole network of objects, or at least there is nothing to stop it being. This is true even of objects who deny communicability with some objects, in that they still appear in the world and so are communicable with the same transcendental as the envelope in question even if they do not communicate with that object. A simple law of appearing: no object appears in the world nonrelationally. After Deleuze, every object is a series even if it is a series of itself and the transcendental and nothing else. If an object appears, it appears in relation. And if it appears in relation, it cannot stop further relations being developed either. There are, therefore, no 'isolates' in a communicable world, no singularities. 'Let us call "isolate" a non-minimal degree of positive intensity such that nothing is subordinated to it, except for the minimum. In other words, there is nothing between it and the nothing. Where everything communicates infinitely, there exists no point' (*LW* 421). The isolate is another name for the atom of an object at the point of its reality. This is the non-decomposable unit that is found at the base of every world, every object in that world, every envelope and every atom. Badiou says correctly that this is the halting point and then goes on to say that in every atonic world there must be a halting point. Let's consider this for a moment.

By our reckoning every world is atonal. An atonal world is so ramified that it has no points. These points can be called isolates. Isolates are the smallest possible elements of any world. They cannot be decomposed. If you want to relate to them, they force you to answer yes or no. Yes, they exist in this world at the smallest possible level, or no, they do not exist in this world. The problem here is that all worlds are based on the halting point. It is not the case that atonal worlds are or are not capable of halting points. For the greater logic to function as it does, you will recall, it needs a halting point, along with a maximum that is not a whole and a degree of relation. This is also the basis for Badiou's belief in events. For any object to enter into a world, it must first of all be a point if it is an atom. The question is, does this being have any relation to this world, yes or no? It is this basic fact of all objects in a world that opens then up to the possibility of that brief, short-circuit where an object is allowed to appear in a world as the inexistent, the object with no relations, the event. At this moment the object is a no, it has no relations, but you have said yes to it, 'I' will relate to it. This is how events find sites in worlds.

The 'decisionist' nature of Badiou's philosophy is where it stands or falls. There is no yes or no ontologically, but the proof of pure Being is such that it first allows one to construct a logics of worlds that is real and not constructible, such that paradoxical objects can appear in that world as inexistent and then operate in that world as isolates forming connections with other isolates due to their being points. There may not be atonic worlds but there may be worlds which are atonic in terms of their transcendental or how they are conditioned and so on. In fact, Badiou ends by saying that 'declaration of the atony of a world might be simply ideological' (*LW* 422). If this is found to be true, then in every world of self-declared atony, the subject must search for a point that is noncommunicable, to which they say yes. Importantly for our perspective Badiou ends this provocative study of the atonal with a quote from Rene Char which supports our own insistence on the relation of worldly atony to the fact of discursive, constructible communicability: 'It is necessary to "forever close the crystal shutters over *communication*"' (*LW* 422). In any world, in fact, it is necessary for an isolate to refuse worldly communication so that it can say yes to a point.

In contrast to atonic worlds, in tensed worlds 'each key moment is an isolate on which one must ground a decision' (*LW* 423). As opposed to atonic worlds which, for me, are all worlds as pure communicability, tensed worlds remain mysterious. They are surely worlds 'under creation' due to commitment to truth and Badiou's examples are from characters trying to negate atonic relativism and push for day-to-day truths. Badiou's position is that most worlds are neither tensed nor atonic and that 'between atony and tension, we wager our worlds, according to opposite imperatives: to find peace within them or to exceed, point by point, that which in these worlds merely appears' (*LW* 424).

Being, event, consequences

Atonic worlds test the limits of our own dual thesis, that being is indifferent and worlds are communicable. Atony, after all, is a meaningless decision or an example of Kant's indifferentism raised up to a principle of life. Democratic materialism argues that because each human life is special, tense, then all human life is sacred, atonic, because human life is radically dissimilar to life as such, tensed; yet, it is animal life as such that we all share in common, atonic, such that we can then aggregate all human life together as uniquely of value, tensed, meaning that we can protect it in a law of universal human rights to life, atonic. This constant interchange between the common, atonic components, and the proper, tensed units, is after all the basis of our reading of the role of indifferential suspension in Agamben's devastating critique on metaphysics, with specific emphasis on the philosophy of difference. If we now consider language, the inability in democratic materialism to favour one utterance over another, because all statements, being truthless, are equally true, means that Kantian indifferentism exists at the level of not only bodies, but also statements, albeit for different reasons. Truthless languages are, I have argued, all atonic at the level of the transcendental, by which is meant no language, no world, no situation can be chosen over any other. In other words, if all worlds are atonic, because their content doesn't matter unless it is subject to truth, then also the relation between worlds is also atonic, no world is better than any other.

I have termed communicability the function of meaning, discourse, power, existence, thanks to category theory founded on the indifference of multiples in extensional, axiomatic set theory. It has a basic maxim, not what is said, the meaning of what is said, but that it can be said. This is the functional effect of the transcendental logic in Badiou typified by the law of universal exposition. What communicability reveals, actually, is that in worlds defined by relationality, in other words languages made up entirely out of differentialism, without a theory of truth, then all said differences, in all their infinite nuance are, in the end, atonic, flaccid, indifferentiated. Does this not account for the two-millennia-long war on indifference in Western thought, the secret intuition that identity-difference metaphysics is, in the end, perpetually destined to arrive at indifferentism? This is another way, I suppose, of saying why we need to choose the event, because the event is not just a radical, pure difference as such, it is also the only source of any kind of differentiation, any manner of meaningful difference. All worlds appear to be fated to arrive at slackness, but after an event, for a glorious period of years, sometimes decades, pointed worlds thanks to event sites, instigate an actual infinity of perhaps daily decisions which actually matter, are tensed. Sure, over time, they come to matter less, certainly it all ends up at atony eventually, but in the meantime, perhaps answering Andrew Gibson's question re: intermittency, conversations take place, actions occur, which appear to matter. Which requires that we think differently about the duration of the event, putting aside the glamour of the revolutionary moment, embracing instead the hard graft of the innumerable post-revolutionary moments where all appears lost, people seem to be about to lose their way, betrayals occur, unpopular decisions need to be made, friendships and relationships suffer, and there is no end to the choices one has to make. Another way to express this is not so much being and event than the habituation of non-transcendental decisions. Not so much being and event as being, event and consequences. Perhaps not logics of worlds, but rather communicability of worlds, because, after all, it is the noncommunicability of the consequences of events, subjectivated into a noncommunicable body, that we are really reaching after.

Book VII

What Is a Body?

In Badiou's general guide to the ideas resulting from *Logics*, his *Second Manifesto of Philosophy*, he makes a definitive statement as to the nature of truth: 'A truth is, then, an event having vanished whose unforeseeable body the world causes to appear little by little in appearing's disparate materials' (*SM* 90). A clear enough statement however makes little or no sense unless you understand what a body is. It is not that Badiou has not already mentioned the importance of the body; in fact, in this final book we have come full circle as Badiou promised that we would. If I can take you back for a moment, we began our reading of *Logics of Worlds* with a proposal as regards the subject and a body. There he said that the body was the worldly dimension of the subject to truth through a point-by-point fidelity to the consequences of an eventual site. Yet at that nascent stage we can hardly be said to be in a position to understand what he really meant by this statement, and he could not at that early point prove the body in any formal way which meant the subject, which depends on a body as the material support for the truth it is faithfully perpetuating by testing, could be nothing other than a proposal. Now, at the very end of the study of the laws of appearing and change, we arrive at what Badiou calls the '"useful" distillate of such a construction: we are able to answer the question "What is a body?"'. This is because the body is a material support for subjective formalism and so is able to play the role of 'agent of a possible truth' (*LW* 451) or we are therefore dealing with what Badiou calls the physics of the body, but best not to get into that phrase as he does not, for example, propose a new, empirical means of dealing with the body. Instead, he recaps the entire 'conceptual strategy that authorizes us to conclude with this physics' (*LW* 451). Before we get into the detail of that which in fact is simply a brilliantly useful summary of the whole book, what matters is the method he has used to prove that bodies exist such that subjects can operate in worlds on behalf of, or due to, truths. It may seem odd to write a complex and brilliant study of worlds, only so as to justify a tiny part of those worlds that destabilizes a profound consistency which, before *Logics of Worlds*, Badiou did not believe had ever been demonstrated by constructivist philosophies of communicability: namely all linguistic-logical theories of being. Yet there is, as ever, method in this madness. Badiou is simply applying to philosophy a retroactive axiomatic method of mainstream mathematics.

Badiou's axiomatic retrogradation across the two volumes of the Being and Event project to date is as follows. What if there were an event? What good would this do for me? What good might it do for the world? Then, if there is an event, what could I use to axiomatically prove that at the very least you cannot say there is not an event? If I can show that nothing can disprove the event, and I can also show benefits to there being an event, perhaps empirical traces in history that suggest events are the only way of explaining certain occurrences, then there is an event in the same way as there is actual infinity or the axiom of choice. However, the process for him is a good deal more complex than for a mathematician. First of all, while there are axioms in philosophy, none of them are able to prove pure being as such without recourse to aporias and onto-theological positions. The result of this has been some philosophers have denied that the question of being is anything other than a metaphysical pseudo-problem, or they have reconfigured being as somehow the narrative of its own metaphysical demise. You are, in other words, an analytical or continental philosopher. Plus, the axiomatic split in philosophy is profound, meaning no philosophical argument will convince the majority of philosophers. More than this, if being helps Badiou because it leads to the event, analytical and continental philosophers work day by day producing countless millions of words all due to the fact that pure being as such is not possible. Faced with the problem of communicable transmissibility, Badiou turns to mathematics for his axioms, a relatively neutral field as most philosophers have a grudging respect for it. In mathematics first he finds the problem of pure being, that being is-not, has been solved decades before without a shadow of a doubt if you are a mathematician. Being then gives Badiou, eventually, the event, the entire purpose of *Being and Event*. The proof of being means you cannot say there is not an event, but the axioms that give you this result ban said event from being produced in being.

Although Badiou tries to lever the event into being in situations due to the subject at the end of *Being and Event*, successfully enough to convince many readers, it appears he remained unsatisfied. It takes nearly twenty years before the second half of the axiomatic, retrogressive proof of the event is complete. Forcing the event due to ontology by paying the price of forcing the event from ontology, *Logics of Worlds* establishes a second axiomatic proof. This time he says, supposing that events cannot be found in pure being, what if they existed instead in the world? How could that happen? Here he realizes that the interdiction against self-predicative nonrelational multiplicities is extremely strong. If an event appears, it appears as an object and if it appears as an object, it is the predicate of at least one concept, the transcendental of that world. More than this, if an event is to be truly new, it must be nonrelational, and if it is nonrelational by definition it inexists in this world. However, he realizes that basing a consistently constructivist world on ontological axioms he gives to constructivist and deconstructivist thinking the one thing they lack: truth, reality, a proof of a material, thinkable precedent to language. At the same time the articulation of ontological and logical means that there are objects which can 'exist' in a nonrelational fashion. All worlds are based on them: they are the inexistents of the minimum. This allows him to say that while something impossible in being really is impossible, something impossible in the world simply means it inexists in that world, although it may be ontologically mundane and possible in any number of other worlds. Pronouncing that something inexists in a world is actually saying a being has not yet become an object in this world. Finally, he realizes that if certain aspects of set theory make it possible to assert the event, some elements of category theory make it possible to assert the site of an event. In particular, self-predicative sets are more possible there, as an object can be considered as the relational identity to itself only. As such it inexists constructively in a world, a function that has a name; it is called the minimum. If one can take the minimum, which is unique and a singularity, and relate it to itself as its own maximum, which in fact it is, remembering that the maximum is also a singularity because it is unique, you have the basis for the construction of a body in a world made up of relational identities built from its own inexistence rather than through relating these elements to the existence of objects already in the world. Perhaps you can even make objects that exist in the world relate to this new body in such a way as they inexist in the world so as to exist in the world of the inexistent. There is nothing logically to stop this in theory.

Thanks to these logically consistent circumlocutions, the axiomatic wager is back on. Set theory cannot prove the event; it just cannot disprove that events might exist. If events exist, they must do so in situations in the world or what he ends up just calling worlds. Worlds do not want events; indeed, the modifications that are objects in the world make real change impossible. Yet all the various logics of worlds have failed to fully found themselves. No constructivist or deconstructivist theory can be more than a language game. Ontology, however, can found worlds. If you link a communicable world to ontological set theory, you can benefit from a halting point, a One that is not whole, and an actual rather than onto-theological infinity. Any theory of worlds benefits immensely from this trade-off. Innumerable problems about worlds disappear and innumerable new things you can do with worlds become possible. However, if you accept that set theory founds logic, then you have to accept the consequences. The first is that set theory says you cannot say there are no events. The second is that the axioms of set theory that you value mean you cannot disallow inexistent objects to be self-predicating and, through yes/no decisive points, proliferating to the point where they become bodies. Bodies then are nothing other than objects that are built out of pointed, value-judged relations (yes/no), to that initial, inexistent, self-predicating multiple, that worlds cannot say do not exist because these minimum multiples are what the consistency of material worlds depend on in a manner parallel to the fact that all sets are based on the inexistence of the void.

Badiou says that he began the second volume by taking the existence of bodies for granted. From that 'we exhibited subjective formalisms capable of being "borne" by such bodies' (*LW* 451). The rest of the book then explored the possibility of such bodies made of points due to a self-predicative eventalic site and found that, given all that I have just said, one cannot say they do not exist. Therefore, if it can be shown that it is good that they do, then like the axiom of choice, you are well on the way to proving this to be the case. Our third axiomatic retrogradation is rather simple. If bodies existed, is there anything to stop subject-truths existing? No, there is not. Leaving us with a simple question of communicability: Do you want them to exist, are there benefits gained from their existence, do old problems resolve themselves and new possibilities open up? Badiou says yes, and for the most part readers of Badiou have agreed.

The formal complexity of this is almost overwhelming, I hope we have made it, in the end, palatable, but to say that this is a result of formalism is to ignore the profound communicability at the heart of this. After all, the two questions of axiomatic retrogradation are both questions of communicability. The first is, what are the benefits of this existing? This is tested against a communicable mainstay, not does this actually exist but what happens amongst us as a community of I say that it exists. It is not the meaning of actual infinity that mathematicians consider, they leave that to the philosophers, but the efficacy of its existing. The second test is equally communicative. If I say this exists because I get benefits from it if it does, is there anyone or anything out there that will say no to this? Basically, if I adhere to the axioms of my community, and the basic formal laws of my conditioned world, recursive deductive reasoning, then there is no one who can say it cannot exist. In other words, the communicable discourse of mathematics has no power to say I cannot say that. What this allows is that a mathematical truth like actual infinity is not accepted because it is true, but because there is nothing about its proofs that does not communicate with mainstream mathematical practice, and there are many things about its existence which means mathematicians will benefit from its existing. Here we have the basic law of communicable existence: an object, here an axiom, exists if it adheres to the formal laws of that world, and if it can find commonality with other objects in that world, other theorems or mathematicians, such that they can relate to this object. In the end, it would seem, retrograde axiomatic reasoning is another, more formal name for the single logic of all worlds, one which I am calling communicability.

Badiou takes us through the steps of his axiomatic retrogradation. The first level of analysis is that of the transcendental relation resulting in three types of appearing: minimum, conjunction and the envelope. He usefully renames these the inapparent (which by definition is inexistent also), co-appearance and infinite synthesis. The second is the nature of the object, in particular its materialism due to the theory of the atom and the reciprocity between being and appearing. Finally, he considers the relations that exist between objects. This leads to the powerful observation of the universal exposition of all objects in the world due to relations, which is another way of saying in a world all objects are communicable to the degree of making the world atonic. From this triumvirate of transcendental, object and relation we end up with a world of absolute consistency based on relations between objects such that all relations are universally exposed. Thanks to this locked-down world Badiou is then able to propose the difference between modifications, facts and real change. Here he defines the site as 'an object of the world that globally falls under the laws of differentiation and identity that it locally assigns to its own elements. It *makes itself* appear' (*LW* 452). Finally, we have what we came for, to some degree, around a thousand pages ago, a clear and consistent definition of the event. The event, he goes on, 'is a site which is capable of making exist in a world the proper inexistent of the object that underlies the site. This tipping-over of the inapparent into appearing singularizes – in the retroaction of its logical implications – the event-site' (*LW* 452). May I just say that, for me at least, this is the first complete theory of the event in Badiou's oeuvre. An object which inexists in a world, and we have explained how this can be, comes to exist in a world in this protected site where its singularity is not lost to modification by the site disallowing the object to relate universally to all other objects. Categorization is basically stymied.

Instead, the object relates to itself to such a degree that the initial impossibility of such self-predication is proven possible by the retroactive application of the logics of appearing to the site as the object in the site. The body, in fact, starts to establish relations.

As this is the first time we can really understand Badiou's event, let us now come at it in a different way. An event gives birth to a new 'world'. But new worlds can be created all the time, in that any envelope, and thus any object, can be taken as a world, the minimum size of any world is one object related to the transcendental, which is also an object therefore. Thus a new world cannot be just another world. Instead a new world, which is also very small initially, only one element and that is inexistent, is created from within an existent world. Its novelty is that it inexists in a world due to the logic of a world that says its existence is impossible in a constructive and banal sense (all words are founded on such an inexistent minimum). This new world grows inside an old world and structurally echoes the old world in terms of its logical relations. It, however, differs in two clear aspects. The first is that the new world is in an old world in a nonrelational fashion. The second is that as it grows through cultivating relations called consequences, it does so through points. Points are important as 'the theory of points allows us to broach the qualitative difference of worlds' (*LW* 452). Points are qualitatively judged, binary relations. They are special relations. For example, they are not universally exposed. If you want to relate to a point you have to wait your turn, as pointed objects grow in a linear, point-by-point, rather than a tabular all at the same time, manner. Second, you need to pass a test. Some objects the point will say yes to, others no. Finally, if the point says yes to an object in the old world, that object now relates to the inexistent object which is the eventual site. To do this it has to now inexist in the world in which it existed. Slowly, precariously, ascetically, judgementally, a new world can drain an old world of its objects, converting them into points, building a body point by point.

Finally, we are left with the body. The body is a singular object with the qualities I have just outlined. It provides the material support for what Badiou calls the subject: 'The immanent agent of the production of the consequences (of a truth), or the possible agents of their denial' (*LW* 453). Subjects may be people but as we know they are not subjective consciousnesses such as you might expect from any of the philosophical traditions, in particular phenomenology, excluding, according to Badiou, Lacan. As you can see, there is a retroactive relation between subject and object or a co-belonging if you prefer. An object supports the subject, but the subject is the agency of acceptance or denial of every point that is added to the object. As the object supports the subject it also supports its subjective formalism, which is worth revising here. We have, you recall, the five operations that organize the field of the subject: subordination, erasure, implication, negation and extinction or −, /, →, ¬, =. Then we have the event accessed only through the trace of its having vanished, careful not to confuse that with a Heideggerian trauma of being as always in withdrawal, although Badiou draws on this quite extensively: the present, which is the predicate attributable to consequences of the event as they unfold, point by point, in present time; the typology of different subjects, faithful, reactive and obscure; and finally the operations that can be derived from the types of subject, specifically production, denial, occultation and resurrection.

Badiou then closes this summary with the following maxim: '*A multiple-being which bears this subjective formalism and thereby makes it appear in a world receives the name of "body" – without ascribing to this body any organic status*' (*LW* 453). I don't think we need to add anything to this. Badiou however reminds us of the precarity of the body based on the five operations that be believes control it. As it can never be a closed whole, a successful body encountered at any point is always under erasure, never complete; yet, it still may serve as a material support for an evental trace, giving force to the production in the present of a faithful subject. Erasure is one of two functions that repress the body, the other being – subordination, operations which are dominated by the negation of the evental trace rather than the production of a body. This results in the material extinction of the present of the event in the form of the reactive subject. In addition, the subject may fall prey to a kind of self-abnegating, self-negation as it erroneously negates the evental trace through the failures of its point-by-point inquiries, the so-called obscure subject. In short, as we have always known, there are very few events because, as we finally realize, the processes of subjectivation are so delicate. Which leaves us with the final question of the study: given the precarity of the body, what is a body, what is the nature of its appearing, specifically 'what marks out a body among the objects that constitute the appearing of the world?' (*LW* 454). This is what the last sections of the whole study set out to explain.

Birth of a body: First description

Valery's remarkable poem, 'The Graveyard by the Sea', is Badiou's chosen example to illustrate the body. The poem describes a world of sun and sea viewed from the location of a cemetery. The sea is 'below' the sun and is thus a sub-object of the sun. Both sun and sea can be seen from the cemetery which then is the pullback or exponention of the relation sun–sea.[1] From the cemetery it can be seen that the sea is totally determined by the sun; thus, the sun is the consequence of the sea which it totally envelopes. For Badiou more generally the surface of the sea is like any world so that the 'sun' 'is that facet of the world the sea-surface takes as its fixed point, its undivided unity' (*LW* 456). In that the cemetery is the exponention of the sea–sun relation, the objects that compose the interior of the cemetery, 'make legible the founding relation' between sea and sun, at least in the way the poem presents them in its 'world'. The introduction of the dead, of monuments and so on results in a description of 'an immobile world, devoid of transformation, a world in which appearing validates Parmenides' ontology' (*LW* 457), and that of the eleatics in general which are invoked later on in the poem as 'cruel'. The poet himself then tests the veracity of the atonic world of sea–sun death and makes clear his desire to escape from it, only to find that at every turn his being is determined by the atonality of this world. At this point the poet gives into the cruel Eleatic logic of Zeno only to then make a clear, pointed decision. He literally says, 'No, no! The future years unfold,/Shatter, O body, meditation's mould' (*LW* 457). Yet, Badiou says, it is not an act of will by the poet-subject that brings real change but the sea itself which allows itself to be transformed by its relation to the mobility of the wind, rather than the hieratic stillness of noon. The wind also refreshes the poet and the atonal, indifferent and reflexive surface of the sea, reflecting only the immobility of the sun, is not broken by the power of the wind. The poet flees the cemetery declaring, 'Let's run at the waves and be hurled back to the living' (*LW* 458).

Badiou notes that in the world of the poem, the world [sea] is 'ontologically invariable'. It is always the sea we are talking about, always the same being. 'What is modified or reversed is the transcendental value of its appearing', initially under the sway of the object sea, now under the sway of the object wind. This also negates the exponention of the cemetery pullback. It is no longer possible to see the sea in full from the perspective of the dead; instead, the poet has to run to the beach or leap into the sea, as is indicated by a central line in the poem 'The sea, the sea, forever starting and re-starting'. Seen from the perspective of the pullback of cemetery observing the relational subordination of sea, world, to sun, power of universal relation to produce atony, this means nothing changes, everything is mere modification. Seen instead from the perspective of being in the sea as the wind disperses the indifference of its surface, means instead a present tense, point-by-point experience of the infinite difference of the sea, perhaps to the point that poet must risk, even lose, his life to drowning.

Badiou sums it up as follows. The world has four objects: sun, sea, the dead and poetic consciousness. The first three objects are universally exposed, 'testifying to their immobile equivalence, their Eternal Return into the Same' (*LW* 459). They are indifferently atonal. Consciousness is the inexistent of the place. It is the poet who struggles to find a place in the world of natural indifference; remember he says no to it yet is forced to succumb to it, which is a typical example of the inexistent described so well in *Being and Event*. At this point, 'in the pure vanishing image of its "elusive foam" the sea is abruptly revealed to be a site, which plunges into the furore of its own evaluation' (*LW* 459). Thanks to this the sea, previously an object in a world, instead drops out of the world to become a site. This is because it allows the inexistent, consciousness and life itself, to 'exist maximally'. Badiou ends by saying 'where the empty excluded of the place used to be there now stands a body capable of breaking the "pensive form" of its submission' (*LW* 459). A body is born in other words, so now what is it composed of?, he ruminates.

Birth of a body: Second description

Poetry is one thing, what about its formal opposite which is, according to Badiou, mathematics? His second example of a body is when the mathematician Galois reconfigures the essence of algebra replacing the analysis of calculations with, instead, a consideration of structures, in particular the nature of the permutations between numbers. This he inherited from the mathematician Legrange who stopped looking for the formulae that would provide solutions and instead looked at the 'functions that link these solutions to one another' (*LW* 461). The idea of groups and bodies, the basis of modern mathematics, was born. As previously mentioned mathematical examples work particularly well for events because the theory of the event is mathematical in essence. In particular, Galois' formula 'the analysis of analysis' gives us a strong sense of the abstract evental nature of the work he was pursuing just as his letters from the time reveal his self-consciousness which Badiou makes much of. At the end of the rather lengthy analysis, Badiou abstracts six levels or degrees of the Galois event, transforming algebra from the consideration of numbers to that of functions. They are useful, I think, for answering questions as to how events come about. First, Galois defines the world he is 'inexistent' in, that of complex, algebraic calculations. Second, he takes the 'stopping-block' of that world, which is that they were unable to take calculations using radical beyond the fourth degree. We don't need to dwell on the meaning of this, its importance being merely that this stopped the thinkers of this world going beyond their accepted methods. Third, Cauchy did develop a theory of permutations, but it 'remained disjoined from any overall vision of algebra' (*LW* 465). In this way we could say his breakthrough was akin to a fact, or perhaps a weak singularity. This implied, fourth, that there did inexist in the world of maths the idea that algebra is the process of 'operating on operations' (*LW* 465), not pursuing ever more complex calculations up to the stopping-point. Five, for Galois, this theory of equations operates as a site for possible new ideas, in particular the analysis of analysis, rather than a stopping-block. Finally, six, 'the fundamental concepts put to work in this site, in particular those of groups, invariants and normal subgroups, sublate the inexistent, and this sublation polarizes the constitution of a new theoretical body' (*LW* 466).

Thus we now have two opposing considerations of the formation of a body, the first is poetic, while the second example is self-predicative in a way as it is the example of the development of the algebraic consideration of structures, functions and groups which first will give rise to set theory and then category theory. In the remaining pages Badiou sticks to these two examples to first show how once a body is born we can define its components. For example, in Valery's poem the body is made up of elements of the sea, responding to the storm 'which entertain with the resurrection of the inexistent (consciousness and life) a relationship of maximal proximity. The function of appearing identifies as far as possible these elements (huge air, wind's reviving, exploding wave …) to what has become … the site's central referent: the inexistent suddenly raised to the maximal degree of existence' (*LW* 466). Hence the elements of a body are those 'whose identity with the becoming existent of the inexistent is measured by the intensity of their own existence' (*LW* 467). In other words, they place the totality of their existence into their relation to the identity of the trace of the event, removing them from the possibility of their forming relations with anything already in the world even if, previous to the end, they entertained these relations. He then says of this property of element with maximal self-identity relative to the event: 'A body is nothing other than the set of elements that have this property' (*LW* 467). The final point here relates to the subject's movement in the poem that dominates all the other elements in that it names them all as part of the same event site. In the poem this is the poet's consciousness, which is a good example as it helps us to realize that consciousness is just a function of gathering, a fiction, not an actual subject. And so we see that the disparate elements of the body are distributed through the poem and are only gathered together into one body of identity relation when the poetic consciousness invokes them with such commands as 'Arise', 'Let's run' and so on.² So that Badiou says of the elements which form the body; 'they are ultimately united in being (here, in the being of the language) by a poetic compatibility that allows them to hold together authorising the cohesion of a body' (*LW* 467).

The final point Badiou proposes is that once in place, the subjective organization of the body of the event does not proceed in a tabular, multi-directional fashion. It isn't a switch so that before 'Arise' say the sea was like this and now after it is like something else. As we saw, there needs to be a point-by-point, step-by-step testing of the sea on the part of the subject to make sure each element registers a yes rather than a no. This leads Badiou to end his consideration of how points are tested in the poem with a detailed and, for us, essential summary of the nature of a body through the processes of its being tested point by point by a subject. A body is what gathers all elements maximally related to the appearance of an inexistent, the trace of an event or it 'depends on the affinities between the other bodies of the world and the primordial statement'.³ The body comes about due to 'post-evental sublimation of the inexistent' (*LW* 470). It attains coherence through the compatibility of all objects internal to it, in that they are all subordinate to that initial trace. For the body to have effect in the world it must have consequences; otherwise, it is just a fact or a weak singularity. To have consequences it must be tested point by point in a linear, sequential, not tabular multi-directional manner. The test is always that of an alternative, yes or no. Thus, 'a point is what directs the components of a body to the summons of the Two' (*LW* 470). That said, these tests take place in organs, defined as 'efficacious regions of bodies' whose job is to test a new possible component against the old world and return a yes vote. He says, the trace is not enough, you also need 'appropriate organs for such a validation' (*LW* 470).

Moving back to Galois, Badiou leaves us with clear conditions for the development of an effective body and so a creative subject.

1. That the new world created is active and not atonic.
2. That there is a site-object and its trace, defined as the maximal-becoming of an inexistent.
3. The elements of the object are maximally correlated to the trace and each other in a compatible fashion, they become, in others words, communicable with each other due to their shared noncommunicability, thanks to their maximal relation to an inexistent.
4. In the body there are 'subsets which are its organs with respect to points', that is, decided upon based on a simple, binary formula.

We have now composed for us a basic sequence: world – points – site – body – efficacious part – organ, which is 'the generic form of what makes it possible for there to be such things as truths. This authorizes the materialist dialectic to contend beyond bodies and languages, there is the real life of some subjects' (*LW* 475). This is not the conclusion of the book but it might as well be. All that is left is to revisit the formal mean by which Badiou says there can be bodies, tied into the greater logic of worlds at large and to detail the relation of the subject-truth to those bodies.

First formal sketch: Definition and existence of a body

The formal theory of the body will remain an important document for any thinkers who wish to develop his idea of bodies in relation to subjects as the central outcome of the two volumes of Being and Event. While we won't then dwell on the formal proofs of bodies, they are elegant and clear and to be recommended. However, in that the formal theory also adds new levels of understanding of the nature of bodies, not just further formal proofs of the existence of bodies, there are points within the formalism we cannot neglect. For example, if we take an evental present, and we wish to relate this evental trace to objects, we can begin to realize a whole set of laws and determinations in this regard which Badiou then goes on to formally prove. First the object in question, x, is defined as that which incorporates itself into the evental present, written as ever: ε. Second, to do so it must conform with the basic law of relation which is that the **ID**(x, ε) is as large as possible, there are no gaps. Furthermore, all the elements that are incorporated into ε are compatible with one another, as indeed they are in normal envelopes and again, as in normal worlds, compatibility is determined by the presence of real atoms. This then allows us to say that a body is simply the set of elements that incorporate themselves into an evental present following the basic laws of greater logic for objects in any world. This also permits us to say bodies are coherent, by which we mean that they are compatible in pairs, as well as to confirm that a body supports a real synthesis determined by the transcendental order $<$. We must remember however that where a body differs is that the order relation $<$ comes with an additional quantity: 1, 0. S, on this stipulation, oversees the process of adding new elements to a set through the 'corporeal synthesis of what happens to differences in the site' (*LW* 486). These differences are filtered in the body through the yes–no decision, in that you can trace this sequence of consequences all the way back to ε. The job of this synthesis is to 'produce the existence of an inexistent' (*LW* 486), best thought of as in the present, responding to the consequences as they occur and in each case making the right decision so that the chain of positive consequences is never broken. If you can achieve this, the synthesis of a body is different to that of a normal envelope because a corporeal synthesis 'is nothing other than the inexistent ε, post-eventally brought to its maximal existence by the site' (*LW* 486). The final point is that aside from ε, the first object, no subsequent object can have a transcendental value equal to the maximum. Each element has maximal relation to the event in terms of its identity but it is always smaller. What this requires is that for the inexistent to become existent through the formation of a body in a world, it must be over-existent as regards all the elements which subsequently belong to it. Badiou summarizes these points in eight formulae, if the reader wishes a more portable version, and thus we can close on the specific nature of a body, relative to any other synthetic envelope of any other world.

Second formal sketch: Corporeal treatment of points

What makes a body different from any other object is first its relation to an inexistent rather than an existent, and second, that it carries with it a quality or a value, it is postivized. The positivization of an object is basically the decision of a determinate subject, again not a person per se. In the section which follows Badiou considers the nature of the point in particular as it pertains to what he is calling the organ. First, as regards ε, every object is positivized by ε; yet, ε is not the organ but the entire post-eventual world, so a mode of differentiation between ε and the organ is necessary. Badiou says: 'The universal efficacy of ε does not really indicate the existence of a coherent efficacious part of the body for a determinate point Ø. It is in some sense an indifferent efficacy' (*LW* 488). Another way of putting this is that all post-eventual worlds are indifferently the same in terms of positivization because without positivization of some order the evental trace never forms a body. Instead, each body formed from an event is different due to the specific nature of its organ or its coherent efficacious part. One might go further and say the real significance of any event is the nature of its organ, the new laws it proposes and sustains, rather than the objects which belong to it. Badiou doesn't quite think so; he is inordinately worried that his events reach an undefined critical mass after which they are 'big enough' to be events which create real change in a world, but in reality what is more important, set theory in terms of its axioms, or the millions of calculations that set theory allows? The millions of calculations prove the communicability of set theory such that the theorem becomes acceptable and axiomatic, but the nine axioms of set theory are, from the wider perspective, its lasting contribution.

Badiou has a very strong set of reasons to find means of organizing post-evental bodies, and it is of utmost importance that the organ be different from the initial ε. Yes, every object is positive in relation to ε, but that is not enough; they must also succumb to the order relation of positivization due to a fixed organ of rules. He says: '*The efficacious part of a body C_ϱ for a point Ø is the subset of the elements of ε other than ε, which affirm Ø*' (*LW* 488). Badiou gives some reasons for this. For example, it is not a given that a body exists for a determinate Ø. You have to build a body using the rules of coherence, being compatible in pairs and the law of positivization. Then, if there is a synthetic element that coheres points into a body, this could simply be ε itself, the transcendental under which all the elements appear. This is legitimate in any other world, but, due to the difficult nature of forming an existent set of objects from a relation to an inexistent, it is not possible for a new world. The new world has to work that much harder to become a world at all and, at the same time, resist becoming simply a subset of the world in which it appears. Every ε needs an organ that is not ε, indifferent efficacy, and more than this, that is internal to ε.

Badiou presents a complex proof to show that an organ is interior to ε but more interesting is why it has to be or what effects it produces. He says, 'Every organ is immanent to its own region of efficacy in the body' (*LW* 489). In that an organ is composed of the coherent and limited rules for the creation of a positivized, coherent body that is more than just ε, it is ε plus objects, the organ is, as we said, the limited set of rules which determine the coherence of the elements of the body such that the new world will be communicable amongst the noncommunicable and also retroactively communicable with already-existing communicable worlds. This again differentiates post-evental worlds from every other world, whilst also relating them. All worlds, Badiou argues, are conditioned and these conditions are effectively the organs of those worlds, although they do not possess positivization as they don't need to. In poetry Badiou says this is the relation of form to matter. In maths, reiterative deductive reasoning. What makes an evental world different is it has a singular organ as well. Said singular organ is indifferent because it is abstract and neutral, but it presents real difference because it must conform to positivization. In that normal worlds do not possess organs, there are no interim levels or organization, as there is no means to stop between the minimum and the maximal and saying anything other than this envelope is bigger than all the elements inside it but smaller than the next largest envelope. What an organ gives to 'new worlds' or real change in worlds is a simple mark of choice based on quality: these objects are good, those are not.

We can end with Badiou's point for formally treating organs and that is to make sure that the potential of ε is tested and fulfilled at each stage. If the world has no points, it is atonal so it must have points. If a world is not tied to an event, then it is stable, and it must be destabilized. If a world does not accumulate enough elements to form a body, he never says what this means which is a major issue, then it has no consequences to speak of and is inconsequential. If in a world all the elements in that world that decide on Ø are in fact just ε, then the efficacy of this world is indifferently anonymous and inactive. Finally, in the world there must be an organ that treats points to form bodies, if not then points are not treated and that world is inorganic. For a new world to be born it must not be atonal, stable, inconsequential, inactive or inorganic: 'This elucidates why the creation of a truth – which requires the treatment of at least one point – is rather rare' (*LW* 491).

Scholium: A political variant of the physics of the subject-of-truth

To end a study of this magnitude celebrating the works of Mao is surely a provocation and explains why Badiou's work remains less communicable than it ought to be. Badiou's Maoism never goes away and in fact is the basis of the most excoriating attack on this work so far, that of Laruelle, who reconfigures Badiou's formal vigour and asceticism in relation to the event along strictly Maoist lines.[4] Perhaps Laruelle goes too far but it is Badiou of course who opens the gate for him. There is no reason that events should result in ethically admirable consequences. In fact, Badiou is quite clear that terror and destruction are intrinsic to the militant subjectivity of any event. If the event is aesthetic the terror is of one order; if the event is political, it will result in death. The Maoist turn is particularly galling because, totalitarian mass murder to one side, the Scholium treats the particular formal quality called subjective induction which answers the important question: Why can a body exist in a world? Therefore putting Mao in brackets, we are left with the quandary: Can we trace the nature of subjective induction without the examples given from Mao's work? I believe we easily can.

1. Subjective induction proves evidentially that there is a subject-body in the world by going back to the initial conditions of its existence, whilst it was still uncertain it would have consequences.
2. Subjective induction determines whether the transcendental characteristics of the world will allow or not allow the appearance of a new body.
3. It then identifies the trace of an event and thinks the space of a new present (evental site).
4. Subjective induction attends to the 'immanent heterogeneity of the body'.
5. It also appreciates the means by which compatibility between objects productive of cohesion can be established.
6. Subjective induction considers the points that must be treated.
7. And finally it examines the organs of the body that are appropriate to the points.

All that is added here is the relation, which began our study, between a subject and a body. The theory of the subject needs a body to support it in a world. Now that we have a theory of the body, we can see that the role of the subject is not deductive, atemporal and neutral, but inductive, occurs in time and in a committed sense. The subject is a historian of the event. Their role is not to formally prove that an event took place; this cannot in fact be done. Instead, all the formal proofs are such simply that, as we said, if someone were to propose a theorem determined impossible in the world, they can then trace back the justification for their faith in the fact that there was an event. Formally, all we can do is set things up so that events cannot be disproved. Then, as regards the ontology of being and the greater logic of existence, we can also show that intrinsic to these proofs is a high degree of likelihood that events do exist. What the subject does is make an event communicable based on its analysis of the body. It does this by establishing first, by wanting the event to be true based on what could be the case for a world if the event had taken place, and second, by bedding the event down through capturing it in communicable norms that mean that the event, that they believe in, will over time come to be widely accepted due to the mass of the body that it created consequentially. The inductive side is important here. Because an event creates a body point by point, it leaves a material trace all the way back to its first flash of inexistence. The deductions allow us to go so far, but it is the inductive commitment of subjects in time that truly make events. Yes, everybody has to have organs, deductive axioms of their fresh existence, but more than this, we all need to have texture, presence, importance and finally history.

Conclusion: What is it to live?

If there is more to life than allowed by democratic materialism, 'preserving the free virtualities of the body' (*LW* 507), what is the nature of this 'more'? This is the question which Badiou ends his entire opus on. He goes further; it is not just that there is more to life than communicable bodies, but that life as such as a question is to be found outside of existence, in excess of our worlds. If at this point we accept this to be true, then when we ask what is it to live we enquire, after Aristotle, what is it to live as an immortal or to live due to the universality of a truth. This is what, after all, Badiou is selling as the basis for our accepting that, given that events cannot be disproved and that further we can show it is very likely they do exist, then his vision of what might be the case such that there are events, subjects to truth, is the correct version of events. Offering us immortality is a means of co-opting us to this new noncommunicable communicability which goes like this. Life is not biologically determined; it is not bodies. Life is not constructible; it is not discursive either. Life is truth as immortality.

Badiou then provides a fifteen-point programme as to how to achieve immortality which, I hope you will admit, is a generous way to end any work of philosophy.

1. If life is something other than existence, then life will not be given in any world. The only way life can be encountered in a world is due to trace of a vanished event. 'Through the incorporation of the world's past to the present opened up by the trace, it is possible to learn that prior to what happened and is no longer, the ontological support of this intense existence was an inexistent in the world' (*LW* 507). The birth of a multiple in a world makes a trace in that world, we knew that, but now he says that is also 'signals towards life' (*LW* 507), which is a new proposition.
2. The trace is not enough, you must incorporate yourself into the trace in terms of how it authorizes its consequences. You then have to become an active element of the body in a process that is ongoing, it is not a one-off.
3. The development of the consequences of an event in a world which you actively participate in proceeds in line with the theory of points, one by one in a binary, decisionist fashion. He says, 'It does not take place through the continuous trajectory of a body's efficacy, but in sequences, point by point'

(*LW* 508). To live is sequential not tabular, and it is classically decisive, not intuitionistic and modal.

4. Life is a category of the subject that needs a body to materially support it. But this body is the result of a 'subjective formalism'; it is not a biological entity, for example, or even the physical body of an actual person. In this way you do not own your body as a subjective right, as would be the case in democratic materialism. This relationship is a crucial difference to the dominant ideas of life and the body, the so-called biopolitical. Badiou calls life a 'wager, made on a body that has entered into appearing' (*LW* 509). Life is a speech act; you make a bet which becomes a promise which is you will allow life to enter into a new temporality that is not negated by the conservative drive of life, to just atonally live, or the mortifying drive either, the death instinct. 'Life is what gets the better of these drives' (*LW* 509).

5. The temporality of democratic materialist life is at odds with the temporality of actual life. Real life is part of a sequential creation of a new present which 'both constitutes and absorbs a new type of past' (*LW* 509). He is calling for an entirely new form of historiography. In contrast, the life of democratic materialism is never created; rather, it 'affirms, in an entirely explicit manner, that it is important to maintain the present within the confines of an atonic reality' (*LW* 509). Or, a historiography that says we live like this today because of what happened yesterday.

6. To live and to live for an idea in the Platonic sense are the same thing. Here an idea is not what exists which you submit to, but what does not yet exist which you are active participant in creating.

7. In that democratic materialism calls for the end of all ideologies; it works tirelessly to negate the very thing it politically and ethically claims to protect with its sanctifying of every body and its refusal to choose one language over another: namely the much-touted concept of the other. Badiou chooses the Greeks as a good example of how to really compose an other, namely an idea of such magnitude that it exceeds human understanding and thus equates an idea with something inhuman and, of course, immortal, because universally true beyond any specific human body or any particular communicable language. The result is a biopolitical process by which anything inhuman is subordinated to the idea of the human. Then the idea of the human is reduced to that of everyday life. This everyday, animal life is subsequently lost in the 'atonicity of the world' (*LW* 511). We can say, therefore, that Badiou agrees with the biopolitical agenda,

except that it misses out the possibility of life being something other than bodies and languages, biopolitical.
8. Badiou considers here the intermittency of the event giving only some subjects the chance to really live, in other words luck. He fails to really answer this objection.
9. He defines why truths are eternal, not because they have already existed but because they have been created. In that a truth is eternal, this does not mean it can escape the process of appearing in a world. Once a truth is created, yes, it appears as eternally necessary, but the process of the creation of that truth is not necessary. As we saw it is precarious and contingent on a host of tests each of which could, and most likely will, fail.
10. Therefore all relativistic and constructivist positions that claim 'the historicity of all things excludes eternal truths' (*LW* 513). In fact the opposite is true. It is because worlds are communicable that they are historical, and it is because they are historical that they are consistent and it is because they are consistent that truths can appear in them as inconsistent. By definition, the constructible, indifferent communicability of every world is what allows for a life or a truth to appear. Our whole study has been orchestrated to show this. Badiou says genuine creation is 'a historicity of exception, has no other criterion that to establish, between disparate worlds, the evidence of an eternity' (*LW* 513). What he is doing he is essentially re-describing the logics of worlds in terms that belong to the discourse of democratic materialism.
11. This section contains perhaps some of the most memorable constructs of *Logics of Worlds*. The apparent grace, inhumanity, immortality and miracle of the event is nothing of the sort. There is no divinity to life at all. Instead all of this is the result of a profound humanism, a humanism that in the future Badiou might be taken to task over. At this point however we should simply savour the celebratory nature of the gift of humanity that Badiou gives to us. 'Man,' he says, 'is this animal to whom it belongs to participate in numerous worlds, to appear in innumerable places. This kind of objectal ubiquity, which makes him shift almost constantly from one world to another, on the background of the infinity of these worlds and their transcendental organization, is in its own right, without any need for a miracle, a grace: the purely logical grace of innumerable appearing' (*LW* 513). This is true. *Logics of Worlds* due to *Being and Event* is a milestone in the history of humanity. It is the first credible description of how we live across multiple worlds with absolute consistency. It is the first fully worked

out theory of communicability, completing a process begun two hundred years before by Kant's third critique. A theory of communicability that is due to the nature of his ideas of being and in particular its indifference. And it is indifference that returns here to spoil the party. For worlds are differentiated through and through but, due to the law of universal exposition which they cannot resist, even though every world is composed only of identities due to differences, and even though we live in an infinite number of these worlds, if we were to stop for a moment in a constant worldly restlessness and looked around us we would see that all the objects in all our worlds which are themselves objects in other worlds and so on, are all, in the end, the same. Perhaps this is why we are errant beings, because constant movement is sufficient to hide from us the truth of absolute stasis. With this in mind it is no wonder that juxtaposed to the constant movement of every living human being to another dynamic multiplicity: 'incessantly, in some accessible world, something happens' (*LW* 514). This is also true. Each of the infinity of worlds we move through is based on a minimum which it excludes so that it can be consistent so yes, by a law of statistical probability, every subject will be exposed to an event 'several times in its brief existence' (*LW* 514). This rejects the accusation of luck but it raises the problem of probability. What does several times actually mean? Finally, Badiou rejects, for ever, finitude. 'The infinite of worlds is what saves us from every finite dis-grace' (*LW* 514). Finitude and death are what he calls the bitter ingredients of democratic materialism which we overcome 'when we seize hold of the discontinuous variety of worlds and their interlacing of objects under the constantly variable regimes of their appearances' (*LW* 514).

12. Given all the above, Badiou declares we 'are open to an infinity of worlds. To live is possible' (*LW* 514). This is a lovely way of saying if there is an infinity of worlds all of which are founded on the axiom of the minimum and the transcendental of the maximal; then it stands to reason that, from time to time, one of these worlds will present to us an event which we can adhere to and thus be able to say that we lived.

13. Badiou then accepts the accusation of heroism but rejects, and this is important, the heroism of sacrifice. It would seem that he has been too free to equate militancy with violence and death, and as we saw even at the very end he is happy to prove subjective induction around the culture of death, Maoism. Here, however, he makes his position clear: 'We could

say that the epic heroism of the one who gives his life is supplanted by the mathematical heroism of the one who creates life, point by point' (*LW* 514).

14. Heroism of this order is based on discipline, this is the centrality of the point-by-point subjective formalism of the system which emulates the point-by-point formalism of set and category theory. That said, the formalism of a subject is a new formalism, it is not the formalism of mathematics because there is nothing mathematical that can prove that there are subject-truths. Instead 'this discipline demands to be invented, as the coherence of the subjectivizable body' (*LW* 514).

15. Our fate is in our hands. Democratic materialism is not a necessity, it is our choice or rather we have the choice not to choose. We consent to the communicability of our horrible age, even if that consent is complicit and even if the logics of worlds make us realize how profoundly stable and atonal all our worlds are. Never has the weight of Foucauldian ideas of control been felt so powerfully than after reading *Logics of Worlds* which is the greatest description of the indifference of communicability we have ever had at our disposal. For me, I would stop there, but for Badiou, this whole portrait of absolute atonality is to provide a profound philosophical chiaroscuro. Yes we consent to a world of communicable indifference, but 'we are shielded from this consent by the Idea, the secret of the pure present' (*LW* 514).

One Conclusion: Communicability and Commutativity

The thesis of our first volume, that being is indifferent, is supported by innumerable instances of Badiou using the term indifference. The thesis of our second volume, that worlds are communicable, cannot make this claim; Badiou never uses the specific term communicability in his major works. Thus the evidence for my second contention seems poor that much I concede. That said, historically indifference, although regularly used as a term, is for the most part cited so that it can be suppressed, dismissed, despised, such that my claim that Badiou's is an ontology of indifference is actually rather hard for my community to swallow. While communicability, admittedly never cited as a Badiou term, all the same forms the basis of Kant's third critique, where the term is first introduced, and from there continues to have mainstream acceptance as a concept, even if the terminology is diverse. It is the basis of Nietzsche's perspectivism and captures the essence of Heidegger's ideas on how art opens up a world for a people. It extends across the analytic tradition, from Wittgenstein's form of life through speech act theory to Quine's indeterminacy of translation. We find communicability debated and discussed throughout the continental tradition of the last century, with Habermasian communicative action locking horns with Foucault's archaeology of knowledge, while Althusser's concept of interpellation looks on. There is surely no Derridean deconstruction without communicability, and Deleuze's insistence that all words are commands means he is, first and foremost, a philosopher of communicability. Finally, it is the essential component of Badiou's only real rival in contemporary thought, Agamben's theory of signatures. In each case what all these thinkers come to realize, thanks to Kant's remarkable intuition, is that what is communicated between two subjects is not primarily the content of the words, but the context of their communication, not what is said, but that such and such a thing can be said by one subject to another and they can both understand that they share said context in common.

Thus although Badiou does not use the term communicability, he is often talking about it and considering its illustrious provenance, there should be no surprise in that. For example, his earlier work calls this context of communicability, conditions. He speaks at length about it in *Being and Event* under the heading of the pure presentation of presentation as such. In *Mathematics of the Transcendental* he defines the axioms of sets as their intelligibility, that which makes the pure multiple legible, communicable, to a specific community, mathematicians. In his very earliest work he defines it as the model.[1] Continuing with this theme, he defines the event as that which is said, within the communicable conditions of a community, which conforms to the conditions of the community and yet remains unintelligible to them. This stipulation is sufficient to determine the idea of communicability being the sanction of a statement, rather than its intelligible content. A truth, actual infinities exist, is rejected because it is an impossible thing to say not because, mathematically, it is impossible to prove, but actually because it is an impossible thing for mathematicians to hear. In *Logics* he makes the same point about Galois and Legrange's revelation when it comes to speaking of algebraic structures rather than formulae. This is Badiou's basic theory of the event, and it is a theory of communicability with numerous examples throughout *Logics of World* and beyond.

These comments ask that we should re-envisage what communication means in this context. If we were to formalize discourse theory using category theory, then to communicate can no longer mean the transmission of meaning between two subjects, for example. Indeed communicability is not directly about the transmission of meaningful content, but the sanction of what is taken to being meaningful in any given world. Even the term 'meaning' needs to be revised. Meaning is only one function of discursive communicability. Rather, what we are talking about is how a statement, object, subject, behaviour, technology can be said to exist in this particular world because of what it does to other elements in said world, under the auspices of the category. To be communicable, an existent in a world needs to exist, intense self-identity, related to at least one other existent, which could be the category, and be visible from the vantage point of the category, through the function of universal exposition. As all three of these existential functions pertain to relation, *we will define communicability as visible or discernible relationality within a well-pointed or defined world, often called a topos.* A unit in a world is communicable when an intelligible multiple is placed within a world such that it can be seen. This updates Kant's original idea that communicability is an objective, inter-subjectivating function: Do you find this beautiful? No, I do not, but I understand the context of the question and accept it as an inter-subjective, objective truth that we are beauty-finding beings. Now communicability is more formally expressible as the basic modality of category theory meaning it does not depend, in any way, on a Kantian subject.

Can we not then make the case that the function of commutativity is in reality the mathematics of communicability? That is what the subtitle of this book is really suggesting; for communicable worlds read commutative worlds. Commutativity is a qualified mode of equivalence or identity. In categories, two objects with the same functional relations are identical, even if they are ontologically distinct. Commutativity on this reading allows for the ontico-indistinction of two ontological multiples, thanks to the composability of functions. The function between A and C called $g \bullet f$ is absolutely equivalent to the composite of the functions f between A and B and g between B and C. Commutativity therefore creates a sophisticated conceptualization of the interplay between identity and difference. It allows two multiples to be the same object in a world because it defines said objects not in terms of what they are composed of but what they do. Commutativity then is the objectivating function of all 'statements', allowing us to make that apparently impossible leap from discourse to material reality. It makes communicable statements objects related by functions.

Yet the topological formalization of categories, commutative triangles, exposes a formal differentiation between two equivalent objects. $A \rightarrow C = A \rightarrow B \rightarrow C$. In the world, these two objects are identical, but in language, they can be differentiated, thanks to the law of association which stipulates either object is the same, for example, you can write $A \rightarrow B \rightarrow C = A \rightarrow C$, without any loss of meaning, as long as you retain the order $A \rightarrow B \rightarrow C$ and $A \rightarrow C$. Unless stated, $A \rightarrow C \neq C \rightarrow A$ or at least does not necessarily do so. This produces, in worldly objects, a hidden tension of symmetry between two objects and asymmetry between three, which is universally exposed by the diagrammatic presentation of commutativity, and the fact that even symmetrical relations can be exposed in a world from a third position. This dynamic interchange between symmetry and asymmetry creates worlds as I have argued. It also means that commutativity is really a means of exposing hidden differences within functional identities such that while two objects can be taken to be functionally different, they can be shown not to be, thanks merely to abstract, indifferent, extensional notation. What this does, in effect, is in-indifferentiate two objects, showing that generically, at least, they retain some vestige of being two distinct multiples. Or, it is impossible to formally show symmetry, without having to admit the formal notation of asymmetry.

The process of making said distinction appear is what I am calling communicability. While communicability can be traced from Kant through both philosophical traditions, I do not think that as yet anyone has been able to formalize it in quite this fashion because none of those thinkers had access to category theory as Badiou at least presents it, and no one in the tradition has been willing to concede the constructive importance of indifference to communicability. Communicability's axiom, not what is communicated but that it can be, finds its formal proof in commutativity. A commutative diagram shows that the content communicated by a function, these two objects are functionally the same, is only possible if the composable and associative relations of said objects can be exposed. In effect, two objects can be taken to be relationally equivalent, if and only if you retain a manner by which their non-equivalence can be exposed. The relation between A and C can only be understood, because the function of exponentiation or exposition allows it to be seen. Commutativity permits us to see that said function can be expressed or better enacted: all functions can be performed (what is said) if their relations conform to associative composability; this is the 'that it can be said' or better 'that it can be shown' that is the fundamental definition of the category. Thus if we say that the essence of the multiple is its indifference, the essence of a category is its communicability. Worlds are communicable because they are commutative, and a logics of worlds is the formal explanation of said communicability.

Why does this matter? Because it is the noncommunicability of events that makes them possible. An event is not a new multiple, there are no new multiples. Nor is it a new object, there are nothing but new objects. Thus it requires a functional means by which it can be expressed, category theory. Categories show that universally all relations between objects are exposed, such that there are no hidden objects that cannot be communicable. Every relation can be made into a commutative diagram through the pull-back of exponention. Communicability alerts us to the fact that something that is noncommunicable is not at all the same as saying it doesn't exist in a traditional sense. A noncommunicable object is one which can be performed or expressed, but in such a way as its relationality cannot be exposed. It exists, it is real, it happened, but it cannot be seen, accepted, sanctioned, related to. Noncommunicable truths are, in fact, noncommutative relations. There is no vantage point from which they can be observed, they are not composable and thus associativity does not matter to them, nor can it be said that they are symmetrical either.

This also gives us a better understanding as to how bodies are formed and why they differ from the objects of worlds in general. Worldly objects expand from the dynamic between symmetry and asymmetry that commutativity facilitates. Multiples expand from a similar dynamic between belonging and inclusion. Finally, the onto-logical relation expands from the dynamic between multiples that belong and objects that are included producing an interdependent, overlapping double augmentation. In contrast, the augmentation and extension of an evental body are not a dynamic oscillation between set and subset (multiples) or between symmetrical relation and asymmetric commutativity (categories). Rather, evental organs extend out in a simple, linear, point-after-point manner. One concomitant of this pointedness is that events are easy to identify simply because they do not resemble multiples or categories. In contrast to Deleuze's definition of events as rhizomatic, real events do not in any way resemble root vegetables, nor are they arboreal or even, as I have said of multiples, alliumatic. Rather, they are simple shoots, slowly extending tendrils, that continue to have power in destroying the status quo of all possible worlds, if and only if they do not split. To give a very English example from our national sport of gardening, they are shoots that are assiduously pruned. Joyce said it first, Derrida followed on, an event is a string of yeses, yesyesyesyesyes. It is Derrida's demand that you say yes to yes, over and over, or better, to modify Derrida, it is necessary that you say yes after yes after yes ...

Finally this explains the centrality of extensional reasoning. Badiou favours axiomatic, extensional set theory. Logic is of course extensional, asking that concepts extend over objects in order to be true. For an evental truth to be extending into a world, however, it must appear to occupy the position of the false, a concept that extends over no objects: actual infinities exist, music should become serialized, we slaves can be free. By the same gesture, thanks to the void, all events are material, real bodies that exist in the world, before they can be constructed through the application of truth-value logic. Yet they are objects which cannot be conceptualized, because the logics of worlds disallows them. What this asks, as I said earlier, is that we change what we take extension to be. Communicability is a process, and so is noncommunicability. In a noncommunicable process of subjectivation, the impossible concept of an impossible object avoids the interdictions of extensional set theory and intensional logics, by occupying the functional ground of what it means for something false to make the arduous journey towards becoming true. Slowly, a concept of an object extends: tentative steps, modest propositions, but also sudden leaps, radical responses. The testing exposition of the conceptual extension is never entirely true, it is a non-whole cardinal infinity, and so it can never be taken to be absolutely false. The more the evental trace can produce objects, statements, actions, expressions, that are 'truthful' relative to the context of noncommunicability, a local yes thanks to a previous yes, or yes as a consequence of yes, the further the initial event travels, as a real object, from false to true. And the more the concept extends, with extension taken as an open-ended process here, the more the impossible object becomes possible such that extension is neither the extension of a concept over an object nor the developing of a concept because of an object, but the slow meeting in the middle of the two, usually opposed, intellectual traditions. Impossible concepts extend over impossible objects such that said concepts become less impossible, while at the same time those objects, those real events, become more possible. If, therefore, events are by definition noncommunicable, then, in terms of categories, they are also non-commutative. The journey from A to C via B as commutatively equivalent as that directly from A to C is banned when it comes to subjectivation of a body due to an event. The only way to get from A to C is through B, the only function between A and B is yes, the only function between B and C is also yes and so on. This being the case then, a well-pointed evental body can never be universally exposed. Events are totally superficial, even more so than categories. If a category entertains no outside, an event will admit to no network, no flattened vantage, no pull-back of any kind. Events possessive of bodies are non-whole, yet delimited, two-dimensional, ever expanding lines of decisions.

In answer to the question: What is an event?, the answer is *a non-commutative category*. It is a response that is totally impossible without a detailed understanding of *Logics of Worlds*, a discipline-disrupting and defining result that has taken Badiou decades to arrive at. Surely, in honour of its implications and revelations, it is time we as a community started to make the book more communicable by reading and re-reading it, with the same militancy that we applied to its predecessor. If *Logics* is, as I believe is the case, the real Badiou event, then take this book as the first yes. I hope there will be many more to follow, although they will not be affirmations extending from my pen.

Another Conclusion: Badiou's Politics of Communicability or Three Functions of Power Structures

That is one way to end the book, but another way would be to say that *Logics of Worlds* is Badiou's most political book, because his is a politics of the event, and it is in *Logics* that the full theory of the event is presented. Fair comment, but not the whole story because *Logics* is also a book about the nature of existent power, before and after evental intervention suggesting Badiou's politics is in the plural because he has at least three political theories: the event, the critique of democratic materialism and an undisclosed third, category theory as a functional description of the tripartite structural basis of all forms of power. In addition, no formal theory of communicability, as was the case in using commutativity to objectivate discursive statements, is meaningful without the sanction function. What can be said is determined by the communal sanction of a conditioned community, meaning that a formal theory of communicability must make room for a political theory of the force of sanction, legitimation, complicity and, of course, exclusion. In the only other credible theory of formalized communicability, Agamben's signatures, the power of the sanction is ever to the fore, albeit at the cost of lacking a truly formalized explanation of the order of categories. In Badiou, perhaps surprisingly, little is said of power and the force of communicable sanction is assumed, but never fully thought. This asks of the commentator then that they do a little digging, indulge in some late-in-the-day extrapolation to find force in categories.

In truth, all three elements of an existent's existence presented by categories accord with a sense of power. The degree to which a multiple is allowed to exist is the first sanction on communicability. A multiple cannot be barred from a world, but the degree of self-identity it is allowed to have in its appearance is not a given. Women existed in the workplace throughout the last century but not initially in any manner that allowed them to use their full potential or skillset. The next is the quanta of functional force between two elements of a world. Foucault famously believes that power is a tautology, an apodictic element of all human relations, such that he feels no direct need to define it or really to justify his point. Such a concept of power as a permanent feature of interpersonal and interdisciplinary relations is communicable because of the prevalence of Nietzsche in the continental post-Existential tradition. Making Foucault's theory of power profoundly communicable: it is not what power says or what we say power is, it is rather what power does.

In contrast, what category theory permits is a way to think about relationality that always has embedded in it something relatively easy to define as power. In terms of two objects, for them to exist as two objects, they must have a relation of function, in which one object dominates the other. For if two objects have the same degree of functional relation, then in our terms they are the same object. This of course suggests that existence is determined by functional force, acting on another existent being. As soon as one thinks of beings as nodes between which travel directional, functional forces, one is forced to accept not that we are always at war, as much as we are always held relationally in an asymmetry of forces. An asymmetry of forces is, surely, the real basis for power and coercive violence, one which we also do not need to essentialize in any sense using Nietzschean social Darwinism. We are not saying there is an asymmetry of forces due to nature, or even due to any universal quality; rather, we are saying that for world-structures to be operative, they can most consistently be presented in terms of structure-preserving formalisms, of which category theory is by far the most consistent. What this implies is that when you are looking at the structural relationality of any world, said relationality is determined by an asymmetry of functional force: associative composability or, simply, commutativity.

There is an argument to be made that two existent beings who wish to differentiate will, by definition, be functionally different and yes, that means one will have some forces superior to the other, but that this alone is not a reason to call their communicability political. For example, different forces do not by definition mean one has greater potency. This is true. However, to understand what is meant by an object, a function, a relation and so on, these need to be placed within a structure, for they are structure-preserving functions, and it is this structure that imposes hierarchy. A category is the name of this structure and of our third theory of power. A category imposes a transcendental functor over all its diagrams so that they can all be seen to be part of this world, such that their relational functions, in this world, are visible, and so communicable. The category then is always a state-function. There is an asymmetry of functional differences rather than just a difference because identity and difference are defined by functional enveloping which is a local and global dominance structure. To see two existents a superior position must be taken from which the relationality of the two objects as existents in this world is communicable such that one of the two will be 'closer' or have a greater degree of intensity of relation to the world than the other. Worlds are differentially relational; objects exist therein in degrees of relation to each other, thanks to a third, the envelope as transcendental functor which is the name of the category or world. If the world is patriarchal, the subject-positions masculine and feminine have a different order of relation to each other because of the world, than if the world is matriarchal.

Put simply, the type of world it is determines the degree of self-intensity of beings that appear in the world, the degree of relational intensity they have with other beings and the degree of transcendental intensity they share with the category of the world they appear in – our tripartite categorization of the functions of power structures. Very strongly sanctioned objects appear intensely in terms of their ontological potential, close to the category of said world, so that they dominate large numbers of other objects also included. Thus power can be determined by three functions of appearing: self-presence, proximity to the category, intensity of relational dominance. Communicability being another name for how category theory formalizes existential functional appearance in a consistent world, read in terms of the asymmetrical functional forces being described as quanta of power. To appear is to have power, to impose power on another, and to be perceived within the wider structures of power for this world. This retains the intuition of the continental tradition, which is that thought is primarily concerned with power, married to the analytical assumption that thought is an indubitable and simple formalism. Communicability is analytical plus power, continental plus formalism.

If the great function of categories is how they allow you to topologically see structural relations, then every category contains an image of what an event could look like, basically the Id arrow morphism (*MT* 20).

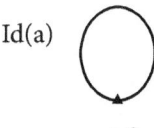

Id(a)

• a

The double paradoxical quality of the identity arrow, a multiple that appears communicable but a part of which remains noncommunicable, an object which self-relates as the precondition of its worldy relationality, is perhaps the most important aspect of category theory for Badiou, typical of the double determination of all categories. Categories are both classical and intuitionist. Categories are both linear-algebraic and tabular-topological. Categories are both sets (ontological) and functions (logical). Categories are both symmetric ordered pairs and asymmetric triangles of relations. Categories are the communicability of the noncommunicability of the multiple. Categories are the functional self-relation of communicable relationality as such. Finally, categories are the indifferential functional relations of a world that is supposedly entirely relational and thus differential.

Coda

It is as if Badiou took a long hard stare at category theory and concluded, if events can be shown to exist anywhere, then it is somewhere in there. And with this, the impossible thought of the event that began two decades ago in *Being and Event*, slowly, point by point, through the pages of *Logics of Worlds*, moved from extensional indifference to intensional communicability. Badiou was able to say events can exist, thanks to the axioms of ontology, but he was only able to see events properly, not in terms of what they are-not, but as what they can-do, once he had discovered a mathematics of the transcendental, or what we prefer to call a communicability of worlds. At this moment Badiou's three theories of political power come together. Events are possible by being noncommutative or noncommunicable objects in a world. Said events are political because they disrupt the tripartite structure of all power: asymmetry of relation. Finally, because they are founded on the void of set theory, are real atoms in a world, evental bodies nonrelationally extending into worlds fulfil our initial political criterion: there are only bodies and languages, *except that* there are truths.

Live by that, decide on that, reflect on that, act according to it, relate to it on a daily, habitual basis and, step by step, point by point, this baleful world we have been complicit in allowing it to be structured for us, can finally be destroyed. Not with one world-shattering hammer blow, a single convulsion in the population, an extinction event that wipes the dirty slate of the global coup of democratic materialism clean, but as a daily, lived, habituated, extending, noncommunicable string of good-faith acts.

Slowly in the nether regions of the garden, the tendrils extend, reaching out, asking of no support, intertwining with no other plant, veering from left to right as a consequence of each of its considered protrusions. Say yes to the tendril, then say yes to yes, and it will continue to grow, until a new world, a developing strand of indifferent yet well-pointed, contextual, real-time, consequential affirmations, overwhelms the old.

A body with organs must be constructed, but not so that the world at large be deconstructed. A new topology of functional dependencies must open out, but not with the aim of deterritorializing. The old certainties of difference, paradoxically, render real difference noncommunicable. It is only a philosophy of indifference that permits the indifferent singularity string, the well-pointed evental body, to exist.

The void is in-different. Being is indifferent. Events are indifferent. Objects are differential certainly, but evental bodies are indifferentially nonrelational. We are entering a new era; we must embrace the experience of the rise of the generic. Nonrelational, indifferent, yet real, functions expressing an extrinsicality, intrinsic to a self-predicating one, which will entirely replace self-present objects, with relational networks of qualitative differences with other self-identical beings. Beings without countable quantity, existing in worlds of relation without describable quality.

Events, dear boy, events. They may, in themselves, be impossibly rare, but it is not the event that matters; rather, it is the indifferential affirmative pointed bodies that concern us. This perhaps answers the final question pertaining to being, events and worlds: events may be intermittent, but their consequences are a daily decision, a constant communicability-test, a persistent accommodation of consequence. Events don't happen; it is their consequences that occur. Consequences that exist, absolutely impossibly, radically noncommunicably, because each consequence is both singular and generic, decisive yet indifferent. We can't think that the philosophy of difference will not allow it, until suddenly one day, impossibly, it is not that we can, but that we begin the capacity to …

An ontology of indifference, an phenomenology of communicability, a generic mode of thinking the singular particularity of everything that appears, thanks to this ever extending, perpetually occurring, yet delimited, well-pointed, real, statement. Indifferent beings can found in communicable worlds, *such that* truths exist. *Such that* rather than *except that*; a language of facilitation not exception, better suited for the impossible, noncommunicable, indifferentially affirmative, worlds of the future that we will build, retroactively.

And with one last glance at her masters, the pupil fled the academy through a forgotten side-door, because she knew what had to happen next, and had decided, fatefully, to say yes to that, which of course demanded that she say no to those who so carefully schooled her. Doomed to failure, she would all the same say yes to her failure, and live like that, day by day, hand to mouth, precarious, like the rest of the population. A zero-hours, almost vagrant thought-function that will never lead anywhere, and in so doing, come to be, in time, bit by bit, positively speaking, the everywhere.

Notes

Introduction

1 Nimrod Bar-Am, *Extensionalism: The Revolution in Logic* (London: Springer, 2008), xx.
2 This study for the most part is standalone and does not require that you have read my *Badiou and Indifferent Being* or even, perhaps, Badiou's *Being and Event*. From time to time however I will make use of concepts from both books. Where I mention a concept I considered in Volume 1, I will not laboriously footnote my own work. The first volume has a very detailed contents page and an extensive index and it is easy for someone, for example, to find out what is meant by being is-not by using those resources. If, however, I think the point I am making is harder to trace in Volume 1, I will give the pagination. The same goes for *Being and Event*.
3 A.J. Bartlett and Alex Ling, 'The Categorical Imperative', in Alain Badiou, *Mathematics of the Transcendental* (London: Bloomsbury, 2014), 2.
4 For more on the bridge between the two great works, see Zachary Luke Fraser, 'Introduction: The Category of Formalization: From Epistemological Break to Truth Procedure', in Alain Badiou, *The Concept of the Model*, ed. and trans. Zachary Luke Frazer and Tzuchien Tho (Melbourne: re.press, 2007), xl–xli. Also Badiou's own comments in Alain Badiou and Tzuchien Tho, 'The Concept of Model, Forty Years Later: An Interview with Alain Badiou', in Alain Badiou, *The Concept of the Model*, ed. and trans. Zachary Luke Frazer and Tzuchien Tho (Melbourne: re.press, 2007), 95–7. Also Bruno Bosteels, *Badiou and Politics* (Durham: Duke University Press, 2011), 199 and Bruno Bosteels, 'Introduction', in Alain Badiou, *Theory of the Subject*, trans. Bruno Bosteels (London: Continuum, 2009), xi–xiii and xxv–xxvi.
5 Hallward was the first Badiou scholar to spend any significant time on *Logics of Worlds* and category theory. That said, at the end of Hallward's excellent thumb-nail sketch of *Logics* and topoi, he rather brutally rejects category theory as being too abstract. He says: 'If the "abstract types" isolated by category theory clearly have their uses in the rarefied domain of pure logic, Badiou is too quick to conclude that they hold the key to relationality as such' (Peter Hallward, *Badiou: A Subject to Truth* [Minneapolis: University of Minnesota Press, 2003], 315). We hope, respectfully, that we will prove Hallward wrong on this point. Category theory does indeed hold the key to relationality as such, as the rest of this book will argue.

6   Badiou was using the term world in this sense early one, for example, Badiou, *Theory of the Subject*, 59.
7   Intuitionist logic is defined by Troelstra's uniformity principle which states: 'Every set of natural numbers can be labelled with a number only if some number labels every set', D.C. McCarty, 'Intuitionism in Mathematics', in Stewart Shapiro, *The Oxford Handbook of Philosophy of Mathematics and Logics* (Oxford: Oxford University Press, 2005), 358. One consequence of this uniformity principle is that it negates *tertium non datur* or the law of the excluded middle, another name for the law of non-contradiction. Said law means, for example, that negation of the false results in the true so that you can state that not-not-A is just another way of saying A is true. As we shall see, category theory's demand that negation be visible thanks to the concept of the reverse is demonstration that, for the most part, the logic of categories is non-classical. All this means is that you have to show negation, you cannot assume it. Many of the concepts in category theory come from intuitionist logic, many from modal logic, but that is not to say it is not also in part classical in its logic. Hence *logics* of worlds.
8   As I was completing this manuscript, the third volume of the Being and Event project, *L'Immanence des Verités* was published. As I wrote my first two volumes back-to-back over a period before its publication, and as length and time were pressing issues, I have decided not to refer to that significant development in this volume, leaving the intimidating task to the next generation of scholars.
9   See Bartlett and Ling, 'Categorical Imperative', 9, *LW* 538 and Robert Goldblatt, *Topoi: The Categorical Analysis of Logic* (Mineola, NY: Dover Publications, 2006).
10 Spreading is a categorical function that allows one to break open sets, a process which, in general, is impossible for category theory because of its extrinsic, functionally relational mode. For more on spreading, see *MT* chapter 8 'Exponention', 45–9.
11 As Bartlett and Ling point out, 'Categorical Imperative', 1, there is a twenty-year gap between the two parts of this 'book', really a collection of two essays on the same topic. What has occurred in the interim is a decided shift from the topological modes of presentation to the algebraic. The preponderance of algebraic presentations of categories is notable in *Logics of Worlds*. Badiou first considered this relational difference between algebraic and topological expression in quite some advanced detail in Alain Badiou, *Theory of the Subject*, trans. Bruno Bosteels (London: Continuum, 2009), 3–50, a 91, 198–9 and 209–14. In this early expression set theory is presented as the algebraic, while topology is not sutured to categories. A major innovation in terms of *Logics*, which is why it permanently supersedes the work of *Theory of the Subject*, is the appreciation that worlds determine apparents due to the double articulation of algebra and topology in one theory, namely category theory.

12 To put this into some kind of perspective, Goldblatt's 'Catalogue of Notation' is ten pages long amounting to way over 300 operations and functions, of which the function of relation for the greater logic, ≤, is but one entry.
13 The evidence in *Being and Event* for the re-count of inclusion is weak. It is replaced instead by the double determination of the onto-logical in this book, which is far stronger and marks a major innovation between the two texts. Badiou doesn't say this but categories provide an advanced formalism for the function of inclusion which is then re-determined as relation. If I were to sum up the differential articulation of the two books, it would be: *count-as-one, act-as-three.*
14 See Michael Potter, *Set Theory and Its Philosophy* (Oxford: Oxford University Press, 2004), 3; and Mary Tiles, *The Philosophy of Set Theory* (Mineola, NY: Dover, 2004), 32–55.
15 Harold Simmons, *An Introduction to Category Theory* (Cambridge: Cambridge University Press, 2011), 2–5.
16 https://commons.wikimedia.org/wiki/Category:Commutative_triangles#/media/File:Category_SVG.svg.
17 Hallward notes that a category made up of consistent commutative triangles and which has a transcendental limit or exponent is called a topos and that topoi are the kinds of categorize that primarily concern Badiou: Hallward, *Badiou*, 307. He goes on to highlight in detail the properties of topoi, ibid., 309–11. Badiou admits in the notes at the end of the book that he has chosen an 'ideal' branch of categories called topos theory (*LW* 537).
18 Hallward with typical perspicacity highlights this feature in his own comments on *Logics of Worlds*; Hallward, *Badiou*, 415 fn. 4 and 298.
19 Robert Goldblatt, *Topoi: The Categorical Analysis of Logic* (Mineola, NY: Dover, 2006), 22.
20 The commitment of Badiou to mathematical structure goes all the way back to his first book. See Alain Badiou, *The Concept of the Model*, ed. and trans. Zachary Luke Frazer and Tzuchien Tho (Melbourne: re.press, 2007), 34.
21 There is an entirely different book that needs to be written on Badiou's engagement with phenomenology which I leave to future scholars more skilled in this field than I am.
22 Universal exposition actually means visible to any other object in a world, but this is sometimes only through the universal position of the category itself. For example, two objects which form the minimum of each other cannot relate directly, but if they both exist in the same world, then a functional line is drawn between the category and each object. On this reading the category operates as a kind of mediation between intractably alien objects of the order of arguing parents who say to a child, tell your father that …
23 I have developed the concept of communicability from its origins in Kant's *Third Critique*, through its development in Foucault's *The Archaeology of Knowledge*,

into Agamben's theory of pure presentation as such and Badiou's presentation of presentation across my last two books. Specifically see William Watkin, *Agamben and Indifference* (London: Rowman & Littlefield International, 2014), 11–14 and William Watkin, *Badiou and Indifferent Being: A Critical Introduction to Being and Event* (London: Bloomsbury, 2017), 19–20. See Hallward, *Badiou*, 296, for the relation with Kantian intelligibility.

24 Hallward was the first to not the indifferent nature of categorical morphisms, Hallward, *Badiou*, 315.
25 You could say categories displace the concept of composition from inside the object to between two objects.
26 Goldblatt, 17.
27 Ibid.
28 F. William Lawvere and Stephen H. Schanuel, *Conceptual Mathematics* (Cambridge: Cambridge University Press, 1991), 3.
29 Goldblatt, 29.
30 Measure is the main function because of the centrality of size, Alain Badiou, *Second Manifesto for Philosophy*, trans. Louise Burchill (Cambridge: Polity, 2011), 34.
31 Simmons, *An Introduction to Category Theory*, 3.
32 Alain Badiou, *Being and Event*, trans. Oliver Feltham (London: Continuum, 2005), 331–4.

Preface

1 An extended consideration of democratic materialism can be found in Badiou, *Second Manifesto for Philosophy*, 15–25.
2 This is the thesis of my *Agamben and Indifference*.
3 This is not to reject the early masterpiece; indeed, it was in *Theory of the Subject* that Badiou has his first intimation of the articulation of sets and categories (Badiou, *Theory of the Subject*, 41).
4 See Alain Badiou, *Ethics: An Essay on the Understanding of Evil*, trans. Peter Hallward (London: Verso, 2001).
5 Ranciere's theory of mute speech is essentially a theory of literary language as an indifferent mode of communicable intelligibility; see Jacques Rancière, *Mute Speech: Literature, Critical Theory, and Politics* (New York: Columbia University Press, 2011), 41–62.
6 Quine's famous 'indeterminacy of translation' argument in Willard Van Orman Quine, *Word and Object* (Cambridge, MA: MIT Press, 1960), 73–9.
7 Naturally I am referring to my reading of *Being and Event* presented in Watkin, *Badiou and Indifferent Being*.

8 This he calls a *calculated phenomenology* which has much in common with the objective elements of phenomenology that have dominated the previous century. Objective phenomenology means rejecting the process of intentional consciousness as the root of the appearing of objects in worlds, so that we end up with a phenomenology of 'pure description, a description without a subject. This "letting emerge" simply seeks to locally test the logical resistance of being-there … to then filter all of this through the sieve of formalization' (*LW* 38–9). This effectively explains the many long examples that make up a good portion of the book.
9 A central thesis of the first two volumes of my ongoing studies on indifference is the constructed nature of difference combined with the concomitant that there can be different 'kinds' of difference: indifferent difference in Hegel, difference within identity in Heidegger, *différance* in Derrida, difference that precedes identity in Deleuze, nonrelational difference, radical non-relational difference and so on in Badiou. The central failing of the philosophy of difference since Hegel, basically the over-valorization and self-blinding presupposition of difference as a radical mode of undermining a metaphysics of presence, is perhaps reducible to the simple fact of a refusal to address the question: which kind of difference?
10 Watkin, *Badiou and Indifferent Being*, 168–9.

Book I

1 See Watkin, *Badiou and Indifferent Being*, Chapter 6: 'The Event, Intervention and Fidelity', 161–88.
2 As we saw in the 'Introduction', a quality in category theory is a function.
3 See section on the 'Axiom of Choice' in Watkin, *Badiou and Indifferent Being*, 175–8.
4 For more on this essential, yet unexpected process, see Badiou, *Second Manifesto*, 91–104.
5 Agamben's theory of signatures is presented in the second chapter of *The Signature of All Things: On Method*, trans. Luca D'Isanto with Kevin Attell (New York: Zone Books, 2009), 33–80. And further explained in Watkin, *Agamben and Indifference*, 18–24.
6 For more on the relation of *Logics* to extension, see Badiou, *Second Manifesto*, 49.

Book II

1 The generic is a mode of treating indifferent multiples in a cardinal infinity wherein specifics of rank are unavailable because the cardinality of the set is nondenumerable. The generic, for example, allows one to treat any multiple

whatsoever as being rankable, even if, given the current situation within a cardinal infinity, you do not know the specific rank.

2. It is a formalization, effectively, of Hegel's 'indifferent difference', or $A \neq B$, which does not however end up in bad indifference of indetermination or of absolute, non-relational determination. Hence no need for the dialectic to solve this aporia, hence no need for a philosophy of difference!

3. 'The fact that a multiple is in some way localized, such that the multiple indifference of its being is assigned to a world, goes beyond the resource of this multiple-being as thought by mathematics' (Badiou, *Second Manifesto*, 30).

4. Badiou's use of the term universe is somewhat confusing. While the text is called *Logics of Worlds* and he makes it clear that universes don't exist because there is no absolute Whole, at other times he speaks of worlds as universes and stipulates that on the whole worlds, at least the Cartesian ones typical of much category theory, are finite and thus closed. This being the case a universe, being a closed world, is by definition smaller than a world taken as an actual infinity, which is what is meant his comments here so that a universe, if it does exist, is smaller than a world.

5. In *Mathematics of the Transcendental* Badiou is clear that categories are not all infinite just as all functions in a category are not all degrees of relationality. So just as we saw that in the categorization of existential appearing it is relationality that is the only functional relation that matters, what this also means is that existentially categorized worlds are all actual infinities. Again in *Logics* this is never clearly stated but because as he says we are dealing with worlds that are never Wholes, then we are able to make this deductive clarification. Not all categories are infinite sets of relational functions, indeed most used by mathematics are not, but as regards the objective phenomenology of appearing, they are. This appears to be a position that shifted between writing the first and second part of the book.

6. Badiou mentions the ease of duality in categories in chapter 6 of *MT*, 37–40.

7. Badiou's first intuition of the place that does not take place, etc., is to be found in his idea of the splace in Badiou, *Theory of the Subject*, 3–50, and in his various comments over the years on Mallarmé's famous dictum: 'Nothing will have taken place but the place', for example *Theory of the Subject*, 7. Traditional views on this idea of communicability, for example, Heidegger's 'language never has the floor', have tended to think of the pure presentability of the place of presentation as a blank space awaiting inscription but which can never itself be inscribed, which is little more than Russell's paradox. It is a characteristic of the philosophy of indifference, Badiou, Agamben and my own work, to think of the communicability function *qua* function, as an operation that is place-making, not a location.

8. See Badiou, *Second Manifesto*, 31 for more on the multiple vs appearing object question.

9. Watkin, *Badiou and Indifferent Being*, 11–13.

10. See Badiou, *Second Manifesto*, 39.

Book III

1. The atemporality of categories is up for debate. For example, the composability of categories requires that you follow relations of functions in order which means they are temporal strings of functions, one function comes before another. On the other hand, the structure of relations does not depend in any sense on time-consciousness and the tabular triangulation of relations itself negates the seriality of the localized order of functional relations essential to composability. Finally, what is patently obvious is that subjectivation is temporal: it consists of a series of yes/no decisions in a particular context, in the present tense, due to an event and which themselves have consequences for future decisions.
2. See Fraser, 'Introduction', xxxix–xl for more on the Kantian elements of Badiou's object.
3. See Hallward, *Badiou*, 302.
4. Badiou is already thinking about place and indexing in *Theory of the Subject*, 6–7.
5. An influential thesis proposed in 1957 by Heidegger is that a being can be the same as itself but not identical, Martin Heidegger, *Identity and Difference*, trans. Joan Stambaugh (Chicago, IL: University of Chicago Press, 1969), 26. This is, as you may be aware, the basis of Derrida's deconstruction of presence. What category theory allows is for a being to be the same being in any world, yet participate in degrees of self-identity from total to nil. This simple innovation negates the entire basis of Derrida's incredible body of work and many other texts taken from the philosophy of difference. Badiou is equally dismissive of Heidegger on this point (Badiou, *Second Manifesto*, 40–1).
6. See Badiou, *Theory of the Subject*, 61 and 70 for Badiou's first thoughts on the relation of void to the real of the atom.
7. The clearest definition of the difference between a thing (multiple) and an object (apparent) is probably to be found in Badiou, *Second Manifesto*, 47–9 and 52. Here he states that things are indifferent, while objects are differential degrees of relation, explaining in relation to Heidegger: 'a thing is between indifference and difference, nothingness and objectivity' (Badiou, *Second Manifesto*, 47), although by this he means what we have called in-difference of the void in our first study. We have in-difference of the void, quality indifference of multiplicities of multiples (thing) and then the object as differential.
8. See 'Three Demonstrations' (*LW* 271–5).

Book IV

1. For a full engagement between Wittgenstein and Badiou, I call the reader's attention to Badiou's *Wittgenstein's Antiphilosophy*, trans. Bruno Bosteels (London: Verso, 2011).

2   Badiou, *Second Manifesto*, 81. The choice of the term surnumerary by the translator is confusing; it seems better that we stick to the supernumerary that is used in earlier translations of Badiou's work.

Book V

1   A simple way to think of this relation is to imagine the Wittgenstein of *Tractatus*' 'the world is all … ' and of *Philosophical Investigations* 'form-of life' and just make both concepts plural so that we have 'worlds are all that is the case' and multiple 'forms of life'.
2   For more on modification, see Badiou, *Second Manifesto*, 74–6.
3   See also Badiou, *Second Manifesto*, 57 and 78–9.
4   Watkin, *Badiou and Indifferent Being*, 50–3.
5   Ibid., 94–8.
6   I am thinking specifically of the fifth 'Theses on Politics' in Jacques Rancière, *Dissensus: On Politics and Aesthetics*, trans. Steven Corcoran (London: Bloomsbury, 2010), 33–5.
7   Badiou himself uses the Foucauldian term statement to describe the event in Badiou, *Second Manifesto*, 87.
8   See *Theory of the Subject*, 'Part III, Lack and Destruction', 111–76.

Book VI

1   Badiou, *Second Manifesto*, 126.
2   This is perhaps best expressed in the diagram inside the back cover of *Second Manifesto of Philosophy* which shows to lines converging on the event, one marked indifferent multiplicities, the other eternal truths. He explains the diagram as follows: 'The line which goes from "indifferent multiplicities" to the evental rupture organizes the *objective* supports of a truth's construction, which are really given in a world, whereas the line which goes from the event to "eternal truths" sets out the *subjective* categories induced by individuals' incorporation within the becoming of this truth. Between these two lies, there is a vertical correspondence' (Badiou, *Second Manifesto*, 115).
3   Tiresome as it is to keep citing my own work, I refer the reader to the only extensive reading of this relation in Watkin, *Agamben and Indifference*, 151–80.
4   Still tiresome but necessary, I refer the reader to my discussion in *Badiou and Indifferent Being*, 84–7.

5   Historically until Agamben, Badiou and my own work, indifference is presented by philosophy as 'bad', for example, Kantian 'indifferentism', lacking the rational means to decide between two opposing systems. Badiou must be thanked for the complex way he has transformed our attitude to indifference, in a sense his indifference is more positive than Agamben's suspensive form. That said, he still, from time to time, presents indifference as a negative adjective as we are doing here in terms of democratic materialism's indifferentism: the inability to choose based on failure to accept that there are truths about which one has no choice.

Book VII

1   Pullback is a categorical limit function that establishes a third object relative to two related objects, exposing their initial relation in such a way as a third point, the exponent, creates a commutative triangle with the first two objects as the base. If we call the initial relation A to B, then an exponent or pullback, called C, makes C to B functionally equivalent to C to A to B. It is the basic categorical function, the foundation of universal exposition, and in addition we have to concede that all relations entertain a pullback. The pullback is the vantage point from which the relation between two objects can be seen by a third, or how a diagram becomes a category. See Hallward, *Badiou*, 305 and *MT* 33-6. Categories that admit pullbacks are typical of topoi.
2   The apostrophe, the invocation, the ode, elegy and so on, all ancient features of poetry across numerous cultures take on a functional clarity here which is quite remarkable.
3   Badiou, *Second Manifesto*, 85.
4   See François Laruelle, *Anti-Badiou: On the Introduction of Maoism into Philosophy*, trans. Robin Mackay (London: Bloomsbury, 2013).

Conclusion

1   Alain Badiou, *The Concept of the Model*, trans. Zachary Luke Fraser and Tzuchien Tho (Melbourne: re.press, 2007), 54.

Bibliography

Angot-Pellissier, R. 2015. 'The Relation between Logic, Set Theory and Topos Theory as It Is Used by Alain Badiou', in *The Road to Universal Logic. Studies in Universal Logic*, ed. A. Koslow and A. Buchsbaum. Cham: Birkhäuser, 181–200.

Agamben, Giorgio. 1999. *The End of the Poem*, trans. Daniel Heller-Roazen. Stanford, CA: Stanford University Press.

Agamben, Giorgio. 2009. *The Signature of All Things: On Method*, trans. Luca D'Isanto and Kevin Attell. New York: Zone Books.

Ashton, Paul, A.J. Bartlett and Justin Clemens (eds.). 2006. *The Praxis of Alain Badiou*. Melbourne: re.press.

Badiou, Alain. 1999. *Manifesto for Philosophy*, trans. Norman Madarasz. Albany, NY: SUNY Press.

Badiou, Alain. 2000. *Deleuze: The Clamor of Being*, trans. Louise Burchill. Minneapolis: University of Minnesota Press.

Badiou, Alain. 2001. *Ethics: An Essay on the Understanding of Evil*, trans. Peter Hallward. London: Verso.

Badiou, Alain. 2003a. *On Beckett*, ed. Nina Power and Alberto Toscano. Manchester: Clinamen Press.

Badiou, Alain. 2003b. *St. Paul: The Foundation of Universalism*, trans. Ray Brassier. Stanford, CA: Stanford University Press.

Badiou, Alain. 2004. *Theoretical Writings*, ed. and trans. Ray Brassier and Alberto Toscano. London: Continuum.

Badiou, Alain. 2005a. *Being and Event*, trans. Oliver Feltham. London: Continuum.

Badiou, Alain. 2005b. *Handbook of Inaesthetics*, trans. Alberto Toscano. Stanford, CA: Stanford University Press.

Badiou, Alain. 2005c. *Metapolitics*, trans. Jason Barker. London: Verso.

Badiou, Alain. 2006a. *Briefings on Existence: A Short Treatise on Transitory Ontology*, trans. Norman Madarasz. Albany, NY: SUNY Press.

Badiou, Alain. 2006b. *Infinite Thought*, trans. Oliver Feltham and Justin Clemens. London: Continuum.

Badiou, Alain. 2007a. *The Century*, trans. Alberto Toscano. Cambridge: Polity.

Badiou, Alain. 2007b. *The Concept of the Model*, trans. Zachary Luke Fraser and Tzuchien Tho. Melbourne: re.press.

Badiou, Alain. 2008a. *Conditions*, trans. Steven Corcoran. London: Continuum.

Badiou, Alain. 2008b. *Number and Numbers*, trans. Robin Mackay. Cambridge: Polity.

Badiou, Alain. 2009a. *Logics of Worlds*, trans. Alberto Toscano. London: Continuum.

Badiou, Alain. 2009b. *Theory of the Subject*, trans. Bruno Bosteels. London: Continuum.
Badiou, Alain. 2011a. *Second Manifesto for Philosophy*, trans. Louise Burchill. Cambridge: Polity.
Badiou, Alain. 2011b. *Wittgenstein's Antiphilosophy*, trans. Bruno Bosteels. London: Verso.
Badiou, Alain. 2014. *Mathematics of the Transcendental*, trans. A.J. Bartlett and Alex Ling. London: Bloomsbury.
Badiou, Alain. 2018. *L'Immanence des Verités*. Paris: Fayard.
Badiou, Alain and Tzuchien Tho. 2007. 'The Concept of Model, Forty Years Later: An Interview with Alain Badiou', in Alain Badiou, *The Concept of the Model*, ed. and trans. Frazer Zachary Luke and Tzuchien Tho. Melbourne: re.press, 79–104.
Bar-Am, Nimrod. 2008. *Extensionalism: The Revolution in Logic*. London: Springer.
Barker, Jason. 2002. *Alain Badiou: A Critical Introduction*. London: Pluto Press.
Bartlett, A.J. and Alex Ling. 2014. 'The Categorical Imperative', in *Mathematics of the Transcendental*, ed. Badiou Alain. London: Bloomsbury, 1–10.
Bartlett, A.J. and Justin Clemens. 2010. *Alain Badiou: Key Concepts*. Durham: Acumen Press.
Bartlett, A.J., Justin Clemens and Jon Roffe. 2014. *Lacan Deleuze Badiou*. Edinburgh: Edinburgh University Press.
Beaney, Michael (ed.). 1997. *The Frege Reader*. Oxford: Blackwell.
Bell, J.L. 1998. *Toposes and Local Set Theories*. Mineola, NY: Dover.
Bosteels, Bruno. 2009. 'Introduction', in *Theory of the Subject*, trans. Alain Badiou and Bruno Bosteels. London: Continuum, xvi–xxxvii.
Bosteels, Bruno. 2011. *Badiou and Politics*. Durham: Duke University Press.
Bowden, Sean and Simon Duffy. 2012. *Badiou and Philosophy*. Edinburgh: Edinburgh University Press.
Carnap, Rodolf. 1947. *Meaning and Necessity*. Chicago, IL: Chicago University Press.
Carnap, Rodolf. 2003. *The Logics Structure of the World*, trans. Rolf A. George. Peru, IL: Carus Press.
Constantinou, Marious. 2009. 'Badiou's Topology of Action as an Ethical Epistemology of the Event', *Environment and Planning D: Society and Space* 27, 771–82.
Constantinou, Marios and Norman Madarasz. 2009. 'Being and Spatialization: An Interview with Alain Badiou', *Environment and Planning D: Society and Space* 27, 783–95.
Deleuze, Gilles. 1994. *Difference and Repetition*, trans. Paul Patton. London: The Athlone Press.
Deleuze, Gilles and Félix Guattari. 1992. *A Thousand Plateaus: Capitalism and Schizophrenia*, trans. Brian Massumi. London: The Athlone Press.
Derrida, Jacques. 1978. *Writing and Difference*, trans. Alan Bass. London: Routledge.
Derrida, Jacques. 1982. *Margins of Philosophy*, trans. Alan Bass. London: Harvester.
Derrida, Jacques. 1992. *Acts of Literature*, ed. Derek Attridge. London: Routledge.
Feltham, Oliver. 2008. *Alain Badiou: Live Theory*. London: Continuum.

Foucault, Michel. 1972. *The Archaeology of Knowledge*, trans. A.M. Sheridan Smith. London: Routledge.

Fraser, Zachary Luke. 2007. 'Introduction: The Category of Formalization: From Epistemological Break to Truth Procedure', in Alain Badiou, *The Concept of the Model*, ed. and trans. Zachary Luke Frazer and Tzuchien Tho. Melbourne: re.press, xiii–lxv.

Gibson, Andrew. 2006. *Beckett and Badiou: The Pathos of Intermittency*. Oxford: Oxford University Press.

Gibson, Andrew. 2012. *Intermittency: The Concept of Historical Reason in Recent French Philosophy*. Edinburgh: Edinburgh University Press.

Gillespie, Sam. 2008. *The Mathematics of Novelty: Badiou's Minimalist Metaphysics*. Melbourne: re.press.

Goldblatt, Robert. 2006. *Topoi: The Categorical Analysis of Logic*. Mineola, NY: Dover Publications.

Habermas, Jürgen. 1988. *On the Pragmatics of Communication*, ed. Maeve Cooke. Cambridge: Polity.

Hallward, Peter. 2003. *Badiou: A Subject to Truth*. Minneapolis: University of Minnesota Press.

Hallward, Peter. 2004. *Think Again: Alain Badiou and the Future of Philosophy*. London: Continuum.

Hegel, G.W.F. 1969. *Science of Logic*, trans. A.V. Miller. Amherst, NY: Humanity Books.

Hegel, G.W.F. 1977. *Phenomenology of Spirit*, trans. A.V. Miller. Oxford: Oxford University Press.

Heidegger, Martin. 1969. *Identity and Difference*, trans. Joan Stambaugh. Chicago, IL: University of Chicago Press.

Kant, Immanuel. 1952. *The Critique of Judgement*, trans. James Creed Meredith. Oxford: Clarendon Press.

Kant, Immanuel. 2007. *Critique of Pure Reason*, trans. Marcus Weigelt. London: Penguin.

Laruelle, François. 2010. *Philosophies of Difference: A Critical Introduction to Non-philosophy*, trans. Rocco Gangle. London: Continuum.

Laruelle, François. 2013. *The Anti-Badiou: On the Introduction of Maoism into Philosophy*, trans. Robin Mackay. London: Bloomsbury.

Lawvere, F. William and Stephen H. Schanuel. 1991. *Conceptual Mathematics*. Cambridge: Cambridge University Press.

Lecercle, Jean-Jacques. 2010. *Badiou and Deleuze Read Literature*. Edinburgh: Edinburgh University Press.

Livingstone, Paul. 2011. *The Politics of Logics: Badiou, Wittgenstein, and the Consequences of Formalism*. New York: Routledge.

MacCannell, Juliet Flower. 2009. 'Eternity or Infinity? Badiou's Point', *Environment and Planning D: Society and Space* 27, 823–39.

McCarty, D.C. 2005. 'Intuitionism in Mathematics', in *The Oxford Handbook of Philosophy of Mathematics and Logics*, ed. Stewart Shapiro. Oxford: Oxford University Press, 356–86.

Madarasz, Norman. 2009. 'The Regularity of Non-Being: Space and Form in Alain Badiou's System', *Environment and Planning D: Society and Space* 27, 796–822.

Norris, Christopher. 2009. *Badiou's Being and Event*. London: Continuum.

Norris, Christopher. 2012. *Derrida, Badiou and the Formal Imperative*. London: Continuum.

Papineau, David. 2012. *Philosophical Devices: Proofs, Probabilities, and Sets*. Oxford: Oxford University Press.

Plotinsky, Arkady. 2012. 'Experimenting with Ontologies: Sets, Spaces, and Topoi with Badiou and Grothendieck', *Environment and Planning D: Society and Space* 30.2, 351–68.

Pluth, Ed. 2010. *Alain Badiou*. London: Polity.

Posey, Carl. 2005. 'Intuitionism and Philosophy', in *The Oxford Handbook of Philosophy of Mathematics and Logics*, ed. Stewart Shapiro. Oxford: Oxford University Press, 318–54.

Potter, Michael. 2004. *Set Theory and Its Philosophy*. Oxford: Oxford University.

Pozorov, Sergei. 2013. 'What Is the "World' "in World Politics? Heidegger, Badiou and Void Universalism', *Contemporary Political Theory* 12.2, 102–22.

Quine, Willard Van Orman. 1960. *Word and Object*. Cambridge, MA: MIT Press.

Quine, Willard Van Orman. 1980. *From a Logical Point of View*. Cambridge, MA: Harvard University Press.

Rancière, Jacques. 2010. *Dissensus: On Politics and Aesthetics*, trans. Steven Corcoran. London: Bloomsbury.

Rancière, Jacques. 2011. *Mute Speech: Literature, Critical Theory, and Politics*. New York: Columbia University Press.

Riera, Gabriel. 2005. *Alain Badiou: Philosophy and Its Conditions*. Albany, NY: SUNY Press.

Roffe, Jon. 2012. *Badiou's Deleuze*. Durham: Acumen Press.

Ruda, Frank. 2015. *For Badiou: Idealism without Idealism*. Evanston, IL: Northwestern University Press.

Shapiro, Stewart. 2001. *Thinking about Mathematics: The Philosophy of Mathematics*. Oxford: Oxford University Press.

Shapiro, Stewart (ed.). 2005. *The Oxford Handbook of Philosophy of Mathematics and Logic*. Oxford: Oxford University Press.

Shaw, Ian and Graham Ronald. 2012. 'Sites, Truths and Logics of Worlds: Alain Badiou and Human Geography', *Transactions* 35.3, 431–42.

Simmons, Harold. 2011. *An Introduction to Category Theory*. Cambridge: Cambridge University Press.

Steinhart, Eric. 2009. *More Precisely: The Math You Need to Do Philosophy*. Peterborough, Ontario: Broadview Press.

Tiles, Mary. 1989. *The Philosophy of Set Theory: A Historical Introduction to Cantor's Paradise*. Mineola, NY: Dover Publications.

Trott, Adriel. 2011. 'The Truth of Politics in Alain Badiou: "There Is only One World"', *Parrhesia: A Journal of Critical Philosophy* 12, 82–93.

Van Houdt, John. 2011. 'The Crisis of Negation: And Interview with Alain Badiou', *Continent* 1.4, 234–8.

Watkin, William. 2015. *Agamben and Indifference*. London: Rowman & Littlefield International.

Watkin, William. 2017. *Badiou and Indifferent Being*. London: Bloomsbury.

Wittgenstein, Ludwig. 1963. *Philosophical Investigations*. Oxford: Blackwell.

Index

A
aesthetic 46, 84, 185, 235
aesthetics 180, 185, 193, 262
affect 50, 61–3, 68
affirmative 62, 73, 214, 254
affirms 32, 51, 124, 141, 238
Agamben 3, 31, 52, 60–1, 103, 197, 204, 218, 243, 258–60, 262–3
agent 63, 185, 221, 226
aggregate 11, 218
algebra 66, 71, 83, 101, 112–13, 116–17, 122, 150, 202, 207, 229–30, 256
algebraic 8, 13, 23, 101, 112, 147–8, 150, 202, 204, 229–30, 244, 256
alliumatic 3, 247
already-existent 34, 46, 93, 162, 182, 189–91, 193–4, 234
alterity 74, 76, 82
Althusser 30, 47, 243
amorous 61, 190
analytical 51–2, 166, 222, 251
anarchist 122–3, 129, 131–3, 137, 141, 145–6, 149
anarcho 126, 128
Angot-pellissier, r 264
animal 29, 60, 218, 238–9
anomic 172
anonymous 41, 40, 43, 235
antecedent 194
Anthropocene 25
anthropological 36, 62
antiphilosophy 261
antisymmetry 106–8, 111, 113, 121
apex 23, 169
apodictic 250
apostrophe 263
apparent 55, 73–4, 83, 87–8, 93–6, 115–16, 122, 127, 129, 131, 144, 162, 171, 177, 212, 239, 261
apparents 87, 94, 99–100, 108–9, 111, 121–2, 127–9, 256

appear 5–7, 17–18, 21, 26, 34, 40, 49, 51, 53, 58, 60–1, 63, 65–6, 68–73, 78–92, 94, 96–100, 104–5, 108, 110, 112, 115–22, 124–32, 135, 137, 140–3, 145–6, 148–50, 152–3, 159–62, 166, 168, 170–4, 176, 181–5, 191–2, 194, 198, 203, 205, 212, 216–19, 221, 225, 227, 234, 239, 246–7, 251
appearance 6, 8, 25, 39, 42, 59, 63, 70–3, 81, 83, 87–90, 92–8, 100, 105, 108–10, 115–18, 120, 122, 124–5, 129–30, 133, 138, 143, 146–7, 150, 159–61, 165, 171–3, 177, 181–2, 184, 190, 192, 194–5, 231, 236, 240, 249, 251
appeared 25, 34, 59, 88, 150, 171, 184
appearing 5, 7–9, 13–14, 26, 33–4, 39–42, 54, 58–61, 63, 65–8, 70–5, 77–90, 92–3, 96–101, 103–5, 107–10, 113–22, 124–36, 138–45, 147–51, 153–4, 162, 170–3, 176–7, 180–6, 189, 192, 195–7, 203, 205–7, 211–12, 214, 216, 221, 225–8, 230, 238–9, 251, 259–60
appearing-in-a-world 66
appearing-in-truth 58
appearing-world 136
appears 18, 25–6, 48, 50, 58, 64, 69–71, 78–9, 81–4, 86–7, 89–92, 94, 97–8, 100, 105, 108, 111, 115–16, 119–20, 124–6, 128, 130–2, 134, 136–7, 140–7, 149, 152, 159–62, 165–6, 171–3, 176–7, 179–86, 192–3, 195, 198, 207, 210, 212, 216–17, 219, 222–3, 234, 239, 251, 254, 260
archetypes 61, 157
Archimedes 37, 59
architecture 5, 210
Ariadne 79–81, 84
Ariadne and Bluebeard 79, 84
Aristotle 1, 11, 59, 75, 108–9, 160, 237

army 50, 52–5, 58, 60–1, 188, 203
arrow 6–7, 11–20, 22, 24, 48, 64, 77, 183, 251
articulation 43, 59, 68–9, 79, 118, 139, 183, 202, 204, 207, 223, 256–8
artistic 61
arts 62
ascetically 226
asceticism 235
Aschenbach 40–1
Ashton 264
associative 11–15, 17, 21–4, 26, 121, 123, 134, 206, 245–6, 250
associativity 9, 123, 246
asymmetry 12–13, 24, 122–3, 136, 183, 245, 247, 250–3
atemporal, a-temporal 34, 57, 116, 236, 261
atom 29, 39, 48–9, 118, 125, 127–37, 139, 142–56, 156, 161, 172–4, 176–7, 216–17, 225, 232, 253, 261
atonal 212, 216–17, 228–29, 231, 235, 238, 241
Aufhebung 31
autumnal scene 87–100, 109–11
axiom of antisymmetry 111
axiom of choice 54, 222, 224, 259
axiom of distributivity 185
axiom of materialism 131
axiom of ontology 118
axiom of relation 165
axiom of replacement 17
axiom of separation 102
axiom of substitutability 18
axiom of symmetry 106, 140
axioms of being 68, 86
axioms of collection 51
axioms of interiorization 214
axioms of ontology 181, 197, 253
axioms of reflexivity 107, 113
axioms of set theory 4, 7, 98, 100, 103, 125, 170, 197, 211, 224, 234, 244
axiomatic 45, 49, 77, 103, 106, 113–14, 131, 139, 167, 180, 183, 186, 218, 222–5, 234, 247
axiomatization 1

B

Badiou
    Being and Event 2–3, 5–7, 9–11, 24–5, 32–5, 40, 42, 45, 47, 54–5, 58, 64–9, 74–5, 86, 99, 101, 104, 108, 116, 130, 135, 159–60, 163–4, 174, 181, 183, 191–2, 213, 219, 222, 229, 232, 239, 244, 253, 255–8
    Concept of the Model, the 255, 257, 263
    Ethics: An Understanding of Evil 258
    L'Immanence des Vérités 256
    Logics of Worlds 29, 30, 32, 34–7, 39–43, 45–8, 50–4, 56–61, 63, 66–73, 75–98, 102, 104–9, 111, 112, 115–27, 129–39, 141, 142, 144–56, 159–73, 175–7, 179–82, 184–91, 193–7, 203–7, 209–17, 221, 224–35, 237–41, 256, 257, 259, 261
    Manifesto for philosophy 258, 264–5
    Mathematics of the Transcendental 11, 24, 49, 65, 66, 169, 251, 256, 260, 263
    Number and Numbers 7, 264
    Paul: The foundation of Universalism 264
    Second manifesto of philosophy 221, 258–63, 265
    Theoretical writings 264
    Theory of the subject 31, 45–7, 61, 236, 255–6, 258, 260–2, 265
    Wittgenstein's Antiphilosophy 261
background 77, 91, 126, 138, 184, 202
banner 120–21
Bar-Am 1, 255, 265
Barker 264–5
Bartleby 204
Bartlett 255–6, 264–5
bathers 123–4
battles 156, 166, 203
Beaney 265
becoming 40, 63, 80, 133, 180, 184, 189, 191–2, 262
becoming-object 132
being as such 34, 67, 76, 80–1, 83, 86, 115, 117–18, 132, 136, 150, 153, 159, 161, 172, 179, 183, 195, 222
being is assigned 260
being is composite 150
being is derived 79
being is determined 65, 228
being is inaccessible 174
being is indifferent 79, 218, 243, 254
being is material 118
being is mediated 79

being is-not 8, 65, 86, 183, 222
being-qua-being 67, 80-1, 85, 130, 165
being-there 8, 30, 33, 66-9, 71-3, 78, 80-3, 85-7, 89, 91-7, 104, 107, 112-13, 115, 119, 121, 125, 136, 138, 147, 150, 159, 161, 181-3, 186, 202, 207, 210, 213-14, 259
being-there-in-this-world 124, 130
being-thereness 71
Bell 265
belonging 1, 3-5, 12-14, 18, 54-5, 66, 76, 83, 92, 99, 111, 123-4, 127-8, 130, 132, 134-5, 140-1, 143, 149, 175, 183, 212, 247
belongs 76, 113, 127, 129, 134, 142-4, 146, 163, 177, 186, 209, 239
bike 88, 91, 93-4
binary 201, 205-7, 211, 214, 226, 231, 237
biopolitical 29, 216, 238-9
bios 31
bio-subjective 60
bi-sexed 62
biunivocal 35
bi-valenced 68
Bluebeard 79, 84, 81
bodies 29-35, 39, 41-2, 45-6, 48, 55, 59, 61, 116, 204, 215, 218, 221, 224, 229, 231-2, 234-5, 237, 239, 246-8, 253-4
bodies and languages 29-31, 33, 35, 39, 215, 232, 239, 253
body 29-30, 33-4, 36-41, 45-53, 55-64, 91, 102, 116, 189, 201, 203-4, 210, 215, 219, 221, 223, 226-38, 241, 247-8, 254, 261
bolshevism 121
Boole 1
Bosteels 255-6, 261, 265
bound 10, 25, 68, 71-2, 86, 98, 111, 122, 138, 142, 144, 149, 151, 157, 181
bourgeois 121
Bowden 265
bracketing 71
Brasilia 209-13
briefings on existence 264
buildings 36, 184, 213

C
caesura 40
calculate 192

calculated 41, 45, 72, 94, 192, 229-30, 234, 259
calculus 59
Cantor 1, 51, 76, 100, 163-4, 175, 185
capitalism 29, 56
cardinal 3, 51, 69, 100, 107, 160, 175-6, 247, 259-60
Carnap 42
categories 1, 4-24, 27, 31, 47-9, 51-2, 64, 70-1, 73-4, 77, 98-100, 183, 202, 245-9, 251-2, 256-8, 260-3
categories and communicability 24
categories and indifference 20
categories and sets 8
categories are infinite 260
categories are intuitionist 23
categories are non-classical 256
categories called sets 16
categories called topos 257
categories entertain posets 10
category 3-27, 31, 33, 38, 42, 47-50, 64, 70, 73-5, 77, 82-3, 96, 98-101, 107-13, 120-3, 127, 132, 136, 138, 140, 149, 155, 160, 167, 172, 186, 202-3, 209, 218, 223, 230, 238, 241, 244-6, 248-53, 255-61, 263
category theory 3-9, 12, 14-21, 24, 31, 38, 42, 47-50, 64, 70, 73-5, 77, 83, 96, 98-9, 101, 107-13, 121, 123, 127, 136, 140, 149, 155, 160, 167, 186, 202-3, 209, 218, 223, 230, 241, 244-6, 249-53, 255-61
Cauchy 230
cavalry 53, 203
cemetery 227-8
Centauri 170
chain 76, 233
chance 173, 187, 197, 239
change 2, 6, 39, 42, 47, 51, 54, 56, 59, 64, 66, 115, 132-3, 151, 156-7, 159, 167, 173-4, 176-7, 179-81, 183-4, 186-91, 203, 213, 215, 221, 223, 225, 228, 234-5, 247
chiaroscuro 241
choice 51, 54, 201, 203-7, 212-13, 215, 222, 224, 235, 241, 259, 263
circular 194, 20
citizen 167-9, 172
city 53, 57, 184, 209-10, 213

civic 53, 173
classes 1, 11, 99, 108, 156
class-essence 21
classification 9, 24–7
classify 24, 55, 61, 25, 206
Clemens 264–5
clots 5, 22
clumps 5, 18, 22, 189
cluster 26, 163
co-appear, co-appearance 66, 72, 87–8, 92, 119–22, 137, 141, 225
co-belonging 79, 131, 139, 142, 226
co-cause 131, 142
co-determines 36
codomain 7, 13–14, 16–20, 48, 77
coexistence 147, 207
Cognitive value 197
Cohen 68, 135
coherence 53, 69, 140, 205, 231, 234, 241
coherent 71, 155, 172, 195, 204–5, 232–4
cohesion 60, 69, 153, 196, 231, 236
co-implicate 36
collection 31, 46, 51, 92, 100–1, 108, 116, 176, 256
collective 33, 51, 131
colonial 59, 161–2
colour 21–2, 25, 39, 95, 121, 127, 131
columns 126–38, 143, 147–8, 154
column-tree 138
commitment 37, 46, 149, 153–5, 199, 215, 217, 236
communards 183, 188
commune 184, 189, 195–6
communicability 1–3, 14–15, 24, 26–7, 33–4, 36–7, 41–3, 46, 48, 52, 57, 59, 78, 104–5, 119, 140, 145, 157, 167, 176, 179, 185, 189, 197, 211, 214–19, 222, 224–5, 234, 237, 239–41, 243–7, 249–54, 257, 260
communicability-test 254
communicable 15, 24, 26, 34–9, 52, 57, 59–61, 63, 77, 80, 87, 104–5, 112, 119, 129, 136, 139, 145–6, 149, 157, 164, 167, 173–5, 184, 187, 190, 193–5, 197, 199, 205, 207, 215–16, 218, 222–5, 231, 234–9, 241, 243–6, 248–52, 254, 258
communism 30, 46
community 1–3, 6, 14, 32–3, 36, 166, 168, 224, 243–4, 248–9

commutative 7, 9, 11–13, 14, 21–3, 82, 123, 168–9, 183, 212, 243–50, 257, 263
compatibility 60, 118, 135, 137, 147–53, 176, 231–2, 236
compatible 20, 30, 120, 137–8, 147–52, 155–6, 176, 231–2, 234
completeness 111, 167, 169–70
composable 9, 12, 14, 19–23, 26, 122–3, 183, 245–6, 250, 261
compose 19, 34, 112, 162, 164–5, 228, 238
composed 3–4, 8, 10, 12, 15, 19, 37, 41, 45, 52, 63, 71–2, 75, 77, 79, 91, 101, 125, 142, 144, 151, 154, 162, 164–5, 175, 179, 185, 198, 204, 229, 232, 234, 240, 245
composes 42, 57, 61–2, 79, 83, 96, 132, 157, 163–4, 169, 175
composing 37, 53, 57
composite 11–12, 14, 20, 22, 42, 46, 125, 150, 168, 245
co-mutual 88
concentric 3
concept of the model 255, 257, 263–6
conditions 2, 4, 29, 34–5, 39, 61, 63–4, 75, 77, 111–12, 114, 132, 138, 181, 185, 231, 234, 236, 241
conserve 161, 176, 211
consistency 5, 60, 66, 68, 78, 81, 83, 87, 92, 98, 100, 115, 117, 131, 136, 139, 150, 157, 159, 163, 197, 199, 205, 210, 222, 224–5, 239
consistent 2, 4, 6, 9, 15, 18, 34, 41–2, 52, 75–6, 81–2, 98–100, 102, 115, 117, 119, 121–3, 139, 164, 169, 173, 179, 197–8, 202, 207, 215, 223, 225, 239–40, 250–1, 257
Constantinou 265
constructability 153, 197
constructed 32, 36, 42, 51, 57, 60, 102, 116, 129, 142, 161, 173, 247, 254, 259
constructible 60–1, 105, 129–30, 136, 154–6, 175, 197, 217, 237, 239
constructivist 34, 38, 42–3, 49, 54, 69, 101, 131, 199, 215, 222–3, 239
content-neutral 3, 46
co-relation 13, 148–9
corporeal 46, 203, 232–3
correlated 48, 231

correlation 72, 74, 91, 116, 133, 204
correspond 102, 130, 154, 166
correspondence 15, 35, 166, 262
count 77, 136, 175, 192
countable 254
count-as-one 65, 257
count-as-whole 65
counted 131, 138, 150
counting 175, 208

D

decide 51–2, 56, 64, 190, 203–4, 207, 235, 253, 263
decided 25, 63–4, 190, 193, 211, 231, 254, 256
decision 24, 52, 55, 70, 130, 201, 203, 208, 210–12, 214, 216–18, 228, 233, 254
decisionist 49, 201, 217, 237
decisions 49, 53, 55, 62–3, 102, 203–4, 207, 210, 215, 219, 248, 261
decomposability 163, 216
decomposition 91, 146, 163, 189
deconstruction 81, 215, 223, 243, 254, 261
deduction 20, 38–9, 74–5, 79, 100, 108, 130–1, 171, 196, 212
deductive 38–9, 46, 49, 76–7, 175, 224, 234, 236–7, 260
Deleuze 2, 36, 40, 80, 82, 91, 139, 144, 202, 204, 216, 243, 247, 259, 264–7
Deleuzian 36, 90, 130–1, 133
demo, demonstration 25, 120–35, 153, 155, 149, 205, 256
democratic 29–30, 32–3, 56, 60, 156, 215, 218, 237–41, 249, 253, 258, 263
denotative 52–5
dependence 8, 72, 84, 94–6, 99, 149, 187
derived 72, 76, 79, 94–100, 102–3, 114, 160–1, 165–6, 202, 227
Derrida 2, 30–1, 74, 81, 103, 202, 243, 247, 259, 261, 265, 267
Desanti 3
destination 48, 52, 56–8, 61
destruction 47, 57, 196–7, 235, 262
desubjectivized 85
determinate 38, 47, 73, 83, 97, 117, 124, 133, 233–4
determination 76, 82, 117, 132, 161–3, 170, 177, 232, 252, 257, 260
diagonal 48, 137

diagram 6, 9, 11–12, 14–15, 17, 23–4, 31, 123, 168–9, 246, 262–3
diagrammatic 7, 9, 14–15, 23–4, 73, 82, 112, 167, 191, 245
diagrammatically 5, 18
diagrams 4, 8, 10, 12, 14, 22–3, 26, 31, 70, 160, 168, 174, 250
dialectic 30–1, 35, 40, 74, 109, 232, 260
dialectical 29, 51, 74, 77
didactics 33
différance 259
difference 1–2, 4, 8, 18, 26, 30–3, 41, 43, 69, 71, 73–6, 81–5, 89, 100, 103–7, 110, 112, 114, 116–17, 120–1, 124–5, 128–9, 136, 140, 145, 163, 165–7, 187, 203, 205, 211, 213, 215, 218, 225–6, 228, 234, 238, 245, 251, 254, 256, 259–61
differences 2, 46, 65, 82–3, 85, 95, 104–6, 116–17, 119, 145–6, 152, 165, 174, 215, 218, 232–3, 240, 245, 251, 254
differential 2, 15, 19, 27, 40, 59, 68, 89, 92, 105, 121–2, 125, 205, 215, 252, 254, 257, 261
differentialism 218
differentially 4, 58, 104, 117, 119, 121, 251
differentiate 82, 122, 141, 163, 177, 250
differentiated 32–3, 38, 43, 50, 71, 81, 117, 127, 207, 240, 245
differentiates 10, 24, 110, 120, 123, 189, 196, 207, 234
differentiating 128
differentiation 17, 42, 51, 76, 172, 188, 218, 225, 233, 245
digital 29, 32
direction 12, 19–20, 22–3, 107, 142, 154, 174
directional 12–13, 15, 17, 66, 250
directionality 12, 20
discerned 24–6
discernible 9, 24, 26, 126, 244
discernment 25–7
discontinuity 60, 179–80
discontinuous 40, 79, 240
discourse 34–5, 57, 60, 156, 218, 225, 239, 244–5
discursive 39, 57, 129, 184, 217, 237, 244, 249
dis-identity 74

disjoined 89–93, 230
disjunction 62, 68, 89–92, 99, 137
disjunctive 40, 88, 91
disparateness 41
disparities 152
disseminating 138, 150, 156, 163
dissemination 66–7, 75, 159, 164–5, 175
dissymmetry 130
distinct 35, 41, 82, 106, 117, 120–1, 129, 143, 145, 159, 169, 245
distinction 70, 104, 110, 120–1, 183, 208, 246
distributivity 112–13, 176, 185
divisibility 75, 83, 107
domain 7, 11, 13, 16–19, 65–6, 77, 106, 255
dominate 91, 94, 109, 111, 149, 180, 227, 230, 250–1
dots 15
Duffy 265

E
either/or 203
element 17, 42, 46–8, 53, 57, 62, 69, 87–9, 92–4, 96, 102–3, 105–6, 108–13, 122, 124–30, 132–6, 138–40, 142–4, 148, 152–4, 156, 161, 164, 171–3, 176, 179, 186–7, 189, 191, 193–6, 198, 203, 206, 208–9, 212, 226, 230–1, 233–4, 237, 250
embedded 4, 22, 168, 191, 250
emerge, emergent 41, 96, 181, 259
empirical 30, 34–5, 42, 49, 61, 129, 139, 186, 196, 221–2
empty set 3, 5, 84, 126, 177, 183
encyclopaedia 24, 64
enquiries 54–5
entailment 187, 193
entails 61, 87, 104, 132, 161
envelop 19, 26, 37, 80, 110
envelope 72, 90, 92–6, 99–100, 109–14, 124, 138, 148, 150–5, 176, 187, 207, 216, 225–6, 233, 235, 251
enveloped 22, 37, 109, 111, 113, 119, 138, 155
envelopes 7, 13, 95, 100, 110, 156, 187, 207, 213, 228, 232
enveloping 97, 111, 138, 160, 251
envelopment 93, 95, 109–10, 112, 119, 196
envelops 91, 100, 111–12
epistemology 2, 255
equality, equalize 26, 29–30, 138, 140
equivalence 12–13, 24, 38, 46, 106–7, 108–9, 125, 150, 215, 229, 245–6, 248, 263
equivalence-relation 140
equivalence-structure 106
erasure 48, 53, 227
errancy 5, 240
essence 1, 2, 4, 11, 14, 30, 42, 58, 65, 69, 99, 106, 123, 133, 155, 167, 201, 203, 211, 229, 243, 246
eternal 33, 35–6, 38–40, 42–3, 58–9, 173, 197, 229, 239, 262
ethics 32, 76, 141, 149, 235, 238, 258
ethics: an essay 258, 264
evaluation 43, 65, 69, 85–7, 106–7, 116, 119–20, 123, 136, 166, 184, 205, 216, 229
event 2–7, 9–11, 14, 24–5, 30–5, 37, 40, 42–3, 45–60, 62–9, 74–5, 78, 86, 99, 101, 104–5, 108, 116, 130, 132, 135, 159–60, 163–4, 166, 173–4, 177, 181–3, 185–95, 197–9, 201–4, 206, 208, 210, 213–14, 217–19, 221–3, 225–7, 229–33, 235–7, 239–40, 244, 246–9, 251, 253–9, 261–2
evental 5–6, 26, 34, 38, 40, 46, 48–50, 53–5, 57, 59, 61–3, 102, 181, 183, 185, 187–8, 190, 193, 196–7, 201, 221, 224, 226–7, 229, 232–4, 236, 247–9, 253–4, 262
events 2–6, 26, 32–4, 37–8, 46–9, 51, 56, 58, 63, 91, 151, 173–4, 183, 186, 191–2, 194, 197–9, 201, 203, 217, 219, 222–4, 227, 229, 233–7, 246–8, 253–4
event-site 225
event-trace 51, 53
except that 30, 32–3, 42, 49, 73, 102, 105, 239, 253–4
exception 29–30, 32–3, 39, 40–3, 164, 181, 185, 189, 239, 254
excess 39–40, 61, 180, 237
excluded 6, 18, 23, 97, 256
exist 6, 9–12, 14, 18–19, 26, 29, 32–5, 37–8, 42, 45–6, 49, 54, 59, 66, 69–70, 80–1, 83, 86, 88, 95–7, 102–3, 106,

108, 116, 124–6, 129, 141–2, 145, 150–2, 154, 157, 160, 164–6, 172–5, 179, 182–6, 189, 191–5, 197–8, 201, 203, 210–11, 213, 215–16, 221, 223–5, 229, 235–8, 244, 246–7, 249–51, 253–4, 257, 260
existence 4, 11, 19–21, 27, 29, 34, 38, 40–1, 43, 46, 53–4, 66, 72, 78, 92, 96–105, 107, 115–17, 119, 123–5, 129–30, 136–9, 141–2, 146–8, 150–2, 154–6, 159–61, 165, 167, 171–4, 176–7, 180, 182–97, 202, 208, 211, 215, 218, 223–6, 230, 232–3, 236–7, 240, 249–50
existent 26, 63, 66, 104–5, 125, 135, 154, 174, 182, 185, 190, 192, 196, 202, 226, 230, 233–4, 244, 249–51
existential 10, 13, 16, 19, 62, 70, 75, 99, 137, 139, 152–5, 165–6, 188, 190, 194, 206, 244, 251, 260
existing 4, 26, 34, 113, 149, 154, 189, 192, 201, 203, 211, 224–5, 254
exists 6, 9, 11–13, 25–6, 31–2, 34, 39–40, 47–8, 51–2, 74, 77–8, 86, 90, 94, 96, 102–7, 109, 111, 113, 122–5, 130, 135, 141, 144, 146, 148, 150–2, 154–5, 159, 163–4, 168–9, 172–4, 176, 179, 181–2, 186–8, 194–7, 212, 216, 218, 224–5, 232, 234, 238, 246
exists-in-the-world 124
expansion 40, 121
exponent, exponentiation 20, 169, 228, 246, 256–7, 263
exposed 5, 19, 162, 169–70, 176, 198, 210–11, 225–6, 229, 240, 245–6, 248
exposes 118, 122, 170, 245, 263
exposition 6, 8, 10, 23, 48, 67, 69, 74, 167, 169–70, 173–4, 184, 198, 218, 225, 240, 244, 246–7, 257, 263
extension 42, 54, 63–4, 164, 197, 247–8, 259
extensional 1–2, 3, 24, 42, 63, 97, 108, 161, 191, 197, 218, 245, 247, 253, 255
extensive 7, 29, 41, 45, 49, 53, 64, 75, 160, 227, 255, 262
exteriority 161, 170

external 49, 73, 76, 96, 102, 163, 165, 169, 210
extrinsic 3–4, 6, 8, 65, 183, 209, 254, 256

F
faithful 49, 56–8, 63, 155–6, 181, 186–7, 221, 227, 236
Feltham 258, 264–5
finite 5, 16, 164, 175, 195, 240, 260
finitude 35, 164, 240
first-order predictive logic 102
fixion 132
force 6, 15, 26–7, 53, 68, 80, 86, 103, 124, 142, 179, 189–90, 195, 205, 207–8, 216, 227, 249–50
forced, forcing 8, 62, 166, 185, 197, 210, 212, 222, 229, 250
forces 48, 50, 189, 195, 197, 206, 250–1
formal 38–40, 45–8, 50–1, 58, 61–2, 67, 74, 77–8, 95, 101, 103, 110, 121, 139, 141–4, 146, 155, 157, 175–6, 186–9, 202–3, 207–8, 213, 221, 224–5, 229, 232–3, 235–6, 245–6, 249
formalism 2–3, 6, 8, 25, 34, 37, 45–51, 57–9, 62, 75, 99, 116, 156, 221, 224, 227, 232, 238, 241, 251, 257
formalization 109, 139, 245, 255, 259–60
formalize 10, 24, 38, 45, 151, 193, 244, 246, 251
formalized 37, 135, 249
Foucauldian 26, 35–6, 59–60, 195, 216, 241, 243, 250, 257, 262, 266
fragment 40, 58, 91–3, 110–11, 210
Fraser 255, 261, 263–4, 266
Frege 1, 42, 64, 102–3, 129, 197
function 5, 7–8, 10–22, 25, 31, 33, 49–50, 52–5, 65, 70, 73–4, 78, 88, 92–3, 98–100, 102–5, 109–10, 113, 116, 119–21, 134–5, 140–4, 146, 152, 154, 156, 160–1, 165, 168, 172–3, 176, 199, 206, 211, 217–18, 223, 230, 244–6, 248–51, 256–61, 263
functional 4, 10, 13–15, 17–24, 26–7, 31, 47, 49–50, 53, 63, 65, 73, 78, 99–101, 105, 116, 120–1, 123, 168, 202, 218, 245–7, 249–52, 254, 257, 260–1, 263
functionality 19–20, 70, 105

Index

functionally 12–13, 17, 19–25, 27, 31, 49–50, 120, 177, 245–6, 250, 256, 263
functions 1–2, 4, 8–9, 11–24, 26, 31, 46, 48, 51–2, 54, 68, 70, 98–9, 114, 140, 160, 165, 168, 176, 183, 227, 229–30, 244–6, 249–52, 254, 257, 260–1
functor 8, 55, 63, 65, 72, 98, 100–1, 136, 151–7, 184, 250–1

G
Galileo 16
Galois 229–31, 244
gaps 5, 18, 109, 112, 232
gathering 100, 213, 230–1
Gaugamela 156
generic 8, 30, 40–1, 43, 46, 48, 54–5, 58, 63, 66, 135, 145–6, 201, 232, 245, 254, 259
Gibson 219, 266
Gillespie 266
global 29, 62–3, 71–2, 77, 83, 93, 104–5, 110, 112, 136, 146–7, 153, 162, 170, 177, 205–6, 211–12, 225, 251, 253
global-local 104, 112, 136, 211
Gödel 5, 49, 76, 161, 164, 175
Goldblatt 7, 14–15, 18, 256–8, 266
greater logic 7–9, 14, 64–5, 113–17, 122, 153, 155, 159, 171, 177, 180, 182–3, 185, 187, 197, 202, 205, 207, 211, 217, 232, 236, 257
Group, grouping 20, 120–2, 129, 131, 133, 141, 144–5, 153–6, 160, 168, 173, 192–3, 213–14, 229–30
Guattari 265

H
Habermas 205, 243, 266
Hallward 3, 255, 257–8, 261, 263–4, 266
halting point 38, 42, 46, 49, 75, 78, 85, 87, 107, 125–6, 134–5, 155, 163–4, 185, 197–8, 205, 209–10, 212, 216–17, 224
Hegel 30–1, 74, 101, 109, 155, 259–60
Heidegger 4, 76, 81, 91, 177, 227, 243, 259, 260–1
Heyting 113, 202
homomorphic 211
Houdt 268

humanimal 33
Husserl 9, 72, 90–1
hyper-consistent 177
hyper-stable 157

I
immanence 9, 68, 115, 256
immanent 1, 32, 68, 75, 97–9, 116, 131, 134, 136, 161, 164–5, 191–2, 203, 226, 234, 236
immanentist 78, 107
immeasurable 111
immortal 58, 237–9
implication 48, 50, 53, 72, 94, 168, 194, 227
impossibility 49, 51, 68, 80, 103, 185–6, 195, 216, 226
impossible 2–3, 6, 9, 26, 39, 45, 47, 49–52, 55, 59, 61–2, 69, 80, 83, 99, 102–3, 117, 124, 143, 145, 174–5, 182–3, 185–6, 191–2, 194–5, 197–8, 201, 203, 223, 226, 236, 244–5, 247–8, 253–4, 256
impotentiality 204
impredicative 51, 197–8
im-predicative 46
inapparent 95–7, 102, 225
inappear 126
in-appear 6
inappearance 6, 90, 96
inappears 98
include 17, 20, 27, 87–8, 91–2, 95, 110, 112, 164, 177, 189, 193, 208
included 10, 17–18, 22, 36, 54–5, 59, 65–6, 76, 89, 95, 100, 109, 111–12, 126, 172–3, 182, 208, 210, 247, 251
including 19, 49, 74, 76, 92–3, 105, 156, 164, 180, 191, 212
inclusion 1, 5, 10, 12–13, 54, 65–6, 87, 89–90, 99, 103, 108, 123, 135, 183, 197, 247, 257
incompleteness 5, 49, 76, 161, 164, 175
inconsistency 67, 75, 78, 102
inconsistent 9, 46, 54, 102, 239
incorporeal 30
indecomposable 37
indeterminacy 243, 258
indeterminate 47, 62, 66
indetermination 260
index 84, 105, 120–2, 124, 126, 128, 132, 172, 181–2, 184, 255

indexed 89–90, 92, 97, 103, 114, 121–23, 133, 138, 141, 146, 152, 176, 181–2, 184
indexing 83, 105, 116–19, 121–3, 127, 131, 133, 144, 159, 165–6, 171, 176, 181–4, 188, 261
indifference 2–3, 20, 30, 32–4, 40–1, 43, 46–8, 58, 66, 68, 71, 85, 104–5, 107, 118–19, 135, 145–6, 172–3, 179, 203, 214–15, 218, 228–9, 240–1, 243, 246, 253–4, 258–63
in-difference 254, 261
indifferent 1–2, 15, 17, 19, 22, 24, 32–3, 37–8, 40–1, 43, 46, 51–2, 63–4, 66–9, 71, 77–80, 82, 85–6, 100, 104–7, 115, 117–19, 121, 128, 135–6, 150, 161–2, 164, 167, 171–4, 185, 193, 203, 205, 207, 211, 215–16, 218, 228, 233–4, 239, 243, 245, 253–5, 258–62
indifferential 3, 6, 15, 41, 117, 121, 218, 252, 254
indifferentiated 3, 15, 47, 52, 107, 174, 218
indifferentiation 3, 15, 66, 103
indifferentism 218, 263
indifferently 58, 82, 104–5, 127, 229, 233, 235
indiscernible 9, 54
indiscerns 204
indistinct 51–2, 120, 184
indistinction 120–1
individuation 33
indivisible 48, 57, 75, 82–3
induction 235–6, 240
inequality 61, 122–3, 137–8, 140, 147, 150
inexist 34, 99, 116, 124, 172, 223, 226, 230
in-exist 34
inexistence 34, 48, 74–5, 99, 101–3, 113, 119, 125, 154–5, 157, 161, 164, 171–2, 176, 185, 192–6, 201, 223–4, 236
inexistent 34, 37, 40, 42, 78, 98–9, 121, 126, 130, 171–4, 176–7, 184, 191–6, 208, 217, 223–6, 229–31, 233–4, 237
inexists 48, 101, 104, 115, 124, 141–2, 163–4, 171–3, 194, 223, 225–6
inextensive 42

infinite 5–6, 16–17, 19, 32, 35, 38, 40, 43, 46, 76, 83, 90–2, 97, 100, 107, 121, 130, 133–4, 140, 157, 160, 163–5, 170–1, 173, 175–6, 180, 185, 191–2, 201–4, 207–8, 210–11, 213, 215, 218, 225, 228, 240, 260
infinitesimals 75
infinities 4, 8, 18, 26, 30, 51, 99–100, 192, 197, 244, 247, 260
infinity 1, 35–40, 51, 60, 69–72, 75, 77–8, 97, 100, 108, 125, 130, 160–5, 170, 172, 192, 198, 203, 205, 210, 219, 222, 224–5, 239–40, 247, 259–60
in-indifferentiate 245
inoperative 57, 74
inquiries 227
intelligibility 24–6, 35, 39, 42, 46, 57, 68, 118–19, 244, 258
intelligible 15, 24–7, 30, 42, 45, 83, 87, 118–19, 149, 190, 193–4, 197, 244
intense 25–7, 95, 98, 101, 119, 125, 166, 188, 237, 244
intensely 124, 126, 251
intensional 25, 108, 197, 247, 253
intensities 6, 88–9, 108–10, 146, 160
intensity 6, 10, 13, 19, 25–6, 34, 46, 62, 66, 70–1, 73, 79, 83, 87–9, 91, 94–5, 98–9, 107–8, 111, 116, 121–2, 124, 126, 128, 130, 133–4, 138, 146–8, 159, 166, 168, 177, 182, 184–5, 188–90, 193–4, 196, 198, 204, 206, 208, 213–14, 216, 230, 251
intensive 111, 180
intercalation 88–9, 99
interior 165, 175, 208–14, 228, 234
interiorization 209–10, 214
intermittent 5, 68, 88, 219, 239, 254
interpellation 243
intrinsic 3–4, 6, 18, 33, 40, 65, 78, 101, 160, 162, 170, 182, 198, 209, 235–6, 254
intuition 1, 34, 135, 141, 218, 243, 251, 260
intuitionist 6, 17, 23–4, 47, 49, 52, 55, 64, 70, 73, 103, 139, 207, 211, 252, 256
invariance 29, 33–5, 39, 79
invariant 29, 34–40, 43, 167, 176, 230
is-not 8, 65, 96, 159, 177, 222, 255
isolates 152, 216–17
isomorphism 50–1

K

Kant 67–8, 72–3, 136, 139, 160, 218, 243–6, 257
Kantian 116, 218, 245, 258, 261, 263
knowledge 26, 39, 41, 48, 61, 83, 243, 257
Koestler's 59

L

Lacan 226
lack 72–3, 107, 189, 193, 223, 262
language 4–5, 8, 14–15, 30, 32–6, 39–40, 42, 53, 59, 84, 90, 102–3, 118, 149, 162, 193, 215, 218, 223, 231, 238, 245, 254, 258, 260
larger 10, 13–14, 20, 26–7, 85, 87–8, 91, 93–5, 97, 99–100, 109, 111, 127–8, 134, 166, 187, 191, 204, 208, 212, 215
largest 87–9, 93, 100, 109–11, 127–9, 169, 187, 204, 208, 235
Laruelle 235, 263
laws 17, 21, 40, 74, 86, 98, 103, 115, 123, 129, 131, 136, 145, 154, 159, 162, 165, 170, 182, 185–6, 214, 221, 224–5, 232–3
Lawvere 16, 77, 258, 266
least largest 10, 93, 100, 110–11
least upper 138, 142, 144, 151
Lecercle 266
legibility 45–6, 87
legible 46, 87, 197, 228, 244
Legitimate, legitimation 25–6, 36, 57, 74, 179, 185, 234, 196, 249
Legrange 229, 244
Leibniz 174
lesser 94, 100, 106, 109, 123, 126, 134, 204
less than 84, 89, 122, 126, 134, 138, 140, 143, 148, 150–1, 166, 187
level 18, 26, 46, 83, 104–5, 109–10, 114, 120, 130, 151, 153–6, 160, 163, 192, 195, 201, 209, 213, 216, 218, 225
Levinas 74, 135
life 30, 33, 53, 157, 187, 212, 215, 218, 228–30, 232, 237–9, 241, 243, 262
linear 23, 31, 57, 63, 123, 167, 197, 226, 231, 247
linear-algebraic 252
line of flight 2, 202
line of sight 10, 25–6
lines 15, 26, 99, 213, 248
lines converging 262
Ling 255–6, 265
live, lived 33, 62, 194, 197, 212, 215–16, 237–40, 253–4
Livingstone 266
local 12, 61–3, 68, 76–8, 83, 92, 94, 104–5, 107, 109–12, 134, 145–8, 153, 164–5, 170, 177, 198, 201, 206, 248, 251
local-global 209, 211
localization 51, 71, 97, 104, 117, 132–7, 146–8, 150, 153–4, 156, 160, 163, 176, 202–4, 206–8, 210, 212, 214
localize 134, 136–7, 156, 208
localized 43, 52, 55, 63–5, 78, 93, 99–100, 109, 114, 118, 136–7, 147–8, 150, 155–6, 207–8, 212, 260–1
locally-globally 66
logical completeness 167, 169–70
logical worlds 33, 106, 171, 174, 215
logicism 64
logics of appearing 7–8, 40, 42, 54, 65–6, 68, 70, 74, 121, 136, 226

M

MacCannell 267
Madarasz 264–5, 267
Mallarmé 31, 260
Maoism 235, 240, 263
mappable 23, 211
mapping 11, 16–17, 20–2, 61, 112
Marxism 8, 21, 31–2
matheme 54, 56
maximal 6, 13, 25, 70, 85, 89–90, 95–8, 100, 105, 120, 124, 126–8, 134–5, 137, 140–5, 154–5, 157, 172, 177, 189–91, 193–4, 196, 198–9, 201, 205–6, 230–1, 233, 235, 240
maximality 195–6
maximally 88, 100, 124, 128, 143, 166, 189, 191, 194, 196, 198, 207, 229, 231
maximum 93, 97–100, 120, 122, 124, 133–4, 152, 192, 195–6, 208, 213, 217, 223, 233
McCarty 256, 266
measure 19, 70, 72–3, 75, 79, 83, 85–9, 93–5, 105, 108, 110–11, 116, 120, 130, 137, 140, 142, 152, 166, 176, 187–8, 190, 258

measurement 82, 106, 147, 152
Melliassoux 83
member 100–3, 128, 156, 192
Messiaen 79
meta-appearance 96
meta-history 34
meta-indifferent 43
metalanguage 14
meta-mathematical 4, 8, 14
metaphysics 31, 101, 218, 259
meta-physics 45
metapolitics 264
meta-relation 136
meta-structural 9
militant 7, 45, 187, 204, 235, 240, 248
minimal 36, 84–6, 89, 104, 118, 126, 143, 171, 206, 213
minimum 4, 6, 13, 70–3, 85–6, 90, 93–100, 107–8, 110–11, 113–15, 119, 124–9, 134–5, 140, 154–5, 163, 172–3, 176–7, 193–6, 198–9, 207–8, 216, 223–6, 235, 240, 257
modal 49, 52, 64, 66, 204, 238, 256
modality 3, 14, 48, 51, 64, 66, 99, 121, 245
modification 132, 135, 180–91, 198, 201–2, 206, 208, 215, 223, 225, 228, 262
modified 55, 69, 112, 180, 201, 205, 228, 247
monism 48, 77
morphism 7, 12–13, 16, 19, 251, 258
multiple 4–6, 13, 18–20, 24–6, 31, 33–4, 49, 54, 60, 63, 65–73, 75–9, 81–4, 87, 91, 97, 100–1, 103–5, 107–8, 116–19, 121, 124–6, 129–36, 138–42, 144–6, 148–53, 159, 161–2, 165, 171–2, 174, 176–7, 180–3, 201, 207–8, 210, 224, 237, 239, 244, 246, 249, 251–2, 259–62
multiple-being 70, 102, 117–18, 132, 139, 141, 164–5, 170, 227, 260
multiple-beings 119, 150, 162
multiples 2–6, 8, 10, 18–19, 24–6, 32–4, 42, 46–7, 54–5, 65–6, 69–72, 75–7, 82, 99–101, 103–5, 107–9, 115–16, 118, 120–1, 127–30, 135–7, 139, 141, 143, 145–6, 149–53, 160, 162, 164, 170, 172, 175–6, 183, 192, 198, 207–8, 218, 224, 245–7, 259, 261

multiplicities 35, 76, 131, 160, 186, 192, 203, 205, 223, 261–2
multiplicity 35, 46, 66, 68, 78–80, 130, 138, 159, 161, 175, 180, 186, 201, 212, 240

N

name 15, 20, 50, 54, 57–8, 63, 72, 111, 127, 153, 191, 198, 216, 223, 225, 227, 250–1, 256
named 18, 31, 54–5, 184–5, 198
natural numbers 80–1, 256
negate 33, 56–7, 59, 63, 73–4, 80–1, 83, 96, 190–1, 217, 238
negated 56, 76, 78, 90, 145, 179, 196, 198, 238
negates 56, 66, 139, 190, 227–8, 256, 261
negating 2, 6, 43, 59, 96–7, 157, 193
negation 31, 48, 52–3, 56, 67, 72–4, 95–8, 100, 102, 196, 227, 256
negative 46, 52–3, 56, 72, 166, 201, 213, 263
neoliberal 29
networks 83, 122, 162, 189–90, 216, 248
neuter 135
neutral 11, 15, 52, 73, 78–9, 117, 172, 190, 215, 222, 234, 236
neutrality 67, 135, 174
Newton-Leibniz event 59
next closest 170
next highest 110
next largest 87, 187, 235
next nearest 170
Niemeyer 210
Nietzsche 243, 250
nil-intensity 108, 183
node 25, 250
nomination 55, 58
non-absolute 138
non-abstract 207
non-apparent 73, 86
non-appearance 72, 99, 108
non-axiomatic 86
non-being 159, 173–4, 177
non-classical 74, 211, 256
non-closed 2, 98, 124
noncommunicability 219, 231, 246–8, 252
noncommunicable 36, 48, 52, 56, 59–61, 119, 193–94, 197, 217, 219, 234, 237, 246–8, 251, 253–4

non-communicable 33, 35, 42, 59
noncommutative 246, 253
non-commutative 248
non-comparative 209
non-compatibility 137
non-conjunction 74
non-constructible 32
non-contradiction 256
non-correlational 74
non-decomposable 1, 20, 130, 144, 172, 216
nondenumerable 259
non-dependence 94
nondetermined 174
non-dialectical 74
non-differentiable 172
non-differentiation 203
non-equivalence 246
non-eventual 24
non-hierarchical 31
non-identical 151
non-identity 50, 105
non-intentional 85
non-maximal 191
non-metaphysical 74
non-minimal 216
non-natural 58
non-nil 120
non-ontological 138
non-participation 121
non-presentable 77
nonrelation 14, 74, 99, 136, 164, 196, 198
non-relation 9, 32, 174
nonrelational 34, 74, 78, 91, 119, 121, 160, 162, 167, 172, 223, 226, 254, 259
non-relational 31, 33, 66–7, 78, 104, 150, 259–60
nonrelationality 79–80, 98, 119, 167
non-relationality 31–2, 67, 80, 174, 215
nonrelationally 182, 216, 253
non-substitutable 106
non-succession 31
non-successor 31
nontranscendental 219
non-translatability 36
non-whole 65, 202, 247–8
Norris 213
not-apparent-in-this-world 86
not-being-there 72, 85–6
nothingness 177, 261

number 3, 7, 13, 18–19, 35, 37–8, 46, 51, 56, 71, 75, 81, 85, 90, 92, 96–7, 103, 124, 129, 133, 135, 140, 164–5, 175–6, 192, 201, 205, 209, 214, 223, 240, 256
numbers 7, 22–3, 35–8, 50, 80–1, 84–6, 175, 229, 251, 256
numerical 37, 46, 175
numerous 58, 154, 239, 244, 263

O

object 1, 4, 6, 10–11, 13, 15–16, 18–22, 25–7, 31, 34–5, 38, 40, 42, 47–8, 50, 52, 62–4, 74, 80, 98–100, 102, 115–18, 121, 129, 131–40, 143–4, 146–7, 150–6, 159–63, 165–74, 176–7, 180–3, 185, 187–98, 202–4, 206–12, 214, 216–17, 223, 225–9, 231–4, 244–8, 250–1, 257–8, 260–1, 263
objectal 115–17, 201, 239
object-component 143, 146
objectivate 249, 117, 182, 245
objective 9, 14, 72, 90, 94, 115, 120, 138, 146, 149, 151, 153, 160, 179, 203–4, 244–5, 259–60, 262
objective phenomenology 9, 14, 90, 94, 115, 120, 259–60
objectivity 116, 132, 145, 261
object-less 116
objects 1, 4, 6, 9–21, 24–7, 32, 36, 42, 46–7, 49–52, 54–6, 60, 63, 66, 68, 70, 72–3, 99, 102, 109, 115–18, 120, 132, 135–6, 138, 147, 149, 151, 154–5, 159–63, 165–73, 175–6, 182–3, 188–92, 196–8, 201–4, 206–7, 209–10, 212–13, 216–17, 223–9, 231–6, 240, 245–8, 250–1, 253–4, 257–9, 261, 263
obscure subject 56–7, 227
occultation 47–8, 56–9, 227
one-at-most 126
one-effect 132
ones 12, 41, 63, 99, 111, 126, 128, 141, 189, 260
ontico-indistinction 245
ontico-ontological 4, 68
onto-logical 31, 52, 139, 160, 247, 257
ontological axioms 103, 173, 223

ontological closure 167, 169–70
ontological composition 119, 130
ontological indifference 68, 104
order 9, 12, 14, 17, 22, 24, 32, 69, 79, 81–2, 92, 100, 106–7, 109–11, 113, 115, 117–18, 120–1, 123, 134–6, 138, 140, 143, 147–51, 153–4, 159, 161–2, 166, 176, 182, 190, 195, 201–2, 205–6, 210, 232–5, 245, 249, 251, 261
order relation 9, 107, 110, 113, 118, 123, 138, 140, 143, 147–51, 153, 159, 162, 202, 205–6, 210, 232, 234
ordered 5, 13–14, 16–18, 65, 69, 76, 83, 107, 110–14, 122, 138, 154, 252
ordered pair 13–14, 17–18, 65, 122, 252
ordered pairs 13–14, 17–18, 252
otherness 29, 32, 74, 82

P
pairing 121, 140, 156
pairs 13–14, 17–18, 72, 122, 151–2, 155–6, 176, 232, 234, 252
Papineau 267
parallel 18, 24
Parmenides 228
partial-ordering 9
phenomenology 9, 14, 41, 45, 47, 71–2, 85, 90–2, 94, 115–16, 120, 226, 254, 257, 259–60
phenomenon 41, 116, 119, 121, 123–4, 130, 141–2
planal 82
Plato 1, 59, 73
Platonism 42, 59, 130, 238
Plotinsky 267
plurality 29, 79
Pluth 267
poem 84, 227–8, 230–1
poet 228–9
poetic 229–31
poetry 21, 39–40, 229, 234, 263
poet-subject 228
point-by-point 40, 53, 55, 57–8, 63–4, 204, 221, 228, 231
pointed 218, 224, 226, 228, 247, 254
points 7, 20, 34, 50–1, 53, 68, 72, 77, 97, 107, 115, 119, 126, 134, 143, 170, 188, 201–8, 210–17, 224, 226, 231–7

political 27, 29–30, 39, 46, 55, 58, 61–2, 120, 128, 141, 149, 156, 168, 172, 184–5, 189, 193, 196, 206–7, 235, 249–50, 253
politically 168, 192, 194, 238
politics 6, 29–30, 32–3, 39, 56, 61–2, 76, 149, 168, 184–5, 189, 206, 212, 249, 255, 258, 262
POSet 5, 10, 17, 20, 107, 109, 118, 189
Posey 267
positive 46, 51–2, 68, 84, 167, 206, 211, 213–14, 216, 233–4, 263
positivization 214, 233–4
post-evental 34, 231, 233–4
Potter 11, 257
power 6, 26–7, 36, 39–40, 56–7, 59, 67, 97, 118, 137, 147, 156, 159, 175, 184–5, 189, 193–4, 207, 218, 225, 228, 247, 249–51, 253
Pozorov 267
precede 166
precede, precedence 31, 36, 114, 130, 166–7, 223, 259
predecessor 201, 248
predicate 102, 149, 166–7, 212, 223, 227
predicative 34, 76, 95, 102–3, 145, 201
presentation 13–14, 18, 46, 73–5, 102, 106–7, 111–12, 123, 132, 244–5, 256, 258, 260
primes 35–8, 80
primitive 3–4, 9, 106–7, 145, 149, 169
production 48–50, 52–3, 56–7, 226–7
proofs 35–6, 68, 82, 101, 103, 107, 125, 129, 135, 146–8, 150, 155, 175, 203, 217, 222–3, 234, 246
properties 1, 4, 9, 20–21, 25, 41, 46, 51, 54, 70, 86, 95, 99, 108, 117, 126, 170, 257
property 16, 21, 24, 52, 70, 92, 107–9, 111–12, 230
protest 120–3, 149
pull-back 7, 228, 246, 248
pure being 4, 79, 119, 130, 133, 150, 159, 164, 172, 174, 179, 217, 222–3
pure difference 218, 146
pure multiple 67, 78, 105, 117–19, 130–5, 140, 150–1, 159, 161–2, 174, 244
pure multiples 82, 135–6, 141, 160, 162, 164, 176

Q

qualitative 66, 146, 226, 254
qualities 21, 25, 46, 49–51, 60, 66, 70–1, 76, 100, 104, 117, 127, 145–6, 156, 174, 226
quality 15, 19, 21, 34, 63, 66, 70–1, 74, 79, 101, 105, 107, 119, 126–7, 136, 138, 154, 162, 170, 174, 233, 235, 250–1, 254, 259, 261
quality-indifferent 135
quality-rich 25, 108
quantitative 71, 176
quantity 71, 104, 106, 145, 232, 254
quasi-causal 131, 139
quasi-complete 54
quasi-negative 96
quasi-rankable 110
Quebec, Quebecois 162–3, 166–7, 169, 172–3, 196
Quine 36, 42, 53, 243, 258

R

Rancière 36, 193, 258, 262, 267
rank 1, 18, 46–7, 51, 82, 100, 259–60
rankable 31, 46, 100, 107, 260
rare 41, 68, 235, 254
reactionary 46, 56, 169
reactive subject 56–7, 227
real atom 132–3, 144, 153, 173, 176–7
real atoms 129–31, 155, 232, 253
real change 157, 159, 173–4, 176–7, 179–81, 184, 186, 189, 191, 215, 223, 225, 228, 234–5
real element 132, 136–7, 147, 153, 176
real events 247–8
realist 34, 58, 130
real synthesis 138, 150–1, 153–4, 176, 232
reascend 139, 152–3
recount 5, 61, 65, 76
recounted 10, 46, 54, 138, 150
reductio ad absurdum 38–9, 50, 59
reflexive 185–6, 228
reflexivity 106–7, 113, 140
region 53, 72, 93, 96, 128, 136, 146, 151, 153, 234
regional localization 136
regional stability 90–1
regions 153, 231, 253

relational 13, 19–20, 23, 26, 33, 46, 66–71, 74, 79, 83, 86, 91, 96, 98, 100, 104, 106, 111, 114–15, 117–22, 125, 128, 133, 136, 138–40, 146, 150–1, 153, 155, 160, 170, 174, 189, 193, 206–7, 209, 212, 214, 223, 228, 250–2, 254, 256, 260
relationality 10, 15, 17, 27, 31, 66, 70, 79–81, 100, 114, 117, 123, 129, 134, 136–7, 145, 150, 160, 162, 166–7, 175, 204, 214, 218, 244, 246, 250–2, 255, 260
relationally 10, 15, 26, 46, 66, 89, 104, 121, 130, 141, 150, 174, 195, 213, 246, 250
relations 4, 9–10, 13, 15, 19–20, 22–7, 32–3, 35–6, 47, 50, 62–3, 65–6, 70, 77, 79, 90, 97, 99, 112, 114, 120–4, 136, 138, 140, 147–9, 155, 160–3, 166–9, 172, 176, 180, 185, 189–90, 204, 210, 212, 216–17, 224–6, 230, 245–6, 250–2, 261, 263
resurrection 48, 57–9, 227, 230
retroaction 132, 134, 136, 138–9, 148, 150–1, 154, 225
retroactive 45, 49, 135, 148, 150, 174, 197, 222, 226
retroactively 6, 45, 49, 133, 136, 138–9, 148, 153, 159, 176, 205, 234, 254
retrogradation 222, 224–5
reversal 73–4, 100
reverse 7, 18, 22, 24, 73–4, 95–100, 113–14, 121, 126, 129, 137, 173, 228, 256
revolt 50, 56, 58
revolution 1, 183, 206, 255
revolutionary 46, 57–8, 120, 193, 206, 219
rhizomatic 247
Riera 267
rights 29–30, 172–3, 218
Robert 123, 125–6, 131, 136
Roffe 265, 267
Romans 53, 61, 129, 203
Ronald 267
Rousseau 190
Ruda 267
rule-bound 184

rule-governed 133, 180
rules 34, 54, 59, 61, 71–2, 112, 121, 127, 151, 185, 193, 234
Russell 5, 63, 102–3, 129, 157, 185, 260

S
sanction 24, 26–7, 36, 145, 184, 193, 244, 249
Sartre 73, 206, 213
Schanuel 16, 77, 258, 266
Schoenberg 46
sedimentation 46
self-belonging 63–4, 182, 188, 193
self-enclosed 13, 183
self-identical 103, 130, 254
self-identity 26, 69–70, 95, 124–5, 140, 207, 230, 244, 249, 261
self-intensity 6, 26, 251
self-mentioned 198
self-mentioning 5–6, 47, 49, 183
self-negation 227
self-predicating 105, 181–2, 192–3, 197, 201, 224, 254
self-predication 5, 102–3, 164, 183, 198, 226
self-predicative 161, 182–3, 223–4, 230
self-refers 183, 198
self-reflexive 185–6
self-relation 6, 9, 99–100, 252
separation 60, 76, 102, 195
sequential 189, 201, 231, 238
seriality 50, 185, 247, 261
sets 1, 4–5, 7–8, 10–14, 16–18, 20, 24–5, 27, 35, 38, 46, 49, 51–2, 55, 71, 74, 76–7, 99–102, 105–8, 112, 123, 125–6, 130, 136, 164, 175–7, 183, 185, 223–4, 244, 252, 256, 258, 260, 262
set-theoretical 4, 10
sexed 62
Shapiro 256, 266–7
Shaw 267
sheaf 156–7, 202
signature 177, 259
signatures 52, 243, 249, 259
Simmons 11, 20, 257–8, 267
singleton 19, 75, 126, 134
singular 5, 34, 40, 63, 76, 78, 80–3, 97, 117–18, 173, 182, 189–91, 207, 226, 234, 254

singularity 2, 5, 40, 69, 81, 83, 105, 122, 141, 154, 179–83, 186, 188–91, 193, 202, 207, 215, 223, 225, 230–1, 254
site 76, 171, 173, 181–91, 193–98, 201, 203–4, 208, 210, 214, 217–18, 221, 223–6, 229–30, 232–3, 236
site-object 231
situation of being 67–8, 78
smaller than 13, 35, 88, 94, 97, 106, 108–9, 111, 127–8, 134, 163, 175, 187, 208, 235, 260
smallest 75, 92, 108, 111, 113, 125, 127–9, 136, 142, 169, 211, 216
Socrates 94
Spartacus event 50, 54, 58, 61, 203
splace 47, 260
spreading 8, 20, 256
state 5, 36, 55, 61, 65, 76, 167–8, 172, 189
state-function 251
Steinhart 267
step-by-step 74, 116, 201, 231
stratified 95, 155
structure-preserving 14, 22, 65, 250
sub-apparent 144
sub-elements 163
subgroups 153, 214, 230
subject 31, 33, 37–9, 43, 45–51, 53–64, 68, 79, 84, 91, 115–16, 133, 137, 169, 174, 182, 187, 197, 199, 203–4, 217–18, 221–2, 226–7, 230–1, 233, 236, 238, 240–1, 243–5, 255–6, 258–62
subject-agent 63
subject-body 204, 236
subject-chooser 204
subject-form 50
subjectivated 50, 63, 68, 188, 219
subjectivation 49–53, 55, 61–3, 102, 227, 247–8, 261
subjective 33–4, 37–9, 48, 50–1, 56–7, 59, 63, 68, 91, 93, 116, 168, 203–4, 213–15, 221, 224, 226–7, 231, 235–6, 238, 240–1, 262
subjectivities 47
subjectivity 37–8, 47, 61–2, 84, 90, 235
subject-less 116
subject-object 116
subject-of-truth 235
subject-positions 251

subjects 33–4, 37–9, 45–6, 56–7, 60–1, 85, 192, 204, 215, 221, 226–7, 232, 236–7, 239, 243–4
subject-truths 35, 151, 224, 241
sublation 177, 230
sub-multiples 18
sub-object 20, 163, 227
subordinate 53, 111, 122, 165, 216, 231, 238
subordination 53, 149–50, 169–70, 196, 227–8
Sub-parts 150, 164–5
subset 13, 35, 61, 65, 76, 93–4, 109–10, 125, 128, 142–6, 152, 154–6, 163, 208, 231, 234, 247
substitutability 17–18, 51, 84, 106
subtracted 33, 35, 171
succession 18, 24, 50, 86, 107, 110, 188
super-consistency 5
supernumerary 57, 190–1, 262
support-being 185
support-set 151
surface 10, 66, 77, 89, 127, 163, 228
surnumerary 173, 262
suspension 31, 52–5, 59, 60, 174, 73, 204, 218, 263
suture 2, 8
syllogistic 94
symbol 53, 106, 121, 126, 214
symmetrical 17, 121, 137, 245–7, 252
symmetry 12–13, 17–18, 106, 108, 121–3, 140, 183, 245, 247
synthesis 40, 71, 74, 91–2, 96, 111, 136, 138, 150–1, 153–6, 176, 225, 232–3
synthetic 60, 92, 136, 155, 233–4
systems 42, 49, 54, 58, 77, 102–3, 179, 207, 263

T
tablet 78
tabular 23, 31, 63, 123, 167, 197, 226, 231, 238, 261
tabular-topological 252
target 13, 20, 48, 123
tautology 49, 95, 110, 162, 250
temple 123–6, 128, 130–1, 133–4, 137–8, 143, 154
temporality 16, 22, 57, 147–8, 180, 192, 238, 261
tensed 212, 214–15, 217–19, 228, 261
territory 111, 156, 162–3, 167, 210
terror 30, 56, 235
test 35, 61, 204, 218, 224, 226, 231, 259
tested 91, 224, 231, 235
testing 40, 51, 53, 57, 197–8, 202, 214, 221, 231, 247
thinkable 76–7, 119, 179, 223
Tiles 11, 95, 257, 268
time-consciousness 261
topoi, topos 7, 156, 244, 255–7, 263
topological 8, 13–14, 112, 146–9, 202–3, 208, 212, 214, 245, 251, 256
topology 4, 14, 150, 152, 203–4, 207–8, 210, 254, 256
totalization 164–5, 175
trace 45–6, 48–50, 52–3, 56, 58, 61–3, 121, 157, 171, 188, 195, 212, 227, 230–3, 235–7, 247, 255
traces 20, 39, 42–3, 58, 102, 132, 171, 222
transcendental algebra 83, 112, 116–17
transcendental degree 97, 124, 134, 136, 142, 144, 211
transcendental degrees 73, 133, 141, 154–5, 187, 208
transcendental function 8–10, 68, 109
transcendental functor 8, 55, 63, 65, 72, 98, 100–1, 136, 151–4, 156, 184, 250–1
transcendental index 105, 124, 126, 128, 132, 182, 184
transcendental indexing 105, 116, 118–19, 121–3, 127, 131, 144, 165–6, 171, 181–3, 188
transcendental inexistence 74
transcendental intensity 251
transcendental logic 114, 117, 148, 150, 159, 179, 181, 218
transcendental measure 83, 86, 88, 166, 190
transcendental operation 73, 107–8, 110, 113
transcendental relation 151, 225
transitivity 17, 106–7, 113, 143, 163–5
transmissibility 15–15, 133, 222, 244
triangle 7, 11, 13–14, 23, 26, 122–3, 168–9, 212, 245, 252, 257, 263
triangular 122–3, 140, 149, 160, 168–9
triangulation 63, 72, 122, 167, 261
Trott 268

truth 24, 29–33, 35–7, 39–43, 47–9, 51, 53–6, 58–61, 63–4, 91, 97, 102, 106, 115, 129, 135, 165, 173, 180, 187, 197, 201, 203–4, 210, 214–15, 217–18, 221, 223, 225–6, 235, 237, 239–40, 244–5, 247, 249, 255, 262
truthful 31, 42, 47–8, 64, 197, 248
truth-less 215, 218
truth-negating 41
truth-object 64
truth-preserving 14
truth-procedure 58, 203
truth-process 204
truths 29–38, 41–3, 45, 47–9, 58–61, 91, 116, 135, 151, 192, 197, 208, 210, 212, 215, 217, 221, 232, 239, 246, 253–4, 262–3
truth-value 247
two-dimensional 82, 248
typologies of subject 47, 56, 60–1, 227
typology of change 186
typology of subjects 60–1
typology of events 191

U

ultra-consistent 5, 198
ultra-stability 2, 64
unconditioned 30, 48
uncountable 163
undecidable 54, 56
unicity 108
unintelligible 35, 167, 244
union 113, 214
unique 2–3, 18, 32, 108, 111, 124, 127–8, 134, 143–4, 169, 173–4, 194, 196, 198, 223
universal 6, 8, 10, 15, 23, 30, 37, 39–40, 46, 48, 58, 62–3, 65, 75–6, 90, 100, 151, 160–1, 163, 167, 169–70, 173–4, 184, 192, 198, 216, 218, 225, 228, 233, 240, 244, 250, 257, 263
universal exposition 6, 8, 10, 23, 167, 170, 173–4, 184, 198, 218, 225, 240, 244, 257, 263
universality 41, 161, 169, 201, 237
universally 14–15, 19, 37, 46, 169–70, 176, 198, 215, 225–6, 229, 238, 245–6, 248

universe 24, 68–9, 75, 97, 138, 157, 260
upper bound 111, 138, 142, 144, 149, 151, 157

V

Valery 227, 230
value 22, 65, 71–4, 76, 84–5, 87, 89–90, 92–7, 105–6, 109, 112, 120–1, 124, 131, 141, 147, 151, 156, 166–7, 171–3, 176, 179, 187, 190, 193, 197, 206, 210–12, 218, 224, 228, 233
values 65, 70–1, 89, 92, 105, 109, 111, 124, 133, 141, 169, 189, 206, 215
vantage point 23, 244, 246, 248, 263
variable 66, 83, 240
veridicality 24
vertical 82, 133, 137–8, 148, 262
virtual 80, 130, 237
visibility 9–10, 14, 24, 36, 60, 128, 131, 161, 169
visible 10, 15, 19, 23, 26, 47, 57, 89, 138, 156, 161, 167, 170, 207, 244, 250, 256–7
vitalism 139
void 1, 5, 8, 12–13, 18, 29–31, 34, 38–9, 42, 48–9, 58, 75–9, 87, 100, 102–3, 107–8, 130, 134–5, 142, 164, 171, 173, 177, 180, 183, 186, 188, 197–9, 224, 247, 253–4, 261
vote 80, 162, 172, 231

W

wager 217, 223, 238
Watkin 258–60, 262, 268
weak 61, 69–70, 120, 149, 156, 186, 188, 190–1, 201, 213, 230–1, 257
Webern 46
well-constructedness, well-ordered 102–3
well-pointed 61, 64, 102, 204, 244, 248, 253–4
wholeness 192
Wholes 260
Wittgenstein 53, 160, 180, 243, 261–2, 265
women 53, 84, 123, 249
workers 149, 184–5, 192–3, 196
worlding 78
worldly atony 217

worldly being 130
worldly communication 217
worldly dimension 221
worldly inclusion 66
worldly logic 195
worldly multiples 24
worldly multiplicity 79
worldly objects 245–6
worldly relations 63
worldly site 171
worldly situation 9, 66, 108, 120
world-sharing 81

world-specific 63
world-structures 250

Y
yes–no 232

Z
Zeno 228
Zermelo 102
zero 86, 100, 107, 120, 134, 163, 212
Zizek 3

www.ingramcontent.com/pod-product-compliance
Lightning Source LLC
Chambersburg PA
CBHW072126290426
44111CB00012B/1793